THE KINDERGARTEN TEACHER

THE

KINDERGARTEN

TEACHER

HELEN HEFFERNAN

Chief, Bureau of Elementary Education
California State Department of Education

VIVIAN EDMISTON TODD

Consultant and Lecturer

D. C. HEATH AND COMPANY

Boston

Library of Congress Catalog Card Number 60-8521

Preface

It is the authors' belief that good kindergarten teaching is based on the understanding of the nature of kindergarten children, which differs markedly from that of nursery school children and also that of first-grade children who are beginning to read. The unique characteristics of kindergarten children need to be understood in relation to the wealth of learning experiences that can enrich their lives. *The Kindergarten Teacher* describes the nature of kindergarten children and effective ways of working with them.

The grown-up who works with kindergarten children at first observes them, then comes presently to understand and enjoy them. The book speeds up this getting acquainted process by taking grown-ups vicariously through real happenings, explaining the happenings in terms of educational and psychological theory, and pointing out related principles of child development. Accompanying these principles are many practical suggestions for learning activities. Situations for Discussion at the ends of chapters present other happenings to consider in the light of theory and practice.

To follow through on these principles and suggestions the busy kindergarten teacher needs to know current findings in research about children and how to guide their learning. *The Kindergarten Teacher* brings her such information in a form which she can use immediately in her classroom and in her conversations with parents and professional colleagues.

The administrator needs to determine the importance of the kindergarten in his school system. The book helps him determine personnel and equipment required, a curriculum that takes into account the needs of children as well as the expectations of the social order, and a program of parent-school relationships.

Even before going to press *The Kindergarten Teacher* had begun to serve grown-ups in their relations to children. A Sunday school teacher borrowed first one and then another chapter of the manuscript so that she could work better with her kindergarten class. A nursery school teacher read it as a means of preparing for her new position as a public school kindergarten teacher. A teacher returning to kindergarten responsibility in Japan used the bibliographies as a basis for purchasing and selecting books for the children and for her colleagues, and plans to use the text as a basis for a series of teachers meetings. While the book was in process a proofreader tried out ideas gleaned from the book and used suggested reading materials and records with the five-year-old friend who visits her on Saturdays. Both she and the parents of the child are finding *The Kindergarten Teacher* a guide to enjoying the child more fully.

The authors hope that the book will result in the greater enrichment of the lives of kindergarten age children, the extension of kindergarten experience, and in more happiness for kindergarten children, and their teachers and parents.

HELEN HEFFERNAN

VIVIAN EDMISTON TODD

ACKNOWLEDGMENTS

Appreciation is extended to the members of the Boys and Girls Department of the Long Beach Public Library who worked with the authors in providing bibliographies of recent books, lists of phonograph records, song books, and other materials for instruction especially suitable to children of kindergarten age.

It is easy and pleasant to acknowledge the help of two members of the faculty of Long Beach State College: Mrs. Molly Morgenroth who read and discussed a chapter in preparation, and Dr. Josephine Burley who was most helpful in the preparation of Chapter 13, "Furthering Artistic Expression."

Mention should be made of the contribution of three children observed and enjoyed twenty-four hours each day: David, Philip, and Susan Mariko Todd, and of their kindergarten teachers: Mrs. Bertram McGarrity of the Long Beach Cooperative Nursery Schools, and Miss Jean Ingold and Mrs. Patricia Tebben of the Long Beach City Schools.

Credit for the illustrations in *The Kindergarten Teacher* goes to the California State Department of Education, Bureau of Audio-Visual Education who supplied all of the photographs.

The Long Beach District School and the Palo Alto District School made it possible to quote curriculum materials in use in their schools. This professional contribution is appreciated, as is that of others, too numerous to mention here, who have shared their experience with the authors over the years.

Contents

THE KINDERGARTEN TEACHER

1

What Is the Kindergarten?

THE KINDERGARTEN EXPERIENCE

The kindergarten is the important beginning of a child's school experience. Before his first day in kindergarten, the child has lived largely within his family group, with brief excursions into his neighborhood and wider world. He has had little experience in social living. Now, he is suddenly confronted with a multitude of new adjustments. He goes forth by foot or car or bus to new experiences at school. Here he must gain acceptance for himself as a participating member of his peer group. For his comfort and security, he must establish satisfying relationships with at least one or two other children. He must adjust to a new adult — his teacher — whose ways may differ considerably from those of his parents. He is aware of certain other adults on the periphery of his new environment — the nurse, the principal, the custodian; occasionally he makes direct contact with one of these adults but is probably not very sure of their relation to him.

The child finds himself in a more spacious and less intimate environment than he has previously known. Many new and attractive objects must be shared with others rather than appropriated for his own exclusive use. Many strange and fear-inspiring objects must be judiciously inspected and tentatively tried out to see how well he can control them. The degree to which the child makes all these adjustments with happiness and confidence depends upon many factors.

How the child adjusts to a new situation depends, for instance, on his social maturity. His behavior shows his teacher how far he has come in learning to get along with others. Is he used to finding himself in a strange situation, or does he withdraw from it and cling to some symbol of security? Does he start right in on an activity by himself or does he watch what others do? Is his approach to the situation mostly a verbal or

3

mostly an action approach? Is he concerned primarily with the other children or with the materials provided? Answering such questions about each child will enable the teacher to work effectively with him, starting where he is and having only reasonable expectations of the progress he can make.

THE KINDERGARTEN TEACHER

Professional Growth. The major factor in how children adjust to the kindergarten is without doubt the teacher. The teacher whom every parent wants to guide his child is a person who understands and loves children and who has had the professional education necessary to carry on a sound program of kindergarten education. The teacher has grave responsibility in helping children to become a part of their social world, so she must have a knowledge and an appreciation of the culture. The teacher knows that the application of science to technology is changing, at a tremendously accelerated rate, the world in which the child will live, so she must be skillful in helping him to understand his scientific environment and to expect and accept change.

The teacher knows that all of the interests which make life rich and abundant for the child must be nurtured early and so she is interested in art and literature, in music and bodily rhythms, and she has learned appropriate ways to stimulate and develop similar interests in children. The teacher knows the importance of the environment the kindergarten provides and how equipment and materials contribute to the child's development.

She knows too that despite her years of professional preparation, her education as a kindergarten teacher is unending, just as the education of a physician or an engineer is unending. Every year, research and the experience of frontier workers are adding to the fund of knowledge about children and about how to promote their optimum development. And so the good kindergarten teacher looks forward to a professional life in which she never ceases to be a learner. Some of this learning will be through formal study in graduate schools of colleges and universities; some in informal study groups with colleagues and parents. Above all, the professional growth of the teacher will take place through increasingly insightful observation of the children with whom she works.

Living with children of kindergarten age is strenuous business and requires vigorous good health, energy, buoyant spirits, and enjoyment of the outdoors. No person should contemplate kindergarten teaching as her life work unless she is certain that she has these physical resources and temperamental qualities.

Personality Requirements. To live with kindergarten children three or four hours a day, five days a week for 180 or more days of the year, a kindergarten teacher must really love four- to six-year-olds and enjoy trying to understand them and work with them. If wriggling, shuffling of feet, and scratching bother her, or if subject matter is more interesting to her than people, she should choose some other occupation. But if she really sees each child as a fascinating individual and wants to have some part in helping him realize his potentialities and find his place in the social and physical world about him, she will be rewarded by the personal satisfaction she experiences in the growth and development of kindergarten children.

Appearance. Although a teacher may not be beautiful by Hollywood standards, she can be one of the most beautiful women in the world in the eyes of adoring kindergarten children. They never fail to appreciate bright and cheerful colors and soon evaluate the teacher's clothing in terms of "the dress I like best." Children provide the teacher's most appreciative audience and, like any good actress, the wise teacher selects her clothing with this in mind. Of course, young children are apt to be "messy"; paint and clay, water and sand, milk and fruit juice have a way of getting out of the hands of the fours and fives. Accidents are inevitable and frequently something gets on the teacher's dress. If the teacher's dress is washable no child need have feelings of guilt about the spilling. Reassurance that it will all "come out in the wash" is comforting to children who have had too many admonitions about keeping clean.

Voice. Since the young child's speech and language habits are in the formative stage, the kindergarten teacher's speech should furnish an accurate pattern. Her voice should be clear and distinct, low pitched, and just loud enough to be heard by the children without undue strain and tension. The calm, matter-of-fact tone of voice of the teacher determines the emotional atmosphere of the classroom.

The Teacher and Her Community. The kindergarten teacher needs to know the community in which she works. Not only does it provide her with resource places which children may visit to broaden their experiences with their social and physical world, but it contains people who are always willing to share their experiences, show their treasures, or lend a helping hand at the invitation of the teacher. Co-operation is fostered by the teacher's expectation of co-operation and friendliness in the community. Everyone likes children and is grateful for opportunities to take part in the nurture of the young when he participates with reasonable assurance of success.

The more the teacher understands the community, the greater will be her success in meeting the needs of its children. She should learn about its history, its geographical features, its climate and seasonal changes. She should know the size of the community and whether its land is used for industry and business, for agriculture, or for homes. She should know the flow of resource materials through the community and the kinds and availability of transportation. She should walk around the community enough to know the people and how they are housed. She should know the important public buildings, parks, and other recreational or cultural institutions and how close they are to the school. The school is an integral part of the community, and education for young children is realistic only when it relates specifically to the area with which the children have firsthand experience.

Attitudes. The success of the kindergarten teacher depends also upon certain less tangible assets. The attitudes with which the teacher approaches her responsibility of guiding children will determine her effectiveness as much as, if not more than, her technical knowledge of child psychology or kindergarten methods. To be sure, a sound psychological and technical foundation has a reciprocal effect upon the attitudes of the teacher. The more one knows about one's task, the more one can approach it with assurance and pleasure, but one's underlying attitudes are still of primary importance.

Fortunate are the children whose teacher has zest for her work. She creates enjoyable learning situations for the children and they reflect her friendly happiness. Less fortunate are the children whose teacher feels that she is merely doing her duty and that they should do theirs. The children reflect the "have-to" attitude of their teacher and their achievement falls short of the "want-to" of motivated learning.

The friendliness of a calm, understanding teacher is most important in helping children grow emotionally. Children judge adults more by what they do than by what they say. So the teacher who is kind, helpful, and dependable in her relations with children will soon gain their confidence and affection. The kindergarten teacher should not impose her personality and her beliefs, biases, and attitudes on the children, nor should she feel that no learning takes place except when she is at the focal point of the activity. The good gardener makes the soil right and permits the plant to grow according to its own pattern with a minimum of guidance beyond the necessary protection from influences which might stunt or distort growth. So must the kindergarten teacher provide the environment, guidance, and protection which are conducive to the child's self-discovery and thus to the fullest realization of the potentialities of his unique personality.

CHANGES EXPECTED IN CHILDREN

Changes Due to Maturation

Kindergarten children will be different at the end of the school year from what they were at the beginning. They will be better able to do what they have been doing, and they will be able to do more things than they have previously done. In part, this difference in their abilities will be due to maturation, or growth. For instance, certain children may be better able to chew their food, simply because they have lost some baby teeth and have gained some new teeth. This change would have happened whether the children were in kindergarten or not.

Changes Due to the Kindergarten Experience

But the teacher is most interested in the way children change as a direct result of their kindergarten experience. In what ways has the social living experience of the kindergarten helped the children develop? Have the science experiences made them more interested in the world around them, or have these experiences dulled their curiosity? Have the musical activities increased the children's liking for music? Has the story program increased the children's interest in literature? In other words, have the children changed? Can these changes be attributed to the kindergarten program? How do the observed changes in the children compare with expected changes? The extent to which expected changes are achieved is a measure of the success of the teaching.

The Teacher Relates to the Changes

The changes expected in children are the *objectives* of the kindergarten curriculum. They may be thought of as the attitudes and interests, the habits and skills, and the large relational ideas that are the outcomes of a successful program. Changes in *attitudes*, *skills*, or *ideas* should result from every phase of the experiences provided.

Objectives for Classroom Activities

The success of the kindergarten program depends upon how fully the guidance given by the teacher is purpose-directed. Differences in communities and changes in social conditions make it desirable for teachers to reconsider their purposes from time to time.

One group of kindergarten teachers met to discuss what they expected of the children in their groups. They agreed on several important objectives of their program, and recorded them in a chart. They did not think of these as a complete list of objectives, nor did they consider them necessarily a list of "the most important" objectives. They thought of them simply as useful objectives to have in mind when planning activities.

DEVELOPMENTAL GOALS FOR KINDERGARTEN CHILDREN

Phase of Program

PHYSICAL DEVELOPMENT

Attitudes
Likes to do tricks on apparatus
Likes running

Skills
Slides down a pole
Does turns on exercise bar
Runs with ease

General Ideas
Rest when tired
Exercise makes muscles strong
Good food makes energy

SOCIAL LIVING

Attitudes
Likes to play co-operatively
Likes to do his part in a group project
Likes to work by himself sometimes
Respects rules and regulations
Respects property

Skills
Takes turns
Shares playthings
Finds a role to play in a group activity
Hangs on to what he is using
Talks over problems instead of hitting or grabbing
Abides by rules
Moves with the group
Puts wraps in their place
Helps clean up

General Ideas
Rules and regulations help people to do what they want to do
If things are put away, everyone knows where to find them

SCIENCE ACTIVITIES

Attitudes
Likes to find out how insects, animals, and plants live
Wants to know about tools and machines, and rocks

Skills
Asks questions about what he finds and observes: "What?" "How?" "Does it?"

General Ideas
Some things are alive, others are dead, and others were never alive
Not all animals are friendly
Tools and machines help people to do work
Rocks are hard and are made smooth by streams and oceans

QUANTITATIVE AND SPATIAL EXPERIENCE

Attitudes
Likes to know how many or how much
Likes landmarks

Skills
Counts forward and backward
Places his structures in relation

General Ideas
People can count how many and can take away
Landmarks help people to find their way

LANGUAGE CONTROL

Attitudes
Wants others to understand him
Wants to talk clearly

Skills
Expresses himself
Speaks accurately
Talks clearly

General Ideas
People like to hear about what others see and do
Stories are about imagined things

LITERARY ACTIVITIES

Attitudes
Likes to hear stories

Skills
Sits still for all of story
Lets others hear too

General Ideas
Story time is listening time
People listen and let others listen too

MUSIC

Attitudes
Likes to hear music
Likes to move with music, or sing

Skills
Sits still to hear
Claps or shakes rhythm instruments with music

General Ideas
Music is to hear and to guide movement
Music is to sing

ART

Attitudes
Likes different art media
Likes to express ideas and feelings with art media

Skills
Uses fingers, brush, and other tools as he wants to
Covers paper as he wishes to

General Ideas
People can draw pictures of things or just draw pretty designs

Objectives for Community Living Experiences

This group of kindergarten teachers found it necessary to make a separate list of the general ideas that the children should get from their social living experiences. The generalizations showed basic relationships. Some of them were:

> Farmers raise wheat for bread
> The bottles or cartons that the milkman brings contain cow's milk
> Many kinds of workers are needed to do all the kinds of work in a community
> Men repair houses and other things that break
> When a fire starts, the fire department comes to put it out
> Traffic officers help people go where they want to safely
> Policemen help protect people and their property

Objectives of Entire Program

After they had focused their attention on changes in children expected from particular phases of the kindergarten program, they turned to changes expected from the program as a whole. They found that they were concerned primarily with changes in attitudes and skills. Their list follows:

Attitudes

A kindergarten child:

> Likes to explore and find out about his world
> Likes more often to be part of a group playing co-operatively
> Likes to express ideas verbally
> Likes to express himself through art media
> Enjoys music
> Carries over his interest in a project to successive days

Skills

A kindergarten child should develop in his ability to:

> Look after his own personal needs
> Share ideas and materials
> Take turns
> Talk about his needs instead of trying to satisfy them by grabbing or hitting
> Help others when they need help
> Carry out simple directions
> Move with the group, helping and not interfering
> Get right to work on a project agreed upon
> Notice differences between objects of similar appearance

Variations in Objectives

Each year in each community the kindergarten teacher has a unique set of objectives, appropriate to the needs and talents of the children and her ability as a teacher. For instance, a teacher in an urban community develops a list of general ideas quite different from those listed by a teacher in a small village. A teacher in an area of new homes expects other skills in climbing than does a teacher where children have trees available in their environment. A teacher in a suburban community of professional people expects other social attitudes than does a teacher in a closely packed area of old tenement buildings. Knowing the needs and abilities of the children in the community, the teacher considers realistically what changes the kindergarten program may or should make in their attitudes, skills, and ideas.

Putting the Objectives to Use

A beginning kindergarten teacher uses the statement of objectives as an aid to teaching. Knowing what attitudes, skills, and general ideas to expect in children, she is able to identify those children who are above the average for the group. She gives them opportunities for greater responsibility. She is also able to identify the children who need to improve their attitudes. By talking with her principal or supervisor she gets help in planning for these children. With objectives defined the beginning teacher can work effectively with her group of children from the first. She does not waste time on fruitless activities, nor does she bypass opportunities for fruitful learning. Knowing what to expect, she is able to see progress and to gain satisfaction from her teaching. As she gains confidence and understanding, she can plan more effectively to meet individual as well as group needs.

An experienced kindergarten teacher is able to use the statement of objectives both in working with the group of children and in working with individuals within the group. Using the objectives as a frame of reference, the teacher identifies children who already have many of the desired attitudes, skills, and general ideas. She provides for them enriching experiences beyond the usual program of activities. Knowing her objectives, she is able to identify children who are developing skills and acquiring important ideas but need more guidance in developing desirable attitudes. For instance, she is soon aware of the "I don't want to" boy who yet manages to keep up with the skills and ideas that the rest of the group are learning. She helps him contribute positively to the group projects, and, as his satisfaction in his new role grows, his negative behavior disappears. The teacher is also able to identify and help the smiling and willing child to whom a cow is a cow and not a milk-producer—the child who has not learned to look for relationships. In short, the experienced kindergarten teacher identifies for each child those objectives especially important for the child to achieve. Then she plans her work with the group so that many individual as well as group needs are met.

Teachers find that listing their objectives not only helps them meet the needs of their group of children but also helps them see its progress. At any time, and especially at the end of the year, they can consider how the children have changed and can view these changes in relation to the expected changes. During the year such an evaluation provides the teacher a basis for improving planning. At the end of the year it gives the teacher satisfaction in the development of the children, and reveals to her the strong points of her teaching. It may also indicate points that might be given increased attention another year. And it may suggest an improved listing of objectives, omitting those that were unrealistic or otherwise inappropriate, and adding others more significant.

When a kindergarten group goes on to the first grade, the next teacher can use the objectives of the kindergarten teacher as a help in planning her work with the group. Knowing the objectives and the accomplishments of the kindergarten, the first-grade teacher knows where to start with the group to promote continuous growth.

SITUATIONS FOR DISCUSSION

In the following situations select each course of action that seems desirable to you, basing your choices and omissions on the ideas presented in this chapter. Add one or more alternate courses of action.

SITUATION I. You are interested in becoming a kindergarten teacher. During your student years, you should:

Baby-sit for your sister who has two children in grade school.
Take care of infants during services at church.
Play with the preschool children living across the street.
Read about five-year-old children.
Observe kindergarten children on their way to and from school.

SITUATION II. As a kindergarten teacher, you should think of kindergarten as:

A child's introduction to a widened community.
Preparation for reading, writing, and arithmetic.
A full experience for five-year-olds.
A place to help children get over being messy.
An introduction to school.

SITUATION III. You have accepted a position for teaching kindergarten in a community new to you. You should:

Use a list of objectives from a book such as this.

Use the list of kindergarten objectives you are accustomed to using.

Talk with your principal about teaching objectives for the kindergarten.

Write down important changes you expect in the children of the new community through kindergarten.

Talk with other kindergarten teachers in the new community about their objectives.

SITUATION IV. You have been teaching third grade, but are interested in teaching kindergarten. When a vacancy occurs among the kindergarten positions in your school system, you make application for it. In talking with the superintendent of schools, you comment on:

Your scholastic average in college.

Your satisfaction in teaching third-grade children arithmetic.

The importance of social development before children learn to read.

Case studies you have made of five-year-old children.

Your practice teaching in the kindergarten.

BIBLIOGRAPHY

Professional Books and Pamphlets

Association for Childhood Education International. *Portfolio for Kindergarten Teachers*, rev. Bulletin #2, General Service Bulletin. Washington, D. C., 1951.

Twelve leaflets give practical help in setting up or understanding kindergarten. Among subjects covered are: "What to Expect of the Fours and Fives," "Kindergarten Housings and Furnishings," and "Kindergarten Responsibility Toward Reading."

Barnes, Fred P., ed. *School Begins with Kindergarten*. Illinois Curriculum Program Bulletin No. C-One. Springfield, Illinois: Superintendent of Public Instruction, 1957.

Helps teachers plan for children. Administrators and others appreciate the importance of the kindergarten as an integral part of elementary education.

California State Department of Education. *Teachers Guide to Education in Early Childhood*. Sacramento: Bureau of Elementary Education, 1956.

Gives for the kindergarten as well as for the primary grades many useful suggestions about how to teach each part of the curriculum in terms of child development.

Foster, Josephine C., and Neith E. Headley. *Education in the Kindergarten*, 2nd ed. New York: American Book Company, 1948.

This book emphasizes the need for pacing education to the individual kindergarten child, and discusses appropriate environment, characteristic activities, needs of individual children, and the use of records and reports.

Gans, Roma, Celia B. Stendler, and Millie Almy. *Teaching Young Children*. Yonkers-on-Hudson, New York: World Book Company, 1952.

Discusses curriculum for kindergarten and first three grades. Emphasizes interests and needs, the emerging curriculum, and the social-psychological approach.

Heffernan, Helen, ed. *Guiding the Young Child*, 2nd ed. Boston: D. C. Heath and Company, 1959.

The California School Supervisors Association presents this comprehensive and insightful book about how to work effectively with children in the primary grades.

Leavitt, Jerome E., ed. *Nursery-Kindergarten Education.* New York: McGraw-Hill Book Company, Inc., 1958.
A book prepared by twelve educators on various aspects of the education of young children.

Monroe, Walter S. *Encyclopedia of Educational Research,* rev. ed. New York: The Macmillan Company, 1950.
This book, prepared under the auspices of the American Educational Research Association, presents excellent history of kindergarten and bibliography of early references to kindergarten education.

National Council of State Consultants in Elementary Education. *Planning for America's Children.* Washington, D. C.: Office of Education, 1955.
This booklet discusses policies, practices, and programs for children below six years of age and includes the legislative provisions and financial arrangements necessary for making kindergarten and nursery school education widely available.

National Education Association. *Let's Look at Kindergartens.* Washington, D.C.: Department of Kindergarten-Primary Education, 1954.
This booklet shows how kindergartens contribute to the well-rounded development of children and to their readiness for later growth.

New York State Education Department. *Child Development Guide.* Albany, 1955.
This booklet includes more than fifty pages of excellent photographs and discusses how children grow, educational provisions for pre-school children and their parents, the role of the teacher, and home-school relations.

Prescott, Daniel A. *The Child in the Educative Process.* New York: McGraw-Hill Book Company, Inc., 1957.
Describes procedures for studying, recording, and interpreting the behavior of children and suggests effective procedures in working with children and their parents.

Wills, C. D., and William H. Stegeman. *Living in the Kindergarten.* Chicago: Follett Publishing Company, 1951.
Useful discussions of the kindergarten child, curriculum, parents, and teachers are presented in a readable and intelligent way.

Film for Teachers and Parents

A Day in the Life of a Five Year Old. New York: Bureau of Publications, Teachers College, Columbia University, 1949.
A fine, sensitive teacher guides the activities of a day in kindergarten. 20 minutes, sound, black and white.

Filmstrips

A Good Day in the Kindergarten. California Association for Childhood Education, Long Film Service, 750 S. Fairmount, El Cerrito, California.
This filmstrip, produced by Helen Heffernan, has an accompanying phonograph record and copy of script and is useful with groups of teachers, parents, or interested citizens in showing what a good kindergarten can be. 60 frames, color, 20 minutes.

Kindergarten and Your Child. Wayne University Audio-Visual Materials Consultation Bureau, 5272 Second Avenue, Detroit 1.
Explains the kindergarten program to parents, pointing out how they can work with the school. 40 frames, black and white.

Tommy Goes to Kindergarten. Eye Gate House, Long Island, New York, 1954.
Tommy visits kindergarten and sees the activities of a kindergarten day. 38 frames, silent, color.

2

Kindergarten Children

THE INDIVIDUALITY OF CHILDREN

What are kindergarten children like? Each of them, of course, is an individual person. No two of them look alike, and no two of them, even identical twins, behave exactly alike. Each has a unique personality. Each has his own pattern of beliefs, his individual set of skills, his own collection of information, and his own potential for growth. To understand what he is like and to be able to predict how he will behave, it is necessary to study and observe the child himself over a period of time.

Each child behaves in some ways like other members of his family, for children in the same family have many characteristics in common. But even knowing the first child in the family, the wise teacher makes no assumptions about the younger children. If the first child is a good learner, she does not assume that the second child will be too. In fact, the good learning of the first child may be the very reason for the second child's seeking a different pattern. Each child develops at his own rate and in his own way.

Although each child is unique, it is not difficult to distinguish kindergarten children from nursery school children and from older children, and to describe them with reasonable accuracy. This can be done in various ways. They can be described as they are now. They can be described in terms of the developmental problems they have already solved. And they can be described in terms of their basic needs. Each of these descriptions is useful to the kindergarten teacher.

CHARACTERISTICS OF KINDERGARTEN CHILDREN

In describing the characteristics of kindergarten children as they are now it is useful to consider them under four aspects: (1) physical, (2) mental, (3) emotional, and (4) social.

15

Physical Characteristics

Muscular Development

Children who have reached kindergarten age are still very much concerned with muscular development. They continue to develop their large muscles through almost continuous physical activity — running, jumping, and climbing over and crawling through objects. They must have freedom to move about. They profit greatly from opportunity for painting with large brushes on large sheets of paper, from hammering and sawing, from finger painting and clay modeling, from building with large blocks and from doing tricks involving balance. In all these activities they have achieved a definite handedness, for nine out of ten a right-handedness. They have gone far in controlling their large muscles, but they will go much further. The incompleteness of their development is evident when, under unusual stress or strain, muscular patterns like those for controlling their elimination go out of control and they have toilet accidents. But on the whole they have, through their unceasing activity, grown remarkably in their muscular co-ordination.

Finer muscular co-ordinations will be mastered later. Kindergarten children are not ready to cut out difficult patterns, to color within the precise lines of a drawing, or to carry on other fine finger movements. But simple cutting, crayoning, and finger activities should be available for short periods of time, since they facilitate small-muscle development. The small muscles that control fusion are not yet developed in most kindergarten children, and prolonged focusing on small pictures, small print, or fine details is apt to damage their eyesight.

Co-ordination

It is important to encourage improvement in muscular co-ordinations but not to press for any expected accomplishment either at home or in school. Each child has his own pattern of physical development, and the patterns vary widely. Girls often show co-ordination and other evidences of physical maturity that make it difficult for some boys to compete with them. Such boys are under undue pressure when parents or older children say to them, "You're not going to let a girl beat you, are you?" Individual competition comes later. In the kindergarten, emphasis is placed on growth and development so that whether a child has developed a particular muscular skill is not so significant as whether he is continuing to improve his skill.

Health

When children enter school they increase their contacts with other children and they often encounter a larger number of virulent pathogens than their bodies can cope with successfully. Fortunately immunizations are available for many of the illnesses that used to plague early childhood. But several communicable diseases — measles, mumps, chicken pox, and common colds — are still part of the experience of children in the early school grades. For that reason each morning the kindergarten teacher checks the health of each child as she greets him. She looks for the symptoms of common diseases, but, more important, she looks for unusual irritability, fatigue, or other evidence that a child is not feeling the way he usually does. An ill child is sent to the school nurse, or, if one is not available, his activities are modified. If he has any temperature, he is immediately removed from the group.

Mental Characteristics

Exploration

The experience a five-year-old has packed into his few years of living is great and yet is only a fragment of what he will have and will need to have in becoming an adult. He seeks out firsthand information. "What makes the light go on?" He presses the switch to find out what happens. He asks questions and he pushes, pulls, and turns whatever is movable. Depending on his individual abilities and past experiences, he explores some things at length but most things rather briefly. Because of his short attention span, his teacher plans activities which are brief and plans repetitions of them in a modified form.

Language

His preschool years of experience with language have given the kindergarten child considerable ability in telling people what he wants and somewhat less in telling them what he has done or seen. Research studies vary in their estimates of the vocabulary of young children. But with a few thousand words in his vocabulary, he sticks mostly to nouns but also uses verbs, adjectives, pronouns, and some conjunctions. The grammatical refinements and subtleties of the language will come later. Meanwhile he builds up a more complete and more accurate understanding of words he already knows, and busily adds on new ideas and the appropriate words for them. His idea of what the word "cat" means changes when he sees a cat of a different color or a tiny kitten. When he sees a strange construction machine busily loading a dump truck, he likes and needs to be told, "That is a skip-loader. It seems to skip around as it loads the dump truck."

The kindergarten child is still perfecting his speech and his auditory acuity. He has been listening to the speech patterns of his family and friends for several years and has been imitating what he hears. Since this learning by imitation is not yet complete, it is highly important that he have a kindergarten teacher who provides a correct pattern, and who speaks slowly and clearly. Like a student of a foreign language, he needs to hear the new language spoken distinctly and deliberately, and always to have the correct name applied to an object.

Egoism

A child understands things by establishing their relation to himself. It takes a multitude of personal experiences before a child can move very far from his egoistic concepts. The kindergarten child says, "I have a kitty at home," "Mine is pink," or "I can do that." When he was younger he had to possess objects before he could learn to share them. Now at five years he must still experience ideas before he can talk about them or learn to do anything else with them.

Abstraction

Another multitude of experiences will be necessary before he is able to go beyond the concrete to the abstract. At his age only the lowest levels of abstraction are possible. Yet, through practice at these levels, he moves on to encompass more and more within a general statement, and later as an adult he will handle abstractions in keeping with his intellectual ability. Now it is a long jump from "This cat says 'Meow' " to the idea that "Cats say 'Meow.' " The kindergarten teacher is constantly watching for opportunities to help children arrive at more general understandings. She is also careful not to use abstractions which mean nothing to children, such as "Hurry" or "Be careful in crossing the street." Instead she uses more vivid and familiar suggestions: "After you finish, we can have our surprise" and "Stop at the curb so you can look and listen for cars."

Property Rights. The abstractions of property rights are confusing to kindergarten children. In the school situation the child is confronted by a new set of rules. The swing is his only so long as he is using it; when he returns from getting a drink, he finds someone else claiming it. He needs help in learning what his property rights are as a member of the group, in distinguishing his own things from the common possessions of the group.

Number

The abstractions of number are also confusing. In family experience he has been one of several, and he has been encouraged to learn to say words that are called "counting." Now he finds himself in a kindergarten group that is much larger than his family group and he learns to deal realistically with numbers beyond ten — but not much beyond. Yet he enjoys stretches into "hundreds" and "millions." The words have pleasant sounds. Much later than kindergarten, they will also have meaning.

Time and Space

Time and space are also abstractions to be coped with later. When a kindergarten child says "In ten minutes," he is merely repeating a phrase to indicate some time later. Furthermore, on his mental map, Japan and Europe are probably located close together, and both are probably near the most distant point he has been to. He needs many experiences with relating his home to his school and to the grocery store and other shops in his immediate neighborhood.

Imagination

Often five-year-olds have not yet learned to differentiate between fact and fancy. Their imaginations take them off into delightful and rather realistic fantasies, and they often need help in labeling their accounts as "pretend" stories. And the listeners, too, need help in distinguishing "pretend" accounts from "real" accounts.

Frequently five-year-old girls use such stories to escape responsibility. Teachers help them move through this phase of development by understanding which labels the story "make believe" and distinguishes it from a true account. A year or two later, other teachers will help the boys to explore this type of behavior.

Emotional Characteristics

The five-year-old runs the full gantlet of emotions. He gets excited about a forthcoming event. He is afraid of what he does not understand and is afraid when others are afraid. He gets angry when frustrated. But mostly he is a happy person with only a few emotional outbursts in the course of a day. And he has an elementary sense of humor.

Need for Expression

The teacher helps the children learn to handle their strong emotions acceptably. She helps them plan their activities so that they can anticipate them with expectation but not undue excitement. She encourages them to talk about their fears and guides them in getting information to alleviate them.

She encourages them to solve their conflicts about turns and the use of materials by talking instead of hitting or grabbing. She gives them desirable language patterns by saying: "Ask Timmy: 'When may I have a turn?'" She helps them realize when they feel "mean" or "like hitting," and helps them find acceptable emotional outlets like punching the punching bag, pounding clay out flat, hammering nails, or scrubbing something clean. She helps them understand that everyone has "mean" feelings and that their feeling that way is quite all right, but that they must vent their feelings on things, not on people who can be hurt.

The Teacher's Attitude

The teacher shares the children's laughter at some unusual noise, some strange mask or costume, or some out-of-the-ordinary dancing, bumping, or falling. She is quite permissive about this level of humor but, if necessary, helps the children see that a bump or fall which hurts someone is not humorous. She helps them to recognize the humor that is portrayed in pictures and in stories.

As a permissive person who enjoys the children and accepts them as they are, the teacher does much to make them feel secure. Her calm appreciation of each child helps the children accept each other and contributes to the stability and happiness of their group. The children feel secure in the daily routine which she establishes, a routine which includes ample time for moving freely from one activity to another. Her consistent enforcement of limits also gives them security. They know other children are not to interfere with their projects and are not to break the playthings. The teacher's voice is also a key factor in the feeling of security within the kindergarten. A calm voice is quieting, and an aggressive voice incites to aggression. To have a climate favorable for sound emotional development, the kindergarten teacher gives attention to the daily routine, consistent enforcement of limits, and a calm and pleasant voice. Then a comfortable feeling tone pervades the kindergarten and fewer conflict situations arise.

Social Characteristics

Gregariousness

The kindergarten child is a social person. He likes to play freely with other children his own age, and does best in playing with them one at a time. A boy likes to play with other boys, with girls, or by himself, and his activities vary accordingly. He plays army with the boys; he plays house with girls and boys; and he paints, draws, cuts, and pastes by himself, or in amiable social relationship to someone near him. By the end of the year many kindergarten children are able to play with others for several minutes in some spontaneous and co-operative group activity: shopping at the grocery store, having a fruit juice party, or taking care of a sick doll.

The child's social development makes him a helpful member of his school group. He willingly volunteers to sing a song or show his picture to the group. He is glad to carry out a request to bring something from across the room. And he adores his teacher. Since her values and expectations are much like those of his parents, and since he knows no others, he accepts them without question. Feeling that his teacher is interested in him and in what he does and says, he goes happily about his play.

Frustration

As the kindergarten child develops socially he learns that his freedom is limited by others. He is free to do only what does not hurt others or keep them from having the same freedom. From time to time his learning involves frustration, and he blames whoever is handy. Suddenly his teacher is "an ole meanie." "I hate you," he says. The wise teacher recognizes his need for an emotional outlet for his frustration. She also recognizes the opportunity for helping him become objective about his frustration and for learning better social behavior. When he is in a good mood later in the day, she talks with him: "This morning you were angry with me because I didn't let you throw rocks where the other children were playing. When you want to throw, you can use the beanbags and set a target away from other people the way you did this morning."

The Teacher's Attitude

By respecting each child no matter what his social skill, attitudes, and ideas, the kindergarten teacher encourages the children to accept their playmates as they are. However, this permissive attitude is sometimes at variance with social discriminations that the children have learned at home or in their neighborhoods. Children sometimes bring to kindergarten undemocratic discriminations based on ethnic background, social class, or religious affiliation. Since they find no opportunity for using these discriminations at kindergarten, they soon discard them. When children are not influenced by older children and adults, they play together democratically.

The kindergarten teacher recognizes her role in promoting the social development of young children. No task is more important to the future welfare of the world. In working with the parents of young children, the teacher can be a potent influence in reducing attitudes of prejudice and discrimination.

No two children are alike, but certain characteristics of growth and development are found in varying degrees in every child. These characteristics are useful to the kindergarten teacher in providing appropriate learning situations for the children and in guiding their development.

The chart on the following page presents the major physical, mental, emotional and social characteristics of the kindergarten child with their implications for the school program.

CHART OF GROWTH AND DEVELOPMENT

Children's Characteristics	*Implications for Teaching*
Are extremely active physically	Provide opportunity to move about freely and play vigorously
Are easily fatigued	Alternate activity with quiet periods Have overstimulated children withdraw
Are susceptible to colds and other illness	Have daily health inspection
Large muscles are more fully developed than finer ones	Plan work with large materials
Incomplete hand co-ordination Eye muscles are not fully developed	Avoid small pictures or print
Children differ greatly in height, weight, co-ordination, and general physical structure	Expect individual variation in energy, strength, endurance and ability to handle materials
Each child matures in his own way	Avoid comparisons
Girls often mature more rapidly than boys	Encourage development but do not impose standards
Auditory acuity is not yet well developed	Speak slowly and clearly
Speech is sometimes faulty and is not yet perfected	Provide correct speech patterns Allow time for children to understand directions and react to them
Span of attention varies greatly according to interest, maturity and experience	Provide a variety of suitable activities
Like to hear, see, smell, taste, touch, and manipulate	Provide learning experiences which appeal to different senses Encourage observation and experimentation Avoid abstractions
Like to ask questions and talk about experiences	Provide opportunities for talking with other children and with adults
Like to react to their experiences non-verbally as well as verbally	Provide for dramatic play, bodily movement, construction, painting, clay modeling, and music
Like to play with other children, without social discrimination	Provide for play groups with companions of their own choice
Are sometimes frustrated and angry	Help them find acceptable emotional outlets Encourage talking in place of hitting
Want to "feel good" about their teacher	Be friendly and understanding Listen to each child and build his self-confidence

Want to "feel good" about what they do and say	Provide for a preponderance of successful experiences
Like security about what to expect	Establish daily routine Be consistent in setting limits
Sometimes evidence tension — thumb sucking, nail biting, toilet accidents, daydreaming	Provide a favorable emotional climate Encourage acceptance by peers Enjoy the children

DEVELOPMENTAL PROBLEMS

In the five years he has been growing, the kindergarten child has already faced and solved many developmental problems. This is clearly seen by considering certain problems of physical development. Being born is the first large hurdle. It takes strength and energy to move down the vaginal canal out into the world, and to start the respiratory and circulatory processes involved in breathing. In the first few days, life itself depends on the baby's ability to solve the problem of learning to nurse. But in a few months the baby learns to eat cereal from a spoon. Eating other foods follows rapidly, and the infant is well started in solving the succession of eating problems which confront a child in our culture.

Muscular Control

Learning to move himself through space also involves the solution of a succession of problems. In the first half year of his life, the infant manages to sit up by himself. A few months later he is crawling around, into everything he can find. Soon he solves the problem of pulling himself erect, and shortly after one year of life he is able to take his first steps alone. In the next four years he focuses his attention on first one and then another problem of moving himself through space. To complicate this learning, he must handle a body that is constantly changing its size and shape. Yet running, climbing, jumping, balancing, and perhaps skipping are successfully added to his repertoire by the time he is ready for kindergarten.

The maturation of nerve endings in various parts of his body is a necessary prelude to solving certain of the developmental problems in our culture. The nerves in his genital area mature between the ages of two and two and a half, and he is interested in controlling his elimination processes all by himself. When he is between the ages of three and four he is able to control his muscles during sleep, and to avoid elimination during those hours.

Learning to Communicate

The problem of communicating his wants and ideas to those close to him constantly occupies the attention of the growing child. His first weak cry as a newborn infant is elaborated and expanded amazingly in five years. From a single cry it develops into a variety of cries, with a hunger cry that is quite different from an anger cry. When the child is nearing two years of age, he has a series of meaningful gestures and a great interest in vocal sounds. The one-syllable words of his private language get closer and closer to the sounds of the language spoken in his home. By two and a half years the child is working earnestly at the developmental problem of learning the language spoken by his family. One- or two-syllable nouns, verbs, short sentences and then gradually all the refinements of the spoken language are mastered by the child by the time he is about eight years old. The kindergarten year greatly aids this process and helps the child in solving his developmental problems of making use of language as a means of communication with other children and with adults.

Irregularity of Development

Many series of developmental problems confront the child as he matures. The precise problem that will catch his interest is sometimes difficult to predict. Today he may spend a great deal of time in practicing some new feat of balance. But tomorrow he may focus his attention completely on some problem in his social development. One can be sure, however, that sooner or later he will work on each of these problems further. Both children and adults are happier when the choice of problems is left up to the child himself and he is free to tackle a given problem when he is ready for it. Instead of planning a fixed schedule of activities for the day, the wise kindergarten teacher provides materials for a wide selection of activities and plans only a minimum number of changes of activity for the whole group to make at the same time. In changing from one activity to another it is important for the kindergarten teacher to allow plenty of time for children (a) to understand what is to be done, (b) to finish what they are doing, and (c) to get started on the new activity. Brief and clear directions with a smile are much better for the young child than lengthy explanations of any kind.

Since the five-year-old has been concerned with so many problems during his few short years, he has not had time to develop a high degree of skill. Nor is he ready to focus attention on what adults consider important. Too many new and fascinating things are still to be explored. As a result of his immaturity he may seem to the uninformed adult to be slow and dawdling. Teachers can help parents realize that they, too, when learning new things impress skilled performers as slow and inept. Skill comes with years of practice.

Individual Differences

Each child is unique in the rate at which he moves through the various series of developmental problems. One child may move rapidly through intellectual problems and much less rapidly through problems of physical development. Another child may move slowly through all aspects of his development for several years and then suddenly begin to develop rapidly in many ways. A child may seem at a standstill in learning to play co-operatively with other children yet be making great progress in handling a ball skillfully. Another child may be an onlooker for weeks during music activities and then suddenly become a participant and in a few more weeks a frequent performer. The wise teacher observes the pattern of a child's development and is confident about his progress, but has no expectations about the timing of his accomplishments. She reminds herself, as she does the children and their parents, "Each child does it when he is ready." She is alert for signs of readiness for a desired learning. She guides and encourages the child in his learning, but she lets him proceed at his own pace. Knowing something of the many developmental problems he has already solved successfully in his five years of growing, she is confident of his ability to continue solving the problems that confront him.

Outgoing-Consolidation Cycle

As children grow and develop they move through a series of two-year cycles. Even years are venturesome and outgoing; odd years consolidate gains made. At four years, the child is apt to go out of bounds and off on tangents. But at three years and even more so at five years the child seems in focus and gives a favorable impression of being in control of himself. The five-year-old is assimilating and organizing what he gained from his preceding expansive and forward era.

The new experience of the kindergarten as well as the fifth-year consolidation period tends to push the five-year-old toward shyness. It is therefore important that the kindergarten teacher be a calm and stabilizing force in the lives of the children. She meets their needs for self-assurance, for belonging to the group, and for achievement. She helps them avoid fears and feelings of guilt. She provides them with new experiences only at a rate they are able to handle. As each child comes to her with some comment or question she bends down and talks with him at his level, listening carefully to what he has to say. In every possible way, she builds the self-confidence of the children, helping them through the five-year-old period of consolidation, and getting them ready for the explosive, brash period of being the six-year-old who so often goes to extremes.

THE BASIC NEEDS OF CHILDREN

The basic needs in our culture are the same for children as for adults, but they vary in emphasis at different ages and under different conditions of living. No two individuals satisfy their basic needs in exactly the same way, because their abilities, values, and purposes differ.

The Process of Learning

Learning and social progress are the result of people trying to satisfy their needs on ever higher levels. Feelings of need arise from dissatisfaction with the *status quo*. These feelings result in a state of disequilibrium. As the individual strives to restore equilibrium, learning occurs and progress is made. However, if feelings of need are seriously frustrated, the result is disorganization of personality and such neurotic behavior that therapy is required to produce order and security. Progress results only from disequilibrium not serious enough to disorganize the individual but sharp enough to stimulate change in behavior.

The Teacher's Role in Meeting Basic Needs

In the kindergarten the teacher arranges the conditions by which the basic needs of the children are met. She helps them meet their physical needs. She notices when children are self-deprecating or overly sensitive and helps them gain a sense of their own importance. She notices when children become hostile or aggressive about conforming to what others suggest and when they become anxious about what others think of them. Then she strives to help them gain acceptance by others and develop a feeling of belonging to the group. She notices when their failures seem to outweigh their successes and helps them develop a sense of achievement. She is alert to expressions of fear and reassuringly helps children rid themselves of their fears. She tries to keep the children free from feelings of guilt. She is constantly aware of their need for a variety of experience and provides them with a balance of familiar security and enticing novelty. She gives them opportunity for quiet rest as well as for exploration and activity. The extent to which she is able to help children meet their basic needs is an important measure of her success as a teacher. She is constantly aware of children's need for:

Self-confidence	Freedom from guilt
Belonging to the group	A variety of experience
Achievement	Love
Freedom from fear	

Every child needs *self-confidence*. He must feel that he is of worth in himself whether he achieves success or not and whether he does what he should or not. When he does something labeled "bad," he especially needs reassurance that people love him and have faith in his ability and willingness to change his behavior when he understands the situation completely.

The kindergarten teacher builds a child's self-confidence at every opportunity. She helps him see good points about his block construction and his paintings, instead of something wrong. She commends the imaginative child on his "pretend" story instead of criticizing him for not telling the truth. When he attempts a new trick on the jungle gym, she says, "That's going to be a really good trick! I like the way you're working it out. Let me know when you get it just the way you want it." When other children try to shame the child who has a toilet accident in the classroom, the teacher calmly smiles at the child and reassures him with, "We all have accidents sometime." At all times the teacher helps children feel sure of themselves.

The common courtesies that every kindergarten teacher practices also contribute to the child's feeling of importance. When talking to an individual child, the teacher stoops down so that she is at his level, not towering over him, and listens attentively to what he has to say. When children are playing, she listens quietly for a bit so that she can enter into and help their activity instead of disrupting it. Before initiating some new group activity, she warns the children of the coming change and gives them time to get ready because she understands that their tempo is slow.

Another need, closely related to the need for self-confidence, is the need for *belonging to the group*. Every child wants to be friends with other children. He wants others to recognize his worth as a member of the group.

The teacher knows that a child needs the security which being a member of a group gives him. She realizes that how children are taught is as important as what they are taught; she knows their need to be treated with understanding, affection, and respect. Sensitive teachers no longer comment on differences between children or banish offenders to lonely isolation as punishment. The teacher is friendly with the children, and because children are imitative they reflect her friendliness. She welcomes new children to the group. When a child returns after an absence from school, the teacher points out that the child was needed and missed. By these and scores of other similar procedures, the teacher contributes to the child's feeling of acceptance as a valued contributing member of his group.

Children need a *sense of achievement*, and the wise teacher expresses her satisfaction with the kind of behavior she wants to promote. Recent studies show that the achievement of school age children spurts when they are given assurance that they are succeeding in their work. Younger children are in even greater need of a sense of achievement.

Children need to work at tasks within their ability — tasks which interest them and for which they see a purpose. They need recognition for their efforts and realistic praise for their accomplishments. They need encouragement to persist when efforts do not meet with success and perhaps a strategic bit of help over an obstacle which seems insurmountable.

The teacher who accepts the facts of individual differences knows that no standards are equally applicable to every child. She therefore avoids competition between children who are not equals, and gives each child opportunity to develop skills and acquire knowledge and understanding to solve his own problems. By providing these positive opportunities, she helps children meet their need for a sense of achievement at a far higher level than they could by competitive striving.

Another basic need of children is *freedom from fear*. Fear can severely limit personality development and can interfere markedly with the attainment of the objectives of the kindergarten curriculum. It is difficult to teach a child who is preoccupied with worries and fears.

The teacher can help children who bring to school superstitions and morbid worries about illness, death, ghosts, earthquakes, or other unusual events. She lets them talk about their feelings; she helps them find out the facts; and she reads stories to them about other children who have mastered their fears and anxieties. A child who studies spiders, who learns how to identify any poisonous species, and who talks about them is not afraid of spiders generally, is wisely cautious about certain spiders, and comes to appreciate their structure and behavior.

Other fears haunt children — fear of failure, fear of embarrassment, fear of ridicule. When such fears are misused to motivate young children, the children may succeed *in spite of* their fears but never because of them. The teacher can help, reassure, and protect the fear-ridden child, and can work with his parents so that they, too, refuse to use fear as a method of controlling children and of imposing the will of the adult upon them.

Teachers and parents can work together in helping children be free from fear of economic insecurity. Parents who express financial worry in the presence of their children often cause them to worry needlessly about matters they understand in part or not at all. One teacher reported that an anxious child asked, "Do you think my Daddy will lose his job?" Such a child can be reassured and helped to understand that economic problems are temporary, are not hopeless, and can be overcome. Certainly teachers should be careful about making demands upon children which may represent a financial burden to certain families and may increase feelings of anxiety and inadequacy in any child in the group.

Close to this need for freedom from fear is the need for *freedom from excessive feelings of guilt.* Old methods of working with children gave approval to the practice of making children feel ashamed of themselves. Standards of attainment impossible for children to reach were set up at home and at school, and then the children were punished for not achieving them.

Modern methods of teaching are based on better understanding of what children can do. Interesting activities adapted to the needs and abilities of each child keep him happy and help him learn with satisfaction. In the modern kindergarten, guilt and shame have no place as methods of guiding children to improved behavior.

When their other basic needs are met, children are curious and active and need *a variety of experiences.* The teacher provides the children with the security of a continuing and satisfying relation with her and the other children, and with the spur of new experiences. Within the familiar setting of the classroom and playground, children have the opportunity to work creatively with familiar blocks, paint, clay, wheel toys, and other equipment. They may repeat familiar play or they may reach out to explore new ideas and materials. Children have the security of daily routines combined with enough of the new to be stimulating but not frustrating. They need time to savor fully the activities of greatest concern to them.

The curriculum of the kindergarten provides experiences which help the child develop as a healthy, well-rounded person. It helps the child understand and enter into the social world of human relations and into the physical world of science. It contributes to his physical development and expands his control of language. It helps him enter into his literary heritage and into his musical heritage. It helps him express himself aesthetically. It helps him understand quantitative and spatial relations. It helps him establish satisfying relations with children and adults. And this variety of experience is provided in such a way that the child has a balance of activity and rest.

Children learn through activity carried on to satisfy their needs. In the process, new needs arise for further activity. The active busy child is a happy child freed from personality-destroying boredom and growing in power to understand and to make himself one with the complex world about him.

Finally the kindergarten child needs *love.* Daniel A. Prescott defines love as "valuing to the degree that one achieves empathy with the loved one and willingness to make one's resources available to promote his self-realization." [1] Love has an important place in the kindergarten. The

---

[1] Prescott, Daniel A. *The Child in the Educative Process.* New York: McGraw-Hill Book Company, 1957, p. 401.

teacher's love assures the child that people outside his own home value him. Going out into the larger world of the school, the child finds a second home in which he has a feeling of belonging and freedom from guilt and fear, a second situation in which it is possible for him to be an important member of the group, self-confident and successful.

Assurance that his kindergarten teacher loves him is a determining factor in whether a child enjoys school. A child who is part of a group loved by its teacher knows that school is a satisfying experience. He looks forward to more schooling.

Sometimes love is confused with putting one's arms around a child or other physical expressions of affection. A teacher puts an arm around those children who like this bodily contact, and avoids putting an arm around those children who do not like to be touched. But she values both kinds of children, and expresses her appreciation of the touch-me-nots verbally. Her tones of voice are those that express affection, confidence, and encouragement; never those that express scorn, belittling, or discouragement.

Occasionally a teacher finds it difficult to like a particular child. Perhaps she is reminded of a person or situation she has feared or disliked, and she transfers her negative feelings to the child. But if she becomes aware of the irrational basis for her feelings, she can often minimize them. By making a detailed study of what the child does, the teacher becomes more and more interested in him, sympathizes with the problems he faces, and shares his successes. Soon the teacher finds that the child she has not liked is a delightful person, and that loving all the children makes her teaching a joy each day.

SITUATIONS FOR DISCUSSION

In the following situations select each course of action that seems desirable to you, basing your choices and omissions on the ideas presented in this chapter. Add one or more alternate courses of action.

SITUATION I. One warm day in the early fall, as the children come into the room, you notice that Johnny has some enlarged capillaries in his eyes. While he is playing a few minutes later you hear him sniffling. You send him to the school nurse, but he returns with a note saying that the nurse is ill today. You should then:

> Let him play outside with other children.
> Let him play on the jungle gym by himself.
> Take his temperature.
> Send him to the office to be sent home.
> Plan quiet activities for him in the room.

SITUATION II. After school one day, one of the girls runs back to your room to tell you that Jean has taken the red clown puppet home with her. The next day when you ask Jean to get the red clown from the puppet box, she reports that it is not there. When you ask her if she put it back when she finished playing with it yesterday, she says that she did. As her teacher you should:

Let the matter drop without further comment.

Call her mother and have her send the clown back.

Have Jean see that she and the other children do not have as much fun without the puppet.

Tell Jean you know she is telling a lie.

Tell Jean, "I'm glad you like the puppets."

SITUATION III. Tim is a fast, hard-hitting boy who is often late for school. His mother works nights scrubbing floors at a hotel. She has a difficult time, she says, in looking after Tim and his two younger sisters. When Tim gets to school, he usually manages to give one or two of the children a good poke before he finds a place to sit down. This morning one of the boys hits back. As the teacher you get the boys separated, and then take care of Tim by:

Letting him pound clay.

Sending him to the office.

Having him sit in a corner by himself.

Talking to him privately about being ashamed of himself.

Getting him started on a carpentry problem.

SITUATION IV. Your kindergarten group is made up entirely of children with European descent. A Japanese doctor and his Canadian wife enter their five-year-old boy, Walter, in your group. The next Monday morning, Tony comes to you and says, "I can't play with Walter. He's Japanese." As the teacher you should:

Have a group discussion about welcoming a new friend into the group.

Tell Tony that he can play with whomever he wants to.

Plan an activity in which both Tony and Walter participate.

Tell Tony that Walter is an American just like him.

Have Walter play by himself.

BIBLIOGRAPHY

Professional Books and Pamphlets

Gesell, Arnold, and Frances L. Ilg, *Child Development*. New York: Harper and Bros., 1949.

This reprint of two earlier books, *Infant and Child in the Culture of Today* and *The Child from Five to Ten*, describes the kindergarten age child as well as the nursery school child and the first grade child. The descriptions are based primarily on observations of children in New England communities.

Hildreth, Gertrude. *Readiness for School Beginners*. Yonkers-on-Hudson, New York: World Book Company, 1950.

How to understand children entering school, methods of studying their behavior, and skills to be developed are related to the concept of readiness.

Hurlock, E. B. *Child Development.* New York: McGraw-Hill Book Company, Inc., 1956.

Films are available to accompany this textbook on different aspects of child development.

Jenkins, Gladys Garner, Helen Schacter, and William W. Bauer. *These Are Your Children.* Chicago: Scott, Foresman and Company, 1953.

Characteristics of children's growth are presented warmly, sympathetically, and with understanding. Five-year-olds are discussed in detail in Chapter 5, "A Comfortable Age."

Merry, Frieda Kiefer, and Ralph Vickers Merry. *The First Two Decades of Life.* New York: Harper and Brothers, 1950.

This text for child psychology takes up such topics as "How We Study Children and Adolescents," "How We Begin Life," and "Interests in Reading, Radio and Movies."

Millard, C. V., and J. W. M. Rothney. *The Elementary School Child.* New York: Dryden Press, 1957.

Case studies of individual children in the elementary school further teacher understanding of child behavior in the classroom.

Murphy, L. B., et al. *Personality in Young Children.* New York: Basic Books, Inc., 1956. 2 volumes.

Volume I deals with methods for measuring the inner life of a child and his perception of a relation to his environment.
Volume II is an intensive study of one pre-school boy.

Olson, Willard C. *Child Development,* 2nd ed. Boston: D. C. Heath and Company, 1959.

Teachers of children from nursery school through elementary school can apply the findings of research on child development.

Olson, Willard C., and John Lewellen. *How Children Grow and Develop.* Better Living Booklet. Chicago: Science Research Associates, Inc., 1953.

As children grow they meet and solve problems at each level of development. Parents and teachers can help them with these problems.

Strang, Ruth. *An Introduction to Child Study.* New York: The Macmillan Company, 1951.

This third edition takes up sequences of behaviors, possible explanations of behavior, how children learn, conditions conducive to development, and methods of child study and guidance.

Films about Children

Children's Emotions. New York: McGraw-Hill Book Company, 1950.

Fear, anger, jealousy, curiosity, and joy are shown in children with suggestions about how parents can promote happiness. 22 minutes, sound, black and white.

Frustrating Fours and Fascinating Fives. New York: McGraw-Hill Book Company, 1952.

The kind of behavior to be expected at four and at five is shown together with methods that help the child in his normal development. 22 minutes, sound, black and white.

He Acts His Age. New York: McGraw-Hill Book Company, 1951.

Typical behavior of ages one through fifteen is shown at a picnic. Interests, actions, and emotions are different at different ages. 15 minutes, sound, black and white, or color.

Long Time to Grow, Part 2, "Four and Five Year Olds." New York: New York University, 1954.

Four- and five-year-old children work and play at Vassar College Nursery School and Poughkeepsie Day School. 35 minutes, sound, black and white.

Principles of Development. New York: McGraw-Hill Book Company, 1950.

Principles of development and factors in individual differences are shown in this film and also in a filmstrip which is correlated with the book *Child Development* by Elizabeth B. Hurlock. 17 minutes, sound, black and white.

Social Development. New York: McGraw-Hill Book Company, 1950.

Social behavior at different age levels is also presented in relation to the book *Child Development* by Elizabeth B. Hurlock. 16 minutes, sound, black and white.

Study of Twins, Part IV. State College, Pennsylvania: Psychological Cinema Register, Pennsylvania State College, 1950.

At ages three, four, and five, children grow in co-ordination and co-operation, and in self-sufficiency in eating, washing teeth, and playing. 19 minutes, silent, black and white.

Filmstrips

From Sociable Six to Noisy Nine. New York: McGraw-Hill Book Company, Inc., Text Films, 1955.

Shows a positive relationship of parents with children from age six to nine; gives parents and teachers of kindergarten children a look ahead. 22 minutes, black and white, or color.

Getting Johnny Ready for School. Bloomington, Indiana: N E T Film Service, Indiana University Audio-Visual Center, 1955.

This film, which is the twelfth in the series, *At Home with Your Child*, describes the $5\frac{1}{2}$ to $6\frac{1}{2}$ age child, a pre-school visit, and tests of readiness, hearing, and vision. 20 minutes, sound, black and white.

Understanding the Child. Bloomington, Indiana: N E T Film Service, Indiana University Audio-Visual Center, 1955.

This series of seven films includes: 1, "How Children Grow," which contrasts the intellectual, social, physical, and emotional growth of two girls, ages 5 and 8; 2, "Physical Development"; 3, "Mental Growth and Achievement"; 4, "The Child as a Whole"; 5, "Social Relations," which shows the social relations of the infant expanding into the community and into the world; 6, "Emotional Development"; and 7, "Child Rearing Practices," which are constantly changing. 30 minutes, sound, black and white.

3

The Social Environment of
the Kindergarten

Modern education has accepted as its major responsibility the job of helping children to develop into happy, well-adjusted, competent citizens of a democracy. Studies of mental health reveal that the realization of this objective involves the development of a person who feels comfortable about himself, who feels right toward other people, and who is able to meet the demands of life.

THE TEACHER AND THE SOCIAL CLIMATE
OF THE CLASSROOM

The teacher creates the emotional climate in the classroom from her own personality. Only the teacher can establish sound teacher-pupil relationships conducive to optimum development. Only the teacher can create pupil-pupil relationships in which respect for the worth of other personalities can grow. The teacher can arrange learning situations in which children experience the satisfaction of working in friendly co-operation with others to achieve worthy group purposes.

Her Own Personality

Teaching is an intensely personal relationship. The teacher's personality has long been recognized as the most important element in the social environment of the classroom. Effective teachers are friendly, constructive, encouraging, and supporting in their human relations. They are interested in and enthusiastic about the things children find intriguing. They are ingenious and skillful in planning challenging learning experiences. They are poised and unvaryingly courteous in their contacts with children. They understand and accept children for what they are and recognize their opportunity to help each child to be and to do his best.

34

The teacher may say this is a large order. To be sure, it is. But the teacher's own potentialities are the creative materials always at hand. No one stands still in the teaching profession. If the motivation is strong enough, personality can be changed. What motivation can offer greater incentive to the teacher than the needs of children and the social significance of teaching?

Knows the Personality of the Children

The emotional climate a teacher provides is determined to a considerable extent by what the teacher knows about each child in the group. In increasing numbers, schools are concerned about providing cumulative guidance records on which pertinent data are kept throughout the pupil's school experience. These records are usually begun in the kindergarten. Reference to such records helps the teacher to get a clear picture of each child — his physical equipment and condition; his native endowment; his experiences and achievement; his family background; problems he has encountered in achieving his developmental tasks; his attitudes and emotional adjustment.

In addition, teachers endeavor to study the behavior of children in the group and to make factual, objective, anecdotal records in order to deepen their insight into the causes of behavior. The teacher knows that unacceptable behavior can be permanently changed only by discovering and eliminating the cause, not by punitive forays directed at symptoms in the form of overt behavior.

Makes Use of Child Psychology Principles

Charlotte Buhler points out that modern techniques for studying individual children are based on certain general concepts of behavior which were discovered by psychological research or through clinical practice. Child psychology has revealed many facts pertaining to the sequence of maturation of functions and behavior. Psychiatry has revealed the necessity of understanding the underlying dynamics, the motivating, and the conditioning of behavior. The three concepts which should be given special attention by school personnel studying individual children are stated by Dr. Buhler as follows:

1. *Maturation* is reflected by the child's mental, emotional, physical, and social development. The level of maturity can be determined through observations made by skilled observers, or through the use of scores from tests standardized for this purpose. It merits particular attention during the early years the individual is in school.

2. *Motivation* includes all things which incite the individual to act. Motivation that underlies overt behavior may exist in any degree of consciousness or unconsciousness. The more closely it approaches

the unconscious state the more difficult it is to identify. Proper motivation is of great importance in the child's education, re-education, guidance, and therapy.

3. *Conditioning factors* are the child's native equipment, his physical condition throughout his life, incidents in his life history, and environmental influences. Each of these factors may be studied through physical and mental examinations or through interviews with the child or with adults familiar with the child's history. Information regarding factors which have conditioned a child should be used in planning a program for his welfare.[1]

Regards the Child as an Individual

The psychologists have pointed out the chief developmental tasks at each level of maturity.[2] They have produced substantial evidence to prove that *all* children are different. Authorities in the fields of teacher education and parent education have pointed out that it is the job of parents and teachers to *accept* children as they are, love them, and help them to achieve *their* best. Psychologists have pointed out the dangers of unrealistic expectations on the part of parents. Parents need to understand their own responses to their children. Children are greatly in need of acceptance by their parents. And parents are greatly in need of the understanding which will make it possible for them to accept and love their children for what they are without feelings of disappointment, shame, resentment, pity, guilt, or resignation. The child's mental health as well as the mental health of the parents depends upon such understanding. Although the responsibility of the teacher is not the same as that of the parent, the teacher, too, must love and accept each child. No child should be made to feel unwanted or rejected in his school or by his teacher.

Parents and teachers need to understand that all behavior is caused. What a person does is caused by things that have happened to him in his life. The causes of behavior are complex, multiple, and interrelated. Individual behavior is aimed at preserving and enhancing the individual as a person. Once an individual has found a behavior useful, he will tend to repeat it. Past successes that the child has had will determine the patterns he will use when he grows up. The same behavior in two children can be the result of entirely different causes. Behavior will not be changed by a direct attack on the behavior itself any more than a fever is cured by direct treatment of the fever itself. The physician seeks to identify the *cause* of the fever and treat that. The fever disappears when the cause is

[1] Charlotte Buhler, "Techniques for Studying Individual Children," *California Journal of Elementary Education*, XXI (February, 1953), pp. 58–59.

[2] Robert J. Havighurst, *Human Development and Education.* New York: Longmans, Green and Co., 1953.

Kindergarten children are extremely active
physically. The teacher should provide the
opportunity for them to move about freely and
play vigorously.

The teacher can arrange learning situations in
which children experience the satisfaction of
working in friendly co-operation with others to
achieve worthy group purposes.

removed. In like manner, the behavior of a child grows out of all the influences which his parents, home, playmates, school, and community have exerted upon him. If changes in his behavior are desired, the teacher will strive to work with causes, but she will know that methods which work with one child will not always work with another. The unit of behavior is the individual and each child is different from every other child.

Makes Use of Specialists' Services

All of these considerations reflect a concern about children that has developed in recent years and that is carried in the term *individualization*. Considerable effort has been made to meet the individual differences of children. An array of new titles has appeared in school directories. Quite properly as knowledge of needs has grown, schools have added nurses, attendance supervisors, counselors, psychologists, psychiatrists, specialists in fields related to the needs of exceptional children, and directors of guidance to the extent that local resources permitted such additions.

As each teacher adds to her growing understanding of children by observation, conferences with parents, visits to homes, and conversations with individual children, needs are sometimes revealed of conditions beyond the knowledge or power of the teacher to improve or correct. At this point, the services of specialized personnel should be available to the teacher. Their service should be largely of a consultative nature, to the only persons who can most continuously bring about change in the child's behavior or meet his problems — his parents and his teacher. With the specialists' aid, the parents may remove causes of frustration in their work with the child at home, or, if this is not possible, bring greater understanding to the conditions responsible for the behavior, and the teacher may better adjust the learning experiences of the school to the child's needs and interests so that he has a greater feeling of adequacy.

In the case of exceptional children the specialists' service may sometimes involve placement in a special class for full- or part-time instruction. It may mean intensive case study, or it may mean consultation with guidance. Special education personnel, the teacher, and the school administrator work with parents to plan for individual treatment.

The teacher with all her daily contacts with children has an advantageous position over any other worker in the school system. Ruth Strang expresses the importance of the classroom teacher in these words: "Teachers hold a key position in the environment of the growing child; and consciously or unconsciously, they wield a cumulative influence on his psychological growth."[3] All of the specialists and specialized services the

[3] Ruth M. Strang, *The Role of the Teacher in Personnel Work*. New York: Teachers College, Columbia University, 1946, p. vii.

school can provide should be available to the teacher for use in meeting the needs of children. The specialists can be of most service as they help teachers to identify the needs in the class and put at the disposal of the teacher the specialists' knowledge, special services provided in the school system, or contact with community agencies in meeting the particular needs.

The teacher needs to be able to fit information about a child together and to develop understanding of him and discover how the school may best meet the child's needs. The teacher needs to know the steps which can best be taken with a child. Through experience with play therapy she learns how to use it as a part of the instructional program and at the same time clarifies her own concepts and feelings about it.

Studies the Child in Relation to the Group

Education in our schools is of necessity a group process. If the group is not too large, the teacher can come to know the individuals reasonably well and can note interaction among the members of the group. The group is important in the educative process, however, and it is possible for a group to be too small to provide adequate opportunity for the interactive process. General agreement seems to exist that twenty five-year-old children constitute a desirable group for kindergarten if the physical environment provides ample space for their work and play.

The kindergarten teacher studies a child best in group situations. The child must be doing something. A child cannot be studied as a child; he has to be studied in relation to a particular context. Descriptions of child behavior are meaningless unless the situation in which the behavior occurs is specified.

SEQUENTIAL STANDARDS OF PERSONALITY DEVELOPMENT

There is accord among experts and acceptance among educators of the steps in personality development as set forth in the report of the Mid-century White House Conference held in Washington, December, 1950. These steps involve the sequential establishment of

A sense of trust
A sense of autonomy
A sense of initiative
A sense of accomplishment
A sense of identity
A sense of intimacy
The parental sense
A sense of integrity

The following statements are taken from *Personality in the Making*,[4] the official report of the White House Conference on Children and Youth:

The Sense of Trust. The component of the healthy personality that is the first to develop is the sense of trust. The crucial time for its emergence is the first year of life. . . . The primitive origin of the sense of trust probably lies in the earliest experience of finding basic needs taken care of in appropriate and consistent ways . . . a sense of trust is the most important element in the personality. It emerges at the most vulnerable period of a child's life. Yet it is the least likely to suffer harm, perhaps because both nature and culture work to make mothers most maternal at this time.

The Sense of Autonomy. The sense of trust being firmly established, the struggle for the next component of the healthy personality begins. . . . Much of his energy for the next two years will center around asserting that he is a human being with a mind and will of his own . . . the sense that he is an independent human being and yet one who is able to use the help and guidance of others. . . .

The Sense of Initiative. Having become sure, for the time being, that he is a person in his own right and having enjoyed that feeling for a year or so, the child of four or five wants to find out what he can *do*. . . . This is the period of enterprise and imagination, an ebullient, creative period when play and phantasy substitute for literal execution of desires and the meagerest equipment provides material for high imaginings. It is a period of intrusive, vigorous learning, learning that leads away from the child's own limitations into future possibilities. There is interference with other people by physical attack. There is intrusion into other people's ears and mind by loud and persistent questioning. There is intrusion into space by vigorous locomotion and intrusion into the unknown by consuming curiosity.

By this age, too, conscience has developed. The child is no longer guided only by outsiders; there is within him a voice that comments on his deeds, and warns and threatens. . . .

The Sense of Duty and Accomplishment. The three stages so far described are probably the most important for healthy personality development . . . with them achieved — and with them caution, self-control, and conscience — progress through the later stages is fairly well assured. . . .

. . . the fourth stage, . . . begins somewhere around six years of age and extends over five or six years, . . . the child wants to be engaged in real tasks that he can carry through to completion . . . children, after a period characterized by exuberant imagination, want to settle down to learning exactly how to do things and how to do them well.

The Sense of Identity. The central problem of the period (adolescence) is (that) the adolescent seeks to clarify who he is and what his role in society is to be.

The Sense of Intimacy. After a sense of identity is achieved . . . the next component of the healthy personality . . . is the sense of intimacy, intimacy

---

[4] *Personality in the Making*, edited by Helen Leland Witmer and Ruth Kotinsky. The Fact Finding Report of the Midcentury White House Conference on Children and Youth. *Children and Youth*. New York: Harper and Brothers, 1952, pp. 8–26. Also in Erik H. Erikson, *Childhood and Society*. New York: W. W. Norton and Co., Inc., 1950, pp. 219–233.

with persons of the same sex or of the opposite sex . . . The surer he becomes of himself, the more he seeks intimacy, in the form of friendship, love, and inspiration.

The Parental Sense. "Parental sense" designates somewhat the same capacity as that implied in the words "creativity" or "productivity." The individual has normally come to adulthood before this sense can fully develop.

The Sense of Integrity. The final component . . . is the sense of integrity. In every culture the dominant ideals — honor, courage, faith, duty, purity, grace, fairness, self-discipline . . . become . . . the care of the healthy personality's integration.

These components of a healthy personality have been delineated at some length not only because of their intrinsic value but for two other important reasons in this particular connection. First, the development of personality follows an orderly sequence — each component is dependent upon the achievement of prior components. For example, a child will not develop a sense of initiative unless he has a well-developed sense of autonomy based on an equally well-developed sense of trust. In the second place, the first three components are of particular interest to the kindergarten teacher because certain problems which children manifest may be due to insecurity growing out of an inadequate development of a sense of trust and a sense of autonomy. But more particularly the component of personality developed during the kindergarten period — the sense of initiative — indicates strongly the kind of educational program needed and the empathy teachers must have with children during this highly significant stage in the development of personality.

THE ORGANIZATION OF PERSONALITY

Organization of the personality is related mainly to the perceptual system (the senses) which acts as interpreter and modifier of the external world in accordance with the biological and social needs of the individual.

The kindergarten child is profoundly engaged in developing his concept of himself — the "I," "me," "self," "ego." These terms indicate the effort of the individual to organize his personality. Each person interprets and modifies his personality in terms of his present concept of himself.

The most important function of the ego is to test reality, to keep the organism from danger. The concept the individual has of the self may not correspond to the picture others have of him. In the process of organizing his personality, every person comes out with a concept of the external world and is certain that others see the world in exactly the same way he sees it.

Children operate on the pleasure principle. They want what they want when they want it. At first children cannot choose deferred values. Part of the maturing process is the development of the ability to make choices which result in the greatest advantage to the individual, to put off immediate pleasure for ultimate results of more significance.

Society operates in terms of moral and logical principles which each child must learn. The psychologist says there must occur an internalization of moral imperatives — the development of the super-ego, or conscience. The deterrent to behavior that is not in accord with these moral imperatives is the feeling of guilt. It is of the utmost importance that a child live in an environment at home and at school in which he may learn these moral and logical principles without undue feelings of guilt for occasional lapses. The kind of personality which emerges from the environment which surrounds the child is determined to a far greater extent by *how* these learnings take place than by *what* is actually learned.

Every young child has an important biological inheritance — the energy part of the organism. Some children have what seems to adults excessive amounts of this biological energy. Certainly it is evident in the ceaseless "on the go" of the kindergarten child — the original "perpetual motion machine." But this energy is important. It powers the organism to activity, and all learning results from the interaction of the learner with his environment. The development of the ego, however, is equally important and here the teacher and the parents give direction through their guidance. They know that the ego is the developed intelligence and personality which uses the biological energy either constructively or destructively.

THE TEACHER AND THE PARENT IN SOCIAL DEVELOPMENT

The kindergarten teacher and the parents of the kindergarten child are concerned with the question: Is this child growing normally? Is there evidence that the child resorts to an unusual number of defenses to protect his ego — projection, repression, rationalization? Does he attempt to escape by withdrawing?

The good kindergarten staffed by an understanding teacher must be in full partnership with parents who know or are willing to learn how to guide the development of wholesome personalities. Education is by no means the sole prerogative of the school. Education is those experiences that affect behavior. Education is not those things a child can talk about but those things he can act about.

POLICIES IN GUIDANCE AND SOCIAL CONTROL

The practices of the kindergarten teacher should be directed toward the ultimate goal of helping each child to grow in self-control and self-direction. The principles followed may be stated briefly because they have been implied throughout this chapter:

1. A positive approach is made to children.
2. A permissive atmosphere to help promote self-control is maintained.
3. The individual is considered in terms of his maturity and background of experience.
4. Kindness, and firmness in recognizing limits, are emphasized.
5. The needs of individuals are anticipated and provision is made for meeting them.
6. The contribution of each child is recognized.
7. The teacher works as a guide and counselor.
8. Emphasis is placed on the effect on the group of an individual's behavior.

With these principles in mind the teacher helps children to understand themselves and acquire the necessary skills for growth in self-control and self-direction.

EVALUATING THE SOCIAL ENVIRONMENT OF THE KINDERGARTEN

A good social environment is one that operates in terms of the democratic faith. Two ideas are fundamental in democracy. The first is *respect for the value of individual lives and personalities.* The second is that *each person shall consider the welfare of the group of prime importance, but, in turn, the group must consider the development of each individual as necessary to forward the highest achievement in group living.* The school in a democratic society exists to perpetuate these basic commitments.

How can the kindergarten teacher know whether she is translating these principles into the day-by-day living of the children? In a truly democratic school, the following situations are the rule, not the exception:

1. The children are carrying on activities and doing work which interests them because it furthers their purposes and makes living richer for them. Child interest is an important criterion for evaluating any teaching-learning situation because interest is evidence of awakening power.

2. The children are engaging in a variety of different activities under the guidance of a teacher who understands the wide range of individual differences represented in any unselected group. The traditional practice of having every child doing the same thing at the same time has disappeared. Now, children interact with an environment designed to meet individual capacities, interests, and needs.

3. The children have opportunity to make choices. In small groups they have periods of planning for work, for trips into the neighborhood,

for dramatic play, which provide opportunities for learning to make sound choices. The process of learning to make wise choices is one of the most important lessons the school can teach.

4. Each child is treated with respect and consideration by his teacher and the other children. Recognition of the sanctity of human personality demands that every child be well treated. The mental health of our people is jeopardized unless every child's self-respect is protected. One of every ten of our population actually breaks under the tension and pressures of modern life and becomes one of life's psychiatric failures. Even more people are in various ways at odds with themselves and their environment and so lead half-lives. Early in the child's school life is one time when wise teachers and qualified specialists can deal with these problems of adjustment before they become impossible to solve. The school can become more concerned with the preventive angle of the problem of mental health. This means avoidance of practices that induce tensions in children or that might make them think less well of themselves.

5. The children are learning to work in groups and are beginning to become aware of group processes. Social values are being taught. Children are learning to look for facts to answer their questions. They are learning to contribute to the group and to accept and respect each child's contribution. Children are respected for their contribution regardless of color, national background, or social or economic status. The satisfactions provided by group participation play a large part in determining the behavior of the individual.

In any evaluation of the educational program of a kindergarten, a qualified observer should be conscious of the teacher's efforts to help each child develop the abilities and attitudes of a truly democratic person. The teacher is working to help each child to become a self-respecting, self-reliant person commensurate with his level of maturity. The teacher is helping each child, by her example and by the experiences she brings to him, to grow in respect for the personality, property, and culture of other persons. The teacher is arranging learning situations in which children may grow in ability to get along with others, to co-operate willingly, and to adjust to new situations and people. Because the teacher knows that in a free society individuals must assume great responsibility, she is patiently guiding children to grow in ability to act responsibly and courageously in accordance with accepted personal and social values.

The social environment the teacher creates in the kindergarten depends greatly on her awareness of social values and social goals within the range of reasonable attainment by children of the maturity level and background she teaches. It depends on the teacher's own full acceptance of the democratic way of life and her efforts to exemplify it in her living with children and with her colleagues.

ADJUSTING CURRICULUM TO ACTUAL NEEDS OF CHILDREN

Every teacher knows that children differ greatly in capacity, interest and background, and in other ways. Efforts to teach a group of children as though they were all alike destine children and teacher to mediocre results.

The old type kindergarten in which all children engaged in the same activity at the same time became obsolete when professional knowledge of individual variation reached its present acceptance.

The modern teacher recognizes that her function is to help each child to make as much growth as possible within the limits of his innate capacity. By her arrangement of an environment which stimulates the children's natural drives to learning and by circulating among the individuals or small groups, encouraging and assisting each child or group of children at the point of need, the teacher provides the guidance necessary to meet individual differences. The kindergarten children are encouraged to help each other and thus the knowledge and skills of each become a resource for the others. The kindergarten teacher is always at hand when children are having difficulty in using materials or making social adjustments. No comparisons are made of one individual with another or of one group with another.

THE TEACHER WORKS WITH THE SCHOOL ADMINISTRATOR

The Public Kindergarten. In the kindergarten that is part of the public school system, the teacher works with other teachers under the direction of a principal. In turn, the principal is directed by the Board of Education, often through a Superintendent of Schools. The Board of Education is representative of the people of the community and is concerned that the schools provide the education needed by school-age children in the community. The kindergarten teacher thinks of herself as a member of a team working for the good of the children. The teachers, the principals, the superintendent, and the Board of Education share the responsibility for educating the children. In working together each is concerned that he do his part and that other members of the team be successful in carrying out their duties. The kindergarten teacher is loyal to her principal, and contributes to his successful administration of the school. In turn, the principal is loyal to her and to the other teachers, helping them do what seems best for the children in the community.

The Private Kindergarten. In the private school, the teacher usually works with other teachers under the director of the school. Through the director, the school is responsive to the community and to the parents who make it possible for the school to exist for the good of their children. The teacher and the director are mutually loyal and co-operative as they further the best interests of the children.

In both public and private schools, either the teacher or the principal of the school may be visited by the parents of an individual child. If the teacher is approached by a parent, she discusses with him any questions he may have about what his child does or about the activities in the kindergarten. However, she is careful to refer the parent to the principal to discuss any question that involves school policy. In turn, when the principal is approached by parents, he refers them to the kindergarten teacher for any information about their child or the activities of the kindergarten. Any questions about the relation of the school to the community or about the policies of the school, the principal discusses directly with the parents.

The Parent Co-operative Kindergarten. In the parent co-operative kindergarten, the teacher may be one of several teachers working with the children under a director, or she may be the only teacher working with the children as their teacher and also working with the parents as the director of the school. As the teacher of the children, she is completely responsible for the activities of the kindergarten day. If she wishes, she may share this responsibility with the parents who assist her. Usually she does so as rapidly as the mothers feel and are sufficiently familiar with children and the activities suitable to their age level. As the director of the school, she attends regular meetings of the parents so that she understands the policies they wish put into effect with the children. She keeps the parent group informed about what is needed in the way of additions or repairs to the equipment. But, more important, she keeps the parents aware of the progress that each child is making, and discusses with the parents, attitudes and activities that will help each child to develop optimally in the kindergarten. As she works with the parents, the teacher constantly furthers their understanding of five-year-old children and of effective ways of working with them.

No matter what the administrative arrangements for the kindergarten, the teacher has an important responsibility toward those who are directly concerned with her work: she must keep them adequately informed about what she is doing with the children. If she is a wise teacher, she does this through the children. An invitation to see an action story that the children have prepared or to see their rhythms is a much more effective report than a highly personalized account of "what I have been doing." The teacher keeps in mind that administrators, boards of education and parents, like herself, have their attention focused on the children. She therefore talks in terms of children, rather than in terms of herself. Thus she is able to keep her administrator informed both about accomplishments of the children and their persistent problems. When the teacher co-operates with the administrator in this way, her feeling of working closely with the school personnel is deepened to the point where it carries over into her work with the children.

Parents are interested in having kindergarten for their children. In parent co-operative kindergartens, the parents take responsibility for policy-making and business arrangements. In kindergartens operated by public school systems or by private owners, parents are not directly involved in providing facilities and teaching personnel. But no matter what the administrative arrangements are for the kindergarten, the parents are concerned about its effectiveness in meeting the needs of the children and are willing to co-operate with the educational personnel to promote the good of the children.

In one state when action of the legislature made it impossible for public schools to continue provisions for kindergartens, parents co-operated with each other in making them available for their children. This co-operation involved different roles for the parents. Some parents enjoyed the business problems in providing facilities and equipment, and in selecting and employing teaching personnel. In one community the parents took turns in doing the janitorial work. In each community, the parents shared by monthly payments the expense of the kindergarten.

In private, co-operative, and public kindergartens, many mothers like to be directly helpful, either in a housekeeping role or in the role of assistant to the teacher. The Parent-Teacher Association encourages mothers to help the teacher by providing aprons for painting, refreshments for parties, and other supplies easily obtained from home. Many mothers find pleasure in this role, and their children take pride in their mother's interest in the kindergarten.

A limited number of mothers enjoy working directly with the children, helping the teacher in providing increased opportunities for learning. Often these mothers were teachers prior to their marriage. In many instances these mothers will be leaders of children or youth groups in Scouts, Campfire, YMCA, or YWCA. Many of them will return to classroom teaching later when their families need less constant attention. Participation in the kindergarten activities enriches their lives and makes them more effective parents and teachers.

With mother assistants a teacher can provide a greater number of activities and more individual guidance for the children. She can introduce and supervise new activities while mother assistants help with familiar ones. A mother assistant can help children put on paint aprons and select their paints. When they have finished painting, she echoes their satisfaction in what they have done, helps them place their painting in a safe place to dry, and helps them in cleaning up and putting away equipment. In the middle of the morning a mother assistant can prepare fruit juice, help serve it, and guide children in cleaning up afterwards. On study trips a mother assistant can help the children in crossing the street safely, in keeping together as a group, in being sure that every child hears new words accurately, and in answering questions. Depending on their interests and abilities, and on the time they have available, mother assistants can participate in the activities that the teacher has planned and can sometimes suggest and provide materials for additional educative experiences for the children. A mother who plays the piano or other instrument is an invaluable aid to musical activities, and a good storyteller is an asset at any time.

It is easy to select and prepare mothers to assist in kindergarten. In cities having an adult education program, a course for mother assistants provides pointers on how to work with five-year-old children at the same time that it is a selective hurdle which eliminates mothers who are not really interested in working with children. Mothers who are taking or have taken such a course are well able to free the kindergarten teacher from routine activities so that she can work with individuals and small groups of children. As the mother assistants gain experience, they become increasingly effective in helping the teacher meet the needs of the children. They provide increased opportunity for meaningful conversation, and make available to the children a greater fund of information and activity.

SITUATIONS FOR DISCUSSION

In the following situations select each course of action that seems desirable to you basing your choices and omissions on the ideas presented in this chapter. Add one or more alternate courses of action.

SITUATION I. As a first-year teacher, you are having difficulty in handling a large group of children. While you work with one small group of children, several of the boys are wrestling with each other instead of carrying on constructive activities. Their noise interferes with what the other children are doing. As the teacher, you should:

Try to work out the problem in your own way.
Say, "Just fine," when your principal asks how you are getting along.
Talk over your problem with your college supervisor of practice teaching.
Find out how the other beginning teacher is getting along.
Reread your college text, *The Kindergarten Teacher*.

SITUATION II. The kindergarten in which you are to teach is a two-teacher unit in which facilities may be shared or used separately. Another new teacher, Miss Simpson, and you discuss arrangements for the school year. Miss Simpson says, "I think we shall each be more happy if we just work by ourselves. I would rather not have a piano than try to work out some plan for sharing it." As the other kindergarten teacher, you should say:

"If you think it best to work separately, let's try it that way."

"Children learn co-operation by seeing how grownups work together."

"We can take turns by the week in using the piano."

"We can talk about use of equipment from time to time during the year."

"That's one way of doing it."

SITUATION III. Your group includes a well-dressed little girl who has pretty features but a rather vacant expression. She seems in a dream world much of the time. Her irrelevant responses and her non-participation in activities of the group make you wonder if she is subnormal. As her teacher you should:

Treat her as you do any other child in the group.

Talk with your principal about her.

Tell her parents you think she is subnormal.

Ask the nurse whether you should refer her for examination by the school physician.

Plan to retain her for a second year of kindergarten.

SITUATION IV. You have been teaching kindergarten for several years in the community in which you grew up. The local school board feels that population shifts make it necessary to use funds at the secondary school level instead of the kindergarten level. Kindergarten teachers are not re-employed and the kindergartens are closed. As a teacher you should:

Talk with leading parents about forming a parent co-operative kindergarten.

Suggest to the president and board members of AAUW that they sponsor a kindergarten.

Apply for a position in a nearby community.

Take a year off from teaching.

Ask for a teaching position at a different grade level in your home community.

BIBLIOGRAPHY

Professional Books and Pamphlets

Association for Childhood Education International. *Portfolio on More and Better Schools for Children under Six.* Washington, D. C., 1949.

Twelve leaflets on such topics as "Children Need Group Experience" and "What Makes a School Good?" contain many suggestions on how to establish, furnish, and staff a kindergarten.

Driscoll, Gertrude P. *Child Guidance in the Classroom.* Practical Suggestions for Teaching, No. 13. New York: Bureau of Publications, Teachers College, Columbia University, 1955.

Presents the view that classroom teachers who understand what lies back of typical child behavior at school can aid the emotional development of children.

Lee, J. Murray, and Dorris May Lee. *The Child and His Curriculum*, rev. New York: Appleton-Century-Crofts, Inc., 1950.

A helpful book for elementary school teachers which contains many suggestions about creating a favorable social environment for children.

Moustakas, Clark E., and Minnie P. Berson. *The Young Child in School.* New York: William Morrow and Company, 1956.

Points out that enhancement of the individual in personal experience and recognition that empathy is an indispensable quality of the teacher are important aspects of the democratic nursery school.

National Education Association. *Creating a Good Environment for Learning*, 1954 Yearbook. Association for Supervision and Curriculum Development. Washington, D. C., 1954.

A good environment for learning is created by relating the people and the physical resources and evaluating the outcomes.

—— *Let's Look at Kindergartens.* Department of Kindergarten-Primary Education. Washington, D. C., 1955.

Supervised activities that children enjoy in kindergarten help them to develop physically, socially, and mentally.

Prescott, Daniel A. *The Child in the Educative Process.* New York: McGraw-Hill Book Company, 1957.

Among other theories expressed, the book defines love in terms of seeing the value of empathy and the willingness to make one's resources available for the self-realization of the person loved, and points out its place in classroom teaching.

Read, Katherine H. *The Nursery School.* Philadelphia: W. B. Saunders Co., 1955.

Discusses interrelations of children and adults in the teaching situation.

Warner, Ruby H. *The Child and His Elementary School World.* Englewood Cliffs, New Jersey: Prentice-Hall, Inc., 1957.

Case studies and teacher record material illustrate the child's reactions to different learning situations.

Film

Growth Through a Two-Year Kindergarten. Carbondale, Illinois: Southern Illinois University, Department of Audio-Visual Aids, 1956.

Each child introduces himself. Activities are planned and carried to completion. 17 minutes, sound, black and white, or color.

4

A Good Physical Environment for the Kindergarten Child

The twentieth century has witnessed notable contributions to the knowledge of human growth and development and of the way learning takes place. The findings of research, the contributions of experimental schools, and the careful observations and records of trained professional people working with young children have pushed out frontiers of understanding. Reliable scientific studies are increasingly being taken into account in planning and equipping new schools for young children or in remodeling old buildings.

General agreement exists among psychologists, psychiatrists, and educators concerning certain basic principles of growth, development, and learning, and their implications for the physical facilities needed in schools.

THE KINDERGARTEN PLANT

In planning the plant and facilities for a new kindergarten, teachers, parents, builders, and architects all have a valuable contribution to make, and since the plant will probably serve many generations of young children, the expenditure of time and effort that teamwork demands is amply justified. The planning group must undertake to answer the question: What are the purposes of education for kindergarten children? Every facility provided should contribute in some significant way to the realization of these purposes.

The planning group may start with a consideration of what is now firmly established by research on the nature and needs of kindergarten children and how they learn. When the group has arrived at a reasonable consensus concerning the kind of persons the facilities are meant to serve, they can

50

BASIC PRINCIPLES AND THEIR IMPLICATIONS

Children's Characteristics

Healthy children are naturally active and vigorous. They need freedom to be physically active as a way of learning, of sustaining interest, and of lessening tension, fatigue, and irritability.

Young children are curious about their physical environment, and physical phenomena provide strong and continuing motivation for learning.

Physical Facilities Needed

Young children need space and equipment that permit freedom of activity. If possible an outdoor classroom adjacent to the indoor classroom should be provided. An ample play area protected by a substantial fence, and safe equipment for climbing and jumping are important. Indoors the need for space suggests the use of light, durable, movable, stackable furniture that will make it possible to free floor space for a variety of uses.

Interest in the natural environment suggests that provision be made for children to have direct contact with their physical world — to touch, to feel, to smell it. The feeling-touching-smelling experiences help them to identify themselves with their world. The building and site can contribute to the opportunity children have for sensory experiences. A well-selected site may give children a chance to live on a piece of ground that has hills, streams, rocks, trees, and birds. In preparing a site for building, the natural environment should be left as unimpaired as possible. Frequently builders denude and level a site which would meet the needs of young children better if the natural features were incorporated into the school grounds.

The school plant should provide outdoor space for gardens and strong, well-built outdoor cages for raising animals or for keeping an animal visitor for a few days of observation. Within the classroom, portable equipment such as aquariums, terrariums, planting boxes, and small animal cages provide for direct experiences with the physical environment. A set of shelves where children's treasures may be kept and shared is an important way to stimulate children's interests and to increase the sources of learning. A box which is too large for a child to move by himself stimulates him to get help from others.

Classrooms equipped with sinks and running water, work tables with stain-resistant and heat-resistant tops, display facilities such as cases, bulletin boards and counters, and storage space for simple equipment will make possible more kinds of direct experiences.

Children's Characteristics	Physical Facilities Needed
Children acquire knowledge and learn attitudes and skills from one another.	The interaction of young children occurs at first between two children. Later they can work and play with increasing numbers until by the end of the kindergarten, many children are able to relate themselves comfortably in a group of five or six of their peers. The school environment should provide opportunity for each child to construct with blocks, pull a wagon, look at picture books, manipulate clay, experiment with rhythm instruments, play grocery store or bakery with another child or in a companionable small group.
	The classroom and its equipment should be sufficiently flexible to provide for individual and group use. If a classroom can be constructed with small alcoves or if movable bookcases and storage cupboards can be placed to provide semipermanent walls, children can have a feeling of intimacy as members of a small group in which the information of one child becomes the knowledge of all and in which social skills important to their present development and their future as mature persons can be learned.
For effective guidance, teachers need as much information as they can acquire about each child.	The richer the environment the school provides, the more opportunity the child has for self-selection of the activities in which he chooses to engage. The teacher learns much about the child as she observes his selection of activities, his interaction with other children, his ability to purpose and plan, his physical vigor, and his emotional attitudes.
	Adequate space for vigorous outdoor play, science experiences, music experiences, use of finger paint and clay, painting at easels, looking at picture books, dramatic play centering in home and neighborhood activities, gardening, and for caring for pets provides the teacher with needed opportunity to observe each child under the most favorable conditions and to interact with him in such a way that he will realize that he is a person whom the teacher knows, understands, and likes.
Children have difficulty in comprehending abstract concepts presented by means of verbal symbols. Learning progresses from the concrete to the abstract.	Children must handle and construct actual objects. The meanings derived by discussion must be continually extended by such activities as painting, construction, dramatic play, and study trips to observe actual processes in the social and physical environment. Again, this calls for space for construction, dramatic play and rhythms, painting, and sufficient storage space to care for needed equipment.

Children's Characteristics	Physical Facilities Needed
The use of audio-visual materials lays a foundation for children to understand abstract concepts.	Good school design and equipment provide for the easy and effective use of objective materials, such as exhibits, models, motion and still pictures, television, phonograph records, and radio programs. At least one room available to young children and their parents should be curtained to permit effective screening of projected materials. Outside light on the surface of the screen should not be higher than one-tenth foot-candle. Adequate electric outlets should be placed at back, front, and side of the room so that lights, projector, or other electrical equipment may be set up wherever needed. In addition to switches regularly placed near doorways for control of overhead lighting, an additional light switch should be located on the wall of the classroom opposite the side of the room on which the projection screen is mounted. Effective use of audio-visual materials necessitates provision for automatic ventilation and temperature control under all conditions. When equipment is too expensive or too infrequently used to justify supplying each classroom, an instructional materials center with easily movable carts to transport equipment to the classroom is a reasonable solution to the problem.

move on to determine what kind of facilities are necessary. They may then move forward to determine the financial ability of the community to meet the needs of children during this strategic period of their development and finally to plan a course of action which will result in the production of a functional school plant.

Planning for Health

Children learn what they live and thus every aspect of the school life becomes a part of the curriculum and a concern of the team involved in planning. The maintenance and development of optimum physical and mental health for each child is the major purpose of the kindergarten. School planners are concerned to provide a safe and hygienic school building which conforms to desirable standards of size, heating, lighting, ventilation and acoustical treatment. Because the kindergarten child is in a period of rapid growth, he tires easily and needs opportunity for comfortable rest on cots or pads in a draft-free area. His rapid growth may require additional nourishment of a kind prescribed to meet his individual needs. Safeguarding the child's physical health necessitates planning for resting equipment and its storage and for kitchen facilities in which midsession nutrition may be prepared and served.

Because the outstanding characteristic of the kindergarten child is his need to be physically active, a large unobstructed room for the indoor kindergarten is needed. Prolonged inactivity is painful to young children and results inevitably in fatigue and tension. The shape and size of the indoor kindergarten should make possible many small group activities which can nevertheless be constantly under the supervision of the teacher. The outdoor classroom and the play area should also be of such a size and shape that all activities can be observed constantly by the teacher.

Mobile units of furniture, storage cabinets, and other equipment facilitate flexibility of use. Where an outdoor classroom can be made available, the floor level should be the same as that of the indoor classroom to permit easy movement of workbenches, blocks, easels, tables, and chairs outdoors when weather permits.

The play yard should be securely fenced. Part of the play yard should be turf, and part surfaced for use with wheel toys. Space outdoors is needed for gardening, a sandbox, and, if possible, a sturdy sink or a small safe pool for wading and water play. Fenced areas or strong, durable cages should be provided for animals. Storage space outdoors that is easily accessible to the children will make it possible for them to share responsibility in putting away wheel toys, blocks, sand toys, gardening tools, and other equipment usually used outdoors.

Young children should spend as much time as possible outdoors, weather permitting. In the photograph which shows a functional arrangement of facilities for a kindergarten, the architect has indicated by the vine-covered pergola and overhanging roof a covered outdoor work area which provides shelter for days that are too cool or too warm. The outdoor play area in this functional plan is oriented so that the building protects the children from the prevailing winds.

Planning for Group Activities

Many kindergarten children are making their first contact with a larger social group. The kindergarten provides an ideal opportunity for social development through group activities. The room and the outdoor play area should be planned to encourage small groups to work together on activities of their choice. All work and play arrangements should foster the interaction of children — the playhouse center requires a family; the airport requires pilots, dispatcher, mechanics, and passengers; the grocery store requires a merchant and customers. Mobile cabinets and easily moved tables and chairs make possible flexible space arrangements so that the block construction of a dairy farm or a harbor may grow with the increasing knowledge of the children.

Planning for Self-expression

The kindergarten program is designed to expand the child's power of expression. Although young children frequently bring considerable verbal facility and rich vocabularies with them when they enter kindergarten, their linguistic power is enhanced by opportunities to share their experiences with interested audiences of their peers. Dramatic play, problem-solving discussions, construction of needed objects, looking at picture books and sharing their discoveries, and study trips in the neighborhood provide the experiences from which new concepts and new vocabulary are acquired and the practice in communicating from which new language facility emerges.

All expression is not of the verbal type, however, and children also express themselves through painting, modeling, construction, and creative rhythms as well as through words. All these forms of expression reinforce the need for ample space for dramatic play and rhythms, for workbenches and tools, for library table and books, for clay tables and clay storage, for painting at easels and using finger paint at tables. The more emotional elbowroom the school can provide, the greater opportunity will the child have to develop his individuality and to learn the social skills which make him an accepting and an acceptable member of a social group.

Since rhythms and musical activities are a part of the daily kindergarten routine, provision must be made for piano, phonograph, records, rhythm instruments, and appropriate storage cabinets to care for valuable materials when they are not in use.

Art experiences of every type appropriate to young children constitute an important part of the kindergarten day. Since young children are inclined to be a bit "messy," it is important to provide linoleum tile or other appropriate floor covering from which spilled paint or scraps of clay can be quickly mopped up with a wet sponge. A sink with water-resistant drainboard is a necessity. Again, size and shape must be kept in mind when storage space for art materials is planned. Since some of these materials are unsightly, cabinets with doors are desirable.

Young children are interested in their physical environment. The indoor and outdoor environment should provide opportunity to observe, to explore, to construct, and to experiment. Provision of aquariums, terrariums, planting boxes, garden areas, cages and pens for the care of pets affords many opportunities for important firsthand experiences designed to develop science knowledge and a scientific approach to problem solving.

The urge to become independent is strong in the kindergarten child. Individual compartments — with hooks to care for his personal belongings or coat hangers firmly attached to a rod — should be placed at a level which makes it possible for the child to hang up his coat or sweater and place other belongings neatly on a shelf above and below. Child-sized toilets and lavatories should be provided for the exclusive use of the kindergarten in numbers sufficient for the number of children to be served. Lavatories are frequently located in the classroom near the toilet door so teachers may assist in establishing hygienic habits of hand washing. A full-length mirror encourages good grooming as well as good posture.

Storage Space

Blocks should be stored on open shelves in easily movable cabinets three or four feet wide. Some other materials may be similarly stored in open shelves to stimulate children to use them freely — library books, musical instruments, and certain art materials. The shelves should be adjustable. The backs of these cabinets can be covered with tackboard and used for display spaces or the backs may be left off so that their contents may be available to children working on either side of the cabinets.

When the nature of the material to be stored indicates the need for closed cabinets, the doors should be attached by hinges and be opened by catches that pull toward the child. Hinges and door catches constitute a hazard to small fingers, and children should be taught to handle this equipment carefully with proper concern for their fingers and the fingers of other children. There is no danger in proper use.

Work and storage space should be provided for the teacher. A work table and sink of adult height are necessary. Open shelves for large sheets of various kinds of paper and slightly tilted upward at the front edge will keep the paper easily available and in the best condition. Similar shelves at least four feet long are needed to store lumber for construction. A closet should be provided for the teacher's wraps and personal belongings. A desk for the teacher provides additional storage space for a register and forms. A four-drawer steel file which can be locked for pictures, professional materials, and confidential cumulative records of the children should be made available in the work space or glass-enclosed cubicle provided for the teacher. A telephone or intercommunication connection with the administrative office should be conveniently located in this area or cubicle.

Location of the Kindergarten in the Building

In placing the kindergarten in an elementary school several recommendations merit careful consideration by school planners. The kindergarten unit should be placed on the site so as to provide a play area for the exclusive use of these children. The kindergarten unit should be located close to the administrative offices, the lunchroom, and the multipurpose room. Although an exclusive play area is needed to protect the children, the primary classrooms should be close at hand, either in a wing reserved for the primary department of which the kindergarten is a part or adjacent to the space assigned to the kindergarten. In planning for kindergarten facilities it is recommended that the play yard be set back 40 feet from the streets on either side. Each classroom in the primary wing should have easy access to the outdoors, ample protection from the street, and an exclusive play area for the kindergarten. Shrubbery planted along the fence will give added privacy and protection from windy weather. Arrangements for offstreet parking for parents near the kindergarten and proximity of the area for school bus loading and unloading are good features where young children must be transported to school by parents or by school bus.

Special Problems

Every group confronted with the necessity of planning facilities for kindergarten education will need to give consideration to many specific problems of construction. When these problems are directly related to the instructional program, the teacher makes recommendations which will facilitate consideration of them. Among important considerations of this nature are the following:

Size of Classroom. Standards vary from state to state but ordinarily provision is made for a classroom somewhat larger than the standard classroom for elementary schools. Classrooms from 960 to 1280 square feet are not considered unusually large to provide for a desirable kindergarten program.

Floors. Since the children are on the floor much of the time, some discussion of floor finish is justifiable. Hardwood may be used, but dirt from the play yard will quickly grind off the finish. Generally, linoleum tile, available in many colors, patterns, and grades, accommodates itself best to variations of taste and budget.

Heating. Many methods of heating are satisfactory. Because young children spend much time playing on the floor, radiant heating has been highly recommended. The climatic conditions in a given area must be taken into consideration in planning facilities for heating.

Lighting. Poor lighting conditions cause many problems for children and teachers. Children exposed to excessively high brightness (glare) for long periods become restless. Their interest spans are shortened and poor behavior patterns develop. Light intensity should be appropriate to the task, which means that variable light controls should be provided in each room.

The amount of light alone does not control how well we see. Once rather low intensities of light (20 foot-candles) have been produced, the balance of brightness becomes the major factor in good lighting.

The difficult problem is to control the areas of high brightness. The unshielded sky and poorly shaded electric light are the two most troublesome sources.

Dark wall areas may be made lighter by painting them with pastel tints. Light-colored furniture, equipment, and floors help to enliven and brighten rooms; however, exclusive use of pastels is likely to be insipid. Skillful introduction of cheerful color will make rooms "sing" a little.

Temperature and Ventilation. Proper temperature and ventilation should be automatically maintained at all times.

Acoustical Treatment. Proper acoustical treatment of walls and ceilings makes it easier for children and adults to hear and lessens the tension caused by noise. Acoustical treatment should reduce noise from outside the classroom and prevent sound within the classroom from being objectionable to outside areas.

Interior Painting. Light, clear, soft pastel shades should be used in durable, washable enamels and paints. Wall surfaces should be without glare or shine. Colors should be so selected and disposed that each room will have its own individuality. Preferably there should be a range of colors which together build a harmony and prevent any single color from being too insistent. Walls and trim should keep their proper place in the scheme of things. Opportunity to experience good color relationships seldom occurs without planning. It is possible to develop habits of care and love of the beautiful in a pleasing environment. The pleasurable feeling of a beautiful room helps maintain eagerness and enthusiasm.

Planning a school is a problem in the housing of a busy community in an environment conducive to learning. Correct housing, furnishings, and play material help children to acquire habits of health, co-operation, skill, concentration, and imagination and desirable attitudes toward work, people, and things that will influence their character throughout life.

PERMANENT EQUIPMENT FOR KINDERGARTEN

A kindergarten equipped to care for twenty children should be
provided with the permanent equipment listed below.

Tables. Tables are necessary for small groups to use when working, lunching, or looking at picture books or display material. Tables should be made of durable wood or lightweight metal with silencers on legs and with water-resistant tops. Linoleum and various types of hardpressed fiber or plastic make desirable surfaces. (Many kindergarten rooms are overfurnished. Arrangement of a few tables about the room in functional groups will leave ample space for vigorous activities.) Tables should be selected with regard for the size of children to be served.

6 to 8 tables with $18'' \times 36''$ and $24'' \times 36''$ tops and 20″, 22″, and 24″ high

4 round tables, 36″ in diameter and 20″, 22″, and 24″ high

1 table of adult height for work or serving.

Chairs. Chairs with hardwood seats, designed to promote correct sitting posture, and varied in seat height to provide for individual differences are recommended. Frames of chairs should be hardwood or light metal. Stackable chairs are desirable. Legs should be equipped with silencers.

25 chairs with seats 10″, 12″, and 14″ high

6 to 10 adult chairs

3 small rocking chairs

Cabinets. Cabinets should be built in sections that are light enough to be moved as the room arrangement is adapted to the changing interests of the children. Some cabinets should have open shelves so that blocks and other equipment frequently used by the children are easily accessible from either side. Cabinets containing toys, equipment for resting, cleaning implements, and the like should have doors. Open cabinets with individual compartments should be provided for children's personal belongings. Such cabinets may be placed four or five feet from the wall with open side facing the wall and ample passageway between them and the wall. The backs of these low cabinets can provide bulletin board or display space.

24 individual cabinets or 3 cabinets each with eight individual compartments, each individual section 48″ high, 6″ wide, and 10″ deep with hooks and with a built-in shelf 9″ from the bottom

6 to 8 cabinets 48″ long, 14″ deep, and 48″ high with open shelves for blocks and toys

2 cabinets with doors, for cleaning equipment and dishes

2 cabinets, adult height, with shelves, for general storage

Display space. Bulletin boards made of soft fiberboard or cork and placed at the child's eye level can be used for the display of children's art work, for pictures of current interest to the group, and for material of seasonal interest. Material placed on the bulletin board should be neatly mounted, well spaced, and frequently changed.

Picture files. Every kindergarten should have two picture files, one for the teacher and one for the children. The teacher's file should contain pictures that supply information for social studies, science, holidays, and seasonal activities. Pictures may be left unmounted and used against a variety of colored construction paper to make desirable arrangements. Pictures for use by children should be mounted on durable, stiff paper of neutral color so children may handle them by the mountings.

4-drawer file for teacher

1-drawer file $18'' \times 14'' \times 12''$ open, on 10″ stand, for children

Bookcases. A good bookcase has wide space between its shelves to accommodate large picture books and still-life arrangements.

2 bookcases 36″ long, 14″ deep, 50″ high

Equipment for resting. The constant activity of kindergarten children and the added stimulation which comes from group living necessitate adequate provision for rest. Lightweight folding or stackable cots of canvas on durable wood or light metal frames are recommended. Quilted pads may be substituted for cots; they should be provided with washable covers to keep the pads clean. The name of each child should be plainly marked near the top of the pad and in storing, the sides with names should be piled face to face to keep them clean.

20 cots 52″ long, 27″ wide, and 12″ high

20 lightweight washable cotton blankets

storage space for 20 cots or pads, and blankets

Miscellaneous equipment. Other items needed as part of the general equipment are as follows:

1 United States flag

1 9′ × 12′ washable rug

4 wastebaskets

1 set nursery stairs

SPECIAL EQUIPMENT AND MATERIALS [1]

The following is a suggested list of special materials and equipment necessary for an effective kindergarten program.

Storage unit for outdoor play equipment
shed with 12′ × 14′ × 3′ sloping roof and removable side panels; ends and one side may be left open

Building play materials
4 large packing boxes 4′ × 4′ × 3′
4 smaller packing boxes of varied sizes
6 apple or banana boxes
3 small nail kegs
6 boards 1″ × 6″ × 24″
6 boards 1″ × 6″ × 48″
4 boards 1″ × 12″ × 48″
4 steering wheels attached to boxes
1 short portable ladder 5′ long
sawhorses for dramatic play

Climbing apparatus (over soft surface)
monkey ring 6′ high
climbing tree 6′ high
horizontal ladder 5′ high
low bar 3′ high
balance board 1″ × 12″, any length

rope ladder hung from tree or frame
jungle gym
1 glazed clay tile, 4′ × 24″ in diameter

Swing (made with tire casing or canvas bucket seats)

Balls (rubber playground balls 8″, 10″, 16″, and 24″)

Wagons
1 with 30″ metal box
1 with 36″ metal box

Tricycles
1 16″ ball-bearing with bicycle spokes
1 20″ ball-bearing with bicycle spokes

Tire casings (to roll around)

Hollow boxes (for indoor and outdoor use)
24 boxes 24″ × 12″ × 6″
24 boxes 12″ × 12″ × 6″

Dolly (for transporting boxes in room and outdoors)

[1] Ruth Edmands, Helen McAllister, and Margaret Rasmussen. "Materials and Equipment Essential for an Effective Kindergarten Program." *California Journal of Elementary Education*, XXIV (August, 1955), pp. 39–45.

Floor blocks (for class of 30)

100 half units $1\frac{1}{4}'' \times 2\frac{1}{2}'' \times 2\frac{3}{4}''$

400 units $1\frac{3}{8}'' \times 2\frac{3}{4}'' \times 5\frac{1}{2}''$

300 double units $1\frac{3}{8}'' \times 2\frac{3}{4}'' \times 11''$

100 quadruple units $1\frac{3}{8}'' \times 2\frac{3}{4}'' \times 22''$

80 pillars $1\frac{3}{8}'' \times 1\frac{3}{8}'' \times 5\frac{1}{2}''$

40 cylinders $2\frac{3}{4}''$ diameter $\times 5\frac{1}{2}''$

20 cylinders $1\frac{3}{8}''$ diameter $\times 5\frac{1}{2}''$

40 circular curves $1\frac{3}{8}'' \times 2\frac{3}{4}'' \times 90''$

20 elliptical curves $1\frac{3}{8}'' \times 2\frac{3}{4}'' \times 90''$

60 large triangles $1\frac{3}{8}'' \times 2\frac{3}{4}'' \times 5\frac{1}{2}''$

20 small triangles $1\frac{3}{8}'' \times 2\frac{3}{4}'' \times 2\frac{3}{4}''$

100 color cubes $1'' \times 1'' \times 1''$

Pine boards (well sanded and treated for water resistance to use with floor blocks)

6 $1'' \times 6'' \times 24''$ 4 $1'' \times 12'' \times 36''$

6 $1'' \times 6'' \times 36''$ 6 $4'' \times 24'' \times 24''$

6 $1'' \times 6'' \times 48''$ 4 $1'' \times 12'' \times 48''$

4 $1'' \times 12'' \times 24''$

Accessory block materials (for use with blocks, all on the same scale)

people — pipe stem cleaners or wood

    family

    community workers

animals — wooden, rubber, or plastic

    farm (horse, colt, cow, calf, pig, sheep, hen, duck, cat, dog)

    wild (elephant, tiger, camel, bear, lion, monkey)

trucks and trailers (all kinds)

freight train set (engine tender, box car, tank, flat, hopper, cattle, caboose)

bus; automobiles

boats (tug, passenger, freighter, sail, motor barge, ferry)

airplanes

Playhouse (outside playhouse, open on one side with overhanging porch for protection from rain)

Playhouse corner (inside)

small wooden screens — wood frame and wallboard center, 24″ × 36″

unbreakable dolls — washable, with easily managed clothing, large buttons, snaps

doll carriage and covers

house furniture, 22″ high (stove, sink, table, chairs, doll bed, dresser, dish cupboards)

ironing board, 22″ high

toy telephone

wooden clock with movable hands

cooking utensils (saucepans, frying pan, bakery set, mixing bowls, measuring cups and spoons, flour sifter, strainer, teakettle)

table service (dishes, spoons, knives, forks)

cleaning equipment (broom, dustpan, dust mop, dust cloths, sponges, aprons, cleanser, cans, soap boxes, clothesline and clothespins, toy iron)

flower bowls

clothing (hats, purses, suitcases, bags, workmen's hats — fireman, painter, postman)

scales, scissors, twine

Play platform

9′ × 12′ for dramatic play, housekeeping, plays, puppetry

Gardening materials

tools — durable, child-size (hoe, rake, trowels, small shovel)

flowerpots

seeds, plants, bulbs

sprinkling can

hose

Water play equipment

wading pool

bucket and tub

toys

miscellaneous articles to float or sink

Sandbox

8′ × 10′ with a wood or concrete frame. (For proper drainage, the ground underneath should be excavated several feet and filled with two or three inches of gravel. Wood should be cedar or cypress. Covers must be provided to protect sand from stray animals. They can become seats or play surfaces when removed and can be hinged or put on tracks.)

Sandbox toys

pails	muffin tins
spoons	pans
sieves	fishing poles
sifters	play fish
scoops	dump truck
funnels	steam shovel
1 3′ × 8′ table	lighthouse
water cans	boats
measuring cups	small cars
	beanbags

Housing plants and animals

glass tank for terrarium 10″ × 12″ × 18″

glass tank for aquarium

cages for animals (large enough to permit animal to move about freely and to be easily cleaned) — made of galvanized iron and wire and with a sliding door and removable pan

glass jars for specimens

Materials for measurement

scales

yardstick

foot ruler

tape measure

6″ wooden level

thermometer (inside) with large figures

thermometer (outside) with large figures

containers of various sizes (quart, pint, and one-half pint cups, bottles, and cans)

Projection equipment (available to the kindergarten)

16 mm motion picture projector with sound equipment

combination filmstrip machine with 2″ × 2″ slide projector, slide carrier, and lift-off case

opaque projector

projector stand, 36″ high with swivel casters and rubber tires for easy rolling

50″ × 50″ portable screen, stand type

stereoscope

Sound equipment (available to the kindergarten)

2-speed tape recorder with microphone jack

classroom radio, AM and FM

television service

Still pictures (study prints)

animals, plants, and other parts of the natural environment

children's activities

Mother Goose

art reproductions

seasonal and special days

transportation

machines

Books for children (This list contains *sources* for titles rather than the titles themselves.)

American Library Association. *Basic Book Collection for Elementary Grades.* Compiled by joint committee of the American Library Association, National Education Association, American Council on Education, and National Council of Teachers of English. New York.

Association for Childhood Education International. *A Bibliography of Books for Children.* 1200 Fifteenth Street, N.W., Washington 5, D.C., The Association.

Cook, Dorothy, and Estelle Fidell (Editors). *Children's Catalogue, 1952- 1954 Supplement to the Eighth Edition,* 1951. New York: H. W. Wilson Co., 1954.

School district headquarters — Bibliographies developed by school district. *The Library Journal; The Journal of Library Work* (periodicals).

Music books

Beatrice Landeck. *Songs to Grow On.* New York: Edward B. Marks Music Corporation, 1950.

——. *More Songs to Grow On.* New York: Edward B. Marks Music Corporation, 1954.

Osbourne McConathy and others. *Music for Early Childhood.* New York: Silver Burdett Company, 1952.

James L. Mursell and others. *I Like the Country.* New York: Silver Burdett Company, 1956.

——, *I Like the City.* New York: Silver Burdett Company, 1956.

Lila Belle Pitts, compiler. *The Kindergarten Book*. Boston: Ginn & Co., 1949.

Ruth Porter Seeger. *American Folk Songs for Children*. New York: Doubleday & Co., Inc., 1948.

Irving Wolfe and others. *Music 'round the Clock*. Chicago: Follett Publishing Company, 1955.

Music equipment
record player
melody bells
rhythm instruments
  sticks ($\frac{1}{4}$ or $\frac{3}{8}''$ dowel)
  wood block
  finger cymbal
  drum — 2 or more sizes
  triangle or nails
  tambourine
  1 or 2 pair sand blocks
  jingle bells

Records
Singing
There are record albums to accompany each of the music books mentioned above for teachers who need them.
Rhythms
RCA Victor Record Library for Elementary Schools — Rhythms, Vols. I and II
Bassett and Chestnut — Rhythmic Activity Album
Phoebe James Series [2] — Elementary Rhythms
Ruth Evans Series [3] — Childhood Rhythms — Series I and II
Listening
RCA Record Library, Listening Albums I and II
Selected individual records from Young People's Records and Children's Record Guild

Construction equipment (Tools should be of best quality, not toys)
1 workbench 20″ × 48″ and 24″ high
2 sawhorses 8″ × 30″ × 24″ high
1 cart or wall rack for tools
2 claw hammers, 10 to 15 ounces
2 crosscut saws, 12″ length
4 "C" clamps, 4″ to 6″ openings
1 pair pliers
1 wood file
1 brace, nonratchet, 6″ × 8″ sweep
1 square
sheets of sandpaper (mount on blocks)

Wood
easy to cut (such as pine)
many lengths and widths
mill ends
dowel $\frac{1}{4}''$, $\frac{1}{2}''$, $\frac{3}{4}''$
Button molds 1″, 1$\frac{1}{2}$″, 2″

Miscellaneous materials (for experimentation)
electric hot plate
magnifying glass (2$\frac{1}{2}$″ diameter)
magnets
nails, hairpins, wire, keys, needles
prisms
straws, balloons, rubber darts
tube for siphon
spools
small pulleys
tin cans (several sizes with smooth opening)
jars, glasses, bottles (various sizes)
plates, saucers, pans
tablespoons, teaspoons, table knives

Painting equipment
Powder tempera
4 double easels or wall easels
15 chipboard easels 19″ × 26″

---

[2] Phoebe James Products, Box 134, Pacific Palisades, California.
[3] Ruth Evans, Childhood Rhythm Records, 326 Forest Park Avenue, Springfield 8, Massachusetts.

12 pounds powder tempera paint —
variety of colors
3 dozen brushes, flat, stiff bristle $1''$
and $1\frac{1}{4}''$, and rubber set varnish
brushes $1''$, $1\frac{1}{2}''$, $2''$
Paper: unprinted news — $18'' \times 24''$,
$24'' \times 36''$
colored newsprint
want ad section of newspaper
wallpaper
construction
towel box liners
3 dozen containers for paint (milk
cartons, plastic glasses, cans)
clips or clothespins for attaching
paper to easels
sponge for cleanup
Finger paint
gloss starch (3 rounded tablespoons
gloss starch, 4 cups boiling water,
$\frac{1}{2}$ cup soap flakes)
wheat paste
prepared commercial starches
drug bond (roll $30''$ or $36''$ wide)
kraft butcher wrapping, white (roll
$30''$ or $36''$ wide)
sponge for cleanup
containers for color (glass jars with
screw-top lids and holes in lids for
shaking dry tempera paint on paper)
bowls for starch
spoons for dispensing starch
Sponge painting
cellulose sponge
calcimine paint

Drawing materials
large colored chalk — assorted colors
crayons
manila paper $12'' \times 18''$, $18'' \times 24''$
chipboards for easels

Modeling materials
Clay
30 pounds of pugged red and white
pottery clay
clay containers (covered stone jar
with wood cover, built-in metal containers)

clay boards $6'' \times 6''$ or $6'' \times 8''$
colored clay slips
soft-haired brushes for use with colored slips
rolling pin or $2''$ doweling for rolling
clay

Baking materials
2 cups flour, 1 cup salt,
2 tablespoons olive oil,
food coloring, knead,
wrap in plastic bag
assorted cookie cutters
buttons for eyes, feet, decorations

Cutting and pasting materials
kindergarten crayons, large size
paste brushes
newsprint $18'' \times 24''$ in various colors
wrapping paper
manila $12'' \times 18''$
wallpaper
colored construction paper $12'' \times 18''$
scissors ($4\frac{1}{2}''$, blunt)
1 gallon paste
discarded materials such as buttons,
yarn, bits of cloth prints, beads, roving,
shells, ribbons, metallic papers, raffia,
string, spools

Printing
*Miscellaneous articles for making print
designs*
corks
spools
blocks — string wrapped
string dipped in tempera
potatoes
pieces of wood
calcimine paint
sponge for cleanup
Paper
newsprint
yellow manila paper
colored construction paper
white kraft paper

Other materials

12 plywood or masonite puzzles (cut in large pieces — 5 to 7 for beginning, more complicated for later use)

boards with pegs (landscape shapes — trees, houses)

mechanical items (bolts, nuts, spacers, screws, lock and key, dials, knobs)

materials with a variety of textures and other objects to feel

materials for making simple booklets
    chipboard cut to size
    papers decorated by children
    yarn or cord to bind

Teacher's materials

pair of 10″ shears

stapler

paper punch

adhesive tape

masking tape $\frac{3}{4}$″

Scotch tape

paraffin

straight pins and safety pins

tongue depressors

spoons for paint

yardstick

foot rule

3 pounds gloss starch

1 pound salt (dough work)

1 small bottle olive oil

1 roll of white butcher paper, 24″ × 36″

1 package of white tissue paper

1 package of colored tissue paper

4 boxes of cleansing tissue

6 cellulose sponges

2 brooms

2 dustpans

3 spools of roving

1 two-burner hot plate

glass jars (quart size) for storing dry powdered tempera

10 sheets of tagboard (for picture frames)

assorted papers for mounted pictures

colored construction paper 26″ × 40″

1 box of assorted food colors

10 pounds of flour

10 pounds of wheat paste

twin tone 26″ × 40″

tagboard 26″ × 38″

The teacher will supplement the items listed with others that she has observed in use by five-year-old children. When she finds new toys displayed by local toy stores and department stores, she examines them to see if they are made from sturdy materials so as to withstand much use, and she questions the children about their experience with such toys to determine whether they are suitable to their age level and capable of holding interest after the novelty is exhausted. In order to keep informed about new toys, the teacher asks that her name be put on the mailing list of a toy store and, to keep informed about new phonograph records, that of a music store. To keep informed about new books for children, she talks with a children's librarian and visits the juvenile section of a book store at regular intervals. Thus she is always in a position to recommend desirable equipment and materials for her class.

SITUATIONS FOR DISCUSSION

In the following situations select each course of action that seems desirable to you basing your choices and omissions on the ideas presented in this chapter. Add one or more alternate courses of action.

SITUATION I. During your first year in a school system, you feel that the custodian is overlooking dusty corners in the kindergarten. The custodian, you realize, is firmly entrenched in his position and will probably be employed as long as he wants to continue. As the kindergarten teacher, you should:

Tell the custodian how well kept the kindergarten was where you did practice teaching.

Discuss the problem of a clean kindergarten with your principal.

Get a mop and a dustcloth and take care of the corners yourself.

Ask the custodian to clean the corners.

Have the children help in keeping the kindergarten clean.

SITUATION II. You are teaching kindergarten in the morning. Another teacher, Miss Hart, uses the same facilities in the afternoon. She is careful to put everything away at the end of her teaching period, and expects you to do the same. As the morning kindergarten teacher, you should:

Talk with Miss Hart about having construction projects requiring a week or more.

Plan construction projects out of small pieces.

Get a wheeled dolly to facilitate putting equipment away.

Allow ample time for the children to help clean up at the end of the morning.

Be sure the children take all personal belongings home at the end of the session.

SITUATION III. The Parent Teacher Association has raised fifty dollars for kindergarten equipment. You are the kindergarten teacher asked to serve on the committee for selecting equipment. You should recommend:

Glass beakers, bar magnets, and other science laboratory equipment.

Sharp saws, strong hammers, and vices for a carpenter bench.

Children's books to supplement those purchased each year.

A savings account for getting a piano.

Playhouse furnishings.

SITUATION IV. The playground equipment is limited and does not include a jungle gym or other apparatus for climbing and the exercise of shoulder muscles. As the kindergarten teacher you should:

Discuss the problem with the principal.

Bring up the question at a parents' meeting.

Arrange for the children to play at a nearby park once a week.

Have the children do arm exercises either indoors or outdoors.

Ask the shop instructor if his students can make a climbing apparatus.

BIBLIOGRAPHY

Professional Books and Pamphlets

Association for Childhood Education International. *Creating with Materials for Work and Play.* Membership Service Bulletin No. 5. Washington, D. C., 1957.

Twelve leaflets suggest how to use materials suitable for kindergarten-primary children and includes useful bibliographies.

—— *Portfolio on Audio-Visual Materials.* Bulletin No. 7. Washington, D. C., 1951.

Includes titles as "How Can We Best Use Audio-Visual Materials in the Classroom?" and "Bulletin Boards and How to Use Them." Also mentions use of films, a record library, and free and inexpensive materials.

—— *Portfolio on More and Better Schools for Children Under Six.* Washington, D. C., 1950.

See Chapter 3.

—— *Recommended Equipment and Supplies for Nursery, Kindergarten, Primary and Intermediate Schools.* General Service Bulletin No. 39. Committee on Equipment and Supplies. Washington, D. C., 1953.

A revision of the popular bulletin of 1947.

Foster, Josephine, and Neith Headley. *Education in the Kindergarten,* 2nd ed. New York: American Book Company, 1948.

Presents useful material on the five-year-old, the teacher and the physical and social climate of the kindergarten.

Gans, Roma, et al. *Teaching Young Children.* New York: World Book Company, 1952.

Deals with the place of the young child in the contemporary world; the organization and evaluation of learning experiences; and the relation of the school to home and community life.

Gesell, Arnold L., and Frances L. Ilg. *Infant and Child in the Culture of Today.* New York: Harper & Bros., 1943.

Deals with the study of infants and young children and the guidance of their development in home and nursery school.

—— *The Child from Five to Ten.* New York: Harper & Bros., 1946.

A study of all aspects of human growth and development during the years of early childhood. Invaluable background material for the kindergarten teacher.

Heffernan, Helen, ed. *Guiding the Young Child,* 2nd ed. Boston: D. C. Heath and Company, 1959.

See Chapter 12, Appendix III.

Heffernan, Helen, and Charles Bursch. *Curriculum and the Elementary School Plant.* Washington, D. C.: National Education Association, Association for Supervision and Curriculum Development, 1958.

Current thinking about the elementary school plant includes provisions for the kindergarten. Includes floor plan for a kindergarten.

Leavitt, Jerome E., ed. *Nursery-Kindergarten Education.* New York: McGraw-Hill Book Company, 1958.

Chapter 12 contains a description of "Plant and Equipment."

New York State Education Department. *Suggested Equipment for Four- and Five-Year-Old Kindergarten Children.* Bureau of Child Development and Parent Education. Albany, 1948.

Pamphlet gives diagrams and measurements and other suggestions for equipment needed in kindergarten.

Sheehy, Emma. *The Fives and Sixes Go to School.* New York: Henry Holt & Co., 1953. Needs of individual children should be met through a variety of school experiences. Records and reports aid the development and guidance of individual children.

Wills, Clarice, and William Stegman. *Living in the Kindergarten.* Chicago: Follett Publishing Co., 1950.
The kindergarten child, curriculum, parent and teacher are presented with emphasis on the importance of the kindergarten in building a sound foundation for the child's later school years.

Wittich, Walter A., and Charles F. Schuller. *Audio-Visual Materials: Their Nature and Use.* New York: Harper & Bros., 1953.
Methods of using audio-visual materials are included as well as their functions in facilitating classroom learning.

Films

Co-operative School Plant Planning. Paul W. Seagers, Educational Author, Audio-Visual Center, Indiana University, Bloomington, Indiana, 1952.
A discussional filmstrip in color — 100 frames.

A Good Day in the Kindergarten. Produced by Helen Heffernan. Distributed by the California Association for Childhood Education. Address: Mrs. Sadye Lewis, 1755 Bel-Air Avenue, San Jose, California.
A filmstrip in color. 60 frames with an accompanying phonograph record. Excellent pictures of arrangement of indoor classroom, outdoor play areas with close-ups of equipment; arrangements of interest centers, storage cabinets, and other facilities of a well-planned kindergarten being used by children.

Sources of Supplies and Equipment for Young Children

American Seating Company. (Offices located in principal cities)

Block Shop, 58 Wall Street, New Haven 11, Connecticut. (Catalogue on request)

Childcraft Equipment Company, 155 E. 23d Street, New York 10, New York. (Catalogue on request)

Community Playthings, Macedonia Co-operative Community, Clarkesville, Georgia. (Catalogue on request)

Creative Playthings, Inc., 5 University Place, New York 3, New York. (Catalogue on request)

Educational Supply and Specialty Company, 2823 E. Gage Avenue, Huntington Park, California. (Catalogue on request)

Mor-Pla Jumbo-Blox. R. H. Stone Products, P. O. Box 414, Detroit 31, Michigan.

Seaver Toys, Burbank, California. (Catalogue on request)

This vine-covered pergola and overhanging roof
provide a shelter for days that are too cool or
too warm.

Each primary classroom should have easy access
to the outdoors, with an exclusive play area for
the kindergarten.

5

What Learning Experiences Should the Kindergarten Provide?

No human being is born with the learnings which will enable him adequately to take his place in the world about him. The modern world is far too complex for society to hope that the process of growing up will, by itself, equip the child with the learnings he requires to make a successful adjustment to life. His quality as a person and his contribution to the social groups of which he will be a part are determined by the experiences with which he is provided and the opportunities they provide him for learning.

THE IMPORTANCE OF THE EARLY YEARS

Of great significance are the initial social, intellectual, and emotional experiences of early childhood. In these early years, the child meets, and in some manner makes an adjustment to many of the persistent life situations which command our attention. For example, he must learn to get along with his family and with other people beyond the family circle; he must learn basic health and safety behaviors in order to survive; he must acquire command of the skills of oral communication sufficient to meet increasingly insistent needs; he must begin to find answers to his questions as his increased power of locomotion brings him into an enlarged contact with his physical and social environment. Guidance in these and in a host of other similar situations constitutes the core of early childhood education.

EDUCATING THE YOUNG CHILD

The curriculum for the young child is as broad as life itself. The major aim of his education is to help him make the best adjustment to life that is possible for a human being of his potentialities. In situations conducive to learning, the child is encouraged to extend his experience, and, in the

69

process, find himself. He is encouraged to use the concrete materials provided in his environment so he may deepen his understanding through sensory impressions. The school affords him a well-planned program which challenges him to extend his horizons through new learnings but at the same time safeguards his security. The school recognizes individual variation as actual and desirable, and consciously provides for flexibility in the program to meet individual needs. It affords the young child an environment in which it is safe for him to be himself, to learn to live with his peers, to interact freely with an environment planned by adults who understand the nature and needs of young children.

The effectiveness of the professionally-educated adult who guides the early education of children will become apparent in their changed behavior. Are they more healthy? Have they discovered better ways of relating themselves to other children and adults? Have they gained power over the skills of communication? Are they more independent? Are they able to accept more responsibility for their own care and behavior? Are they understanding more about their physical and social world? Are they extending their interests in creative activity?

All these and many similar questions not only reveal the scope of the learning experiences appropriate for kindergarten children but they provide the basis for determining how well the school is meeting the needs of the children. Education must be evaluated by its success in achieving for each child *all* the objectives to which it has made commitment to the society that the school serves.

In this chapter, various types of learning experiences usually found in a comprehensive kindergarten curriculum will be discussed briefly. In subsequent chapters each type will be treated more fully. Such an approach does not imply any separation of curriculum content into traditional subject-matter fields. Each type of development is examined separately only for purposes of analysis. To serve kindergarten-age children well, the school must meet their unique needs through unified experiences. To meet this challenge will be sufficiently demanding on the time, energy, and ingenuity of the qualified teacher.

Neither the organization of curriculum nor curriculum content adapted to more mature children should be transferred to the kindergarten program. The teacher's aim should be to provide a richly developmental experience consonant with the young child's present growth characteristics and needs, in complete confidence that such a course of action is the only way to prepare the child to meet his next developmental task with the inherent strength of a wholesome personality.

Learning Experiences in the Kindergarten

The kindergarten teacher is aware of the purposes of the educational program and strives to make every activity of the day contribute to the realization of one or more of these purposes. A program for kindergarten children may be said to be truly purpose-directed when it contributes to helping each child to:

Develop and maintain optimum health
Further his physical development
Extend his understanding of the social world
Enter into his scientific world
Grow in understanding of spatial and quantitative relationships
Expand his control of language
Enjoy his literary heritage
Express himself aesthetically through art media
Become acquainted with and learn to enjoy his musical heritage
Establish satisfying relationships with children and adults

The degree to which each child will attain these goals differs according to his individual ability, background, and interest. But if the kindergarten teacher checks her preparation for each day's work against these purposes, she will find herself always working toward defensible goals. These purposes of kindergarten education are dynamic. Each involves significant forward movement in an important aspect of development. The parents of kindergarten children, as well as people in the community generally, should be well informed concerning these purposes and their educative significance in the present and future progress of young children. The popular misconception of the kindergarten as a pleasant place for children to play or a "kiddie parking station" for harassed mothers can only be replaced by an understanding of the kindergarten as a significant first step in the educative process as teachers themselves fully understand the purposes of kindergarten education and are capable of interpreting them with enthusiasm and reflect a dignified respect for their chosen field of professional service.

Developing and Maintaining Optimum Health

Safety. The kindergarten teacher is deeply concerned with many activities designed to help each child maintain and develop optimum health. Because the child is moving into a wider environment, special emphasis is given to establishing understanding of the need to practice sound safety habits while coming to and from school, while using the school bus or other transportation facilities, and while using school facilities and equipment. Careful instruction followed by adequate practice is given so that children learn to respond quickly to fire and air-raid signals.

Health Services. The health services the school provides can be learning situations for young children. The periodic medical examination, vision and hearing tests, immunization services, visits to the school nurse, and the daily observation of each child by the teacher are among the usual health services of the school, but each provides teachable moments which are highly impressive for the young child. He comes to understand the values that adults associate with health practices, the importance of safeguarding himself from infectious and contagious diseases, and the need to accept momentary discomfort in order to secure immunity from possible future infection. The entire school health personnel can contribute to the learning which accompanies these events in the child's school life.

Health Practices. The entire routine of the school day is designed to safeguard the child's health. The mid-morning snack, the careful washing of hands before eating, the rest period on comfortable cots or mats, and the vigorous outdoor play with suitable apparatus and equipment are all planned to promote health, strength, and co-ordination.

The simple health instruction program helps to develop appropriate knowledge, habits, and attitudes. Children learn to cover a cough or a sneeze with a clean handkerchief or disposable tissue, they learn the importance of cleanliness and frequent hand washing, they learn about nutritious foods, they learn the relation of nutrition to dental health, they learn the importance of adequate rest and sleep, they learn that vigorous play — skipping, climbing, jumping, and running — contributes to the growth of strong muscles, they learn to play safely with other children, they learn to recognize adult judgment in matters of health and safety. The school continually reinforces the health practices the children are learning at home and works with parents toward a common acceptance of what is good for the health of young children.

Mental Health. The kindergarten teacher is aware of the importance of providing an environment conducive to the mental health of the child. She realizes that he is a single organism with physical, intellectual, social, and emotional aspects inextricably interrelated. A sound mind and controlled emotional reactions contribute to physical well-being and, conversely, a well-equipped body in good health is essential to intellectual development and emotional stability. The kindergarten teacher, therefore, creates a relaxed atmosphere free from strain, tension, and unrealistic expectancies. She is aware of the need of a rhythm of activity and rest. She chooses more activities which involve large muscles than those requiring fine muscle co-ordination. She knows that only a few activities in the kindergarten day should involve all of the children; she feels no necessity to introduce subject matter content in reading or numbers which is better suited to older children and which may be damaging to the kindergarten child if prematurely introduced. She knows that when each child is ready, he will take his next developmental step and that no amount of teaching will hasten the process any more than a parent can hasten the eruption of the first tooth. Much damage to a child's mental and physical health will result from unwise forcing by teacher or parent before there is proper physiological and psychological readiness to attack the next developmental step.

Furthering Physical Development

Much that has been said about the role of the kindergarten in maintaining and developing optimum health is equally applicable to its role in furthering each child's physical development.

The Environment. The environment of the kindergarten contributes to the child's physical development. All of the activities incident to living in an environment planned for five-year-old children make their contribution to the growing-up processes. Coats and hats must be hung in the proper place, rubbers or overshoes neatly placed on the designated shelf, and housekeeping responsibilities carried out to make kindergarten a pleasant place to be. All such activities further physical development.

Work Periods. The kindergarten work period is a busy time of building with small or large blocks, of using long and short boards, boxes, and kegs in building boats, trains, or airplanes. Children move about freely as they use the workbench, wood, and tools, model with clay, paint at easels, use the finger paint, and draw with large crayons.

Rest Time. Brief rest times in a busy work period contribute to physical development. Storybooks available in a library corner or a comfortable chair near the aquarium or animal pen provides for a few minutes of relaxation in an interesting spot.

Dramatic Play. Dramatic play — fishing off the boat, keeping a grocery store, housekeeping with dress-up clothing, playing airport and airplanes, bakery, dairy farm — provides for almost limitless physical activities of a highly creative nature.

Music Time. Music time provides opportunity for rhythmic response to music played on piano or phonograph. Creative rhythms may also grow out of experiences such as a visit to the zoo and subsequent efforts to show the ponderous walk of the elephant or the agility of the monkey. The teacher may enhance and give form to these efforts by accompaniment on the piano or on percussion instruments. Sometimes the children enjoy walking, skipping, running, jumping, and galloping to music.

Play Time.   Play time in kindergarten gives children opportunity to use the slides, swings, or jungle gym.   The wheel toys — tricycles and wagons — provide further means for fun as well as for the development of large muscles and co-ordination.

Games.   Kindergarten children are not yet ready for highly organized games involving large numbers of children and intricate rules, but simple games with only four or five children participating can provide valuable opportunity to learn to share the use of balls or other toys, to take turns, to accept minor bumps and mishaps with courage, and to show good sportsmanship.

Extending Understanding of the Social World

Study Trips.   Kindergarten children need many opportunities for first-hand experience with the wider world of their neighborhoods and community.   Short study trips to the fire station, the bakery, the market, a nearby farm, or a house or bridge under construction are appropriate. When the children return to school, they relive their experiences through dramatic play and thus get inside each experience and understand something of the work of the different people in their neighborhoods and the source of the products that come into their homes.

Role Playing.   After visiting a house under construction, one group used the boxes, blocks, planks, and kegs for many days of house building. They took the roles of carpenters, plasterers, bricklayers, plumbers, and electricians.   Vocabulary expanded.   Ideas were clarified in discussion as problems emerged.   The children grew in knowledge about the different workers needed in building a house, the materials they used, and how they worked together and depended upon each other.

Children discover that play becomes more satisfying as they work together.   The fisherman must have a fish market to which the "catch" can be delivered and the merchant must have customers to whom he sells his fish.   The housekeepers must have a grocery store where they may shop for supplies, a bus to ride down to the shopping center and a baby sitter to take care of the children.   Gradually, the kindergarten play becomes interrelated as life is interrelated.   The children learn that the play is more fun when they take turns, respect the rights of others, co-operate, and exercise a reasonable amount of self-control.

Imitation.   The teacher realizes the importance of imitation in the learning of young children and shows them by her own example that courteous behavior, a well-modulated voice, consideration for others, good temper, and a sense of humor are effective ways of getting along with other people.   She demonstrates the truth of the statement that "Love begets love and savagery begets savagery."

History. Young children are not ready for much formal history. "Long ago" has little meaning to the five-year-old, but through the observance of such holidays as Thanksgiving Day, Christmas, Washington's Birthday, Lincoln's Birthday and Columbus Day, young children enter into their social heritage and learn the stories of important people to whom all of us owe so much.

Geography. Young children are not ready for much formal geography. "Far away" has as little meaning as "long ago." A neighboring city may seem farther away to a child after the inactivity of a hundred miles through heavy traffic in the family car than a city ten times as far after an exciting airplane trip which included a visit with the pilot in the cockpit.

All of these learnings are the important beginnings of the social studies program. As he goes on, the child will deepen his understanding of how people live and work together, of how people use the things nature has given them and how man has built institutions such as schools, churches, and governments to regulate and improve his relationships with other men.

Entering the Scientific World

Natural Environment. The child cannot begin any exploration of the modern world in which he lives without making immediate contact with the world of science. A walk in the school yard or a nearby park or garden reminds children of their unanswered questions about all the things in nature that surround them. The kindergarten program affords children opportunity to satisfy their curiosity about the insects, animals, and other growing things in their environment. Seasonal changes and changes in weather and temperature afford opportunity for observation and experimentation.

Science Materials. Many activities suitable for five-year-old children are rich in opportunities to help children understand scientific principles and a scientific approach to learning. Gardening either outdoors or in window boxes or pots indoors and caring for birds, guinea pigs, hamsters, or turtles indoors, or for ducks, chickens, a lamb or other appropriate animals for short periods in well-protected outdoor cages are all ways to deepen interest in nature. Young children enjoy playing with such things as magnets, prisms, pulleys, magnifying glasses, and scales.

Growth of Scientific Attitude. Anyone who has worked with young children understands the values in science experiences. Young children have many "how" and "why" questions that can be answered by observing, experimenting, reasoning, and evaluating outcomes. Not only is the material of science fascinating to young children but the opportunity to begin the development of a scientific attitude in a group of questioning, wondering children is a rewarding experience for the teacher. The materials of science can be observed and as children feel satisfaction in seeing for themselves, they are stimulated to increasingly more careful observation in other situations. As a group of children observe scientific phenomena together, individuals will note different things and offer a number of different explanations. This encourages other children to look again and compare their original impressions with those of their friends; as they discover the accuracy of other children's observations they grow in respect for the opinions and ability of others. When questions are raised which seem to baffle everyone, the young seeker after knowledge may be guided to a book or an authority or be helped to devise an experiment to help answer the questions. Other experiments may be set up to test the validity of his concepts still further. These are all important steps in acquiring a scientific method of attacking problems, and five-year-olds are intrigued by such a logical way to find answers to their "hows" and "whys."

In a world changing at a tremendously accelerated pace because of the application of science to technology, the importance of science experiences in the kindergarten curriculum cannot be overemphasized. Children must be helped to understand and accept change and to adjust to it. No better way can be devised than providing direct experience with the natural and physical environment.

Understanding Spatial and Quantitative Relationships

Building Concepts. Similar to the ways of building understanding of the social and scientific worlds are the ways in which young children build understanding of space and quantity. Beginning with their preschool years, children are steadily in the process of developing comparative concepts of tall and short, dark and light, more and less, large and small, fast and slow, wide and narrow, thick and thin, heavy and light, as much as, older than, bigger than, thicker than. These are not easy concepts for the young child, particularly since they change somewhat in meaning, depending upon the object to which they are applied. All of these concepts enter into the kindergarten program as children work with a wide variety of objective materials.

Space and Time. Trips, again, afford opportunity for children to develop understanding of distance and time. How far is it to the new highway being paved? How far is it to Timmy's house where we visited his baby sister? The kindergarten teacher begins an understanding of geography by helping the children make a map first of a walk in the neighborhood and later of more ambitious trips to the zoo or harbor.

Number. A trip to the grocery store to buy the things needed for a party to celebrate "all the birthdays in November" brings out questions of

"How many . . .?" and "How much . . .?" The beginning of an understanding of how much things cost and of buying and selling comes out of such experiences.

Before the five-year-old comes to school, an adult may have taught him to count by rote. Many children are proud of the accomplishment of saying the numerals in the conventional order. But many adults who assure you that Betty "knows her numbers" mean only a memoriter repetition of words in order. Many experiences in kindergarten will help Betty to understand "three" as her friends Judy and Sharon make cakes with her to sell in their bakery. She may even chant, "Three girls making cakes, making cakes for the bakery." "Four" will come to have meaning when the number of wheels on the wagon are counted. And "three" will have a still different meaning when it means one large wheel and two small ones on the tricycles. Later "twenty" cookies will mean that Jerry's mother sent one for every child in kindergarten to help him celebrate his birthday.

The kindergarten teacher builds into the activities of every day the insightful experiences which give meaning to spatial and quantitative relationships. Setting each table with four places, putting the small blocks away by two's, and using a cup, a pint, and a quart measure give children real experiences with differences in quantity. Looking at a ruler with space divided into inches and using it to measure the length of the boards needed to make an airplane or a boat is the beginning of understanding of linear measure and its usefulness.

Not every child will acquire mathematical insight to the same degree or at the same rate. A few will be fascinated by the manipulation of number. Nuts and pebbles will be marshaled into rows by two's and five's. One will be taken away and the child will wish to share his discovery that "five take away one leaves four." Thus does the future mathematician or engineer take his first pleasurable steps into the world of number.

Expanding Control of Language

From birth the child has been engaged in extending his power to communicate with others, first to let the adults about him know of his unmet needs, but later to share his ideas and feelings because human beings are just naturally gregarious.

Vocabulary Building. A good kindergarten puts no premium on silence but encourages much free conversation among the children and with the teacher and other adults. The richer and more stimulating the experiences are, the more rapidly will children develop interesting and vivid vocabularies and master more complex grammatical forms. The success that children experience in their later school work depends to a very considerable extent upon the accuracy of the concepts they attach to the verbal symbols.

Trips. Again, firsthand experiences by means of trips into the community build up a wealth of concepts. If the teacher is careful to see that accurate words to express these concepts are learned at the same time, she has made an immeasurable contribution to the child's future educational progress. A trip to an airport should yield command over many such words as jet, pilot, propeller, stewardess, engine, helicopter, tail, landing gear, mechanic, control tower, ticket office. Not all children will acquire all these words but many of them will. The teacher can offer "propeller" when the child wishes to tell her about "the thing that goes round and round" or "landing gear" when the child talks about "the little wheels underneath." Children learn new words easily if they are associated with an object and are then spoken clearly and distinctly.

Stories and Songs. Picture books, stories told by the teacher, rhymes or short poems learned in small groups, the words of songs understood and clearly enunciated in singing — all contribute to growth in language power.

Dramatic Play. Dramatic play is carried on largely through language. No one who listens to a group in the kindergarten playhouse or to a group playing airport or fire station can question the unparalleled opportunity for language development that dramatic play affords.

In fact, social living in the kindergarten moves ahead in an atmosphere of friendly chatter as children compare their prowess with that of their peers on jungle gym or slide, as they work with clay in a companionable group, or as they wrestle with tools and materials to construct a boat. Frequently, there are moments of concentration on painting a picture, drawing with crayon, observing the baby chicks, or looking at a picture book, but these are interludes for most children, whose desire to communicate with their peers is an insistent one.

Writing. Little need arises in kindergarten for the child to use written symbols. He may occasionally draw short vertical lines or make circles, and he may even attach names to them, "one" and "zero." Or he may put the circle on top of the line and call it a "head." The teacher observes such drawings and remembers that writing as well as reading is part of the curriculum in later grades and not in kindergarten. Many children learn to identify their own names in manuscript or cursive writing; a few who have good co-ordination may write their names themselves. Occasionally, a child may ask for a sign for his store and the teacher obligingly prints it on tagboard for him. But the kindergarten teacher who really understands the growth characteristics of the child realizes that building a rich oral vocabulary based on accurate concepts produces a more useful foundation for later development in the language arts than any premature smuggling in of written symbols.   The adult's motivation to engage in procedures which are totally without approval by pediatricians, psychologists, and psychiatrists is difficult to understand when the welfare of children is at stake.

Enjoying the Literary Heritage

It would be almost impossible to find a child who does not love stories. In the kindergarten, there is never a day when a small or large group of children does not settle down comfortably to listen to the teacher tell or read a story or poem.   The kindergarten teacher has untold resources to draw upon because many writers of children's stories have produced and are producing a wealth of literary treasure for children.

The story time is one of complete enjoyment for most children and perhaps that is the reason it influences their language development, stimulates their imagination and creativity, and develops empathy for other girls and boys everywhere throughout the world.

The artists have collaborated with the authors in a labor of love for children expressed in the exquisite color and design to illustrate the author's patterns of beautiful words.   Another collaborator should be mentioned — the publisher of children's books — who has done his full part in enriching the lives of modern children by his generous use of the bookmaker's art.   Could all these adults who worked to produce fine books for children see the wide-eyed delight of the fives as they gather around their teacher, chime in to finish a sentence, draw a deep breath at a lovely illustration, squeal with mirth at a ridiculous incident, and sigh the deep sigh of satisfaction as the teacher gently closes the book on the finished story, they would feel well repaid for their efforts.   Together the teacher, the author, the illustrator, and the publisher have opened the door so today's children may joyously enter their literary treasure house.

Expressing Ideas Through Art

The kindergarten affords the child a wide range of art materials and sets the stage so that he may use them freely.   He is not *taught* to paint although he has a standing invitation to paint at the easels, or on the table, or with his fingers, hand, or entire forearm in his so-called finger painting. All of the materials are his to manipulate, to explore, to experiment with, and ultimately to use in expressing his own honest thoughts and feelings in colors of his choosing.

The kindergarten affords the child clay and a safe place to use it but the kindergarten teacher does not *teach* him to model.   He rolls, pounds, and pinches this satisfying material.   And some day, he is moved to model a turtle, or a duck, or anything else he wishes. Sometimes it comes out to his satisfaction and sometimes he turns to his teacher for advice. She may show him the solid structure of another ceramist's work or advise pulling out the smaller parts from the mass of clay rather than trying to make them adhere as separate bits. She may pick up a piece of clay to show very simply what she means, because a good teacher shows a child new ways to use his material if he is unsatisfied with his present accomplishment.

The kindergarten affords the child a workbench, tools, and materials for construction and helps him in learning to use the tools to make them do what he wants them to do, but the idea is his idea and no patterns are provided.

The kindergarten affords the child many opportunities to arrange things — science collections, pictures on display boards, furniture in the playhouse — because art *is* arrangement.

The child's art efforts in the kindergarten are likely to be at the manipulative level, and the teacher should never impose adult standards on him. Without full opportunity to live through this manipulative level of expression, the child can never move on to the next steps in his artistic development. But again, the beginning is important and should be safeguarded in a classroom — by a teacher who understands this period of artistic development and allows no adult evaluations to lessen the child's joy in his creative work.

Becoming Acquainted with Music

Music plays a large part in the lives of young children. Many bring to school a background of joyous experiences provided by wise parents. The school affords further opportunity to extend musical experience in a variety of ways.

In the atmosphere of freedom of a good kindergarten, children hum as they build with blocks or model with clay. Original chants may accompany the "pumping up" in a swing or a rhythmic climb on the jungle gym. Children are encouraged to sing in small groups with the teacher, around the piano, or with a phonograph recording. Rhythm instruments are arranged for experimentation during outdoor play. The phonograph is equipped with earphones so three or four children may enjoy listening to records without disturbing others in the room. The teacher brings a few musical instruments into the room and shows the children how the musician uses them. Perhaps a parent of one of the children will prepare a short concert on an instrument, perform it for the children, and follow the presentation by answering the children's questions about the instrument and learning to play it. All musicians like to be "in on the act" of widening the music horizons of children.

The kindergarten teacher who can accompany on the piano the children's skipping, running, and galloping to music is equipped with an exceedingly worth-while accomplishment, but a wealth of recorded material is available so that no child need be denied the opportunity for rhythmic response to music.

The influence of music in the lives of people justifies the emphasis given music in the good kindergarten. Music becomes an integral part of work, play, and relaxation. It contributes to the child's feelings of security and understanding. Every child has an opportunity to participate regardless of whether he has found his singing voice or not. Many children will find it as they listen to the teacher and the other children and their own voices. Some will find it more quickly than others, depending upon natural differences in auditory discrimination. The richer the music environment in singing, listening, experimenting with rhythm instruments, and responding rhythmically to music, the more rapid will be the child's progress. Children learn to do by doing; the more joyous experiences they can have with music the more they will love it and grow in musical power.

Establishing Satisfying Relationships with Others

The kindergarten makes one of its major contributions to the growth and development of the child through the social situations it affords for living and learning as a member of a group. Only in such a situation can a child develop social values by coming to attach feelings of satisfaction to the sharing of materials and experiences and to the recognition of the rights and abilities of others. In the periods of group discussion the child learns that each person must take turns in talking and listening, that other people have good ideas and suggestions, and that he too can make a contribution to a group project by presenting his ideas in a way that others can understand. But he is not hurried into group participation; the kindergarten day affords plenty of time to do interesting things alone or with another child. Gradually, the child can adjust to a number of other children and find his way in making friends among his peers. The entire experience of his kindergarten day is designed to provide an environment conducive to his growth as the kind of social being who behaves in keeping with democratic principles and ideals.

In helping the children develop in the kindergarten, the teacher sometimes has them working in one large group, sometimes individually, but most frequently in small groups. For matters that concern all of the children, she works with the group as a whole. When a matter is of importance for one child only, she works with him individually. When several children have the same or related interests, the teacher works with them in a small group. Meeting needs of individual children is highly desirable but often several children can learn as easily as one. To teach effectively the teacher needs to know the needs and activities of children as they are provided for individually *and* in small and large groups.

THE TEACHER WORKS WITH THE CHILDREN

Working with the Entire Group of Children

In a democratic kindergarten where responsibility is shared by children and teacher a few situations concern every member of the group and should be handled by the entire group. These include situations in which the group needs to plan some new activity (*e.g.*, how to get safely into the school bus); or to evaluate some current experience (*e.g.*, working and talking so loudly that it is difficult to hear); or to enjoy an audience situation (*e.g.*, a special radio program or a motion picture). When children come together as a large group only in such situations, they see that the large group is important and they learn quickly how to participate helpfully in it.

Helping the children to learn to move from place to place or from activity to activity as a single group is generally recognized as an important objective of the kindergarten. When a group of children is in a school building, that group must be able to leave the building quickly in case of fire, or get to a shelter in case of an air raid. Whether children survive may depend on their ability to move with the group. Although no difference of opinion exists about the importance of the objective, kindergarten teachers differ in their opinion about its relative importance and the proportion of the kindergarten day needed for practicing it. In the democratic classroom, the entire group comes together briefly when necessary but most activities are carried on by individuals or in small groups. In the teacher-centered classroom great emphasis is put on group and audience activities involving all the children as a unit.

The Group in the Teacher-centered Classroom

In the teacher-centered classroom the teacher gathers the children as a large group at the beginning of the day; she plans small group and individual projects only as deviations from the large group activities; she keeps the children in one large group for the greater portion of the kindergarten day. This use of the large group is contrary to the five-year-old's tendency to be in motion and results in a large amount of discipline imposed by the teacher, rather than in discipline imposed by the children themselves as they grow in self-control and self-direction. Furthermore, excessive organization of children in the large group leads to making audience situations out of what really concerns only one child or one small group of children. In a teacher-centered classroom, a teacher's conversation often includes such remarks as

We're not acting silly, Jim.
Class, do we think acting silly is funny?
Tom, you're disturbing us.
Let's each sit in his own place, Ted.
Show Miss Teacher you know how to sit.
Wait until you're chosen, Mary.
Dan, are you helping Tom be a good helper?
Sam, can you wait in line with the rest of us?

Thus individual behavior is brought unfavorably to the attention of the entire group. Such undesirable attention is resented by many children. Even favorable attention from the large group tends to increase the timidity of certain children. Furthermore, when the large group situation is used for what concerns only one or a few children, others are disinterested and restless. Their time would be better spent on their own projects.

A mother reported an incident which reflected what her son had learned from a teacher-centered kindergarten:

One Saturday morning towards the end of the school year, Dan was having breakfast with his family and his grandmother, who was a special overnight guest. Dan interpreted the breakfast situation at once as one calling for especially good behavior. His younger brother made no such distinction and was busy stirring up pancakes for the family while Mother encouraged his efforts and wiped up after him. Dan talked with his grandmother and his father for a few minutes, and then ate silently for an interval. Suddenly he burst into tears, directing his anger toward his mother. When she had finally re-established good rapport with him, he was able to explain his problem: "I sat there a long time and no one chose me to stir the pancakes!"

Dan's mother explained to him that his kindergarten was the only place in which he had to wait for someone to choose him to do an activity. At home he could do it whenever he could arrange for a turn.

The teacher-centered kindergarten with its great emphasis on teacher authority and the children as an audience is probably better adapted to countries where people are taught to be followers than to a democracy, in which each person is a valued individual. In the democratic kindergarten the children learn how to achieve their purposes without interfering with the rights or property of others. At the same time they learn desirable ways of working in small groups as well as individually and in one large group.

Working with Small Groups of Children

Working with children in small groups requires a minimum of teacher direction and offers opportunity for a maximum of pupil initiative. Many five-year-old children have had nursery school or family experience which prepares them for small group projects. Even left to their own resources, the children go on growing in their social relationships and in their understandings. But with well-timed teacher guidance they gain more from each situation. The teacher notices when a group of children need some further technique or information and steps skillfully into their play to make a needed brief explanation or guide them in discussing a problem. As her time permits, she may occasionally take part briefly in a bit of dramatic play or read the group a story closely related to their interests. However, since she is responsible at all times for all the children, she does not get absorbed in the activities of one group to the exclusion of others.

At the first of the year, the teacher who appreciates the importance of children working individually or in small groups on projects of their own choosing lets them work primarily in this way. However, she also helps them learn to work together as a single group. She and the children agree upon a signal for coming together to discuss a plan or a problem of concern to everyone. Gradually the children learn to work together purposefully as members of either a small or large group. The primary objective of the teacher is to help the children achieve their purposes. But at the same time she helps them understand their roles in groups.

Helping the Individual Become Part of the Group

Although the children may be working in small groups or by themselves, the teacher thinks of them and works with them as individuals. She respects each of them as an important person. When any child has something to tell her, she listens appreciatively and with interest, stooping down to his level and giving him her complete attention. She helps him do what he wants to do insofar as it is possible and does not interfere with others. She co-operates with each child and, in turn, each child co-operates with her and with others. Thus the teacher creates a happy climate of co-operation.

In helping the children work together democratically, the teacher makes a point of seeing that no child gets more than his share of turns, teacher attention, or group attention. She keeps in mind that hurting others or destroying school property are limits beyond which no child can go, and in meeting the needs of each child, the teacher helps him understand the limits needed in the group situation of the kindergarten. She helps him achieve his purposes, working sometimes alone, sometimes as a member of a small group, and sometimes as one person in the total group.

PARENTS PREPARE CHILDREN FOR KINDERGARTEN

It is the responsibility of parents to help their children be ready to enter school. In most states, parents are not required to enroll their children in school until the age of six, seven, or eight. But where kindergartens are provided in connection with public schools, parents have the privilege of sending their children when they are ready to profit from the experience. The age of entrance is usually established by legal provision or by action of the governing board of the state educational system. Both public and private kindergartens usually retain the privilege of excluding any child whose behavior interferes with the welfare of the children's group. For instance, a child who spends the first several days of kindergarten crying and screaming interferes with what the other children want to do and is obviously not ready to profit from the experience himself. If separation from his family is so emotionally disturbing that he is unable to recognize the attractive play situations of kindergarten, unable to relate himself to the teacher, or unable to relate himself to another child, he needs to take part in many simplified social situations before he is ready to come to kindergarten.

The teacher identifies children unable to profit from kindergarten, and works with the principal and with the school counselors in helping the parents to recognize their responsibility for helping the child develop socially. An emotionally dependent mother must learn to release her child, and to give him consistent affection as he ventures away from her. The overly-protective mother must learn to let her child learn from his own experience and from play with other children. The asocial mother must arrange for her child to have playmates and to visit back and forth with them. The mother who is intent on meeting her own needs must learn how to provide for her child's needs at the same time. Often the child who is not ready for kindergarten when he is about five years old has a parent who needs counseling or psychiatric help in facing the realities of life situations. Fortunately, few five-year-old children come to kindergarten who cannot be stimulated by the environment and the warm acceptance of the teacher to meet the new situation with a minimum amount of emotional distress.

SITUATIONS FOR DISCUSSION

In the following situations select each course of action that seems desirable to you basing your choices and omissions on the ideas presented in this chapter. Add one or more alternate courses of action.

SITUATION I. You are a member of an elementary school committee assembling information about the community in pamphlet form for the use of teachers. You recommend that the pamphlet include:

The flow of resources through the community.
Recreational opportunities for people of all age levels.
History of the community.
Problems in further development of the community.
Maps, charts, and pictures.

SITUATION II. Whether or not your college program included courses in science, as a kindergarten teacher you should help the children:

Avoid hazards of the community.
Observe characteristics of migratory birds.
Enjoy bringing in pets, rocks, insects, plants.
Look for relationships, especially likenesses and differences.
Try out their ideas.

SITUATION III. You have never been able to carry a tune. As a kindergarten teacher you should:

Assemble a good record recollection.
Encourage children to make up songs of their own.
Chant while the children sing.
Have more art and less music for the children.
Learn to play the piano.

SITUATION IV. You want to introduce creative dramatics and have decided to begin with "The Three Bears." You should:

Have a mother assistant help.
Work with a small group of interested children during a free play period.
Work with the entire group of children.
Choose the children to play each part.
Take one of the parts yourself.

BIBLIOGRAPHY

Professional Books and Pamphlets

Association for Childhood Education International. *Curriculum at Work*. Washington, D. C., 1948.
Pamphlet includes anecdotal accounts of the kinds of curriculum experiences needed by children.

Battenberry, Hilda L., and Phyllis Van Dyke. *Wonderland in Kindergarten*. New York: Exposition Press, 1957.
Twenty-four handicraft units concerning the seasons, holidays, the farm, and the zoo to help teachers in planning activities for children.

Clapp, Elsie R. *The Use of Resources in Education*. New York: Harper & Bros., 1952.
A county school in Kentucky and a community school in a farming-mining area in West Virginia develop meaningful education for children and parents by studying and using environmental needs and materials.

Culkin, Mabel Louise. *Teaching the Youngest.* New York: The Macmillan Company, 1949.

A book written primarily for the student teacher and her supervisor.

Forrest, Ilse. *Early Years at School.* New York: McGraw-Hill Book Company, Inc., 1949.

The curriculum is planned to meet the needs of the continually growing child. "The curriculum in early childhood education" is one topic discussed.

Hymes, James L., Jr. *Before the Child Reads.* Evanston, Illinois: Row, Peterson and Company, 1958.

Author makes the point that the school cannot "build" readiness; children are ready, work with them; parents are ready, work with them.

Lambert, Hazel M. *Teaching the Kindergarten Child.* New York: Harcourt, Brace and Company, 1958.

This book for prospective and in-service kindergarten teachers has chapters dealing with art, music, dramatic play, language, social studies, health, science, and quantitative concepts.

National Council of State Consultants in Elementary Education. *Education for Children below Six.* Washington, D. C., 1955. % Elsa Schneider, 1711 Massachusetts Avenue, N.W.

General statements of policy for the adequate education of children under six are included.

Sheehy, Emma Dickson. *The Fives and Sixes Go to School.* New York: Henry Holt and Company, 1954.

Needs of individual children should be met through a variety of school experiences. Records and reports aid the development and guidance of individual children.

Ward, Muriel. *Young Minds Need Something to Grow On.* Evanston, Illinois: Row Peterson and Company, 1957. 192 pages.

Anecdotes portray vivid logical ways of teaching young children.

Wirick, M. M. *Kindergarten Year.* New York: Exposition Press, 1954.

A pamphlet of practical experiences adapted to the developmental needs of children.

Filmstrip for Parents and Teachers

The Kindergarten Way Is to Learn Each Day. Santa Ana, California. Books That Talk Programs, 1956.

Classroom activities show the value of dramatic play, craft activities, show and tell, educational trips and story telling. 65 frames, $33\frac{1}{3}$ r.p.m. disc recording, color.

6

Health in the Kindergarten

Entrance into school provides many opportunities for the young child to learn about health. Eager, reluctant, curious, cautious children come to school. The help they are given in adjusting to the group, the conditions which the school provides, and the understanding they acquire about themselves as living organisms have an effect upon the attitudes they develop and the health practices they employ. The school aims to make its contribution to the health of each child. If a child is to have health, his body must function well, he must recover from fatigue quickly, he must have a mental outlook that meets life with poise and confidence, and he must get along well with others.

MAINTAINING GOOD HEALTH

Unless children are in sufficiently good health to attend kindergarten and to take advantage of the environment provided for them, all the money invested in well-equipped classrooms and playground and in salaries for their teachers is wasted. Realizing this, the kindergarten teacher prepares the children for having physical examinations by the school physician, immunizations by the school nurse, and dental examinations by the dental hygienist or dentist. She follows up the findings of the various examinations by providing any modified program indicated and by encouraging parents and children to follow recommended remedial measures. Each day she looks carefully at each child to see if he is his usual alert and happy self, ready for the activities planned for the day. And each day she guides the children as they acquire health knowledge and form good health habits. When she talks with parents she helps them understand the school health program and interprets school policies established in the interests of the children. Above all, the teacher constantly keeps herself in the best possible health, having regular physical examinations and making use of

88

what she knows about keeping free from illness and disease. She is an example to children of the buoyancy that health can give to life.

Inspections and Health Examinations. When a child enters school, both the parents and the school need assurance that the child is in good health and able to profit from the school program to the best of his abilities. Many parents through their family physician or pediatrician have their children examined prior to the opening of school. However, many parents may not have had their children examined. And even if they have, it is still necessary for the school to be assured of the fitness of each child and to provide an examination by a physician.

Daily Inspections. In addition to knowing that the child is in general good health, the school needs to know that the child is well each day and is not a health menace either to himself or others around him. The teacher is responsible for inspecting each child daily. Although a child is usually well when sent to school, he may at any time in the course of the day begin to have symptoms of a cold or other contagious illness. The teacher notices:

Eyes watering, nose running
Forehead warm, face flushed, fever
Sneezing, coughing
Sweating or chilling
Pallor, lips colorless
Swollen neck glands
Headache, earache, or other ache
Rash, skin irritations

Whenever a child has such symptoms, the teacher takes immediate steps to get help for the child and to protect the other children from possible contagion.

The teacher notices not only signs of acute illness but also any sign that a child needs medical attention:

Little or no gain, or actual loss, of weight between regular examinations
Little or no gain in height between regular examinations
Frequent colds; frequent absence
Disinterest; poor posture; excessive fatigue
Frequent rubbing or other attention to eyes, ears, or scalp
Cracks at corner of mouth; sores or rough patches on skin
Excessive withdrawal or attention-getting behavior

Referrals to School Doctor and Nurse. If a child is not his usual self — alert, energetic, bright-eyed, happy, and clean — the teacher refers him to the school nurse or physician. Such referrals are apt to disclose a remediable health situation which might otherwise be overlooked. Referral examinations are an important part of the school health program.

In making a referral, the teacher is careful to describe what she has observed and to avoid any guesses about the exact nature of the child's difficulty or its treatment. She avoids making remarks such as, "I think Don needs glasses. He has been rubbing his eyes a great deal lately." But she may say, for instance, "Julia seemed so alert at the first of the term. She was interested in every activity we suggested. But now she seems to slump down as if she were tired, and to avoid entering into new projects. She was out of school with the measles a few weeks ago, and since she came back, she does not seem like herself. I wonder if she should have a thorough medical examination." In this way the teacher reports what she has observed. She leaves to the physician both diagnosis and recommendation of treatment.

Dental Health. The teacher also notices children with discolored teeth, inflamed gums, or teeth that do not come together correctly (*i.e.*, malocclusion). Increasingly schools are arranging for examinations of teeth by a dental hygienist or by a dentist. For kindergarten children such an examination is especially important since they are beginning to lose their first teeth and gain their permanent set.

Visual Difficulties. The kindergarten teacher is particularly observant of the children's appearance and behavior to discover signs of visual difficulty. Red-rimmed, encrusted or swollen eyelids, dizziness, nausea following close use of eyes, complaints of blurred vision are frequently indicative of serious vision problems. Rubbing of eyes, blinking, shading eyes from the light, holding a picture book or work close to the eyes are signs readily observed by the alert teacher. These conditions should be drawn to the attention of the school nurse and the parents. The teacher will, of course, arrange physical conditions in the classroom in ways conducive to the optimum comfort of the child with visual difficulty.

Hearing Difficulties. The teacher is also sensitive to evidences of hearing difficulty. She observes restlessness and inattention in children. She notices the child who often fails to follow suggestions and needs to have statements repeated. She makes notes regarding such behavior and she looks for further symptoms of difficulty in hearing. Does the child turn his head to one side to hear better? Is his speech as well developed as that of the usual five-year-old? Does he have earaches and head colds frequently? Does he make an effort to watch the face of a person speaking? Does he tire more readily than other children? Is he overly aggressive, or timid? Does he hang back as activities get under way? What the teacher observes and records, she takes with her to discuss with the school nurse.

The evidence that the kindergarten teacher presents to the medical personnel of the school may make the difference between a child who gets help with his hearing problem and goes on to successful school experiences and a child whose hearing problem remains unidentified for a considerable time and who may go on to further problems in his school life.

At the same time that the teacher refers children with possible hearing difficulty for further examination, she arranges for them to be near her when she is talking, and she gets their attention before she gives directions. She speaks to such children just as she does to other children, naturally, without obvious exaggeration, simply and briefly.

Remedial Work. After the children have been examined by school physicians, dental personnel, or eye and ear specialists, any remediable disabilities will be known but must still be corrected. The teacher then is a key person to work with the school nurse in encouraging parents to obtain the medical and dental care needed. In parent conferences and meetings, the teacher emphasizes the possible handicaps a child may have both now and later in life if disabilities are not remedied as soon as possible.

Depending upon the nature of their remediable disabilities, the teacher makes adjustments in the programs of certain children. Children who are hard of hearing she seats where they can readily see the speakers during talking periods. For other children, the teacher arranges for rest, modified physical activities, supplementary nutrition, or whatever other treatment prescribed by the school physician can be carried out as part of the school program.

HEALTH RECORDS

The kindergarten teacher frequently begins the cumulative records which will be continued throughout the child's school life. His bodily equipment, health conditions, and health needs are important entries on the cumulative record. If any detrimental health condition continues or recurs at intervals, a detailed anecdotal record of the situation together with an indication of referral or treatment secured may be added to the child's individual folder. The child's attendance record may indicate health conditions responsible for excessive absence.

Height and weight records should be made at regular intervals every two or three months. Each time height or weight is recorded, the previous records should be examined to see if there has been any marked or unexplained deviation from anticipated normal growth. Whenever such deviation is noted, the child should be referred to the school nurse for further study to ascertain the cause. Such a condition merits a conference with the parents so that appropriate action may be taken to correct the condition.

HOME AND SCHOOL WORK TOGETHER

Much information concerning a child's health can be secured only from the parents. Many schools gather this information in conference with the parents. Parents are invited to be present during medical and dental examinations and to discuss findings with the doctor or dentist. The school recognizes full partnership with the home in safeguarding and improving the health of children.

San Francisco Unified School District has developed a form called the *Health Inventory* which is filled out by parents. Excellent co-operation has been secured from a high percentage; parents respond completely to the *Health Inventory* and return the form promptly. The data recorded by the parents have proved helpful in identifying children with physical and emotional problems which require subsequent follow-up. Parents indicate their interest in the health problems of their children and frequently request opportunity to discuss these problems with the school personnel.

The teacher working with the school health personnel can be an effective member of the team because of the opportunity the school affords to build good health practices, to provide needed health instruction, to integrate health instruction with the health services the school provides, and to work closely with parents in securing the services of the private doctor, dentist, or specialist in meeting the health needs of children.

The *Health Inventory* [1] form used by the San Francisco Unified School District follows on pages 93–97.

HEALTH TEACHING

When children enter school is probably the time when most can be done about helping them form desirable health habits. Studies of upper-grade children and high school youth show that health habits are already well established by the time the children reach those grades. Apparently if the school is going to help children improve their health habits, it will have to start with them when the children first come to school. The primary objective, then, of the kindergarten health program is to build sound health habits with the accompanying attitudes and generalizations for reinforcing them.

One kindergarten teacher thought that she could help the children begin to develop the following lifelong health habits:

stretch when tired of sitting

get a drink when thirsty

[1] Charlotte Singer-Brooks, M.D., "The Value of Health Inventories Filled Out by Parents," *California Journal of Elementary Education*, XXIII, No. 2 (November, 1954), 95–104.

HEALTH INVENTORY
For Elementary School

San Francisco
Department of Public Health

San Francisco
Unified School District

I. Pupil's name_____Sex____Birth date_____

Address_____Phone no._____

Father's name_____Mother's name_____

Employer's address_____

Employer's telephone no._____

In case of accident, this information will assist
the school principal in notifying parents.

How many members in immediate family?____Mother_____

Father_____Brothers_____Sisters_____Others_____.

Does this child live at home with _____Mother,

_____Father; if not, with whom is child living?

_____. Give relationship_____.

II. Past illness (please check those which your child has had)

____measles   ____smallpox

____whooping cough   ____diabetes

____infantile paralysis   ____heart disease

____rheumatic fever   ____chorea (St. Vitus Dance)

____scarlet fever   ____epilepsy (convulsions)

____diphtheria

Please tell any other serious illness, operation or
injury, and age when incurred:_____

_____

III. Has your child been vaccinated against smallpox?

No_____ Yes_____. Does he/she have a scar? Yes_____
No_____. What was the date when he/she was last
vaccinated?_____.
Has your child been immunized against diphtheria?

No_____ Yes_____. Year_____.
Has he/she been reimmunized (booster protection)?

No_____ Yes_____. Year_____.

IV. Has your child ever been around anyone known to have
tuberculosis? No_____ Yes_____. Year_____.
Has he/she ever had a skin test for tuberculosis?

No____ Yes____. Year_____.
Do you know if the test was: Positive___ Negative___.

Has he/she had an X-ray of the chest? No____ Yes___.

Year_____. Where was the X-ray taken?_____

_____.

V. Please check any of the following symptoms which have
been noted recently:

____4 or more colds each   ____allergy
    year
                                  ____persistent cough
____frequent sore throat
                                  ____speech difficulty
____frequent headaches

____blurred vision   ____running ears

____frequent sties   ____hard of hearing

____frequent pains in legs ____frequent nose bleeds
or joints
                            ____night sweats
____dizziness
                            ____tires easily
____fainting spells
                            ____shortness of breath
____abdominal pain
                            ____hernia (rupture)
____frequent urination

VI. Information which will help you, the school staff and
physician understand your child better. Please check
which of the following you observe in your child:

____nail biting   ____is self-reliant

____thumb sucking   ____dependable

____bed wetting   ____jealous

____shy   ____likes to play with
                            others
____happy disposition
                            ____resentful
____orderly
                            ____is generous with
____helpful around home   playmates

____has many friends   ____selfish

____is a leader   ____excitable

____has few friends   ____angers easily

____prefers to be alone   ____suspicious

____becomes discouraged   ____very easy to manage
easily
                            ____thoughtful of family
____worries a great deal   members

____has many fears   Other_____

VII. What time does your child usually go to bed _____,

get up _____? Does he/she eat breakfast_____,

lunch_____, dinner_____ every day? What is the

average amount of milk he/she drinks each day_____?
Check any other beverage which he/she usually drinks
daily:

_____	_____	_____
tea	coffee	fruit juices

_____	_____
cola or other soft drinks	other

VIII. What does your child like to do when he/she is not in
school, such as (circle): outdoor games, movies,

T.V., music, other_____.

IX. Do you take your child to a private physician? No___

Yes_____. What is his/her name?_____.

How often do you take your child to him/her?_____.

Do you take your child to a clinic? No_____ Yes____.

Which clinic?_____. How often?

_____. For what reason and when
did you last take your child to a private physician

or clinic?_____.

_____ Date_____

Do you take your child to a private dentist? No_____

Yes_____. What is his name?_____.

How often does your child visit him?_____.

Do you take your child to a dental clinic? No_____

Yes_____. Which clinic?_____

How often?_____.

Are there any problems or other matters which you
would like to discuss with the school staff (physi-

cian, teacher, nurse, other)?_____

_____

Date_____ Parent's signature_____

use the bathroom properly
have regular physical examinations by a doctor
have a dental examination regularly
obtain immunizations as needed
wash hands before eating
keep pencils, fingers, and other objects out of mouth
cough or sneeze in a tissue or handkerchief
rest when tired
stay home when ill
eat wholesome food and avoid excess of sweets
brush teeth and gums at least once a day

BUILDING HEALTH HABITS

In building health habits the teacher makes her health teaching program a great deal of fun. She knows that children like those experiences which are happy and satisfying ones. She avoids "health telling" and provides ample opportunities for the children to ask questions and talk about health, for dramatic play in which children take the parts of parents and children, doctors, nurses, and dentists, and for songs, poems, and stories related to health.

The teacher takes advantage of opportunities for teaching about health whenever they occur spontaneously. Perhaps the children want to look at a book that was taken home overnight by a child who came down with chickenpox. Perhaps a child has seen a nurse wearing a gauze mask and wants to know why she wore it. Perhaps a child says, "Daddy is sick today. Will I get sick?" The teacher is alert to find "teachable moments" for health instruction in children's questions or comments, and in the happenings of the day. When interest is high, discussions are more meaningful and information becomes increasingly significant. In this way the teacher guides the children to develop desirable attitudes, habits, and generalizations about health.

The teacher can use pictures effectively in teaching health lessons and in finding out how children feel about certain health practices. Pictures of health activities may be shown to small groups of five or six children. The children will usually talk freely about the pictures if the group is not too large. While he is talking, the child frequently reveals his food preferences and dislikes, the time he goes to bed at night, what time he rises in the morning, or his attitudes toward his doctor or dentist. These revealing talks help the teacher to make her health instruction more realistic for the individual children.

Health Habits in School

Teachers help children form the habit of stretching after sitting. They have a talking or listening group interrupt its activity for a stretch whenever children seem restless. Five-year-old children are not used to sitting for any prolonged length of time. They are used to being active. Even when they watch television programs, they watch for a few minutes and then move about for a few minutes. In school some of the children may find it difficult at first to sit with a group and keep their hands to themselves for more than a minute or two. To help them keep from disturbing others, certain restless children should feel free to leave the group for a brief interlude of activity — to punch the punching bag, to play with clay, to stretch and yawn, to walk about a bit — and then return to the group when they are ready to join comfortably in the activities in which the group is engaged.

When the teacher senses general restlessness in the group of children, she may interrupt their sitting with a stretching game, perhaps jack-in-the-box, or perhaps the following:

Head, shoulders, knees, toes (*touching each part*)
Head, shoulders, knees, toes (*touching each part*)
Head, shoulders, knees, toes (*touching each part*)
We all stand up together (*standing up*)
Head, shoulders, knees, toes (*touching each part*)
Head, shoulders, knees, toes (*touching each part*)
Head, shoulders, knees, toes (*touching each part*)
We all sit down together. (*sitting down again*)

Some kindergarten children need to develop the habit of getting a drink when they feel thirsty. The teacher talks with them about the body's need for water and encourages them to get a drink from time to time. Of course getting a drink must be both sanitary and convenient. A drinking fountain in the room and another on the playground are desirable to help children establish the habit of drinking an adequate amount of water.

Not all five-year-old children have established complete bathroom routines as part of their elimination processes. The kindergarten teacher helps many children to learn to flush the toilet and to wash hands as part of their toilet routine. When the kindergarten classroom has its own lavatory, it is easier for the teacher to supervise children as needed, and it is easier for the children to take care of themselves. In a general lavatory with large toilets and large washbowls, small children are uncomfortable, and they may feel crowded and hurried. Furthermore, going to a toilet at a distance may contribute to toilet accidents or to constipation. Certainly kindergarten children who have their own lavatory as part of their classroom are helped to establish good toilet routines.

Furthering Nutrition

Undernourished children do not progress in school as well as other children do. The malnourished kindergarten child is usually identified in the examination by the school physician, and provisions for rest or supplementary food are made as required. But both the malnourished and the adequately nourished children need to begin learning what foods are necessary to help a child continue through school in good health. The advertising that the five-year-old hears on television or radio is not necessarily conducive to the best food habits. The school must provide interesting as well as scientifically accurate information about nutrition if it is going to compete effectively with other information media and have girls and boys adequately nourished and able to profit from the educational program of the school.

The kindergarten teacher uses the flannel board to show children pictures of desirable food and to help them identify foods to be eaten regularly and those to be eaten only in limited quantity, if at all. "What is this?" she asks, putting up a picture of a beautiful red apple. "How many like to eat apples?" "Are apples good for us?" Later she guides the children in making simple choices. "Which will you drink this afternoon after school?" she asks, displaying an inviting glass of milk and a bottle of highly colored carbonated beverage.

Mid-morning juice is an opportunity for contributing both to the nutritional status of the children and to their health education. "My, this juice is good, and it's good for us too," says the teacher. Functional health teaching is also carried on in planning for a party. What drink should the children have at their party — fruit juice, synthetic juice popular in the community, milk, or chocolate milk? Thinking about what to eat and why in an interesting situation provides realistic health teaching that lays the basis for good habits of nutrition.

Encouraging a Rhythm of Rest and Activity

A rhythm of activity and rest is necessary for the well-being of a person. In the kindergarten such a rhythm is provided for the children. At mid-morning the children stretch out each on a low cot or a small mattress, and have a few minutes of relaxation. Sometimes soft music helps establish a restful mood. Sometimes the teacher softly sings or chants some simple and repetitive song such as, "Jamie's resting. Johnny's resting too." This quiet time gives the children renewed energy for activities during the remainder of the kindergarten period.

Although the rhythm of activity and rest is important to the well-being of the children, it is also important in teaching them to meet their own needs for rest and relaxation. After a period of activity, the children should feel the need for an interval of quiet. At the first of the year the teacher says, "We've been playing so hard that we need to rest before we do another thing." But later in the year the children will say, "I want to rest now." The teacher knows that important growth has been achieved when children recognize their own need for rest.

The attitude of the teacher has much to do with helping the children relax. Her quiet expectation that everyone is going to rest, her acceptance of the fact that many children will require weeks and months in learning to relax completely, and her own good stretch and yawn help the teacher to set an example of real relaxation. She avoids "You're going to rest now whether you want to or not" as well as the tight muscles and taut figure that stimulate restlessness in children. She may prepare the children for their rest by talking with them about Raggedy Ann and Raggedy Andy. Arms and legs go limp, jaws drop, and faces relax as the children think about the dolls resting.

In setting a good example for the children, the teacher gets her own interval of relaxation. She knows the value of a good stretch and makes the most of it for the benefit of her own well-being. Loosening her neck and shoulder muscles as she stretches, she too gets ready for the activities of the rest of the kindergarten day. Her genuine feeling that rest is important for each person — for herself as well as for each child — is probably the key to having a real period of rest and relaxation in the middle of the session.

The mid-morning snack, the careful washing of hands before eating, the rest period, and vigorous outdoor play are all planned to promote health, strength, and co-ordination.

The teacher incorporates into the daily program
such quantitative activities as setting a table
in two or more places.

Preparing Children for Health Examinations

At the first of the school year, the kindergarten teacher prepares the children for their health examination by the school physician, and then follows up the examination so that the children assimilate it as a pleasant and interesting experience. After several weeks in which the health examination has been the center of interest in health teaching, children should be pleased with the opportunity of going to see their friend, Dr. School Physician, and of having him look at them. When children ask, "Do we see the doctor today?" or "When do I have a turn to go?" the teacher can be assured that her teaching has been successful.

In starting to think about health examinations with the children, the teacher helps them remember their experiences in going to visit their family doctor. At least some of the children will be on friendly terms with a family doctor or pediatrician and will be happy to talk about him. Perhaps some of the children will have unhappy memories of their visit to the doctor. Often these are due to their dislike of "shots." Since immunizations are usually given by the nurse and not by the doctor, the teacher can guide the children in understanding that the doctor only examines the patients. If for some other reason they have unhappy memories of visiting a doctor, talking about the visits gives the children a chance to relieve their minds, and, through the guidance of the teacher, to replace their memories with pleasant anticipation of future visits.

The teacher provides a few simple properties for the children to play doctor and patient: a stethoscope and a white apron. One of the children who enjoys visiting the doctor probably will want to play the part of the doctor, at first, and will furnish a good example of his role. From time to time the teacher, after carefully listening to know what the role playing situation is at the moment, contributes a question or comment, or enters the play for a few moments in order to enrich it with health teaching: "Isn't it fun to have the doctor examine you?" "The doctor looks at ears too." The teacher does not enter the dramatic play when it is serving as a vehicle for a child to express verbal aggression toward the doctor or patient. She realizes that the child is finding release from emotional tension and will be better able to cope with the doctor's examination later.

It may be possible for the teacher to have the school physician come to say at least a friendly "Hello" to the children. He may not want to take time to show them how he examines a patient, but just a greeting reassures the children that he is really the friendly person they have been talking about. Playing doctor takes on new meaning after his visit.

Dramatic play also becomes more meaningful after the children are examined. Then the play gives them opportunity fully to assimilate this experience. As the memory of the examination takes its place among other remembered experiences, playing doctor will be replaced by other play. However, the children should be encouraged to play doctor whenever they wish.

From time to time the teacher provides opportunity for the children to talk about visiting the doctor and having him examine them. She guides them in these discussions to help them understand the importance of being examined as a safeguard against illness.

In much the same way that the teacher prepares the kindergarten group for physical examinations, she prepares them for an examination by the dentist or dental hygienist. Knowing what to anticipate, the children are not afraid and, in fact, look forward to the new experience. They play dentist, examining a doll's mouth, and they practice opening their own mouths wide.

When a five-year-old child loses a tooth, he is delighted with this evidence of his maturity. He enjoys talking about teeth. He likes to hear *One Morning in Maine* [2] and any other stories that have to do with this experience of getting a new tooth in place of a baby one. The teacher encourages the children to talk about their teeth and leads them into further understanding about care of their teeth.

Even in the kindergarten, children can begin to understand the relationship of dental health to general health and to appreciate the importance of a healthy mouth. They can begin to understand the importance of an adequate diet and the necessity of restricting candy and sweet drinks to prevent damage to the teeth.

The most important factor in a sound program of dental health is a teacher who is completely aware of the importance of proper care of the teeth. Such a teacher will find many ways to help children understand that their health and comfort depend upon safeguarding their teeth through a good diet and frequent vigorous brushing of teeth and gums.

Immunization

Most kindergarten children have been immunized for the common diseases of childhood and are familiar with having "shots." They like to talk about these experiences, and they like to play nurse and give "shots." The teacher encourages them in dramatic play which will help them assimilate their immunization experiences. If the children are to be given immunizations as part of the school program, then the teacher, well in advance, introduces dramatic play about being immunized and provides white caps and aprons for the nurses and a large doll for a patient.

---

[2] Robert McCloskey. *One Morning in Maine*. New York: The Viking Press, Inc., 1952.

Although most children like to play nurse or doctor, not so many are willing to be patients. The teacher occasionally plays the role of patient and adds glamor to the role. Sometimes she plays the howling patient, and sometimes the brave and stoical patient. Each time she has so much fun doing it that the other children want a turn in the same role. Of course, whenever she participates, the teacher guides the children in appreciating the importance of having immunizations. "Please, nurse, let me have a shot. I don't want to get sick." "Let me see. I have had a shot for whooping cough. I think I'll take one for diphtheria today." "There, now the germs can't make me sick."

During talking time the teacher encourages the children to bring stories from home about how their parents had whooping cough or tetanus or some other illness that children avoid today. Now children have a moment of hurt instead of the weeks of illness that children used to have before immunizations became available.

Absence Because of Illness

Children usually know when they do not feel well, but they need to learn what to do about it. If they have a permissive teacher with whom they like to talk, they readily report when they are not feeling well. They learn that they should be at home when they feel ill.

Parents, as well as children, need to understand that the child who is coming down with a cold should stay at home. If a mother has made plans for her morning, she may send her child to school hoping that he has not contracted the cold he seems to have. Parents need to be reminded that:

When a child is coming down with a cold or other illness he is especially apt to give the illness to others.

By keeping a child home when he may be getting a cold, other children are protected and maintain better health. They are less likely to expose the first child to an illness later.

Getting rest, liquids, nourishment, and medication as needed when a cold is starting helps to minimize its effects. Attention to a child when he is getting a cold results in less need for attention on subsequent days.

Five- to six-year-old children are absent about one day in ten, and more often than children of any other age range.

Respiratory diseases account for about half of children's absences.

Germ Theory

Teachers sometimes feel that five-year-old children should not be weighted down with germ theory. They are quite right that the children should not be burdened with the theory, but they need also to recognize that teaching the beginnings of the germ theory can be interesting to the children. The important factor is to teach children what they can do about germs. If they are taught only the dangers of germs without being taught what to do about the dangers, then they are burdened with fears of what they do not understand. But if they are taught at their level of understanding how to cope with germs, then they avoid fears and learn to avoid the germs.

For instance, the teacher can tell the story about John who did not feel well one day. He sat and chewed a red pencil for a while until the teacher came and asked if he wanted to go home. John put down the red pencil and went home. He had the mumps. As soon as he left, Carl, who liked red pencils, picked up the red pencil John had been chewing and put it in his mouth. What, the teacher asks, did Carl do that he should not have done? And what may happen to Carl as a result of what he did? How can Carl, or anyone, avoid the danger of getting sick in that kind of situation?

A child can have as much fun out of guarding his nose and mouth from germs as he has from guarding a fort or castle from an enemy. Children protect their bodies by keeping out of their mouths horns, whistles, balloons, spoons or anything else that has been in another person's mouth. They put in their mouth only food, utensils that have been thoroughly washed, or their own toothbrush.

In dealing with children, the teacher should be realistic. Complete freedom from illness is probably unattainable at our present level of medical knowledge. Although we would like every human being always to enjoy abundant vigor and strength, it is well for children to understand that perfect health is not always attainable. The teacher strives to prevent children from acquiring fear of disease or injury because fear can be as incapacitating as the disease itself. However, the child should be helped to acquire the knowledge which will enable him to live with the optimum amount of satisfaction and ability to participate in worth-while activities regardless of disease or injury.

Daily Health Habits at Home

Teachers and parents can work together to promote good health habits. Eating wholesome food, getting enough sleep, and brushing teeth regularly are desirable habits which concern the parents and are taught by the parents. At the same time these habits are so important in keeping children healthy enough to profit by school that they also concern teachers. How can such habits be effectively taught to five-year-old children?

To have children report at school on health habits carried out at home may encourage inaccurate reporting and emphasize the reporting rather than the health habit. Furthermore, conditions in all homes are not equally favorable to forming desirable health habits. Children who come from certain homes are handicapped in obtaining suggested diets, for instance. A quart of fresh milk a day for a child is not possible in all family budgets. Teachers who know the community in which they teach modify the health-teaching program according to local customs. For instance, a teacher in a fishing community encouraged fish as a staple of the diet. She realized that the local custom of cooking the small fish bones with the fish gave the children a source of calcium that was less expensive than fresh milk.

Certainly the kindergarten teacher should not emphasize health habits at variance with those in the community. If she attempts it, the children are confused and do not learn. But if she encourages desirable health habits which are being taught at home, health teaching at school and at home reinforce each other and the children establish acceptable habits more quickly.

Safe and Healthful Environment

The teacher maintains a room and a play area that are both healthful and safe. In doing so she encourages the children to be aware of their environment and to help in regulating it. When a child finds a piece of broken glass he puts it in the wastebasket or gives it to the teacher. When something breaks he reports it. Thus, primarily by teaching the children how to handle themselves, the teacher helps them to be safe. At the same time, of course, teachers daily check the grounds for any unusual hazard — broken glass, nails, sharp sticks, defective playground apparatus — and they check indoors to be sure that difficult spots such as stairs are well lighted.

The teacher helps the children develop habits of safety. If a child sees a drawer or cupboard door that has been left open, he learns to close it before someone bumps into it. If something is spilled, he helps clean it up before someone slips. He learns to keep toys out of passageways and from under foot. He learns to look where he is going before he starts moving, and to stop moving when he wants to look. He learns that beanbags and balls are for throwing and blocks, sand, or dirt are not for throwing. He learns to throw bags and balls only when people are not in the way.

The teacher maintains a uniform temperature for the children and encourages them to regulate their own warmth. When they come inside after playing in the cool outdoors, they take off their outer clothing. If the room gets too warm, they tell the teacher, "I'm hot," and the teacher finds out whether it is the child or the room that needs attention.

The Healthy Teacher

To learn well, a child should be healthy. To teach well, a teacher should be healthy. An annual health examination is as essential to the teacher as it is to the child. It should include a chest X-ray and immunizations. The teacher should refer herself to a physician at any time that she notices:

Feeling tired frequently; lack of usual energy

Increased negative reactions toward suggestions

Disinterest in the children; dislike for teaching; irritability

Feelings of depression; tendency to withdraw from people; difficulty in getting along well with people

Headaches

Any recurring ache or pain; persistent irritation in throat, breast, and the like

With the antibiotics now available, a teacher can minimize her absence from school. At the first feeling of an approaching cold or other illness, she gets help from her physician. She takes care of herself during illness, gets plenty of rest, and returns to school shortly. The children need an alert and healthy teacher. A teacher who is coughing and sneezing is exposing the children to a cold or other illness and has no place in the classroom.

School Health Policy

In every school, health policies are in effect although they may not be completely defined. They can be inferred from what is said and done by the administrators and other school personnel. It is the responsibility of every teacher to know what the policies are, to help get them defined in writing, and to help interpret them to children, parents, and other members of the community.

In finding out what the policies are, the teacher observes what is done in practice. One teacher defined the health policy in her school by answering the following questions:

What provisions are made for first aid in case of an emergency?

Are definite regulations available concerning communicable diseases?

Is there a room where a child can rest by himself?

Can ill children be taken home when necessary?

What provisions are made for medical examinations? Dental examinations? Eye and ear examinations?

Are children of indigent parents able to get needed medical care? dental care? other care?

Are children provided with needed food regardless of parental inability to pay?

Are children and school personnel protected from undue noise by acoustical treatment of ceilings and walls?

Are chairs, tables and other equipment selected for safety?

Are facilities and equipment suitable to the size of the children?

Are facilities and equipment kept clean and in good condition?

Is it easy to maintain an even temperature in each classroom?

Are the outdoor play area and facilities up to standard?

Are rest rooms well supplied with soap, towels, and toilet paper?

Is there a teacher's room? Is a cot provided for the teacher to rest?

Is there provision for a substitute teacher in case a regular teacher is ill?

How often are fire drills conducted?

The school health policy should be arrived at through a teacher committee working with administrative personnel. It should be developed in writing so that everyone can refer to it as needed. It should take into account each age level of children, including the kindergarten child. Arrangements should be made for carrying it out as planned. The policy on paper and the policy in operation should be one and the same, and should be developed in terms of the greatest good of the children.

SITUATIONS FOR DISCUSSION

In the following situations select each course of action that seems desirable to you basing your choices and omission on the ideas presented in this chapter. Add one or more alternate courses of action.

SITUATION I. Tommy goes suddenly to the bathroom. Through the partly open door you see that he is vomiting into the toilet. As the teacher you should:

Clean him up and give him a drink of water.

Get him to the school nurse.

Have him sit down quietly in the story group.

Tell the children that Tommy does not feel well.

Get Tommy some Seven Up.

SITUATION II. Mary is a quiet child. When she comes in the morning she gets a book and sits down by herself on the rug, turning the pages of the book and looking closely at the pictures. In the talking circle when pictures are held up or articles are shown, she often rubs her eyes. On the playground on a sunny day she squints almost in a frown. As her teacher you should:

In the talking circle have Mary sit toward the front.

Talk to Mary's parents about taking her to an eye specialist.

Refer her to the school physician for an examination.

Tell her not to rub her eyes.

Talk with the children about keeping their hands away from their eyes.

SITUATION III. Bobby is an only child whose mother is proud of the way she has trained him. "Bobby always minds," she says.

You notice that Bobby leaves the bathroom without flushing the toilet. As his teacher your procedure should be:

The next time Bobby goes to the bathroom, remind him to flush the toilet after using it.

Ask his mother to have Bobby flush the toilet when he uses it.

Talk with the group about what to do when using the bathroom.

When the toilet has not been flushed, ask the group, "Who used the bathroom?"

When Bobby leaves the bathroom without flushing the toilet, ask him with a smile, "Did you flush the toilet?"

SITUATION IV. You wake up tired one school morning. By the time you get to school you have a headache. By mid-morning you feel as if you are getting a cold. You should:

Finish the day with the children.

Tell the principal that you feel as if you were getting a cold.

Call for an appointment with your doctor.

Have the school nurse take your temperature.

Plan activities in which you will not be close to the children.

BIBLIOGRAPHY

Professional Books and Pamphlets

Association for Childhood Education International. *Educating for Healthful Living.* Washington, D. C., 1950.

Pamphlet discusses such topics as "The First Prerequisite — A Healthy Teacher," "What Makes a Healthful School Day for Children and Teachers," "Sex Education and Its Relation to Health," "Safety Is a Cooperative Venture, Too."

Fisher, Aileen. *Health and Safety Plays and Programs.* Boston: Plays, Inc., 1953.

Plays, skits, group readings about health and safety for kindergarten and primary grades.

Gallagher, J. Roswell. *Your Children's Health: A Handbook for Parents and Teachers.* Better Living Booklet. Chicago: Science Research Associates, Inc., 1952.

This pamphlet for parents and teachers contains up-to-date information.

Grout, Ruth E. *Health Teaching in Schools.* Philadelphia: W. B. Saunders Co., 1953.

Book for prospective teachers and teachers in service discusses "Guides to Health Teaching in the Kindergarten."

Metropolitan Life Insurance Company. *What Teachers See.* New York, 1951.

This illustrated booklet describes the signs that tell when a child needs to see the school health personnel, and is an example of the excellent health materials available through insurance companies.

Oberteuffer, Delbert. *School Health Education.* New York: Harper & Bros., 1954. Book for medical, dental, or school personnel participating in the school health program. Discusses basic problems, curriculum, and administration of the program.

Schneider, Elsa, and Simon A. McNeely. *Teachers Contribute to Health.* Washington, D. C.: Department of Health, Physical Education, and Recreation, Office of Education, 1951.
A clear and concise description of the school health program.

Walker, Herbert. *Health in the Elementary School.* New York: Ronald Press, 1955. Contains many suggestions to make health instruction interesting and meaningful to children.

Books for Children

Bemelmans, Ludwig. *Madeline.* Little Golden Book #186. New York: Simon and Schuster, Inc., 1939, 1954.
In rhyme, Madeline goes to the hospital and has her appendix out.

Brown, Margaret Wise. *Doctor Squash, the Doll Doctor.* Little Golden Book #157. New York: Simon and Schuster, Inc., 1952.
Besides this book of special interest for girls, *Doctor Dan, the Bandage Man* was written by Helen Gaspard telling about a little boy who plays doctor and uses band-aids.

Green, Mary McBurney. *Everybody Eats.* Eau Claire, Wisconsin: E. M. Hale, 1950.
Simple words and pictures tell what each animal eats, as well as what boys and girls eat.

McCloskey, Robert. *One Morning in Maine.* New York: The Viking Press, Inc., 1952.
A little girl loses a tooth one morning in Maine.

Paullin, Ellen. *No More Tonsils.* New York: Island Press Cooperative, 1947.
Karen has her tonsils out at the hospital.

Schlein, Miriam. *Deer in the Snow.* New York: Abelard-Schuman, 1956.
The way deer lose their antlers each year is compared to our losing our teeth.

Sever, Josephine A. *Johnny Goes to the Hospital.* Boston: Houghton Mifflin Co., 1953.
Johnny has a matter-of-fact trip to the hospital and back.

Woolley, Catherine. *Lunch for Lennie.* New York: William Morrow and Co., 1952.
Lennie gets more and more hungry as he explores being first one animal and then another. Finally he is a boy who eats his own lunch.

Films for Children

Judy's Smile. Hollywood 38: Avis Films, Inc., 1948.
Judy learns to take care of her teeth — brushing them and going to a dentist twice a year. 10 minutes, sound, color.

Kitty Cleans Up. New York: Young America Films, Inc., 1950.
Kitty's interest in being clean leads to first prize in a pet show given by the first grade children. 10 minutes, sound, color.

7

Furthering Physical Development

The five-year-old is more restrained than younger children. He is capable of maintaining one position for a longer interval than is a four-year-old. He can sit for a while, or stand for a while, or squat for a while. Yet even with his greater control, he is still a very active child. He is used to being in motion most of the day and has to learn to sit with a group or move at the pace of others.

This great activity of a five-year-old, of course, exceeds that of older children. Each year in school, children develop greater skill in sitting quietly with other children. The kindergarten year is often the child's first year for being inactive physically for even a brief period of time.

The five-year-old has come a long way from the time when he was learning to walk and was using literally every moment of his waking hours for diffuse muscular movement. Even eating and getting dressed were accomplished in motion, with mother trailing around with garments trying to dress, or a spoon trying to feed, a child who was primarily engaged in achieving the developmental task of walking. This urge for activity has lessened somewhat by five years of age, but muscular development and control are still a major task. In every phase of the curriculum, through every activity of the kindergarten, the child is busy in activities which further his physical development. It follows, then, that the entire program of the kindergarten is shot through with activities that help the child further develop his large muscles, start to co-ordinate some of the finer muscles and increase control essential for balance and co-ordination. Physical development is an integral part of every phase of the kindergarten.

OBJECTIVES OF PHYSICAL EDUCATION ACTIVITIES

Besides being interwoven with other parts of the curriculum, physical education has a place of its own in the kindergarten program. Through physical education activities, children develop rhythm, balance, and co-

110

ordination as well as muscular strength. They also develop the game skills needed to participate successfully in out-of-school recreation. The child who does not have these skills has difficulty in finding a place among his peers in his playground and neighborhood play groups. Since the school endeavors to help children lead a full life now as the best preparation for a full life in succeeding years, it provides opportunity for physical development through games and through free play on apparatus.

Through the physical education games and activities and through the physical development that is an integral part of other aspects of the curriculum, the children change materially during their kindergarten year. They increase their muscular development, their rhythmic movement, their co-ordination, and the control of their sense of balance. They develop many physical skills, and they modify their attitudes and their ideas in relation to their new skills. In one school system a group of teachers listed the following attitudes, skills and generalizations as reasonable outcomes of the kindergarten program as it furthers physical development of children.

Skills [1]

He develops sufficient strength and endurance to perform his daily activities effectively with a margin of energy in reserve.

He develops as high a degree of physical skill and motor co-ordination as his motor educability will permit.

He utilizes correct body mechanics in all of his daily activities — walking, running, sitting, lifting, carrying, climbing, pulling, changing direction.

He responds rhythmically to music and accompaniment appropriate to his age group.

He handles his body correctly while handling objects.

He is able to recognize and experience relaxation of the body as a whole.

He is able to use all the common pieces of playground apparatus and toys suitable for his age.

Knowledges

He has a repertoire of . . . activities which he can initiate during his leisure time.

He knows the rules of safety to be observed on play areas and for play activities.

[1] *Guide for Teaching of Physical Education in the Elementary Schools.* Committee of Long Beach Teachers, Office of Curriculum Development, Long Beach Public Schools, 1949, pp. 1 and 2. The items printed here were selected as pertinent to the kindergarten age child.

Attitudes

He respects and observes rules. . . .

His emotional stability is suitable to his age level.

He has developed a desire for the type of recreational activities which are organically stimulating, and which will send him on to his other activities mentally refreshed with a confident approach to the next problem of living.

PHYSICAL DEVELOPMENT THROUGH CURRICULAR ACTIVITIES

The kindergarten teacher provides for the well-rounded physical development of the children through the various activities of the kindergarten curriculum. Development of the pelvic girdle through pulling, pushing, walking, running, climbing; development of shoulder muscles through pulling, pushing, reaching, and climbing; development of the torso through turning, twisting, and reaching; development of leg and arm muscles through pulling, pushing, reaching; development of eye, wrist, and finger co-ordinations through the use of tools, balls, and apparatus — all of these and more are possible within the scope of the modern kindergarten. It is of interest to consider different phases of the curriculum as they contribute to the physical development of the children. A few examples serve as illustrations of the methods and materials used.

Social Studies

When children think about their home living, they think about the ways that the members of the home use its equipment. They play house and use household tools built to their size. As they have fun, they further their physical development. For instance, rearranging the furniture in the playhouse brings their large muscles into play with back, arms, and legs in action. Cleaning up the playhouse, sweeping with brooms the right size for them contributes to their large muscle development as do all the vigorous activities the children engage in as they imitate the work which adults do in their homes.

Physical activity goes on continuously in the playhouse. Children set the table and wash dishes; wash table covers and doll clothes; iron them; hang them up to dry on a line high enough to require stretching. They look after the dolls, dressing them, feeding them, and carrying them around. All such activities further arm and hand co-ordinations. Dressing up in grown-up clothing, the children practice finger movements necessary for tying shoe laces, buttoning large buttons, and hooking large hooks into large eyes. In dressing up as the mother or father, the children tie each other's aprons and help each other into the various garments. In this way they develop hand and finger co-ordinations both in relation to themselves and to another person.

Physical development as well as dramatic play are furthered when children have a tree house or an elevated platform about seven or eight feet above the ground. The top of the playhouse may be used for house play with a staircase up to the house. Or a large tree may be used, with a ship's ladder or a stout climbing rope as well as with the more usual types of ladders to help the children develop skill in climbing. Children who have such apparatus available have opportunity for developing shoulder and arm muscles as well as leg and abdominal muscles. They also learn how to handle themselves safely at a height.

The children develop leg muscles and leg alternation as they play messenger on their tricycles or play delivery man with a wagon in back of their tricycles. When they pull the wagon by hand with both hands on the handle in back of them they develop back and shoulder muscles on both their right and left sides. When they pull a wagon with one hand, they should be encouraged to do it first with one hand and then the other as an aid to equalizing muscle development.

When the teacher considers the various experiences kindergarten children have in social living, she finds them full of physical activities. In playing grocery store the children reach and stretch as they handle goods on the high shelves, and they stoop and reach as they handle goods on the low shelves. The customers carry bundles of goods, often contriving at the same time to manage high heels and long skirts and other difficult costumes appropriate to their buyer role. In playing fireman, children handle ladders, hoses, and wagons. In playing train, they load and unload freight, mail bags, and baggage. In short, they further their physical development in all the dramatic activities of social studies, strengthening large and small muscles and developing co-ordination and balance.

Science

In carrying on science activities the children likewise have opportunity to develop large and small muscles, as well as to co-ordinate hand and finger with eye movements. Outdoor gardening is great fun and affords exercise for back, arm and shoulder, and leg muscles. In preparing the soil, the child uses tools designed for his size: spade, hoe, and rake. He moves dirt in a sturdy wheelbarrow scaled to his measurements and works hard in loading and unloading it.

In planting seeds, the child sprinkles the seed where he wants it, thus co-ordinating eye and finger movements. Watering the garden area each day with his watering can requires co-ordination of eye and hand movements. As the plants grow, the child develops control and balance as he avoids stepping on the seedlings. Of course the weeds grow, too, and pulling them exercises many small muscles.

Indoor gardens also afford opportunity for co-ordination and muscle development. The child prepares soil, plants seeds, and waters and weeds the flower boxes. When children have pets to care for, they develop muscular control in carrying water containers and finger skills in manipulating cage door fasteners.

In both social studies and science activities children engage in construction projects that further their physical development as well as their social, emotional, and intellectual development. They stoop and stretch to pick up blocks and move them into position according to the plan of their imaginative play.

Packing boxes of all sizes and shapes also are useful in dramatic play. Children reach around the boxes and push, pull, lift, and guide them into place. They arrange them end to end for a train, pile them into pyramids or other buildings, equip them as rowboats, ships, cars, trucks, airplanes or rockets, and arrange them for a farm area or a city block. The children use very large packing boxes as tunnels or houses if appropriate openings are cut out of the sides. Walking boards, with cleats at each end to hold them in place, bridge the space between packing boxes and give the children opportunity for balancing as they walk across them. Of course, boxes and boards are checked for safety each time they are rearranged. Nails should be firmly in place with no sharp ends protruding, splinter edges should be sanded off, and boards should not teeter or slip to pinch fingers.

In co-operating with other children on a construction project each child furthers his own muscular control. For instance, two children carrying a sturdy six-foot ladder learn to walk in relation to each other. In moving a large packing box that is too big for one child to move by himself, children also learn to control their movements in relation to other people as well as in relation to the objective to be accomplished. The teacher has both equipment adapted to one-child manipulation and equipment which necessitates co-operative handling.

Children take sturdy automobiles and trains into the sandbox, across the lawn, and over the dirt. They crawl on hands and knees pushing the wooden cars and engines up hill and down hill and around an imaginary track, getting excellent exercise as they do so. With improvised rockets the children raise themselves from a squatting position beside the staging area to a standing position as the rockets blast off and then to a tall stretch as the rocket reaches outer space en route to some distant planet or satellite. The children also stretch and move about with airplanes that are structurally strong rather than accurate in design detail.

When the children make their own airplanes and ships at the work bench, they use large and small muscles as they reach and stretch to get out tools and materials, to hammer and saw, and finally to put the tools away again. Keeping their fingers out of the way of the saw and the hammer develops eye and muscle co-ordination. Then, when the weather permits, the children float the boats they have made. As they bend and stoop and reach, their muscles stretch and contract, and their co-ordination of eye and muscle movements develops.

Besides playing with trains, the children enjoy playing the game of Railroad Train. The teacher gives them each the name of one car in the train: engine, gondola car, stock car, ore car, and so on. Then she acts as train master and tells a story about the train. As she mentions each car, the car adds itself to the train by placing hands on the shoulders of the child in front. When the train is all made up, the engine signals and the train moves off around the room. Thus, in a game situation, the children learn to control their motion in relation to the motion of others.

Quantitative Relations

Several games further physical development at the same time that they help the children develop skill in counting. In physical education activities the teacher is alert to capitalize on any situation which can be used for practicing counting. A simple game for an individual child to play with a ball is called "Hear Me Count." The child bounces the ball, counting each bounce. If his ball-bouncing skill is better than his counting, he will be interested in improving his counting, and if his counting is better than his bouncing, he will want to improve his skill with the ball.

One group game uses the counting rhyme: One, two, put on my shoe; three, four, shut the door; five, six, pick up sticks; seven, eight, run or you'll be — *late*. Two lines are drawn some distance apart, and the children line up along one of the lines. When they all say "late," they run to the opposite line and back. The first person coming back across the first line is the leader for lining up the children for the next game.

Space Relations

A child's entire physical development is probably the outgrowth of his adventuring forth into an increasing life space. At five he explores, twists, turns, and makes other body movements in the small space around the exercise bar, the jungle gym, or other apparatus. He also ventures forth from home to school and into an increasingly larger neighborhood, some-times on foot and sometimes on tricycle. He develops mental maps and pictures and translates them into physical action. As his muscles strengthen and his balance, co-ordination, and rhythmic movement develop, his understanding of space relations also develops.

Language Expression and Literary Heritage

When a small group of children sit and listen to stories or participate in discussion, they develop the basic skill of sitting comfortably. As the kindergarten year progresses, the children are able to sit for an increasing number of minutes and are able to keep from disturbing other children sitting near them.

Music and Creative Rhythms

In swinging or in bouncing, five-year-old children move according to rhythms of their own devising. They like to determine the frequency of their rhythmic movement. They also like to adapt the frequency of their movement to a drum beat or to music being played. At five, children express themselves spontaneously and rhythmically. They are not ready to fit into the more structured rhythmic situations of gymnastic exercises.

Children enjoy exploring the musical medium through rhythmic bodily movement. They learn to relax and move freely with the music. As they do so they strengthen their muscles and develop co-ordination and balance. Of course, they learn primarily how to move in response to auditory stimuli.

In helping children listen to the music and move with it, the teacher often begins with a group of children gathered around her sitting on the floor. She plays a good recording of some folk music, for instance, "Pop Goes the Weasel." Then she and the children clap to the music. When Mary claps on one side, the teacher does too and says, "We can clap at the side the way Mary is clapping." When the teacher wants to introduce additional movements, she may say, "We can clap up high over our heads," and start the children moving their clapping up and down. When the teacher thinks the children are ready to go on to arm movements other than clapping, she simply says, "We can do it this way in the air," and then she pushes her hands rhythmically into the air. Thus the children begin to move their arms in time with the music in a free and spontaneous way.

As easily as she guided the children into free arm movements, the teacher guides them into using all the space of a large room. As the children stand grouped around the teacher, they pretend they are bouncing balls. They bounce and bounce with the music. Then, as the music grows somewhat louder and fills the room, the bouncing balls go wherever they wish, bouncing and bouncing all over the room. The teacher bounces and whirls with them, guiding them into motion around the room. Thus the children are moving muscles all over their bodies in response to the music.

The teacher guides the children, timing her few suggestions to come just as they are ready for some further idea. As they move with the music she imitates the graceful variations of first one child and then another. As much as she can, she follows the lead of the children, thus giving them pleasure in the motions they create for themselves. In the course of twenty minutes of this musical experience, each child in the group has had the satisfaction of having the teacher imitate or praise verbally something he has created. This is the essence of encouraging creativity in children.

Children thoroughly enjoy moving with music when their movements are their own creation and not imposed suggestions. Doing it themselves without any patterns to be learned or fitted into gives them a free experience which encourages them to develop, each at his own rate. At no time does the teacher say, "This is the way to do it," or "Don't do it that way." She simply encourages the most graceful and relaxed movements of each child and the less desirable movements drop out presently from disuse.

Toward the end of the year the children have explored movement to music at length and are well accustomed to listening to the music and moving according to its rhythm and its mood. For instance, the teacher may say, "The piece I am going to play next is called 'The Golden Cock.' Where the cock stretches himself up and crows, I'm going to stretch and crow. You may want to do that too." In this way the teacher encourages the children to enjoy dramatic activity within the permissive freedom of creative rhythm.

Many of the experiences children have lead to dramatic play and to rhythmic bodily movement. Some children watched a dairy herd move slowly from the pasture to the milking barn and were fascinated as each cow took her place in the stanchions. When they returned to school, a child suggested that they could play it. Quickly, lively five-year-olds became lumbering cows walking slowly along, one behind another, until they quietly stopped at their stanchions in the milking barn. When the children decided to "do it again," the teacher went to the piano and played slow "walking music" which ended in a crash as the stanchions were fastened in place. The music made the bodily movement "more fun," but the *idea* preceded both the musical accompaniment and the rhythmical muscular activity.

Aesthetic Expression

When children use various art media they bring into play arm and shoulder muscles, as well as small muscles of wrists and fingers. They develop eye and finger co-ordinations, too, as they lay the foundation for drawing, painting, modeling, and craft work of all kinds. At five, they are exploring art media, and certain ones are ready for the beginnings of symbolism and of representation. They create what they wish. The wise teacher simply encourages their use of art media without telling them what to make and without holding up any standards of attainment. In this way she helps the children work with easy relaxation that is favorable to muscular development. The materials she provides make for large muscle movements rather than extended co-ordinations of small muscles unsuitable for five-year-olds. She encourages each child to work only so long as he wishes and accepts his definition of when he is done. In this way she helps the children avoid undue tension or nervous strain.

Children develop finger muscles and co-ordination when they have fun with soft clay or dough. They pinch off bits, they squeeze, they push, pat, and pound as they enjoy working with the medium. As they become familiar with it, they roll and fashion it into three-dimensional shapes and objects. They use finger, hand, and arm co-ordination as they mold and model.

With a stick of charcoal and a large piece of paper at an easel or with colored chalk at a chalkboard, children develop hand, arm, and shoulder movements. With large pieces of newsprint or butcher paper mounted on an easel, children, clad in painting aprons or smocks, develop arm and hand co-ordinations as they stand and paint with stiff-bristle brushes of a size suitable to their hands. With softer brushes that are not so wide, they use water colors at a table or on the floor and gain further control of arm, wrist, and fingers. With finger paints they also further their co-ordinations of fingers, wrist, and arm.

Five-year-old children enjoy cutting strips and triangles and other shapes, cutting freely for as long or as short a time as they wish, and thus further finger and hand co-ordinations. Sometimes they like to use large crayons, drawing with the ends or making wide sweeping lines with the side of a broken piece. Sometimes they like to put together picture puzzles logical in design and made of large substantial pieces of plywood. Often they enjoy using cotton string or cord for tying knots, for braiding, or for weaving such simple items as belts and doll hammocks. All such craft activities further finger dexterity and co-ordination.

Health

The familiar phrase, Health and Physical Education, indicates the close relation between these two parts of the curriculum. The healthy child has good posture that is the outgrowth of good physical development and is an aid to further physical development. The child with ample opportunity for well-rounded physical exercise outdoors furthers his own good health.

In both health teaching and physical education, children are guided to learn habits and skills which keep them safe and contribute to the safety of other members of the group. A few important rules for safety inside the building are:

Look where you are going.
Move or roll toys; do not throw them.
Close drawers or cupboard doors.
Keep blocks and toys out of places where people walk.
Get the sponge or wastebasket and clean up spills and messes getting them out of people's way.
Bring broken toys to the teacher.

The physical development of children incidental to social studies, science, music, and other aspects of the curriculum is great. Yet it may not be well rounded nor complete without a place in the kindergarten program for physical education. Special attention to physical education gives the children opportunity to think about their physical skills. They become aware of how parts of their body can move and they experiment with hopping on one foot, a jump turn, or some other newly discovered movement. They realize how skillful they are and they appreciate their need for developing other skills further. They see the movements of others and try them out for themselves. As they play games and perform on the apparatus, they feel the thrill of some new realization or accomplishment.

In physical education the kindergarten teacher shares the enthusiasm of the children in what they can do and suggests new goals only a little more difficult than those already mastered. She carefully avoids any comparisons of one child with another as she does so. She shows the children desirable ways of handling themselves and furthers their awareness of how they are able to do their stunts. The goal of each child is to move himself through space in the direction he wishes and with whatever speed he wishes to use. The teacher encourages this aim whenever possible.

Children need a variety of activities, but they also need opportunity to pursue a certain activity until they have exhausted its learning possibilities. Realizing this, the teacher notices when a child or group of children is monopolizing a piece of equipment or a play area. Then she rearranges the environment so that the children have opportunity to develop new interests. However, if they have not played out their original interests and make a definite request for their former equipment, she assures them that they will have another turn with that equipment very soon. In this way the teacher broadens the interests of the children and provides for their well-rounded physical development, but also helps them achieve the security which comes from deciding for themselves when they are finished with an activity and are ready to move on to new experiences.

Apparatus

At the playgrounds in the park, children enjoy exercising and trying out different ways of moving themselves through space. On the school playground it is important to have similar apparatus so that the children can be guided in developing safe and efficient ways of handling themselves. If the apparatus at the park is different from that at school, then the teacher should arrange to take the children to the park playground where she can help them learn the skills required to enjoy taking part in out-of-school recreation. Their physical, social, emotional, and intellectual development is greater when children feel successful in doing what they want to do and in belonging successfully to groups of their peers.

In order to move themselves easily through space, children need to develop rhythm in movement. Swinging is one of the first activities through which children discover enjoyment in rhythmic motion. They develop it better when swinging themselves than they do when an adult or another child pushes them. By the time children are in kindergarten they should be pumping to make the swing go. The teacher gives a start to children who are just beginning to develop pumping skill and helps them verbally with their pumping rhythm. She does not push them each time, and she discourages the children from pushing others.

In the interests of safety, the swing seats are of leather or canvas rather than wood. An acceptable variation of a swing is a discarded tire hung from the limb of a tree or other strong support by a rope. Both the soft-seat swing and the tire encourage the kindergarten child to lie on his stomach sometimes as he uses the swing.

The bouncing board is as important as the swing in developing rhythmic movement. The children thoroughly enjoy bouncing up and down on a ten- or twelve-foot plank that is only a few inches above the ground. A child finds he must adapt the rhythm of his motion whenever another child steps on or off the board.

The jumping pit is another aid to developing rhythmic movement. Children who are not ready for the precision and balance of the bouncing board like to jump up and down in the sawdust or shavings that fill a hole about eight inches deep and six or more feet across.

The teeter-totter or see-saw also furthers rhythmic movement. In learning to use it safely the children are taught to keep their fingers and legs out from under the board and to tell each other when they want to get off.

Some of the kindergarten children develop the ability to go across an overhead ladder. Doing so depends on an easy swinging motion co-ordinating bodily movement with reaching for the next rung. It also depends on arm strength. Another rhythmic activity that only a few of the kindergarten children are ready for is rope jumping. Yet some of them have the co-ordination of arms and legs necessary to enjoy this activity.

The jungle gym is the basic climbing apparatus on the kindergarten playground. Even if it includes a fireman's pole, it involves skills well within the abilities of the five-year-old child. At that age the child is able to build up speed in moving over the apparatus and is able to play co-operatively with other children on it and to develop dramatic play with them. It is important for the teacher to guide the children in watching where they step or cling so that no fingers or toes are stepped on. Sometimes a child asks others to clear part of the apparatus so he has room to do his stunt. The jungle gym thus makes it possible for children to judge space needed for movement.

The horizontal bar like the jungle gym gives opportunity for muscular development all over the body: neck, arms, shoulders, abdomen, pelvis, legs. A child uses an exercise bar individually and works out his stunts at his own rate. The bars are of different heights so that a child can select the one which seems right for him. They have loose sand below them so a child will not be hurt if he loses his hold on the bar. No toy or other object should be left under the exercise bar since it might get in the child's way.

The kindergarten child is old enough to meet easily the requirements for using the slide safely. He can climb the ladder, change to a position for sliding, slide, stop by pressing his feet against the side of the slide, and come off the slide onto his feet. Since the skills required are well within his abilities, the slide, like the jungle gym, affords opportunity for the child to control the speed with which he moves through space. When he was younger, the slide determined his ride. Now he is able to control the speed and nature of his slide. The slide and the jungle gym contribute to a child's sense of achievement and self-confidence, especially when the teacher comments descriptively on his prowess, "You used your brakes to slow down at the bottom."

Playground apparatus should also help a child develop effective use of his sense of balance. A child walks on curbs and walls on his way to and from school, and he takes advantage of exploring any new building under construction. At school he should have bouncing boards and walking boards. In fact the five-year-old is ready for a narrow walking board, the school yard equivalent of the railroad track. He enjoys walking on a two-by-four set on edge and kept from overturning by a cross board secured at each end.

In addition to the safety rules for each piece of apparatus, children need to learn some rules that apply to the use of all apparatus:

> Have both hands free. Before you start using the apparatus, leave any toys on the ground out of the way of others and out of your way.
>
> Leave dirt on the ground and sand in the sandbox. Do not throw them. They hurt eyes.
>
> Walk around a play area, not through it. Keep out of the way of other children.
>
> In taking turns on apparatus be sure the child in front of you has plenty of room.

In supervising the use of apparatus, the teacher helps the children apply the rules to their situation. She also watches the safety of the children herself. Knowing that fatigue is a frequent cause of accident, she plans for physical education when the children need activity as a change from sitting but are not tired or hungry.

Games

The out-of-school life of kindergarten children makes it important for them to learn simple games so that they can fit into their peer culture. They must learn the importance of playing by rules, but must have games so simple that they can focus their attention on the game itself. They must have games in which they do not have to wait long to participate, for their attention span is short when they are not actively involved in the game. Kindergarten children are not ready for "organized games." These come later. Nor are the children ready for the testing activities that are an important part of physical education activities for older children.

Ball games play an important part in American culture. Five-year-old children need to develop skill in running and in handling a ball so they will be ready later to participate in neighborhood ball games. In kindergarten they like to play simple ball games with simple rules: *Dodge Ball* which emphasizes keeping out of the way of the ball and of other players, *Toss Ball or Hoop Ball* which emphasize throwing, and *Catch the Ball* which emphasizes getting the ball.

Children need ball games; they also need games which further skills not often included in the kindergarten activities: hopping, jumping, kicking, turning, changing direction, breath control, hiding and finding, and throwing, catching, and bouncing balls. *In and Out of the Pond* is a jumping game the children enjoy. They stand in a circle. When the teacher says, "Into the pond," they jump in, and when she says, "Out of the pond," they jump back. The children who are slow in responding to the command are eliminated each time.

Few kindergarten children have learned how to control their breathing. Yet breath control is as basic to physical movement as is rhythm. In fact, the rhythm of breathing is related to the rhythm of an activity. Swimming, of course, is an excellent example of an activity that requires breath control in relation to other movements.

Kindergarten children enjoy blowing bubbles, and as they experiment with the blowing, they develop the abdominal muscles and the oral muscles which give them control. They like to blow bubbles using bubble pipes or a detergent solution in a juice or other small can. The teacher makes blowing bubbles at school with other children a simple group activity, a pleasant rudimentary game.

PHYSICAL EDUCATION AND EMOTIONAL RELEASE

Within physical education activities, a child finds relief for his pent-up emotions. When a child is frustrated, glandular secretions pour into his blood stream and drive him toward physical expression of his anger and resentment. The kindergarten teacher realizes this and guides him in finding suitable physical outlets for his strong feelings. She provides a punching bag and the child exercises hand, arm, and shoulder muscles as he relieves his feelings. He can think of the punching bag as the adult or child who got in his way or interfered with what he wanted to do. Or he can throw big soft beanbags at a target which represents to him the person who caused his frustration. Or he can kick a ball across a line the way he would like to kick someone. By using these acceptable emotional outlets a child is gaining control over his emotions. He must learn to use verbal outlets for minor feelings of frustration and acceptable physical outlets for his strong emotions. The importance of this learning cannot be overemphasized.

While physical education provides expression for the strong negative emotions, it also provides for positive feelings of pleasure: the satisfying feeling of having exercised to the point of fatigue, but not beyond it, the feeling of accomplishment in achieving a new skill or in becoming aware of an existing skill, the pleasure of having played with others in a game situation, and the satisfaction of contributing to the game.

The teacher who recognizes the emotional needs of the children provides activities in terms of those needs. But in game situations where the group feeling may rise easily to a high pitch she is careful to see that emotional elements are kept within the emotional tolerance of the group.

WELL-ROUNDED PHYSICAL DEVELOPMENT OF EACH CHILD

Within the total kindergarten program each child has opportunity for well-rounded physical development. Both large and small muscles grow stronger. Muscles develop in arms, wrists, hands and fingers, neck, shoulders, abdomen, pelvis, legs, ankles, and feet. The child learns to co-ordinate movements of different muscle groups, and to alternate both arm and leg movements. He develops the use of his sense of balance.

Through the different curricular phases of the kindergarten program he has physical movement as an integral part of activities that further his intellectual development.

Through the co-operative activities of the kindergarten program, each child experiences pleasant and satisfying emotions as he furthers his physical development. Through the competitive aspects of the program, he learns to cope with negative emotions in socially acceptable ways that provide physical outlets for his frustrations.

Each child gains self-confidence and a sense of achievement as he builds his physical skills. His new skills help him find a place in his peer groups. He feels that he belongs to the group and is wanted by the other children. In game situations he explores the roles of leader and follower, of winner and loser, and observes that other children do also. On the apparatus he takes turns with others, and plays in co-operation with, or parallel to, others. Thus each child develops socially at the same time that he develops physically.

In fact, the whole child comes to kindergarten and develops in his entirety as a child. The teacher furthers this development in all its aspects: physical, intellectual, social, and emotional.

SITUATIONS FOR DISCUSSION

In the following situations select each course of action that seems desirable to you basing your choices and omissions on the ideas presented in this chapter. Add one or more alternate courses of action.

SITUATION I. Janey is a sturdy and solidly built girl whose father is a physical education teacher. She is one of two or three children who use the overhead ladder. She is the only child who has a good, rhythmic motion that carries her easily across.

Today Janey's friend, Marie, comes to you and asks, "Will you help me go across the ladder?" You smile and say, "Of course." In helping Marie, you should say to her:

"Shall I help you get into the swing of it?"

"Do it just the way Jane does."

"I'll help you down whenever you wish."

"Good for you!"

"You and Janey certainly are strong."

SITUATION II. David, who pumps stiffly, moving only his feet, does not care to swing for any length of time. He gets the attention of the teacher by being helpful. Today he has decided to push Kathy, a small girl who is quite capable of pumping and swinging by herself. Kathy says, "Leave me alone!" but David keeps on pushing her. As the teacher you should say to David:

"Thank you for pushing."

"Kathy likes to swing herself by pumping."

"This swing is free, David. May I give you a start away up high?"

"Look how Kathy leans into her pumping."

"Let's see you pump the way Kathy does."

SITUATION III. One warm day in early fall Tom is playing with the big cargo airplane when it is time for the group to go outside. He flies the airplane in long sweeps across the room and out the door. He runs to the exercise bar, dropping the sturdy wooden airplane in the sand below it, and starts to do a stunt. As he swings, his hand slips and he falls to the ground bumping his head on the plane. As the teacher you should:

Feel guilty about not picking up the toy airplane.

Wring a cloth out of cold water.

Comfort Tom.

Ask Tom how to avoid getting bumps like that another time.

In talking time ask what safety rule we should help Tom remember.

SITUATION IV. Yesterday John asked you about climbing up the hill of the slide, and you reminded him that we all use the slide only as a slide. Today John is about to have his turn at the easel when it is time for the group to go outside to play. Without asking you, John goes straight to the slide and starts climbing up the hill side. When he is about half way up, two girls run over and start up the ladder of the slide. As the teacher, you should tell John:

To ask the girls to wait until he gets to the top.

To climb the hill after everyone goes home.

That you cannot let him hurt himself or get in the way of others.

That missing a turn and not being able to go up the slide hill makes anyone feel like hitting.

That he can punch the punching bag if he feels like hitting.

BIBLIOGRAPHY

Professional Books and Pamphlets

American Association for Health, Physical Education, and Recreation. *Children in Focus.* Washington, D. C.: National Education Association, 1954.

This yearbook of the American Association for Health, Physical Education and Recreation, presents the point of view of the organization regarding elementary education. Material of specific interest to kindergarten teachers is on pages 88 and 149. Pages 123–131 deal with safety.

Andrews, Gladys. *Creative Rhythmic Movement for Children.* Englewood Cliffs, New Jersey: Prentice-Hall, Inc., 1954.

In addition to some music and suggestions for rhythm instruments, this book presents basic ideas of creative rhythms for elementary school children.

Cowell, C. C., and H. W. Hazelton. *Curriculum Designs in Physical Education.* Englewood Cliffs, New Jersey: Prentice-Hall, Inc., 1955.
Sequential development in physical education activities.

Evans, Ruth, Thelma I. Bacon, Mary E. Bacon, and Joie L. Stapleton. *Physical Education for Elementary Schools.* New York: McGraw-Hill Book Company, Inc., 1958.
A practical program for young children is included.

Geri, Frank H. *Illustrated Games and Rhythms for Children in the Primary Grades.* Englewood Cliffs, New Jersey: Prentice-Hall, Inc., 1955.
Simple rhythms and games are classified according to grade level.

McNeely, Simon A., and Elsa Schneider. "Physical Education in the School Child's Day." Office of Education Bulletin, 1950, No. 14. Washington, D. C.: Office of Education, 1950.
The objectives, the physical education program itself, and its contribution to the growth and development of the elementary school child are discussed with suggestions as to how activities may be carried out effectively.

Miller, A. G., and Virginia Whitcomb. *Physical Education in the Elementary School Curriculum.* Englewood Cliffs, New Jersey: Prentice-Hall, Inc., 1957.
A general treatment of the physical education program.

Neilson, N. P., and Winifred Van Hagen. *Physical Education for Elementary Schools,* rev. New York: A. S. Barnes and Company, 1954.
Part 1 — pages 3–129 — deals with "Basic Considerations" about physical education in the elementary school.

O'Keefe, Patric Ruth, and Anita Aldrich. *Education Through Physical Activities.* St. Louis: The C. V. Mosby Company, 1955.
Pages 45–49 and 70–72 emphasize teaching children to recognize and deal with hazards to their safety. The book as a whole is for elementary schools.

Sehon, Elizabeth L., and Others. *Physical Education Methods for Elementary Schools.* Philadelphia: W. B. Saunders Company, 1953.
In addition to Chapters 1 and 2 — pages 1–48 — regarding the elementary school program as a whole, Chapter 8 "Creative Rhythms" is of interest to the kindergarten teacher.

Books for Children

Steiner, Charlotte. *Kiki Dances.* Garden City, New York: Doubleday and Company, Inc., 1949.
Kiki is able to realize her ambition of being a dancer. *Kiki Skates* (1950) and *Kiki Goes to Camp* (1953) are by the same author.

Wright, Ethel. *Saturday Walk.* New York: William R. Scott, Inc., 1954.
A walk with Daddy on Saturday is full of trucks and trains, and is fun.

Yashima, Taro. *The Village Tree.* New York: The Viking Press, 1953.
The village children in Japan climb the big tree, swim in the stream below, and enjoy other physical activities.

Films for Children

Building Children's Personalities with Creative Dancing. Los Angeles: Educational Film Sales Department, University of California, 1957.
A group of children learn to express their feelings creatively in dancing. 30 minutes, sound, black and white, or color.

Primary Safety: In the School Building. Chicago, Illinois: Coronet Films, 1955.

A game with stop and go signs is used to help pupils learn safe practices in the school building. 11 minutes, sound, black and white, or color.

Primary Safety: On the School Playground. Chicago, Illinois: Coronet Films, 1955.

Pete knows that the right way is the safe way in swinging, seesawing, sliding and playing ball. 11 minutes, sound, black and white, or color.

Recreational Game Series. Bloomington, Indiana: Audio-Visual Center, Indiana University, 1950, 1951.

This series of short films are for teaching attitudes and skills desirable in: "Beat Ball" (4 minutes); "Squirrel in Trees" (5 minutes); "Three Deep" (6 minutes); "Skip to My Lou" (5 minutes). Sound, black and white.

Safety in Winter. Chicago, Illinois: Coronet Instructional Films, 1952.

Sensible rules are developed for walking, sledding, snowballing, and skating. 11 minutes, black and white, or color.

Filmstrip

Child Cooperation and Self-Discipline Series. Chicago: Society for Visual Education, Inc.

"Share the Sandpile," 24 frames; "Share the Ball," 31 frames; and "Schoolground Discoverer," 23 frames, showing how to have a tidy playground, are included. Silent, black and white.

8

Furthering Understanding of the Social World

THE GROWTH OF CONCEPTS

Adults are inclined to forget that a child is born into the world with no knowledge of how the world operates, how it came to be the way it is, or what values the grownups in his world have accepted. In a whole lifetime, many adults do not acquire the understanding, develop the habits and skills, or achieve the behaviors essential to a successful adjustment to life. Objective evidence of this failure may be found in the fact that in this country the cost of public assistance because of ill-health, social inadequacy, delinquency, emotional maladjustment, and inability to secure and hold a job is in excess of thirteen billion dollars annually. This monumental figure does not take into account the millions of human beings who may never actually receive public assistance in any form but who live half lives with a narrow fear-inspiring margin between a tenuous security and actual inability to cope with the problems of life and living.

And yet, only too frequently, adults scold or even punish young children because they do not somehow *know* what life has not yet given them an opportunity to *learn*. Sometimes, for example, even young children are subjected to severe reprisals because they violate the sanctity of private ownership. The adult may react to such behavior in judgmental terms and say "he steals." But private property is not a concept inherent in the germ plasm. Like hundreds of other concepts and values of our complex society, it must be learned. Probably this particular learning about "mine and thine" is begun best in a home in which certain loved toys, a favorite mug or bowl, articles of clothing, a space in a closet, *belong to the child*, are reserved for *his* exclusive use, and shared only as a result of *his* decision to share.

128

Parents and teachers need to give thought to the complexity of the world into which each child is born. Archaeologists and anthropologists cannot tell exactly how long human beings have inhabited the earth but the most conservative of estimates indicates that a hundred thousand years ago and more, men and women not greatly unlike those who currently live on this planet were engaged in the processes necessary to meet basic life needs. A hundred thousand years and more of human striving, experiencing, and experimenting have gone into the building of today's world. This accumulated learning constitutes the social inheritance of every new human being born into the world.

The lifelong task of every person is one of becoming increasingly a functioning part of his world. From helpless infancy, the human organism must move through a series of developmental tasks to a maturity in which he is capable of making his individual and unique contribution to human progress. It is no easy task; the road is long and beset with obstacles. The hopeful promise that it may become easier lies in our expanding knowledge about growth and development and the way human beings learn. Without doubt, there is much more to be found out than is now known about human growth and development and the learning process. To the revelation of greater insight in these fields, qualified research workers address their efforts, but opportunity for tremendous progress lies in putting to use at each maturity level what is now firmly established by experimentation and systematic experience with children.

THE JOINT RESPONSIBILITY OF PARENTS AND SCHOOLS

What is the role of the school in helping a child to become an adequate person in today's world? This is a question which teachers and parents in every school in the country should be studying together because, at best, the school is only a supplementary institution in the education of young children. The home is the primary teacher. Only as parents and teachers become full partners in the joint enterprise of rearing children can worthy goals be achieved. In general, parents and teachers agree that the goal in both child-rearing and education is to help each child to develop to the highest degree he is capable of attaining. To realize this goal, home and school are jointly responsible for the development of each child in body, mind, character, and feeling, and in personal, economic, home, and civic competence. The most futile business is the mutual blaming of home and school for failure to fulfill responsibility. Not until parents and teachers together accept as their major task that of replacing the present adult generation with one better able to cope with the individual and group problems of the world will any real progress be made. Inevitably, this means a dynamic kind of educative experience for young children at home and at school. It means an adequate investment of the time and resources of the adult generation. No alternative exists.

THE CHILD'S INTERACTION WITH THE ENVIRONMENT

Why is it possible for human beings of normal endowment to achieve the generally accepted goals of education? Because nearly every child is born equipped to become one with his world. Every normal child can see, hear, feel, smell, and taste. Every normal child has ability to move. As the child grows in strength he is able to use his sensory equipment and his power of locomotion to interact with his environment, and all learning is the result of this interaction of the learner with his environment.

A child cannot learn the difference between sweet, sour, and bitter, or the varying intensities of these qualities, except through firsthand sensory experience with them. A child cannot know hot and cold and all the temperatures that lie between the extremes, except through experiencing. A child cannot know the quality of redness until he has seen the color in a woolen coat, a gay Valentine, a summer sunset, a cranberry glass pitcher and a score of other relationships. In this way, in innumerable contacts with reality, children accumulate a store of impressions and meanings.

As the child begins to move about under his own power, he gains understanding of distance. It may take considerable time to *creep* the length of the living room to examine with eyes, hands, and even tongue a shining silver bowl on a low table, but relatively less time a little later to disappear from view in a neighbor's garden or around the corner. Through all these experiences the young child is in the process of becoming one with his world.

GENERAL REQUIREMENTS FOR ALL KINDERGARTENS

In a rapidly changing world, it is difficult to define precisely the nature of experiences the school must provide. It is impossible to defend the point of view that every kindergarten situated in the same community should provide identical experiences, because differences in individual children and in the particular neighborhood served require differentiation in the program. Because of the youth of the children, experiences must of necessity deal with the familiar concepts of home and family living and orientation to the new institutions in the child's life — the school, the immediate neighborhood, the workers who serve the basic needs of the family, and to a certain extent the broader community with its contact with other communities far beyond the child's firsthand experience.

Fostering the Democratic Way of Life

Two factors operate, however, to make the experiences in all kindergartens highly comparable. The first factor is the responsibility of the school always to underwrite the basic principles of the democratic way of life. Schools in any culture are maintained to preserve the way of life and government to which the culture is committed. Teachers in our country are fortunate that democracy provides the best way of life man has yet devised for each individual to be and to do his best. Democracy is based on the supreme worth of the individual, and is the complete antithesis of political and social philosophies which would subordinate the individual to the position of a mere instrument of the state.

The teacher, therefore, in whatever area of experience she may be guiding the development of children emphasizes the human values. She emphasizes the principle of equality and human freedom incorporated in the fundamental law of the land. In guiding children in their study of home and family living, she emphasizes the affectionate and mutually supporting relationships which make a worthy family unit rather than a stereotype family group; she emphasizes the wholesome, happy, shared experiences of a home, rather than the rooms, facilities, and furnishings of a house. In studies of neighborhood and community, she emphasizes the quality of services people render each other and builds understanding that respect for the worker does not inhere in the specific work he does but in the honest and conscientious way in which he renders the service. The teacher emphasizes the dependence of people on one another for goods and services. Throughout all the experiences the school provides, children come to understand that democracy means an ethical way of running life not because this concept has been verbalized in pious utterances but because they have lived day-by-day under the guidance of a teacher who has accepted the principles of equality and human rights as the basic values by which she chooses to live. Any class guided by such a teacher is not greatly dissimilar in its essential human relations to any other class guided by a teacher who has a like commitment to democracy.

Recognizing the Role of the Environment

The second factor which makes for similarity is acceptance by the teacher of the importance of the environment in stimulating children to wish to interact with it. The great task of the teacher is to create an environment favorable to learning. No doubt the most indispensable single element in the environment is the teacher herself. The teacher determines how free the children feel to use the environment, how free the children feel to seek the guidance and counsel of the teacher, how free the children feel to interact with other girls and boys of the group. From her own personality, the teacher creates a democratic climate in which children can be themselves and work out their problems, continually assured that a wise adult will set the essential limits to make school a safe and comfortable place in which to be.

Anything worth doing merits advanced planning. And therefore a wise teacher thinks of broad areas of human experience likely to be developmental to kindergarten children. She thinks of what things she can bring into the environment which will stimulate their interest and curiosity and will thus cause them to wish to move into the environment and interact with it. And so she brings in the raw materials from which children can begin to build an experience — pictures and books, real objects, tools and materials for construction, clay and paint, musical instruments, appropriate science materials, and other things which her ingenuity and experience may suggest. When the children are ready, she guides them as they move out into their larger environment on study trips.

The classroom environment does not remain static. Children change it with the things they make and the arrangements they devise to increase their satisfaction in playing and working in it. The teacher changes it by removing items to which the children do not seem ready to react or by bringing in new materials to satisfy emerging needs or to suggest new leads into activity. Learning moves forward as children develop their purposes and endeavor to satisfy them.

The teacher is conscious of her goal of democratic citizenship. In all the guidance of young children, the teacher with due regard to the maturity of the group strives to help the children to gain understanding of how human beings satisfy their basic needs in the world today. Even in the kindergarten, modern children may be interested in how mankind is satisfying these needs in other parts of the world. The experience of even young children in today's world has been immeasurably broadened because of the mobility of our population and because of the access children have to the mass media of communication. As a popular advertisement points out, "never underestimate" the power of children to acquire understanding.

Through their experiences in democratic living, children begin to acquire the patterns of action necessary for them to move forward courageously and adequately as participating and contributing members of a democratic society established to safeguard human progress.

THE TEACHER'S GOALS FOR HER CLASS

Like other teachers, the kindergarten teacher has clearly defined concepts of her goals in helping children acquire the behaviors that character-

In playing grocery store the children reach and
stretch as they handle goods on the high shelves,
and they stoop and reach as they handle goods on
the low shelves.

The child learns to co-ordinate movements of
different muscle groups, to alternate both arm
and leg movements, and to develop the use of
his sense of balance.

ize a democratic person. She has asked herself, "What are the characteristics of a democratic person?" From time to time as social needs seem to demand she may expand her definition but in general the socially-minded teacher believes that a democratic person is one who:

Acts on the basis of responsible thinking. This involves considering all the factors in a case, judging on the basis of these factors, holding solutions tentatively but acting on the basis of conclusions resulting from this process

Shares with others generously and courteously

Co-operates with others in a friendly, willing spirit

Respects the rights of others. This involves respect for human personality, appreciation for other cultures than his own, respect for public and private property, respect for the opinions of others, and acceptance of properly constituted authority.

Appreciates the worth and contribution of others

Has independence in thought and action

Has self-control, self-respect, and self-reliance

Acts responsibly and courageously in accordance with accepted personal and social ideals and principles

The kindergarten teacher accepts these as the characteristics of an adequate person in a democratic society and sees her greatest responsibility in providing the experiences and the guidance essential for each child to grow steadily toward the acquisition of these behaviors. She realizes that day-by-day growth may sometimes be imperceptible but that if her own activities are consistently directed toward the achievement of these purposes, the development of the children must result and be wholesome.

One teacher who was sensitive to the importance of teaching democracy throughout the kindergarten day, started on the first day of school to observe the children's appreciation of individual differences. The day the children began finger painting she observed that Elsie and Marie were getting acquainted with each other by touching and being competitive. As the girls worked side by side finger painting, they talked together, and with Jane who was also at the table:

JANE: I like to do this.

MARIE: Look what I made!

ELSIE: (*Looking at Marie's painting*) It's ugly.

MARIE: It is not!

ELSIE: Teacher said your picture is ugly.

JANE: No, she didn't.

The teacher, who was moving among the children as they worked, recognized as typical of her age Elsie's remark that "Teacher said your picture is ugly." The teacher knew that girls at kindergarten age, and boys about two years later, often try to escape responsibility by saying what is not true. She made a mental note then, and a written note later, to help Elsie with her individual problem. Now, however, the teacher took up with the group the democratic point that all three girls needed to understand: that each person has the right to do things his own way so long as he does not interfere with the rights of others — what is good for one person may be quite different from what is good for another person.

> TEACHER: (*Reassuringly to Marie*) It's a lovely picture, Marie. I'm sure you enjoyed mixing the colors to make it. You and I like it, don't we?
> Elsie likes her picture, too. It's quite different from Marie's picture.
> Elsie, do you like the green color of your picture, but not the brown color of Marie's?
>
> ELSIE: Yes.
>
> TEACHER: That's all right. Each of us likes some colors better than others.

In this way the teacher initiated a discussion about favorite colors, and how the choice of a favorite color changes as people grow older.

During the next few days the teacher found opportunity to read *A Bunny, A Bird, A Funny Cat*[1] to a group of children including both Elsie and Marie. The girls made no special response to the story, nor did their teacher expect them to. She realized that fundamental beliefs are not easily changed and that it would take a series of experiences to help the children appreciate individual differences. She planned to capitalize on conflict situations as they occurred, and to read *It Looks Like This*[2] to stimulate verbal expression about differing points of view. She felt confident that the children would increase their appreciation of the rights of others during their kindergarten year.

THE TEACHER'S GOALS FOR HERSELF

In order to help children become increasingly more mature democratic persons, teachers must themselves be growing toward an increasing professional maturity. Professional maturity for the kindergarten teacher involves:

> Valuing the role of the teacher in maintaining and expanding the democratic faith

[1] Schlein, Miriam, *A Bunny, A Bird, A Funny Cat*. New York: Abelard-Schuman Limited, 1957.
[2] Webber, Irma E., *It Looks Like This*. New York: William R. Scott, Inc., 1954.

Becoming increasingly sensitive to the differences in children

Developing techniques that encourage the interaction of children such as planning, work periods, evaluation, discussion, play, construction, going on study trips, and the like

Providing flexible working arrangements

Providing a wide variety of experiences and materials essential to meet the needs of the children

Utilizing the playground, the neighborhood, the people in the community to provide firsthand experiences designed to help children understand and become participating members of their world

MAJOR CENTERS OF INTEREST FOR THE SOCIAL ENVIRONMENT

The kindergarten teacher helps the child understand his social world by the centers of interest she arranges in the kindergarten. She arranges several centers of interest and adds to these as interest in any of them seems to lag. The teacher must use her knowledge of the children and the community in which they live to determine which centers are to be set up first and which may follow. Work with kindergarten children reveals that they are especially interested in these aspects of the community: transportation facilities, food production and distribution, the home, schools, and public services. Birthdays, Christmas, and other special days appeal and introduce a break in routine. Other interests may appear from time to time but they are usually transitory. Children return again and again to use the materials the teacher has arranged, especially when *things that move* form the center of the particular interest.

A Visit to an Airport

Preparation

In a community near a large airport, the teacher arranged the classroom environment to deepen understanding of this aspect of community living. She believed that kindergarten children can be helped to understand that:

Airplanes are used for many purposes

An airport is a place where airplanes can land and take off safely

Many different buildings are needed at the airport

Many different kinds of work are needed

Every airport worker has specific tasks

Automobiles, buses, and trucks bring people and things to the airport

To help children acquire these understandings, the teacher arranged a corner of the room with sturdy toy airplanes, floor blocks, pipecleaner "people" in costumes of airport workers, small toy trucks, automobiles, and buses. On the library table nearby, she placed copies of:

Gramatky, *Loopy*
Lenski, *The Little Airplane*
Lent, *Straight Up*
Lewellen, *The True Book of Airports and Airplanes*
Maloy, *Toby Can Fly*
Park, *Here Comes the Postman*
Pryor, *The Airplane Book*
Smith, *Joe's Story of the Airport*
Weir, *The Wonderful Plane Ride*

Excellent, large, colored pictures of different kinds of airplanes were attractively mounted at the eye level of the children.

When the children came to school, some of them were attracted by the playhouse, others by the farm animals, some by the easels and paint, some by the clay table, but five boys took the toy airplanes and flew around and around the room. After the newness wore off and the play was becoming confusing, the teacher directed a discussion with the five boys along the lines of where a plane lands and where it stays when not flying. From this discussion, the children decided that they needed to build hangars and runways.

With the definite purpose of building hangars, the teacher guided them to look at pictures of hangars, and to discuss which of the available material was best to use. The children decided on the builder-boards, selected sizes, and tested to see if the proposed hangars would be big enough to house their airplanes. They learned how to bolt the boards together and to use some of them for a roof.

Then they were ready for their runways. Again, they looked at diagrams and pictures of runways, decided to use more builder-boards, and experimented to find out how to bolt runways together in a V-shape.

With this new equipment, planes were pulled out of the hangars. They taxied down the runways, took off, and landed. More children joined in the fun, and crashes were inevitable. The teacher felt that to make the play more meaningful it was important to arrange for a trip to the airport. In the meantime, the teacher led the discussion into what makes a good pilot. The children had a surprising amount of information to share because some of the fathers were pilots or airport personnel. They knew that pilots must have licenses because they fly planes in which people ride and these planes must be safe. They learned that a pilot must study hard for his license, pass tests, and show that he is capable of handling an airplane. After that, when crashes occurred, children explained that the pilot was "only a student" and not "fully licensed." Much information was exchanged about the different kinds of planes, parts of planes, and airport facilities. Such terms as "helicopter," "cargo liner," "passenger plane," "weather station," "runways," and "control tower" were added to the vocabularies of the children in the group.

The Visit

Finally, the study trip to the airport was arranged. At the airport the children saw the parking lot with thousands of parked cars, the station with its ticket office, baggage desk, and waiting room, the passenger canopy to the air field, the wind sock, the beacon lights, different kinds of airplanes, the hangars, the gas truck, baggage truck, and the workers: pilot, co-pilot, ground crew, stewardess, gasoline attendants, dispatcher, and ticket agent.

The children climbed the stairs to the balcony of the terminal building to observe other activities of the airport. They watched the dispatcher signal with the automatic control projector and listened to him as he explained the signals. They watched the stewardess put lunches and thermos bottles into their compartment in the plane. They watched the ground crew load mail and baggage. They watched a passenger check his baggage and the conveyor belt carry the baggage out of the station. They watched the gasoline attendants refuel a plane. They watched the ground crew prepare a plane for take-off. They watched the plane taxi down the runway and take off. They watched the helicopters land, discharge passengers, cargo, and mail, and take off. They watched a big cargo plane being refueled and loaded.

Follow-up on the Visit

How much did they see and understand on this study trip? For each child the answer to this question was different, depending upon his background of experience, his alertness, and his interest. The next day and subsequent days, the teacher answered the question in terms of each child's reaction to the experience.

Many children deserted the playhouse, the farm, and other activities to join the airport center. The need to build a ticket office and a baggage desk emerged the morning after the study trip. The play in the airport became more realistic. The children now were calling plane departures and arrivals over the loud speaker, checking baggage, and playing the parts of all the airport personnel.

During this play in the indoor airport, a big plane constructed of large hollow blocks and boards was built out of doors with a ticket station and a control tower. Children were busy selling tickets, loading and unloading passengers, cargo, and mail, checking with control tower, checking with ground crew, and observing the direction of the wind for take-off. Wagons became trucks carrying mail and cargo and limousines, taxis, and cars carrying passengers.

As the play progressed, the teacher read stories to correct misconceptions and to give the children new material with which to work. A filmstrip "Seeing the Airport" helped to clarify relationships, and two motion pictures: "Airport Passenger Flight 376" and "The Airport" provided additional information.

Some of the children constructed airplanes, nearly every painting reflected airport interests, and nearly every child was eager to listen to airplane stories, to sing songs about airplanes, and to participate in airplane rhythms.

Although some children devoted most of their time to playhouse activity, even the homemakers made trips to the airport to "see friends off" or to become passengers, especially in the big outdoor plane.

Other Centers of Interest

Many school systems have developed suggestions for teachers concerning appropriate centers of interest. The following is a typical section from such a course of study: [3]

FARM

Understandings	Play possibilities	Sources of information

Farm animals help man to make a living and to feed and clothe himself and his family.	Using the horses for plowing and for pulling the wagon
	
	Feeding the chickens and ducks
	
	Gathering eggs
	
	Washing and milking the cows while they are in their stanchions
	
	Selling milk and eggs
	
	Shearing the sheep
	
	Feeding pigs and selling them
	
	Using a dog to help the farmer take care of the farm animals
		BOOKS
		  Hartwell, *Animals of Friendly Farm*
		  Lenski, *Animals for Me*
		  Lenski, *The Little Farm*
		  Lindman, *Snipp, Snapp, Snurr and the Buttered Bread*
		  Read, *Grandfather's Farm*
		  Slobodkin, *Friendly Animals*
		
		EXPERIMENT
		  Making butter
		
		MOTION PICTURES
		  Frisky the Calf
		  Our Foster Mother the Cow
		  Patty Garman, Little Helper
		  Pig Tales
		  Shep the Farm Dog
		  Sparky the Colt
		  The Red Hen

[3] *A Teacher's Guide for Kindergarten Education.* Long Beach: Long Beach Public Schools, 1954, pages 55–67.

Understandings	Play possibilities	Sources of information
Farm animals are housed in a variety of ways.	Keeping farm animals in proper areas Having stables for horses Having chicken houses for chickens Having pens for pigs Having hutches for rabbits Having barn and pasture for cows	BOOKS Flack, *Angus and the Ducks* Gay, *Hi-Ho for the Country* Hader, *Cock-a-Doodle Doo* Hader, *Farmer in the Dell* Hall, *Barnyard Animals* Lent, *The Farmer* Martin, *The Little Lamb*
Trucks take the products to the city to be sold.	Loading and driving trucks full of produce to the city Carrying milk from the farm to the creamery in trucks or wagons	Bonino, *The Cozy Little Farm* Werner, *The Fuzzy Duckling* Woodcock, *This Is the Way the Animals Walk*

Everyone on the farm has a specific responsibility.	Being mother — cleaning, cooking, and working in the house
	Being father — working in the fields
	  Using farm machinery
	  Plowing fields
	  Caring for crops
	  Harvesting crops
	  Storing crops
	  Caring for animals
	Being children
	  Collecting eggs
	  Helping mother
	  Weeding the garden
	  Helping with animals	

FIRE STATION

Fires should be reported.	Telephoning the fire department
	  Reporting the fire
	  Giving correct address
	Driving the fire truck to and from the fire
	Putting out the fires, using hoses, ladders, and axes
		BOOKS
		Brown, *The Little Fire Engine*
		Johnston, *Jamie and the Fire Engine*
		Lenski, *The Little Fire Engine*
		Scott, *Binky's Fire*
		Smith, *The Fireman*

Understandings	Play possibilities	Sources of information
	Cleaning fire truck; drying hoses and other equipment	Zaffo, *The Big Book of Real Fire Engines*
	Living at the fire station while on duty	EXCURSION A walk to a nearby fire station
		MOTION PICTURE *The Fireman*
Caution should be taken to prevent fires.	Taking precautions at school and home	

THE HOME

There are many kinds of houses.	Making and playing with different sizes, types, and shapes of houses	BOOKS Bertail, *Time for Bed* Burton, *The Little House* Flack, *The New Pet*

Each room in a home serves a different purpose.	Living in each room of the house
	Living room — visiting, watching television, resting, playing
	Dining room — eating breakfast, lunch, dinner
	Bedroom — sleeping
	Kitchen — cooking, baking, ironing, washing
	Taking care of each room — cleaning, dusting, sweeping
		Leaf, *Health Can Be Fun*
		Leaf, *Manners Can Be Fun*
		Lenski, *The Little Family*
		Lenski, *Papa Small*
		MacGregor, *Tommy and the Telephone*
		McCullough, *At Our House*
		
		EXCURSIONS
		A walk through the neighborhood to see
		  Houses
		  Pets

A family usually lives together.	Having a father, mother, and children in each house (varying the size of the family)	Construction
		  Gardens
		  Mother cooking
		  Mother bathing baby

All the members of a family should help in the home and help each other.	Playing that father works away from home Playing that mother cooks, cleans, makes beds, washes, irons, takes care of babies Having father help at home after work or on Saturday, doing such things as washing car, caring for yard, and helping mother	MOTION PICTURE *Patty Garman, Little Helper*

Understandings	Play possibilities	Sources of information
	Letting children help both mother and father by putting toys away, hanging up clothes, taking care of pets	
	Buying groceries, furniture, clothes, and baked goods	

SHIPS AND HARBOR

Ships are used for specific purposes.	Transporting passengers on liner and ferry	BOOKS
	Sailing ships out of the harbor	Becker, *Judy Goes Sailing*
	Carrying cargo from one place to another	Coplan, *Down by the Sea*
		Flack, *Boats on the River*
		Gramatky, *Little Toot*
	Helping large ships to dock, enter, and leave the harbor	Lenski, *The Little Sail Boat*
	Using tugboats to push and pull ships and barges	Read, *A Story about Boats*
		Swift, *The Little Red Lighthouse and the Great Bridge*
	Using pilot boats to guide ships into harbor	Zaffo, *The Big Book of Real Boats and Ships*
	Going for a cruise on a sailboat or motor boat	
	Fishing with nets or poles on fishing boat	EXCURSIONS *The Long Beach Harbor*
		MOTION PICTURES
		Boat Trip
		Coco at the Beach
Many people are needed to work on ships and in the harbor.	Being a member of ship's crew	*The Fireboat*
	Being captain and steering the ship	*Freighter in Port*
	Being steward and waiting on passengers	*Harbor Pilot*
	Being ticket agent and selling tickets	*No Vacancy*
	Painting and repairing ships	*Tugboats*
	Being a longshoreman	
	Operating a crane	
	Driving a tractor	
	Driving a Ross carrier	
There are many facilities and safety devices in the harbor.	Tying ships to dock for loading and unloading	
	Using crane to load and unload	

Understandings	Play possibilities	Sources of information
	Loading and unloading cotton, lumber, paper, oil, and other cargo	
	Using tractor to pull dollies in and out of transit shed	
	Loading and unloading barges and using tugs	
	Following rules and regulations in the harbor	
	Keeping ships away from dangerous areas by noting lighthouses, buoys, and other warnings	
	Sounding foghorn and proceeding slowly in foggy weather	
	Anchoring ships safely inside breakwater	
Transportation is needed to carry materials to and from the harbor.	Taking cargo to and from the harbor by trucks and trains	

TRAINS

Understandings	Play possibilities	Sources of information
Trains carry passengers, mail, and freight.	Building and using passenger cars Engine Tender	BOOKS Burton, *Choo Choo* Cross, *The Engine That Lost Its Whistle* Hurd, *Engine, Engine No. 9* Lenski, *The Little Train*
Passenger and freight trains are made up of different cars serving special purposes.	Baggage and mail car Coach Pullman Dining car and kitchen Building and using freight cars Engine Tender Mail car Boxcar Flatcar Stock car Tank cars Caboose	Meeks, *One Is the Engine* Ross, *The Little Red Engine Goes to Market* Slobodkin, *Clear the Track* Tatham, *The First Book of Trains* (teacher information) Wooley, *I Like Trains* Zaffo, *The Big Book of Real Trains* FILMSTRIP *Tommy Takes a Train Trip*

Understandings	Play possibilities	Sources of information
Many people are needed to operate and service trains.	Being member of train crew (primarily outdoors)	MOTION PICTURES *Diesel Engine*
	Driving train, signaling conductor, observing signals (engineer)	*Freight Train* *Passenger Train*
	Stoking coal, minding tender on steam engine, checking motors for fuel supply (Diesel), observing track conditions (fireman)	
	Operating switches, coupling cars, oiling cars (brakeman)	
	Collecting and punching tickets, signaling engineer, notifying passengers of departures and arrivals (conductor)	
	Serving passengers and making up berths (porter)	
	Preparing meals (chef)	
	Building and using the freight yard	
	Icing cars	
	Taking on water	
	Fueling tender	
	Coupling cars	
	Loading cars	
	Building and working in roundhouse (primarily indoors)	
	Building and working in railroad station	
	Being ticket agent	
	Being passenger	
	Being redcap	
Trains may stop en route to discharge and pick up passengers, freight, and freight cars.	Loading and unloading passengers at passenger stations	
	Loading and unloading freight at stations en route, at harbor	
	Stopping to take on water or fuel	
	Picking up and dispatching mail while en route	

Understandings	Play possibilities	Sources of information
	Loading and transporting livestock to stock yards or ranches (primarily indoors)	
	Filling tank car with oil and delivering it to the harbor	
	Loading and dispersing cargo at the harbor	
Safety rules and signals are important for the safe operation of the trains.	Using signals Semaphore Crossing gate Hand signals Wigwag	

TRUCKS

There are many kinds of trucks used for transporting different materials.	Using furniture truck to move furniture from store to home (primarily indoors)	BOOKS Elting, *Trucks at Work* Hurd, *Benny, the Bulldozer*
	Using lumber truck to carry lumber back and forth from lumberyard, trains, and harbor (primarily indoors)	Johnston, *Jamie and the Dump Truck* Johnston, *Jamie and the Fire Engine*
	Using mail truck to pick up and deliver mail to and from train, post office, airplane, and helicopter	Lawndes, *Traffic* Leaf, *Safety Can Be Fun* Lenski, *The Little Auto*
	Delivering bakery goods to homes, groceries, and cafés with bakery truck	Lenski, *The Little Fire Engine* MacDonald, *Red Light, Green Light*
	Using milk truck to bring milk from farm to creamery and to deliver to stores and homes (primarily indoors)	Reichert, *My Truck Book* Smith, *The Fireman* Zaffo, *The Big Book of Real Fire Engines*
	Fueling planes and filling storage tanks at gas station with gas truck (primarily indoors)	Zaffo, *The Big Book of Real Trucks*
	Using fire truck to put out fires	EXCURSIONS A walk to a nearby fire station
	Using delivery truck to carry cargo to and from the harbor and to deliver goods from stores to homes (primarily indoors)	A walk to a busy street A walk to neighborhood area where trucks are used
		FILMSTRIPS *Buses at Work* (color) *Roadbuilders at Work* (color)

Understandings	Play possibilities	Sources of information
Drivers must observe safety rules and signals.	Driving carefully in order to avoid accidents Stopping at stop signs and crossing gates	*Trailers at Work* (color) *Trucks at Work* (color) MOTION PICTURES *Our City* (12 min. sound) *Streets and the Community*
Trucks need fuel in order to run.	Servicing trucks with gas, air, oil, and water	*The Fireman* (11 min. sound) *Trucks That Serve Our City*

BAKERY

Many foods are made at the bakery.	Using the sandbox to make bakery goods (outdoors)	BOOKS Cridland, *The Baker*
Trucks bring supplies to the bakery.	Being the clerk or the baker Arranging baked goods Selling baked goods to customers	EXCURSION A visit to a neighborhood bakery EXPERIMENT Making cookies at school
Some bakeries have trucks to make home deliveries.	Buying baked goods Delivering baked goods by truck	

DEPARTMENT STORE

Many different things can be bought in a department store.	Buying clothes for small dolls (indoors) Buying luggage for trips (outdoors) Buying furniture (indoors) Being the clerks in the department store (indoors)	

FURNITURE STORE

Many kinds of furniture may be purchased at a furniture store.	Buying furniture Using the small furniture and dolls Selling furniture from the furniture store	EXCURSION A visit to a store

Understandings	Play possibilities	Sources of information
Trucks bring furniture to the store.	Delivering furniture	
Trucks deliver furniture to homes.	Making and painting some of the furniture	

GAS STATION AND GARAGE

Gas stations are maintained for the servicing and refueling of vehicles.	Being the gasoline attendant Selling gas Checking oil Checking water Washing windshield and windows Receiving money Checking, repairing, and changing tires Greasing cars Taking care of station equipment and grounds Washing and polishing cars	BOOKS Smith, *Filling Station* EXCURSIONS A visit to a nearby gas station A visit to a nearby car wash
Gas and oil are delivered to service stations by truck.	Filling gas storage tank with gas Delivering oil Paying for gas and oil	
A garage is a building in which cars may be repaired, stored, and parked.	Being a mechanic at the garage Replacing and repairing parts Towing cars Greasing cars Changing and fixing tires Storing and parking cars	

GROCERY STORE

Food may be bought at the grocery store.	Shopping in the store Taking milk from refrigerated cases Selecting vegetables from bins	BOOKS Lent, *The Storekeeper* Miller, *To Market We Go* Miller, *Jimmy the Groceryman*

Understandings	Play possibilities	Sources of information
Food in a grocery store is arranged in many ways.	Taking canned goods from shelves Buying meat at the meat counters Going to the check stand Paying cashier Clerking in the store Arranging the food on the shelves Checking out the groceries and taking the money from the customers Carrying the groceries to the customer's car	Price, *The Grocery Store* EXCURSION A walk to a neighborhood grocery store

LUMBERYARD

Lumber may be kept and bought at the lumberyard. Lumber is used to build many things. Lumber comes from trees.	Stacking lumber neatly Buying and selling lumber Delivering lumber with the lumber truck Putting the lumber on the lumber truck with a crane or Ross carrier Using trucks to transport lumber to and from the harbor	BOOKS Zaffo, *The Big Book of Real Trucks* EXCURSION A walk to watch a building under construction

POST OFFICE

Stamps are necessary for mailing letters or packages. Many people are employed by the post office. Letters may go long or short distances by trucks, trains, and airplanes.	Buying stamps Mailing letters and packages at the post office or in mail boxes Being the clerk at the post office and selling stamps Being the mailman delivering mail Delivering mail to the harbor or airport Picking up and delivering mail at the helicopter landing	BOOKS Baker, *Friends for Every Day*. "The Letter," pp. 52–58 Beaty, *Story Pictures of Our Neighbors*. "Helen Writes a Letter," pp. 105–109 Brown, *Seven Little Postmen* Gehres, *Everyday Life, Book 2* Hahn, *Everyday Fun*. "Mr. Postman," pp. 49–52 EXCURSION A walk to a neighborhood post office MOTION PICTURE *The Mailman*

GUIDING INTERACTION OF CHILDREN WITH THE SOCIAL ENVIRONMENT

Much of the guidance of the kindergarten teacher is achieved through the arrangement of a stimulating environment. The teacher must decide the elements of living which are desirable, wholesome, and capable of enriching the lives of the individuals in the particular group.

When the kindergarten child enters school he is familiar with his home, the neighborhood, and the immediate community. Through centers of interest that the teacher arranges in school, such as the playhouse, the bakery, the grocery store, the harbor, the airport, and the like, the child learns to understand the function of each. He begins to interpret and broaden ideas of things he took for granted before coming to school.

Guided study trips to the bakery, the fire station, a house under construction, and the airport widen the child's world to include ideas of relationships beyond his neighborhood and community.

Talking with others about his interests makes them more fun. Planning with others helps him to think about what needs to be done, what should be done next, and how to have a better time doing it. He finds he can get ideas for building his airplane by looking at books. He likes to hear his teacher read about activities in which he is engaged and promptly incorporates the ideas, the attitudes, and the language patterns of story characters into his own reenactment of the activity. The young child is constantly finding new things to do and new places to seek information. The teacher's guidance takes into account that:

The child moves naturally from one experience to another

He moves continuously

He moves toward the learnings and behaviors he needs only when he is ready for them

He makes a part of himself only those patterns of behavior which he needs at his particular level of development

Evaluation of Centers of Interest

Observation of the behavior and knowledge of the growth and development characteristics of kindergarten-age children lead the teacher to guide them according to the following basic ideas:

Centers of interest appropriate for children at this level of maturity are those related to home and community living.

One center of interest sometimes leads unexpectedly into another and they become inextricably linked together in the children's work and play. In the arrangement of the environment, thought should be given to facilitating the discovery of such relationships. For example, the "airport workers" have "homes and families" and live in the homes in the "community," drive cars to work, shop at the market, and participate in the various activities of community life.

Interest is not continuous in any one center. It may be compelling for a time and then seem to be completely lost. But an interest is often recurrent as the child acquires new knowledge and power to manipulate the environment with more satisfaction to himself.

Increasingly children's understandings of man's activities in the world develop as relationships between areas of experience are established.

The children are eager for stories about the things they are working or playing with such as ships, trains, airplanes, trucks. They are ready to pore over pictures of them endlessly. Their interests are expanded and heightened by the trips they take. Curiosity is sharpened. They talk together about what they have seen and done and the routes they have taken. They sing and paint pictures and create rhythms about their experiences. Often they lay out the whole scheme on the floor with their blocks, pooling and organizing the knowledge they have gained. With this block building their sense of orientation is being established and strengthened.

Materials of instruction are relatively large and flexible, capable of being used for manipulation and construction.

Tools are good ones. Wood is soft, surfaced on four sides, and cut to a size the child needs so he can achieve his purposes without too much difficulty.

Play with their age mates and with materials adaptable to their purposes constitutes the chief means of learning for kindergarten children. Such play results in understanding of themselves, their age mates, and the material environment, because they are capable of identification with persons and things. Play gives them an opportunity to express their feelings and helps to satisfy their great need for fellowship and acceptance. Play occurs easily and naturally in a stimulating atmosphere when there is a feeling of freedom and where the friendliness and sympathy of the teacher are continuously apparent to the child. Play is not a meaningless repetition of activity but becomes more comprehensive, more accurate, and more stimulating to learning as the teacher continues to "feed" the interest through all the activities of the kindergarten day.

SOCIAL LEARNING EXPERIENCES

In the kindergarten, much learning takes place through sharing and discussion, well-planned study trips, and the re-creation of experience through play and through construction.

Discussion and Sharing

Through sharing and informal conversation each child can increase his ability to communicate his ideas, to listen with interest and courtesy to the ideas of others, and to build concepts based on their ideas. Because these skills are difficult to learn, the teacher is content with briefer explanations from the less verbal children and keeps the more loquacious from usurping too much of the sharing time. The teacher's goals are to encourage observation and wise selection of things to share and to help the children grow in power to express themselves effectively and to listen to others.

The following is an example of an early sharing period: [4]

DAVID: (Holding up a picture)
Here's a picture from Hawaii.

TEACHER: Look at the tall trees they have in Hawaii.

DAVID: Yes, palm trees.

TIMMY: What is growing on them?

DAVID: Coconuts.

TEACHER: How could they pick them?

DAVID: Climb up the tree.

TEACHER: What is that building behind the trees?

DAVID: A church.

TEACHER: How do you know?

DAVID: It has a steeple.

TIMMY: Yes, and a cross on it too.

Later in the year, the following sharing period occurred:

TEACHER: I see that lots of you have brought things to share with us this morning. Joey, what would you like to share with us?

JOEY: Our family made some Christmas tree ornaments and I brought some to you.

TEACHER: How thoughtful of you, Joey. May we look at them together? Oh, Joey, they are lovely! Will you tell us how you made them?

JOEY: Well, these balls we found on the street.

TEACHER: Remember, these are like the seed pods that Billy brought in and we read about in his little nature book. They are still on the science table. Billy, will you bring them up so we can see again how the seed balls look before they are decorated? Thank you, Billy.

JOEY: We took the seed balls and put them in paint — different colors. Then my sister and my brother and I — we put these shiny things on.

TEACHER: Does anyone know what they call the shiny stuff?

JOEY: My mother got it at the store.

TEACHER: It is called "glitter."

JOEY: We made lots of them; it was fun.

---

[4] *A Teacher's Guide for Kindergarten.* Palo Alto Unified School District

TEACHER: They are beautiful, Joey. Would you like to hang them on our tree?

JOEY: Yes.

TEACHER: If any of you would like to bring some seed balls, some people might make ornaments at school.

CHILDREN: I can. We have some at our house.

TEACHER: Thank you, Joey, for sharing your fun.

The periods devoted to sharing, planning, discussion, and evaluation are exceedingly important. Most of the discussions are carried on with small groups and for a brief period of time. The values in terms of social adjustment, self-realization, acceptance and appreciation of others, language development, and broadening social and scientific concepts are so apparent that such periods merit the most careful planning on the part of the teacher.

Study Trips

Trips provide vital firsthand experiences which give children new insight and deeper understanding of the world about them. Through a carefully planned succession of trips, children expand their knowledge of their world and grow in ability to make detailed and accurate observations. The planning for a trip, the questions during the trip, and the discussion which follows provide for much growth in vocabulary and oral expression. Shared experience creates a new feeling of oneness in the group. Little by little children grow in appreciation of their fellows because of the interesting reactions of the other children to the trip and their understanding of what has been experienced together.

Every school system has its own policies concerning school trips. The teacher needs to be fully informed about these policies and adhere to them rigidly because liability for the school district may follow any deviation from the established regulations. A pre-trip conference with the principal or consultant may be included in the regulations but, in any event, it is desirable to discuss trip plans fully. Many valuable suggestions concerning arrangements will probably be made and problems of weather, safety and health can be checked. Whether the trip is a short walk or one involving the use of the school bus, plans should be made as far in advance as possible with the administrator or consultant designated in the local district.

The teacher needs to know the immediate neighborhood and the wider community in order to select appropriate trips in terms of content, distance, and any possible hazard to the safety of the children. The teacher always takes the trip beforehand in order to determine the specific items to be emphasized. She confers with the person who will serve as guide. She estimates the time the visit will take, and the most convenient time to schedule the trip. Young children are easily distracted and overwhelmed by too many details at one time. The children will acquire more substantial outcomes from the trip, when the teacher directs attention to the most significant items.

Many excellent learning experiences may result from a visit to some point of interest close to the school and within easy walking distance. A house under construction, a neighborhood fire station or a market will yield many vital impressions which will later be reflected in discussion, play, painting, and construction. If it seems desirable to take a longer trip by bus or other means of transportation, it is of the utmost importance that travel time to the destination not exceed a half hour.

Before the children take a trip, the teacher prepares them by discussing reasons for going, by telling or reading appropriate stories, or by showing them pictures relevant to the trip. Preparation for the trip may be spread over three or four days, using a variety of interesting materials to serve as background. As was stated earlier in this chapter in connection with the airplane activities, the need for a trip grew out of an activity in progress because the children wanted to find answers to their questions about airplanes and airport operation. Occasionally, teachers may reverse the process and use the study trip to initiate or stimulate an interest. For example, a trip to a nearby dairy farm may be taken in order to clarify concepts concerning the source of dairy products and the cleanliness observed in handling food for human consumption. Such a trip helps children to develop concepts about the interdependence of city and country people. In the pre-planning the teacher and children consider safety precautions, self-responsibility, manners, and the proper way to speak to guides and other adults. Parents are usually eager to assist on study trips. A short meeting with parents who are going on the trip concerning the purposes of the trip, special points of emphasis, vocabulary which may be anticipated, and safety rules to be observed increases the contribution parents can make to the success of the trip and their confidence in fulfilling their role in the undertaking. Knowing how to conduct a worthwhile study trip has much value for parents when they select and guide family excursions to broaden the experiences of their children.

After the study trip, much discussion centers about what was seen, heard, felt, and tasted. Any subsequent expression in play, construction, words, painting, or rhythms grows out of the accumulation of information and sensory impressions gained through firsthand experiences. Subsequently children participate in planning with the teacher, letters of appreciation to all the people who helped make the trip a success.

What types of study trips are appropriate for young children? Walking trips, often not more than three or four blocks from the school, include:

Visits to neighboring homes or gardens
Neighborhood park to see plants or animals
School library
Service station
Fire station
Market
Road or bridge construction

Trips at a distance from the school and possibly requiring transportation include:

Airport
Dairy farm
Creamery
Harbor
Passenger and freight railway station
Zoo
Post office

Learning Through Play

Healthy normal children are physically active and constantly on the move. Infants flail the air with their arms and legs and reach out for objects near them. They satisfy their urge for activity by their bodily movements and by pushing objects around. They feel increasing power over their environments as they move objects from one place to another. As their bodies grow stronger, they run and skip and jump, reveling in the ability to control and manipulate them.

Young children use their bodies to identify themselves with the life they see and hear about them. Crawling on their hands and knees they suddenly are dogs or ponies or bears. As quickly they change to steam engines, tractors, or motorboats. Spreading out their arms they are airplanes. Adding imagination and sound they identify themselves more realistically. "I am a bear" means I am a bear to a three-year-old. When a four-year-old says "I am a big engine" as he puffs around the room he means just exactly that. Young children are masters of their world. They can be whatever they want to be and they are limited only by their experience.

At first each child is interested in his own play and his own use of objects in his environment. Four- and five-year-olds may even engage in similar activities as individuals without interacting with one another. Gradually, however, co-operative play begins and the size of the co-operating group steadily increases.

The child selects objects from his environment to help him in this identification with and re-creation of the life about him. He places chairs in a row and — using his imagination — he has a train. He places one stick across the end of another and has an airplane. A corner of the room is marked off by blocks for a garage, a store, or a farm. When toys are provided, however, the need for improvising is minimized; two sticks crossed may make a more satisfactory airplane than a toy one. The child's identification varies. At one time he may be the truck or engine he is pushing around the room. At another time he may be the truck driver or the engineer.

Children are physically active: they desire to explore and to control objects in the environment, and they have an urge to re-create the adult activities they see and hear. This drive to physical activity, this urge to identify with and to re-create life, finds its fullest satisfaction in play.

The child comes to school from a world of play. He has been imitating life as he knows it, and he has been identifying himself with the people, animals, and objects about him. He has enriched his identifications by imagination and by utilizing the materials available.

From the many possible experiences, the school selects for emphasis those which are of most value in helping the child understand his world. The school uses those objects and materials which will direct the child's play into these selected experiences. If given the opportunity to move about the classroom and to handle objects and materials, the child immediately begins to play. What he plays and how he plays, whether alone or with others, constructively or destructively, depends upon his past experiences and present maturity. To provide a basis for learning he must have the opportunity to play and the play must be satisfying and fun.

Play helps children develop social relationships. The modern school recognizes the value of play and utilizes it in many kinds of learning. Through play children grow socially. They find that playing together is more fun than playing alone. They practice sharing materials, co-operating with each other, and learn many other important skills of democratic living. These skills become surrounded by a pleasant aura because they are learned with many satisfactions. Thus favorable attitudes toward democratic skills are developed and the basis for democratic living becomes firmly rooted.

Play stimulates language development. Play provides opportunity for children to grow in language power. They need to communicate ideas to each other to further their play. They learn word symbols for the materials they are using and the experiences they are having. Through play they add new meanings to word symbols already acquired. The planning of the play and the sharing of the fun provide many opportunities for language expression.

Play stimulates curiosity and interest. Play is characterized by its spontaneity. The skillful teacher directs play into learning without losing this spontaneity and helps the children to develop satisfying patterns for play. As children develop a pattern for their play, they need information to further or enrich it. This information may be obtained in various ways: through study trips, audio-visual materials, listening to stories, or talking with people. Thus play becomes a dynamic way of learning information and skills, increasing understanding, and extending interest and curiosity.

Play is a means of evaluating learning. The school uses play to measure the child's attitudes, acquisition of skills, and understandings. Observing the child during play, the teacher obtains evidence of his social adjustment. The child reveals his attitudes toward himself and toward others of his group. He reveals the information and understanding he has acquired. On the basis of these observations and evaluations the teacher plans for his further growth. Thus play is not only a way of learning and of stimulating interest and curiosity, but a test of the skills, information, and understandings already acquired.

Helen Christianson has developed a useful guide to the evaluation of children's play at kindergarten level. Since so many activities of young children are play activities, this guide will serve the kindergarten teacher in evaluating the educational values of play. See pages 156–158.

Construction

Construction helps play. Construction and play are closely interrelated as children explore an area of experience. Play gives purpose to construction and construction in turn enriches play. As children play, they select from the environment objects and materials to use. They are not too exacting in the realism of the objects and the materials for use in play. A piece of wood held in the hand and curved through the air serves as an airplane. The same piece of wood held at a different angle serves as a machine gun. A large box may be a barn for the horses or it may be the counter at the supermarket. Blocks may be set out in many designs or serve as buildings. The child needs properties that will make his play more realistic.

Toys help to meet this need for properties to give satisfaction to play. This is particularly true of toys that can be pushed around: trains, trucks, boats, planes. Young children are interested in things that move and they

EVALUATION OF PLAY [5]

Generalizations regarding children's play needs	Criteria for evaluating environmental arrangements to meet these needs	Clues to the role of the teacher giving guidance
Young children crave vigorous bodily activity with opportunities to develop new motor skills in their own time and way.	Is there ample space for freedom of movement without disrupting other activities?	Are the children encouraged to be inventive in bodily movements, evolving new ways to swing, slide, or use the bars?
	Is the equipment sufficiently varied in size and intricacy to challenge the children and lead to new skills?	Does the teacher show imagination in varying arrangements and supplementing equipment to challenge all children in the group?
	Is the standard playground equipment supplemented with plenty of movable boxes, boards, ladders, and wheel toys to suggest various possibilities?	Does the teacher recognize and encourage use of big equipment for dramatic play?
Young children seek understanding of the world of things by investigating, manipulating and exerting control over a thousand and one common objects.	Is there an abundance of materials and objects to provide rich sensory experiences? Are there occasional changes of materials to provoke new discoveries of color, form, weight, texture, mobility and other qualities?	Is the teacher resourceful in furthering children's interests in materials (1) by helping them make comparisons; (2) by encouraging verbal expression of sensory experiences?
	Is there opportunity for finding out about and using various mechanical devices, gadgets, and tools?	Does the teacher help children find answers to their questions: "What is it for? How does it work?"
	Are there study trips to see men and machinery at work?	Is the teacher able to assist children with scientific information when needed?

[5] Helen Christianson. "Play as an Educative Factor in Early Childhood Education," *California Journal of Elementary Education,* February, 1949. Pp. 153–158.

Young children delight in contacts with living, growing things as a part of their everyday play environment.	Are there pets that invite children to observe, handle, feed, carry about, make pens?	Does the teacher share children's enjoyment, and encourage the shy child to have satisfying contacts?
	Does the outdoor play area invite acquaintance with trees and shrubs, insects and butterflies, flowers and gardening?	Do teacher and children garden together sometimes — digging, planting, watering, or raking?
	Are nature materials used for beauty indoors as well as for manipulation and science observation?	Does the teacher show appreciation of children's discoveries and provide appropriate containers for insects, flowers, pods, and other treasures?
Every young child needs opportunity to identify himself with the world of people through dramatic play with other children of his age.	Is there a variety of play centers invitingly arranged indoors and outdoors to suggest home, neighborhood, and community activities?	Is the teacher ingenious in providing meaningful supplementary material to enrich the content of children's play?
		Are the children free to launch social activities in terms of their own readiness?
		Does the teacher help the young children with quick construction of a setting for dramatic play when needed?
	Are there carefully selected transportation and construction toys for use with sand, building blocks, boxes, and boards?	Do children have a chance to carry over absorbing play activity and construction from one day to another?
	Are there walks and trips to places of interest so that children may have a shared experience and common understanding to form background for dramatic play?	Does the teacher study the personality needs of each child and vary the play environment to stimulate developing interests?

Generalizations regarding children's play needs	Criteria for evaluating environmental arrangements to meet these needs	Clues to the role of the teacher giving guidance
Every child needs to find media for expression of his feelings and ideas in an environment where he may grow at his own pace in sharing the feelings and actions of others.	Do the available materials include sand, clay, earth, water, paints, blocks, wood, and supplementary tools?	Does the teacher show understanding of children's needs for emotional outlet as well as for manipulation and construction? Does she encourage individual expression?
	Is there a variety of equipment to stimulate experimental play with sound, rhythm, melody, and movement (drums, rattles, bells, simple tonal instruments)?	Does she have an appreciative eye and a listening ear for creative activity? Can she contribute to a high moment of experience by her spontaneous use of melody, rhyme or rhythmic accompaniments?
	Are there plenty of pictures and books to help children recall and relive familiar scenes and activities and share fresh experiences imaginatively?	Does the teacher use picture books and story time as an opportunity to encourage children's own language expression?

derive tremendous satisfaction from being the manipulators and from exercising control over the things they move.

As children mature in physical strength and in muscular co-ordination, they construct things with which to play. While their limited use of tools often results in crudely constructed objects, these objects are adequate for the purposes intended. One piece of wood nailed across another to make a plane may not be much improvement over the single piece of wood that had served adequately earlier, but the child gains additional satisfaction because he has made it.

The modern school recognizes and provides tools, materials, and time for construction. The materials should lend themselves easily to the things that are to be constructed. The child is interested in making the thing quickly so that he can play with it. A skillful teacher places materials in his environment that are suggestive and that lend themselves easily to the things to be constructed. A flat piece of wood can be sawed quickly into a point at one end and made into a satisfactory boat. Without too much work a wooden box can be converted into a satisfactory house or barn. Pieces of awning pole or a broomstick can be cut into proper lengths to make gasoline pumps for the filling station or smokestacks for a ship. When suitable materials are available, children can construct many of the community features which they will need in play.

As children grow in physical strength and in muscular co-ordination they acquire skill in using tools. Girls and boys should be helped to use tools and materials correctly from the beginning. Otherwise the construction period can be full of danger and frustration. A child soon becomes discouraged when wood splits or is otherwise spoiled because he uses a tool incorrectly. The proper use of tools insures success and encourages children in their construction. The alert teacher is sensitive to the children's needs and gives them help when it is necessary.

Construction helps children develop social relationships. In construction the skills of democratic living are practiced. A child who makes a filling station and adds it to the community readily recognizes his contribution to the group enterprise. He sees how his filling station contributes to the activities of the community. The child who makes a truck appreciates the work of the farmer who grows the vegetables he eats and the work of the storekeeper who buys the vegetables. He enjoys buying gas at the filling station and groceries at the grocery store. He begins to understand the relationships involved in community living. He finds that sharing what he has made and enjoying what others have made makes living in the community richer. Girls and boys have opportunity to practice co-operation as they carry on the activities of the community. Within the group activity individuals contribute according to their different abilities. The concrete experiences in construction help them to see how each individual contributes to the welfare and enjoyment of the group.

Construction provides many opportunities for growth in language. Through the use of tools and materials girls and boys extend their vocabularies. They acquire verbal symbols for the experiences in construction and these activities add new meanings to the word symbols already acquired. They need to communicate ideas to further the work being carried on together. The planning and evaluating of construction provides opportunities to express ideas and to practice using language. Discussion of construction demands accuracy of expression. Through construction children have something about which they wish to talk and something definite to say.

Construction leads to problem solving. Because of the concreteness of construction, girls and boys are helped to recognize and to define their problems. A child can quickly see when the wheels are not turning on his truck. He can figure out that the wheels are nailed too tightly or that the axle is not wide enough to permit the wheels to clear the platform of the truck. All of his problems in making a truck may not be so easily solved. Other children may contribute ideas to help him with his problem. He may find his answer by looking at a real truck or by looking at a picture. He learns to use sources of information to help him solve problems.

Construction provides motivation for learning skills and information. Children construct things with which to play or to add to play. They are not interested in the thing actually being in a completed state at a given time because their imagination adds the lacking details. Young children are satisfied to play with unfinished things that are only suggestive. A child pushes a truck around with satisfaction before the wheels are attached. With more maturity and as more elaborate plans are developed, interest centers in the properties themselves and in the details of the construction. If possible, the children want the things they make to work. Construction provides opportunities for learning quantitative relations and for concrete experiences with numbers. Skills in the use of numbers are needed and are used in realistic situations. In construction the children's information is organized and skills are practiced.

Construction enriches social studies experiences. Objects constructed should enrich rather than minimize the opportunities for play. When a large store or post office is constructed there is often little space left for further construction. The number of children who can play is limited and those who play merely repeat the few activities of the store or post office. Because of its size the store or post office cannot be related to other activities of the community. Such large-scale construction limits rather than broadens the play. When the construction is on a smaller scale, more construction can be carried on, more children can play, and more community relationships emerge. The size of the objects made should be suited to the size of the children.

Construction is a vital part of the exploration of a broad area of human experience. Combined with play it provides dynamic purposes and interests which extend and deepen children's understandings.

SITUATIONS FOR DISCUSSION

In the following situations select each course of action that seems desirable to you basing your choices and omissions on the ideas presented in this chapter. Add one or more alternate courses of action.

SITUATION I. You think it important for the kindergarten children to get acquainted with the school they attend. As their teacher, you should have the children:

Take a walk through the school.

Look at a floor plan showing the kindergarten, the office, and other points of interest.

Dramatize how a child introduces himself when he goes to the office.

Talk about the families of the married people on the staff.

Discuss what each member of the school staff does to help the school.

SITUATION II. You would like to have the children visit a real farm. In planning for this study trip, you should:

Announce it to the children for the first time the day before the trip.

Show the film, *One Day on the Farm.* [6]

Encourage the children to talk about farms they have visited.

Send home notices for the parents to sign and return.

Have the children play "The Farmer in the Dell."

SITUATION III. One day when you are near the playhouse you hear Jane saying, "This is mine, and you can't have it!" and Theresa saying, "These are mine and don't you touch them!" As the teacher, you should:

Let the girls work out their problem of property rights.

Guide Barbara, a more mature girl, into the playhouse.

Knock on the door of the playhouse and say, "Hello. I'm your neighbor."

Use your teacher role in helping the girls work out their problem.

Call the children into a group to discuss property rights.

SITUATION IV. You have taken the children to the local airport where they saw the control tower, runways, different kinds of airplanes, and were shown through a passenger plane. In getting ready for the next day, you should:

[6] *One Day on the Farm,* 11 minutes, black and white, or color. Chicago: Coronet Instructional Films, 1955.

Look at your file folder on "airplanes."
Ask the children's librarian for suitable books.
Borrow model airplanes made by upper-grade boys.
Check the construction supplies for wood of appropriate size for making airplanes.
Put away the paints and painting easels to make room for airport construction.

BIBLIOGRAPHY

Professional Books and Pamphlets

Adams, Olga. *Children and the City.* Chicago: Reginald R. Isaacs (% Michael Reese Hospital Planning Staff), 1952.

Helping five-year-old children understand the city around them is described and evaluated.

Association for Childhood Education International. *Adventures in Human Relations.* Washington, D. C., 1948.

This pamphlet describes everyday experiences of children which contribute to better relationships.

Bathhurst, Effie G. *Where Children Live Affects Curriculum.* Washington: Office of Education Bulletin 1950, No. 7.

Shows how the curriculum is varied in terms of children's personal needs — in using their environment; health and nutrition activities; social and civic understanding; and family living.

Foster, Josephine C., and N. E. Headley. *Education in the Kindergarten,* 2nd ed. New York: American Book Company, 1948.

Meeting the needs of five-year-old children makes it important to help them understand the community in which they live.

Hanna, Lavone, Gladys L. Potter, and Neva Hagaman. *Unit Teaching in the Elementary School.* New York: Rinehart and Company, Inc., 1956.

An integrated curriculum in the elementary school helps children to see relationship between content fields. Typical units for young children are included.

Heffernan, Helen, ed. *Guiding the Young Child:* Kindergarten to Grade Three. 2nd. ed. Boston: D. C. Heath and Company, 1959.

"Experiences in Social Living" and "Teacher Guidance in Social Living Experience" are two of the chapters that show how children's interest in home and school are guided into broader understanding of their world.

Houdlette, Harriet A. *Growing into Democracy.* Washington, D. C.: U. S. Government Printing Office, 1948.

The Elementary Division of the Office of Education prepared eight pamphlets with suggestions for guiding children in the democratic way of life.

National Society for the Study of Education. *Social Studies in the Elementary School.* Part II of the 56th Yearbook. Chicago: University of Chicago Press, 1957.

Current developments in social studies curriculum prepared by contributors from various parts of the country.

Turner, Marion E. *The Child Within the Group.* Stanford, California: Stanford University Press, 1957.

This reports a two-year experiment with a group of four- to six-year-old children given opportunity for increasing self-government.

Willcockson, Mary, ed. *Social Education of Young Children.* Washington, D. C.: National Council for the Social Studies, 1956.

Descriptions of programs; suggestions about audio-visual, book and community resources; and discussions about child growth and development are valuable to the kindergarten teacher.

Books for Children

Brown, Margaret Wise, and Edith Thacher Hurd. *Two Little Miners.* Little Golden Book #66. New York: Simon and Schuster, Inc., 1949.

How the miners do their daily job is told clearly, interestingly and with an occasional rhyming verse. *Five Little Firemen* (#64; 1948) and *Seven Little Postmen* (#134; 1952) are by the same authors.

Ipcar, Dahlov. *World Full of Horses.* Garden City, New York: Doubleday and Company, Inc., 1955.

The pictures and information presented in this book enhance any study of farms and farm animals.

Jackson, Kathryn. *The Little Eskimo.* Little Golden Book #155. New York: Simon and Schuster, Inc., 1952.

The story of the little Eskimo is the story of how Eskimo families live.

Kingman, Lee. *Peter's Long Walk.* Garden City, New York: Doubleday and Company, Inc., 1953.

When he gets to be five years old, Peter takes an early morning walk to school looking for friends to play with and learns that children start to school only in September.

Krauss, Ruth. *Big World and the Little House.* New York: Schuman, 1949.

The little house and its activities have the world as their setting.

Kravetz, Nathan. *Two for a Walk.* New York: Oxford University Press, 1954.

Grocery store, barber shop, pet shop, construction work and the fire station are explored by John and Tony.

Lewellen, John. *The True Book of Airports and Airplanes.* Chicago: Children's Press, 1956.

Simple and accurate information in this well-illustrated book helps children study airports and airplanes.

Liang, Yen. *The Pot Bank.* Philadelphia: J. B. Lippincott Company, 1956.

With the money they saved, Bao and Dee Dee buy presents at the Fair and another pot bank. *Tommy and Dee Dee*, 1953 is by the same author.

Mitchell, Lucy Sprague. *A Year in the City.* Little Golden Book #48. New York: Simon and Schuster, Inc., 1948.

Billy and Jenny enjoy each of the four seasons as they come to the city. *A Year on the Farm* (#37; 1947) is by the same author.

Puner, Helen Walker. *Daddies, What They Do All Day.* New York: Lothrop, Lee and Shepard Company, Inc., 1946.

This book is an answer to a child's question: "What does Daddy do when he goes to work?"

Radlauer, Ruth S. *Fathers at Work.* Los Angeles: Melmont Publishers, Inc., 1958.

Daddy is a steam shovel man, truck driver, jet flyer, newspaper reporter, gardener, carpenter, or lineman.

Schlein, Miriam. *How Do You Travel?* Nashville: Abingdon Press, 1954.
A bird travels in the air. Hans goes by skis. How do you travel?

Schneider, Nina. *While Susie Sleeps.* New York: William R. Scott, Inc., 1948.
While Susie sleeps the people who work during the night carry on their jobs.

Tresselt, Alvin, and Roger Duvoisin. *Follow the Road.* New York: Lothrop, Lee and Shepard Company, Inc., 1954.
A boy, a frog, leaves, trucks and wagons go along the road as it runs from the country into the city and out again into the country. By the same author are *Wake Up, Farm* (1955) and *Wake Up, City* (1957).

Yashima, Mitsu and Taro. *Plenty to Watch.* New York: The Viking Press, Inc., 1954.
A child on his way home from school in Japan sees the activities of the community.

Films for Children

The Airport. Wilmette, Illinois: Encyclopaedia Britannica Films, Inc., 1948.
What goes on at a large airport is shown: ticket selling, packing food, handling baggage, checking the plane and loading it. 10 minutes, sound.

Beginning Responsibility: Taking Care of Things. Chicago: Coronet Instructional Films, 1951.
This film shows how and why children care for things at home and at school. 10 minutes, black and white, or color.

Firehouse Dog. Chicago, Illinois: Coronet Films, 1956.
A Dalmatian dog views the routine of a fireman and the operation of a fire engine. 11 minutes, sound, color.

Freighter in Port. Hollywood: Academy Films, 1948.
A freighter arrives at the port, unloads and loads for its next voyage, and then departs. 15 minutes, sound, color.

Frisky the Calf. Chicago: Coronet Instructional Films, 1950.
Boys and girls from the city visit a barnyard and see a calf. 10 minutes, sound, black and white, or color.

Helpers Who Come to Our House. Chicago: Coronet Instructional Films, 1955.
The newspaper boy, milkman, postman, garbage man and others of the community help a family move into a new home. 11 minutes, black and white, or color.

On the Way to School. Chicago: Coronet Instructional Films, 1952.
On the way to school, children learn about transportation. 11 minutes, black and white, or color.

One Day on the Farm. Chicago: Coronet Instructional Films, 1955.
Kenny Lane and his parents do the daily chores and work on a farm. 11 minutes, black and white, or color.

Our Foster Mother, the Cow. Hollywood: Frith Films, 1947.
This film shows how dairy cows are handled. 11 minutes, sound, color.

Patty Garman, Little Helper. Hollywood: Frith Films, 1946.
Patty helps her mother and father with the work of house and farm. 11 minutes, sound, color.

South Pacific Island Children. Wilmette, Illinois: Encyclopaedia Britannica Films, Inc., 1951.

Fiji Island children fish, go to school, help with the garden and help with building their family home. 11 minutes, sound, color.

Filmstrips for Children

The Farmer's Animal Friends. Detroit 11, Michigan: The Jam Handy Organization, 1954.

"Cats on the Farm," 25 frames; "Chickens on the Farm," 23 frames; "Cows on the Farm," 24 frames; and "Horses on the Farm," 23 frames; each show how animals care for their young, what they eat, where they live and how they are useful to man. Silent, color.

Living and Working Together. Detroit, Michigan: Jam Handy Organization, 1954.

This series of six filmstrips shows: "The Family Begins the Day," "The Safe Way to School," "A Busy Morning in School," "Lunch and Play at School," "A Birthday Party at School," and "The Family at Home." Color.

9

The Child Enters His Scientific World

Science experiences are an important part of the kindergarten program. These experiences help the child learn about four aspects of his environment: (1) plants and animals, (2) machines and tools, (3) rocks and geologic events, and (4) weather, fire, and water. Through his experiences the child develops the beginnings of the scientific attitude, skill in observing science aspects of his environment, in reporting accurately what he sees, and simple concepts concerning scientific relationships.

Through his science experiences the child should learn how to keep himself and his friends safe. He should develop understandings which free him from fears or superstitions. He should develop understanding of and a feeling of control over his biological and physical environment. He should find his environment a never-ending source of interesting adventure.

Since he is only five years old, the child's science experiences are beginning ones, an introduction to what may be a lifelong interest. Yet right beginnings are of great importance and beginning science experiences should be accurate and satisfying ones.

The kindergarten teacher encourages science activities. She guides the children in exploring their environment and in trying out ideas about it. But she does not restrict them except to keep them from injury. She avoids the "don'ts" that so often go with "messes" because she (1) provides durable and easily cleaned equipment in safe situations and (2) she makes the cleaning up an integral and happy part of the activity.

SCIENCE AND THE SHORT ATTENTION SPAN

The teacher also realizes that beginning experiences are often of short duration. As children become more familiar with an activity, their span of attention for it increases. But they start many interests and may give

166

each only brief attention. The teacher therefore plans short experiences and ones that will show results quickly. For instance, in planning the spring garden, she chooses radish and other quick-growing seeds. In showing how water changes to steam, she starts with hot water that is almost ready to boil, not with cold water that takes much time to warm up. In this way, children have a pleasant feeling of success with science activities, and are interested in having more such activities.

CHANGES IN CHILDREN THROUGH SCIENCE EXPERIENCES

When science activities of the kindergarten are planned to meet their needs, the children are different at the end of the school year from what they were at the beginning. They improve their attitudes, skills, and ideas of relationships.

The children develop the beginnings of the scientific attitude. They are curious about the biological and physical aspects of the world about them. They want to find out about plants, animals, rocks, machines, and weather. They want to know the facts. "Is it pretend or real?" they ask on hearing a story. "Let's find out," they say when a question is asked. "Let's try it" implies for some of them at least the limits of experimenting: no one is to be hurt in the process. Science experiences in the kindergarten result in the beginning of the scientific attitude.

New Skills

The selection of skills to be learned will depend upon what science experiences are considered by the teacher to be important for children in her community. Skill in gardening, skill in caring for pets, and skill in handling water, for instance, may be outcomes of the program. No matter what the precise content of the science program, the children should grow in their ability to observe accurately what they see, in their ability to report accurately using correct terminology, and in their ability to see relationships. These three skills — observing, reporting, and seeing relationships — are significant objectives of the science program because they are the basis of the scientific method.

New Ideas

The general ideas of relationships which the five-year-old gains from his science experiences vary with the experiences provided. In cold parts of the country, the safety of the children makes it necessary for them to learn about water solidifying into ice. In other parts of the country, such understandings are interesting but less vital. In each community, the generalizations that the children learn through their science activities should be primarily those which free them from fears, make them safe, or give them control over their immediate environment.

Nine generalizations commonly thought important for five-year-old children are listed below:

In trying out an idea, see that no one is hurt.
In trying out an idea, use small amounts of material.
The world has both living and nonliving things.
Living things move, breathe, and feel.
Living things die when they wear out or have an accident.
Baby animals grow inside their mothers until they are born.
People must have air coming into their lungs to live.
People can tell when storms are coming.
Fire can be controlled.

TEACHING METHOD

In helping children develop scientific attitudes, skills, and generalizations, the kindergarten teacher uses the questioning method as much as possible, and keeps her statements to a minimum. The following anecdote illustrates this method of teaching.

When she went to the playhouse the teacher found several children clustered around Johnny who was standing precariously on a chair placed on top of a table. She went over close to Johnny to catch him in case of need and smiled. The following conversation ensued:

TEACHER: What's the problem?

JOHNNY AND OTHERS: The light won't go on.

TEACHER: Let's sit down here on the floor and talk about it. (*The teacher helps Johnny down from his perch; the children are seated.*)

SUSIE: Why won't it go on?

TEACHER: Let's find out. Is the switch on?

CHORUS: Yes! No!

TEACHER: Timmy, you go over and try it. (*Timmy does so. No change.*) Try it the other way again too. (*Again no change.*)

SAM: The bulb's burned out.

TEACHER: What makes you think so? Is the bulb black?

SAM: No, but it's burned out. I know it is. Ours at home was.

TEACHER: It may be, Sam, but let's see if there is some other reason for this light not turning on. Is the bulb screwed in all the way?

JOHNNY: I wanted to turn it.

TEACHER: Johnny wants to see if the bulb is screwed in tightly. When he climbed up, the chair on the

table was pretty wiggly and not very safe.
How can he climb up safely? (*The ladder is
suggested, and children go to bring it. Then
it is set up.*)

TEACHER: Is the ladder safe now for climbing? (*They
check the safety catch.*) Is it safe for Johnny to
climb up now and turn the bulb?

CHORUS: Yes!

TEACHER: The ladder is safe, but are we sure the electricity is? We don't want Johnny to get an
electric shock. How can we check to be sure
he won't?

The light switch was checked to be sure it was off. Then Johnny
climbed the ladder and screwed the bulb all the way in. When the switch
was turned on, the bulb lighted.

MEETING THE BASIC NEEDS OF CHILDREN THROUGH SCIENCE

The importance of the science program in the kindergarten is emphasized when newspapers report fatalities of five-year-old children. The
child who suffocated in the abandoned refrigerator that his friends per-
suaded him to climb into; the child who accidentally hanged himself by
a rope placed around his neck in play; the child who turned on the gas
stove while his mother was resting; the child who got into the neighbor's
pool and could not get out; the child who tried sliding on the thin ice of
the pond; the child who pointed the loaded gun at another person or at
himself; the child who touched a high-power line; the child who tasted
the ant poison or a poisonous plant — these are the children who warn
teachers that the science program must teach living children how to be
safe and how to help others to be safe. Life itself depends on such teaching.

The science program in the kindergarten is first and foremost a survival
program. But after the science program has provided for survival, it
provides also for meeting other basic needs of children. Children need
freedom from fear if they are to live and to learn happily. When they
have knowledge of scientific facts to replace their fears, they can explore
safely the infinite variety of experiences available in the biological and
physical aspects of the world about them. Learning to control the science
aspects of their environment gives them a sense of achievement and helps
build self-confidence.

Fortunately not all the hazards to young children occur in every neighborhood. By checking the following list of generalizations, the teacher
can identify those important for the children of a particular community to

know. Then she can plan science experiences to help the children keep themselves and their friends safe.

SCIENCE GENERALIZATIONS NECESSARY FOR SAFETY

1. People and other animals must have air at all times.

   Keep out of chests, refrigerators, or airtight small rooms.

   Keep the neck free from ropes or anything that might squeeze it.

   Keep away from gas or anything else that might prevent getting air to breathe.

   When swimming, put the nose out of water to get breaths of air.

2. Moving cars, tricycles, and other vehicles need time before they can stop.

   Keep out of the way of cars.

   Stop at the curb to look and listen for cars before crossing the street.

3. Ice floats on water.

   It takes days of continued cold weather to make ice thick enough for sliding or skating.

4. Before stepping on a loose rock, thin ice, or other dangerous object, put weight on it carefully, ready to jump back to a safe place.

5. Electricity in a broken power line or in an electric socket can hurt people.

6. Guns should be pointed at targets, not at people.

7. Some plants are poisonous. Eat only those plants served at meals.

8. Some animals are poisonous. Avoid them and the places they live.

9. Medicine, strong cleaning agents, and poisons are for adults to use.

10. Before eating, wash hands with soap and rinse them well with water.

11. Fire can be controlled by a fine spray of water or chemicals.

12. Storms and other kinds of weather can be predicted.

It is important for the kindergarten teacher to be objective, casual, and not emotionally concerned as she guides children in understanding how to be safe. Overemphasis can result in undue concern on the part of certain children who find satisfaction in being anxious or timid. The child who has been taught "Keep away from poison ivy" may be afraid to go for a walk in the woods, unless he knows that poison ivy is a vine that has a three-pointed shiny leaf which should not be picked and that washing at once with soap and water helps to get rid of the poison. Children are not afraid of what they know about. Knowing how to avoid accidents and knowing what to do in case of an accident make a child feel safe.

Understanding that hazards can be prevented and controlled does not imply responsibility for their prevention and control. Children share responsibility with adults, and five-year-old children have only limited responsibility. But they can learn a great deal about what needs to be done and this learning gives them confidence and a foundation for increased responsibility later.

The child who knows that fire can be controlled is not the child who is transfixed by fear when a fire starts to spread, but the child who goes and gets help. The child who has learned about electrical storms is not the child who cowers in a far corner but the child who enjoys watching the progress of the storm confident in the ability of man to cope with any effects of the storm. In short, the kindergarten child through science experience gains confidence in the possibility of control. This is a necessary foundation for learning methods of control later.

Freedom from Fear

Science knowledge is a means to help children free themselves from fears. Whenever children have fear of fire, fear of death, fear of darkness, fear of animals, or other fears, the science program should provide them with the experiences necessary to free themselves from these fears. Superstitions also must be dealt with and replaced with accurate understanding and beliefs based on reality.

The child gains control of his biological and physical world through understanding it. Fears are simply evidence of the areas in which the child feels least able to exert control. Through science experiences the child can rid himself of his fears and then move ahead to gain a sense of achievement through learning to control what he had previously feared. The wise teacher helps the child control situations in which danger is involved rather than merely avoiding the situation.

Fear of the dark, a most common fear to children, is the joint responsibility of parents and teachers. At a parents' meeting, the kindergarten teacher can help parents understand why children are afraid of the dark and how children can gain control of their fear of the dark. A child goes to sleep in a room with which he is thoroughly familiar — in the daylight. If he awakens at night, his eyes, unaccustomed to the dark, show him not the surroundings in which he went to sleep but a strange environment with many shades of grayness and unfamiliar shapes and sizes. If he can control the dark by turning on a small night light by his bed or a flashlight that goes on very easily, he can reassure himself and go back to sleep. But if he cannot control the darkness, he becomes afraid and may cry out for help.

Of course, what children need is to play in the dark and have fun as they grow increasingly familiar with it. Because they are able to move about safely in the dark, they feel secure and in control of darkness. A walk outside with daddy or mother just before going to bed; looking at the clouds, the stars, and the moon as part of the going-to-bed ritual; and an evening game of blind man's buff or hide-and-go-seek are all delightful experiences for the child and, at the same time, ways to prevent fear of darkness. At school children enjoy taking fluorescent puppets, pictures, or other objects into a dark room to see them glow.

A Sense of Achievement

The kindergarten teacher plans science activities so that the children gain a sense of achievement from them. Children learn by doing. When they see a rainbow, the teacher can help them relate this phenomenon to themselves and gain a sense of control over light. Indoors a child may use a triangular prism or the bevel edge of a mirror to spread a beam of daylight into the many colors of which it is composed. Another child can hold a piece of white paper in a position to show the tiny rainbow made by the prism. Other children can catch the rainbow from the prism on their clothing. Outdoors the children can see the rainbows made when the sunlight passes through the spray of the sprinkler. By spreading sunlight into its colors, the children get a sense of achievement because they are able to control miniature rainbows. The wise teacher plans science experiences so that the children are active participants, not passive observers.

Variety of Experience

Children need to have a variety of experiences which they can assimilate at their own rate. The biological and physical aspects of their environment provide them with a limitless reservoir of experience, and their teacher guides them in tapping its resources at a rate commensurate with their levels of development.

The Physical World

The physical world around him is filled with items of interest to the five-year-old. As the kindergarten year progresses the child samples here and there, selecting from the multitude of topics those that impinge on his life. The kindergarten teacher is not surprised when his questions deal with any aspect of the physical world: telephones, highway signals, electrical appliances; simple machines; sound; light; pull of gravity, centrifugal force, magnetism; what air is made of; stars, planets and moons; rocks and soil and what the neighborhood used to be like in previous geological eras; weather and how to predict it; water and how to control it; fire and how to control it.

The Biological Environment

His biological environment also offers the five-year-old opportunity for a lifetime of learning. During the kindergarten year he samples this environment and pays attention to those bits of it which for one reason or another briefly catch his interest. His teacher is alert to guide him in observing accurately and in seeing relationships, for instance, the changes in plants and animals associated with each of the seasons. She follows the leads of his questions and is ready with field glasses to help him observe the movement of birds and other animals and with a hand lens to help him observe the detail of a fly or a mold or whatever has caught his interest.

Birth

Children need to understand what happens at home and in the community. During the school year almost every kindergarten group is interested in the new baby arriving at the home of a child in the group. A new litter of kittens or puppies is a topic of conversation at least once or twice during the school year. These births offer an excellent opportunity to help children answer their questions about "Where did I come from?" Incidentally, too, they learn differences between boys and girls. However, in certain social groups in our culture, it is the custom not to discuss either sex or reproduction. The teacher needs, therefore, to discover through parent meetings and conferences with individual parents how much help the school can give children in acquiring understanding about these important aspects of life.

Even in communities where human reproduction is not discussed, reproduction in plants and animals is recognized as an important school topic. Since five-year-old children are so interested in babies of all kinds, reproduction is an essential part of their science program.

An aquarium of guppies is of great interest at any time, but especially when the next generation of guppies is visible inside their mothers. This circumstance is the occasion for the teacher making it clear that babies grow in a special place inside a mother, not in her stomach. This distinction is essential for certain five-year-old children who have superstitions and fears growing out of their confusion about the reproductive and the digestive systems and the system of elimination.

Appropriate science experiences fortify the kindergarten child against emotional disturbance over infant deaths, miscarriages, or birth abnormalities. The wise teacher, for instance, brings in fresh peas in the pods. As the children hold a pod up to the light, they see how many mature peas are in the pod. Then they open the pod and confirm their count. They notice that a pea that did not grow up occurs quite often. In fact, about one out of five peas, on an average, does not mature. Some peas have what it takes to grow up and others do not.

Similarly, kindergarten teachers may guide children in their observations about nuts and other seeds that they harvest in woods and fields. When the children garden in the spring, they may again be guided to observe that some seeds are able to develop into a hardy plant while others are not. Litters of animals, the children may observe, are composed of babies that are able to survive and others that are frail and probably cannot survive. With such background experiences in science, it is easy for a child to understand that reproduction in human beings may likewise result in perfect and imperfect babies.

Death

Many teachers and parents avoid teaching children about death. Their reluctance in doing so is understandable. Perhaps their own experiences with death were upsetting emotional ones. Or perhaps they feel that death is a religious question to be explained to children by religious teachers. Nevertheless, teachers and parents should help children develop the basic science concepts which enable them to avoid fears related to death and to cope with death whenever they encounter it. These science concepts are:

> When an animal dies, it stops feeling, moving, breathing.
>
> Sooner or later every person dies, either by accident or by having some vital part wear out.
>
> The life span of most people includes childhood, growing up, working as an adult, getting married, having children, having grandchildren.

Such concepts should be brought out casually just as any other relationships are. In one kindergarten group, the teacher was helping the children measure off garden plots when one child pointed to the five-inch mark and said, "That's how old I am." The children gathered around to talk about the numbers, and the teacher seized the opportunity to show the children how old parents and grandparents are, compared with children. She pointed out how far her age was down the tape, how far her mother's was, and how old her grandfather was when he died. The children saw that the long time they had already lived was just a small part of how long a person lives in order to be a grandparent. Then, as casually as the little group of children had formed, it broke up to go about the business of measuring garden plots again.

THE SCIENTIFIC METHOD

A misconception common among teachers and other people is that science teaching requires magnets, prisms, and other special apparatus. The fact of the matter is that such materials contribute to science teaching but are not essential to it. Especially at the kindergarten level, science teaching should concern itself primarily with what is already familiar to the children — things they live with in their homes, things they bring in, and things they observe and ask about in their daily environment. But the essence of science teaching is the method by which the children are guided to think about these familiar things. The children experience the scientific method and use it themselves in observing and inquiring about their physical environment.

Steps in the scientific method, and likewise in science teaching, include:

Identification of a problem or question
Setting up a hypothesis or guess about its answer
Planning some method of testing the hypothesis
Trying the method and observing what happens
Interpreting the observations, and making sure of what was found out
On the basis of the findings, drawing conclusions
Planning further experiments to prove the hypothesis or to extend learning further

Children gradually learn the scientific method if, consistently, it is the method by which problems are tackled. The following description of what happened when a boy brought a box of rocks to school illustrates use of the scientific method with kindergarten children. The teacher skillfully guided the children in observing and finding out more about the rocks.

Jimmy brought a box of rocks to school. The rocks were of a great variety of sizes and colors. The children admired them.[1]

MARY ANN: Oh, what pretty red color.
TOM: Why are they different?
TEACHER: (*Referring questions to children*) Does anyone know why Jimmy's stones have different colors?
RICHARD: (*Making a suggestion*) They have different pieces in them.
TEACHER: Yes, those colored "pieces" or "specks" are minerals.
BETTY: Are they pasted on?
MARCIA: Will they come off?
TEACHER: (*Guiding children to experiment*) How can we find out?
MARY: I'll show you. (*Mary tried to scrape off the color with a steel spoon.*) No, they don't come off.
JACK: I'll bet they'd wash off with soap and water. May I try?
TEACHER: Jimmy, shall we let Jack wash your rocks? (*Jimmy wasn't certain and so wouldn't risk too much.*)
JIMMY: Well, let him wash this one. I have another one like it.

Madge helped Jack and all the class watched expectantly.

JACK: Look, we scrubbed this one with soap and it is brighter.
BETTY: Are the rocks colored inside?

---

[1] *A Teacher's Guide for Kindergarten Education.* Long Beach, California: Long Beach Public Schools, 1954. Pp. 215–217.

MIKE: Sure, all the way through.

SUSAN: No, they are black inside.

TEACHER: (*Helping children to find out*)   Since you don't agree, how could we find out for sure?

MIKE: If Jimmy doesn't care, we could break it with a hammer and look at the pieces.

CHILDREN: Yes, let's do that.

JIMMY: You can break the same one Jack washed.   I have two like that.

TEACHER: (*Practicing safety*)   I am afraid to do it unless you figure out a way to protect our eyes.   If we hit a rock hard enough to break it, splinters might fly and hit us hard enough to hurt.

MIKE: Could we hit it under the table?

MARY ANN: Oh, I know.   It's just like breaking ice when we make ice cream.   You put it in a bag and hit the ice right through the bag.

CHILDREN: Let's try Mary Ann's way.

TEACHER: Maybe this piece of heavy cloth would do.   May I break it?

A piece of scrap lumber was put under the rock to protect the floor. Pupils wrapped the rock and the teacher struck it sharply several times with a hammer.

TEACHER: Watch how hard I have to hit it.   Listen to see if you can tell when it breaks.

RICHARD: There!   Hear the two pieces crack together.

Everyone examined the pieces.

SUSAN: Yippee!   They are pretty inside.   I was sure they'd be black.   Mike was right.

TEACHER: Well, he was right about this rock.   We will break other rocks later.   Maybe someone will bring us more rocks we can use.

The teacher should break some more rocks later so that the children will not determine that one example proves the rule.

This description of a lesson using the scientific method illustrates the seven steps in the method, as follows:

1. Identify problem	Betty and Marcia ask if the specks are pasted on and if they will come off.
2. Set up hypothesis	
3. Plan to test it	With a spoon, Mary tries to scrape off the color.
4. Test it	
5. Interpret findings	Mary reports that, "No, they don't come off."
6. Conclude	
7. Plan further experiments	Jack proposes seeing if the specks wash out.

After Jack's experiment, Susan proposes the hypothesis that the rocks are black inside (1, 2). Mike suggests a method for testing the hypothesis by breaking the rock with a hammer (3). The teacher helps the children plan a safe way of breaking the rock and helps with the hammering that is beyond the skill of the children (4). Then various children report and interpret their observations (5). Susan concludes that "The rocks are pretty inside" (6). The teacher is aware of the danger of drawing conclusions beyond the data at hand and helps the children think of further experiments with rocks for other days (7).

LABORATORY AND FIELD EXPERIENCES

Science study depends on both laboratory experience and field trips. The field trip in biology, for instance, shows the interrelation of plants and animals in their natural environment. The biological laboratory on the other hand shows the close-up detail of the plant or animal. On a fall field trip, kindergarten children see the colored leaves on the trees, each kind of leaf on its own kind of tree. Then the children bring the colored leaves into their kindergarten laboratory. There they look at the leaves in detail through a hand lens, if possible. Perhaps they count the leaves, put the same kinds of leaves together in boxes, or study their shapes by drawing them.

On a field trip in the spring, the children look for spring flowers. When they find one they like, they notice whether it grows in the sun or in the shade; whether it grows in a damp or in a dry place. Carefully they dig up one plant and bring it back to their kindergarten laboratory. There each day they can watch it grow and can see whether it needs the same conditions of sunlight and moisture that it had where it grew outdoors.

Laboratory Experience

The kindergarten laboratory is primarily a try-out place. In the sandbox, children experiment with construction projects of all kinds: road making, laying a water system, and making dams, caves, bridges or walled structures of one kind or another. In the sink, children experiment with hydraulic projects: pouring, filtering, using funnels, mixing, siphoning, making balloon fountains, making bubbles, spraying.

Now that new materials are available, water play is an important part of the kindergarten program. Soft plastic (polyethylene) and aluminum containers do not rust and do not break. Furthermore, they are available in gay colors. Plastic aprons protect the child's clothing. If the sink is indoors, two rules keep the water play under control: (1) keep the water in the sink, and (2) turn the water off when it is not in use. Sometimes it is desirable, also, to have a rule about the number of children using the sink at one time.

Water Play. Water play is especially valuable for children who have toilet accidents. When children gain control over water from the faucet, they have a sense of achievement which helps them in taking responsibility for themselves. With timid children especially, it is important that any spilling of water be quietly and casually taken care of. Sponges are handy and the children enjoy helping clean up any water that spills on the water-proof floor around the sink. As children gain increasing control, spilling occurs less and less often, both at the sink and in activities with paints, juice, or other liquids.

The Workbench. The workbench is another important part of the kindergarten laboratory. Here children try out construction with tools, wood, and nails. As they build boats of all kinds, trucks, and airplanes, their teacher guides them in observing differences in the materials they use and differences in where the nails go, depending on just how they are hit by the hammer.

The Garden. Probably the most important part of the kindergarten science laboratory is the garden. In the fall and winter, gardens may be planted indoors: carrots placed in water to grow a carrot top, aluminum foil dishes of bird seed on wet cotton, beans sprouting on a wet sponge or blotter, mold growing on pumpkin or squash, avocado seed or sweet potato sprouting in water, or narcissus bulbs growing in a glass jar so children may observe the developing root system. When the ground is ready to work outdoors in the spring, each child should have his own garden plot, and the teacher, too, should have at least one plot.

The teacher constantly keeps in mind that the reason for a child's garden is for him to answer his questions about seeds and how they grow. With this in mind the teacher encourages each child to plant two kinds of quick-growing seeds, so he can see which comes up first and so he can continue to make comparisons within his own project. The child must be completely responsible for and in charge of his own garden. If he wants to plant his seeds in bunches instead of rows, if he wants to dig the plants up, if he wants to flood them with water — no matter what he wants to do with his garden — he should be free to do it. The wise teacher lets him try out what he wants to. She talks with him about what he wants to do. If he wants to see if the seeds he planted yesterday have sprouted, she helps him see that digging up two is as good a way to answer his question as digging up many of them. If he leaves most of them, he will have other seeds to use in answering other questions on other days.

Of course the reason why the teacher has a garden plot of her own is that she wants to demonstrate that plants continue to grow bigger until they make vegetables, or flowers which develop into seeds.

Animal Life. The garden is a laboratory situation for animal life as well as plant life. As the plants grow they create a favorable environment for small insects, spiders, earthworms, and birds. A toad or garter snake may move in. A garden that is flooded daily soon attracts snails and slugs. The children thus have ample opportunity to observe animal life and to find relationships between plant and animal life.

The kindergarten should also provide a laboratory for other animals. Children may bring their pets for a day at a time. By inquiring in the school community, the teacher may be able to have a cage of white mice, or hamsters, or an aquarium for several weeks. These pets require a minimum of care and afford a maximum of experience for the children.

Field Experience

The kindergarten child profits from two kinds of field trips: (1) a walk that helps him see science aspects of his environment, and (2) the study trip which combines science experience with social studies. In the first, the purpose is to help children see interrelationship among science phenomena and in the second, to see relationship between science phenomena and people.

The Science Walk. The kindergarten teacher plans science walks to help the children answer their questions about:

construction projects in the neighborhood
(road making, bridge building, house, store or other building construction)

repair projects in the neighborhood
(road repair, reroofing or other house repair, fixing telephone or electric lines, replacing street lights or highway signals)

plants and animals as they are during the current season

weather (clouds, winds, moisture — fog, dew, rain, snow)

rocks and what they tell about the geologic history of the neighborhood

Of course, if their walk takes them to some mechanical object of interest, for instance a car with a wheel off, their questions are encouraged and discussion enlarges their understanding about machines and tools as well.

The Study Trip. On study trips, whether a child is dealing with social science or with natural science depends not on the situation but on how he is thinking about it. For instance, if children are watching a road construction project, they want to see how the road is dug up, how the dump trucks are operated, how the scraper blade is raised and lowered, what the steam roller does, and how the asphalt is put on. Considering these topics about their physical world, the children are dealing with natural science. But when they consider the daddies who are driving the machinery and earning money to buy food, clothing, shelter, and other things for their families, they are dealing with the social sciences. The kindergarten teacher who understands this distinction between social and natural science provides a full program in which the children consider situations from both points of view.

The experience which is primarily a social science study trip always has science aspects. Both in planning for the trip and in conducting it, the kindergarten teacher needs to check to be sure that natural science as well as social science aspects of the trip are brought out. In the following chart are given some of the field trips which are apt to be a part of the program for kindergarten children. For each of the field trips, two or three science aspects are mentioned.

Field Trip	*Some Science Aspects*
Airport	Loading baggage and mail, starting motors
Barber shop	Chairs going up and down, mirrors, lights
Dairy or creamery	Keeping utensils clean and milk free from germs
Factory or mill	Machinery, changes in materials, making of sounds
Farm	Feeding and caring for different kinds of animals
Filling station	Getting under the car, storing and handling gas and air
Fire station	How the pump works, sirens, how ladders are carried
Grocery store	Wheeled carts, lights, how the cash register works
Hardware store	What items are made of, and what they are used for
Laundry or laundromat	Use of power, use of water, use of chemicals
Library	Classifying, lighting, wheeled cart
Park	Different kinds of trees and shrubs, watering provisions
Police station	Use of carbon paper, devices for writing
Post office	Weighing, gluing, sorting
Printing plant	Different kinds of paper, printing process, machinery
School	Heating system, ventilating, lighting
Train station	Engines, car hitching, brakes, drinking fountains
Zoo	Kinds of animals, care, cleanliness, food

A study trip to a small bakery is an example of a trip which provides opportunity for learning in social studies as well as in science. On such a trip, children ask science questions dealing with the chemical process of bread making, with mechanical and electrical processes for simplifying work, and with psychological processes such as sensory reactions in people. The children also ask social studies questions dealing with the lives of the people in the bakery and with buying and selling activities. The following chart helped one teacher to be sure that a field trip to a small bakery would aid the children in understanding both people and processes, both social studies and science.

QUESTIONS ABOUT A SMALL BAKERY

Natural Science

Why are cakes and pies kept in glass showcases?
Why are some cakes and pies kept in refrigerated cases?
What makes things move on a cash register?
What is bread made of?
How are the ingredients mixed?
Why is bread kneaded?
How are cookies rolled out?
How are they cut?
How is bread cooked?
How are cookies cooked?
How are doughnuts cooked?
How can a person tell when bread is done or cooked too much?
What makes the kitchen feel so warm?

Social Science

Does the woman selling bakery goods have any children?
Where does she live?
When she is at the bakery, who is at home?
How much does a dime buy? A quarter?
Who brings the flour to the bakery?
Where does he get it?
Does the baker have children?
When is he at home, and when is he at the bakery?
Does he like to bake?
How did he learn to be a baker?

THE SUBJECT MATTER OF SCIENCE

What should kindergarten children study in science? One group of children may learn about quite different things from those explored by another group of children. Two sources of content have been pointed out: (1) the need of each group of children to learn how to be safe in spite of the hazards of the community and (2) the observations on walks and while playing outdoors that each child makes of the plants, animals, machines, tools, rocks, and weather of his environment. A third source of science content is the local superstitions which the children talk about. The teacher helps the children understand that the bad luck of a black kitten crossing one's path is imaginary. She encourages them to distinguish what they really observe from what they imagine. Watching how a kitty drinks milk, eats food, and cleans itself can be observed.

It has also been pointed out that the needs of children should be met through science teaching. The safe behavior of children, the fears especially of the five-year-old, and the interests of children in the world around them are observed by the teacher and should be used in planning the content of science activities. The questions asked by children are also a good basis for science teaching. However, many of the studies of children's questions have been made in school situations where teacher interests and enthusiasms have encouraged child interests beyond those that appear repeatedly in intimate conversation with children at home.

Listening to children and helping them find answers to their questions result in experiences that are the beginnings of all the branches of science. Beginnings of biological sciences are readily observable in such generalizations developed with children as:

A person must have air at all times (*biology*)

Plants need water and good soil (*botany*)

Animals need food each day (*zoology*)

The beginnings of geography and mathematics are discussed at length in Chapter 10 in this book. The beginnings of chemistry and physics are also apparent in generalizations developed with the children, such as:

Fire must have air to burn

Ice melts to water, and water freezes to ice

Wheels make it easy to move heavy things more quickly

Five-year-old children should develop an interest in what things are made of and in the strength of materials. A child should learn to ask: "Will that rope hold me without breaking?" and "Can I swing from that branch?" As he continues to grow he finds that materials which used to be strong enough to hold him now give way under his increased weight. His teacher can help him develop awareness of the strength of materials by providing a safe learning situation at kindergarten. Miss Kelly, for instance, brought in a cardboard carton, an orange crate, and an apple box of about the same size and shape. With the children she considered which boxes were strong enough to hold a child's weight. Then the children tried out the boxes to see if they would really hold their weight. Johnny suggested jumping up and down to see which cartons would break. When the children tried this, they observed that a small child could jump up and down on a carton which cracked under the weight of a large child. Miss Kelly guided the children in developing ideas of relationship such as: thick boards are stronger than thin ones, wood is stronger than cardboard.

Miss Kelly also helped the children observe the shape of an object before trusting it with their weight. With different shapes of stepping stones to walk across the children learned to ask themselves, "Will this rock turn under me if I step on it?"

At Christmas time the children in Miss Kelly's room went on a trip to a nearby shop to see what kind of toys they might get for gifts. Miss Kelly bought the bright red and yellow plastic clothes sprinkler which intrigued some children as a gift for their mothers, and also another sprinkler made of soft plastic. She bought a sturdy toy boat of wood and another toy boat with metal parts. The next day when the children talked about their shopping trip, Miss Kelly guided them to understand that the brittle plastic sprinkler broke when it was dropped, but that the soft plastic one did not. That day the two boats floated equally well, but a week later the one with metal parts was rusty and its rudder would not turn easily. Thus Miss Kelly helped the five-year-olds see that what something is made of is important in terms of what you want to do with it. Such lessons about materials are an important part of a five-year-old child's introduction to physical sciences.

The kindergarten teacher provides science experiences so that the children learn how to be safe from hazards in their community. She helps them replace fears with understanding, and, if possible, with skills that give them control over what they previously feared. Throughout the kindergarten year the teacher guides the children as they sample the biological and physical aspects of their environment and develop the beginnings of scientific attitudes and interests and of the concepts basic to further scientific explorations. The teacher carefully listens to the children's questions and uses skillful questioning herself as her principal means of guiding the children's thinking. With the children, she plans for gardens, construction projects, water play, care of pets, and other science activities the children can carry on themselves within the kindergarten laboratory. She also plans for field trips where plants and animals, rocks, machines and tools, weather, fire, and water can be seen in relation to other science phenomena and to the activities of people.

SITUATIONS FOR DISCUSSION

In the following situations select each course of action that seems desirable to you basing your choices and omissions on the ideas presented in this chapter. Add one or more alternate courses of action.

SITUATION I. At the beginning of the school year early one Monday morning, Janice comes in to find you. She seems excited and anxious. She says, "There's a spider in the playhouse!" As the teacher you should:

Put your arm around her to calm and reassure her.

Ask her how she knows there's a spider in the playhouse.

Did she see its web? Did she see the spider? Did someone tell her?

Go with her to look for and kill the spider in the playhouse.

Ask the children if they kill spiders outdoors as well as indoors.

On the next science walk, look for spiders and spider webs.

SITUATION **II.** Carl, a small boy, is standing on a kindergarten block at the sink. As he reaches for the faucet at the back, his rubber-soled shoes slip on the wet surface of the block and he falls down, squeezing the syringe in his hand. The syringe squirts water all over the wall, all over the children by the sink, and all over the floor under the sink. As the teacher you should:

Pick up Carl and laugh with him about, "What a mess!"

Tell the children it surely was a good thing they had their plastic aprons.

Let the children get out the sponges and wipe up the water.

Ask the children how Carl happened to fall.

Plan with the children how to avoid such accidents.

SITUATION **III.** The kindergarten room has blinds that are pulled up and down with cords. When something goes wrong with one of the cords so that it will not pull up, you should:

Ask the janitor to fix it when the children are out of the way.

Do some simple demonstrations with a pulley for the children to watch.

Make no mention of the blind unless some child asks about it.

Tell the children they must learn to leave the cords of the blinds alone.

On the next field trip, point out similar blinds and pulleys.

SITUATION **IV.** Several of the children bring you the remains of a bird they found in the bushes on their way to school. The condition of the bird, especially its smell, suggests that it has been dead for several days. As the teacher, you should:

Listen carefully to what the children tell you.

Have the children put the bird in the trash barrel.

Ask the children to show the bird to the group.

Go on to another activity at once.

Read *The Dead Bird* by Margaret Wise Brown.

BIBLIOGRAPHY

Professional Books and Pamphlets

Blough, Glenn O., and Paul E. Blackwood. *Science Teaching in Rural and Small Town Schools.* Office of Education Bulletin 1949, No. 5. Washington, D. C.: Office of Education, 1949.

A wealth of science awaits the children whose teacher encourages them to find answers to their questions by observing the science materials at hand and by trying out their ideas.

Blough, Glenn O., and Albert J. Huggett. *Methods and Activities in Elementary School Science.* New York: Dryden Press, 1951.

This book shows simply and clearly how science subject matter is treated in teaching.

Dunfee, Maxine, and Julian Greenlee. *Elementary School Science; Research, Theory and Practice.* Washington, D. C.: National Education Association, 1957.

The Association for Supervision and Curriculum Development published this booklet.

Freeman, Kenneth, and Others. *Helping Children Understand Science.* Philadelphia: John C. Winston Company, 1954.

The principles of good teaching are presented in descriptions of desirable practices.

Hubler, Clark. *Working with Children in Science.* Boston: Houghton Mifflin Company, 1957.

Discusses how to work with children and what science experiences to provide for them.

Kirkendall, Lester A. *Helping Children Understand Sex.* Better Living Booklet for Parents and Teachers. Chicago: Science Research Associates, Inc., 1952.

This pamphlet discusses the role of the school in the sex education of preschool as well as older children.

National Education Association. *Science for Today's Children.* Department of Elementary School Principals. Washington, D. C., 1953.

The school and its principal have a responsibility to help children understand their physical and biological environment and how to control it.

National Society for the Study of Education. *Science Education in American Schools.* Forty-sixth Yearbook, Part I. Chicago: University of Chicago Press, 1947.

Philosophy, methods, material, and evaluation of science teaching in elementary and secondary schools.

Navarra, John G. *The Development of Scientific Concepts in a Young Child — A Case Study.* New York: Bureau of Publications, Teachers College, Columbia University, 1955.

Parents of a high-average boy used a nondirective approach in furthering his scientific concepts from age three years and two months into his sixth year. The father emphasizes that the boy had "ample opportunity to explore, to manipulate, to experiment, and time to re-evaluate and integrate information which he could then apply for himself as a partial answer to his own questions."

Books for Children

Alexander, Anne. *ABC of Cars and Trucks.* Garden City, New York: Doubleday and Company, Inc., 1956.

Colored pictures introduce the bulldozer, X-ray truck, and other cars and trucks along with the letters of the alphabet.

Cook, Bernadine. *The Curious Little Kitten.* New York: Young Scott Books, 1956.

The kitten gets acquainted with the turtle and what he does that is different from a cat.

Daly, Kathleen N. *About the Seashore.* Little Golden Book No. 284. New York: Simon Schuster, Inc., 1957.

Pebbles, shells, crabs, birds, seals, and the occupations of the seashore are pictured and described.

Downer, Mary L. *The Flower.* New York: Young Scott Books, 1955.

A plant, a flower, and new seed grow from a tiny seed and go on growing with the girl and boy who care for the plants.

Ets, Marie Hall. *Play with Me.* New York: The Viking Press, 1955.

A little girl learns that by sitting still and letting animals come is the proper way to play with them.

Gay, Zhenya. *Who Is it?* New York: The Viking Press, 1957.

Questions and footprints lead to animals.

Hall, Katherine. *Barnyard Animals.* Garden City, New York: Garden City Publishing Company, 1950.

Baby animals play and grow on the farm.

Horwich, Frances R., and Reinald Werrenrath Jr. *Growing Things.* A Ding Dong Book. Chicago: Rand McNally and Company, 1954.

A girl puts a sweet potato in a bowl of water and watches a vine grow from it.

Parker, Bertha. *The Golden Book of Science.* New York: Simon and Schuster, Inc., 1956.

Colored pictures make this introductory science book both attractive and useful.

Podendorf, Illa. *The True Book of Weeds and Wild Flowers.* Chicago: Childrens Press, 1955.

This well-illustrated book can be used for identifying commonly found weeds and flowers. *The True Book of Birds We Know* (1954) and other such books are similarly useful.

Webber, Irma E. *Up Above and Down Below.* New York: William R. Scott, Inc., 1953.

Demonstrates how plants grow both below and above the ground.

Zaffo, George J. *The Big Book of Real Building and Wrecking Machines.* New York: Grosset and Dunlap, Inc., 1951.

The series of *Big Books* is notable for the large pictures and brief factual text. It includes books about fire engines (1950), trains (1949), trucks (1950), boats and ships (1951).

Zolotow, Charlotte S. *The Storm Book.* New York: Harper and Brothers, 1952.

Pictures and text describe how a summer storm passes over the country, the city, and the seashore.

Films for Children

Animals and Their Homes. Chicago: Coronet Instructional Films, 1955.

Shows how different kinds of homes are made from materials at hand to protect each kind of animal. 11 minutes, black and white, or color.

Animals Growing Up. Wilmette, Illinois: Encyclopaedia Britannica Films, 1957.

The rapid development of baby animals is shown by a hen with her chickens hatching and ten days later, a mother dog with her puppies, and a cow with her calf. 11 minutes, black and white.

Autumn on the Farm; Spring on the Farm; Summer on the Farm; Winter on the Farm. Wilmette, Illinois: Encyclopaedia Britannica Films, Inc., 1947, 1948.

Incidents and information about the year-round life on the farm are presented slowly. 11 minutes each, sound, color.

City Pets: Fun and Responsibility. Chicago: Coronet Instructional Films, 1954.

A child is responsible for caring for his pet dog and for playing with it. 11 minutes, black and white, or color.

Farmyard Babies. Chicago: Coronet Instructional Films, 1952.

Baby animals are shown on the farm in the spring. 11 minutes, black and white, or color.

How Animals Help Us. Chicago: Coronet Instructional Films, 1954.

In a visit to his grandfather's farm a boy learns how animals help us. 11 minutes, black and white, or color.

How Machines and Tools Help Us. Chicago: Coronet Instructional Films, 1955.

How tools make man's muscles more effective; how natural forces work for us; and how engines and motors work for us. 11 minutes, black and white, or color.

How Plants Help Us. Chicago: Coronet Instructional Films, 1954.

Steve does not like weeds in his father's lawn, but he sees the value of useful plants when he visits his uncle's farm. 11 minutes, black and white, or color.

Spring Is An Adventure. Chicago: Coronet Instructional Films, 1955.

Describes plants and animals that are noticeable in the spring. 11 minutes, black and white, or color.

Water, Water, Everywhere. Chicago: Coronet Instructional Films, 1954.

The cycle of rain and evaporation and the everyday uses of water are learned by the boy hero. 11 minutes, black and white, or color.

We Explore the Beach. Chicago: Coronet Instructional Films, 1955.

Betty and Billy learn many things about birds, seashells, water animals, and the wonders of the sea itself during a walk along the beach. 11 minutes, black and white, or color.

Zoo Babies (Observing Things About Us). Chicago: Coronet Instructional Films, 1955.

Six baby animals grow up with their parents. 11 minutes, black and white, or color.

Zoo Families. Los Angeles: Film Associates of California, 1956.

On a visit to the zoo, a child sees several animal mothers with their babies. 11 minutes, color.

Filmstrips for Children

Autumn Is Here. Detroit, Michigan: The Jam Handy Organization, 1957.

This series of six filmstrips of 22 frames each includes: "Birds Get Ready for Winter," "Animals Get Ready for Winter," "Plants Get Ready for Winter," and "People Get Ready for Winter." Silent, color.

Growing Things. Detroit, Michigan: Jam Handy Organization, 1954.

This series of 7 filmstrips includes: "Plants Grow," "Trees Grow," "Butterflies Grow," "Toads Grow," "Birds Grow," "Rabbits Grow," and "We Grow." Color.

Proper Care of Pets. Wilmette, Illinois: Encyclopaedia Britannica Films, Inc., 1954.

This series includes six filmstrips of 46 frames each: "Gordon's Goldfish," "Kathy's Kitten," "Paul's Puppy," "Peggy's Parakeet," "Roger's Rabbit," and "Terry's Turtle." Silent, color.

10

Understanding Space and Quantity

Closely related to both science and social studies are the kindergarten activities which develop understandings of space and of quantity. Physical geography and mathematics are classified as natural sciences. In fact, mathematics is considered basic to all other sciences. At the same time, social geography is considered one of the social sciences. Whatever their technical classification, the beginnings of geography and of mathematics are important in the kindergarten. Five-year-old children need to understand spatial relations and quantitative relations at their level.

Actually the children are ready for only a few kinds of experiences, yet these are highly important and bear endless repetition in first one setting and then another. Repeating the same setting teaches the setting rather than the attitudes, skills, and understandings desired. Children learn to count, for instance, not by repeating the numbers day after day, but by counting sometimes one thing and sometimes another: how many children are in the group, how many blocks are needed to build the bridge, how many sheep are in the picture, how many times you can bounce the ball.

In helping children develop natural and social science concepts, the teacher is careful to use terms correctly and to encourage the children in doing likewise. Of course the distinctions that each child makes depend on his abilities. One five-year-old child may distinguish hundreds, thousands, and millions; another child will think of them all as big numbers. Yet each child is helped to understand more completely by hearing terms used correctly. When he is ready to cope with distinctions, the correct patterns help him set his mental maps in order.

Not only does the skillful teacher cultivate the habit of using words correctly, she also tries to explain simply, giving the child the main idea in terms he already knows, and in doses he can assimilate. When Tom asks, "What's a dozen?" the teacher says, "Twelve of anything. Twelve pencils are a dozen. Twelve children are a dozen." Later in the day she finds opportunity to reteach the concept: "How many books are there on the library table, Tom? Twelve? I thought there were a dozen." Tom's broad grin and his reply, "There are," show that he knows that a group of twelve books is a dozen books.

When the teacher uses correct terms, she has no expectations that the children will also use them. Many concepts that the teacher uses are far beyond five-year-olds. For instance, the teacher constantly uses time concepts: "We have only ten more minutes. Let's finish what we are doing and put our things away." "The special radio program begins at ten o'clock. Do you know where the hands of the clock will be then?" This use of time concepts gives the children an idea of their importance. Readiness for telling time increases through familiarity with adult usage of it.

UNDERSTANDING SPACE RELATIONS

When they enter kindergarten, five-year-old children suddenly enlarge their life space. Up to that time their experience has been with their home as it is related to their yard and to the homes of near neighbors. But when they enter school they must relate themselves to the new situation of the school, and relate their school to their home and their neighborhood. Encountering these new problems creates new learning opportunities for children. Their teacher helps them learn a method for relating themselves to new situations: identifying landmarks on the way and then using the landmarks as guides in finding the way back. An important objective of the kindergarten program is to help the children get around in their enlarged life space without fear of being lost.

In this modern age of transportation devices, children must relate themselves to trips by automobiles, bus, train, or airplane. They do this in their play with cars, buses, highways and service stations; with tracks, trains, and train stations; and with airplanes and airports. On an actual trip their teacher or their parents guide them to see that cars and trains take people greater distances than they can cover in walking. They can also see that distant mountains are different in color and clarity and that distant figures of people look like tiny dolls.

The child needs help to learn how to avoid getting lost on a car trip. In the car, he is with his teacher, his parents, or his friends. But when he gets out of the car or bus, he needs help in knowing how to take care of himself. One teacher talked to the children before they got out of the bus and said, "We are going to keep together so that no one will get lost. Each of us will hold the hand of one friend as we walk around to the front door of the factory. When we are ready to leave the factory we shall come back here to this green bus. How will we know where to find it?" The children then figured out landmarks which guided them from the parking lot to the factory and then back to the bus.

Boats and ships, airplanes and rockets are part of the environment of the five-year-old. He sees them on television and in motion pictures. He hears them talked about by other children and adults. He plays with boats and ships of all kinds, those he makes and those he has at hand. He plays with airplanes, and he makes airplanes and rockets which, held in his hand, take off, fly around, and land. Through his play he works out relationships: "My airlift gets there before your ferryboat does." "Your car is slow. I get there fast in my plane."

A Place for Everything

The kindergarten teacher helps the children understand the usefulness of the idea: "A place for everything." When a child is running across the room, the teacher reminds him, "We walk inside. Running is for outside." When a voice gets loud, the teacher reminds the children, "Let's use our indoor voices." When the water splashes out of the sink, the teacher may say, "Let's keep the water in the basin." By such reminders the teacher helps the children associate a place with an activity. Such association is basic to understanding geography.

MARIE: Hear my whistle! I just got it. (*Whistles loudly*)

TEACHER: My, what a good whistle. Do you know where we use loud whistles like that?

MARIE: Where?

TEACHER: Whistles are for outside. We would not be able to hear ourselves talk with whistles like that inside. You save it until you are outside.

In this way the teacher encourages a child in a newly found activity and helps her explore the limits of its use. If the teacher had said, "Marie, stop whistling," she would have cut off Marie's activity instead of channeling it toward an appropriate setting, and Marie's frustration might show itself sooner or later in socially undesirable behavior.

Daily the teacher also helps children understand that each object has a place and when they return it to its place they can find it easily when they want it.

JOHN: Where's my jacket?

TEACHER: Where did you hang it?

JOHN: In the closet.

TEACHER: Then that's where it is.

Through such conversations the teacher helps five-year-olds understand and use the idea of "a place for everything and everything in its place."

Meeting Basic Needs

Finding Your Way

Five-year-old children are afraid of getting lost. In social studies they learn to ask help from policemen, people working in a shop, or people living in a house when they are not sure how to find their family or get home. But they need also to learn how to find their way when help is not available. A child who lives in a city or in a village learns to notice landmarks and to use them in retracing his route. A child who lives in open country learns to pick out a distant landmark and then walk directly to it. A child who lives in a wooded area also learns to use landmarks and walk in a straight line until he comes to a stream or highway. Then he goes down the stream or down the highway until he finds someone to help him get home. Since survival may depend on these basic concepts of geography, the teacher makes every effort to help the children understand and use them in realistic play situations.

When the children are in a park or other large wooded area, they learn to pick out some landmark and then go directly to it. At first, the landmark will be some large object, perhaps the little house where the bathrooms are. Later the landmark will be a particular tree not so easily distinguished from other trees. Later, too, the landmark will be approached by winding one's way over and around obstacles. The first easy game becomes more and more realistic at the same time that it remains great fun for the children.

Self-orientation. Science walks are an excellent occasion for helping children understand space relations. Perhaps a walk around the block is planned. The teacher draws a simple map in the sand or on the dirt of the playground. On the map she shows where their principal landmark is located, perhaps a house painted green. Then the children see that the front of the house is visible at one point of their walk, and that the back of the house is visible at another part of their walk. While taking the science walk, they stop in front of the green house and then they go around the block to where they can see the back of the green house. Then they keep on going around the block until they are again in front of the green house. The teacher guides them in understanding the relation between where they are and what they see, as well as the relation between their simple map and where they go. They look again at the map on their return from the science walk and then answer questions and point out the house painted green and where they went in relation to it.

Some five-year-old children profit from direct help with their personal problems of identifying landmarks and getting a mental map of the route between home and school. The kindergarten group plans a science walk going as far as the house of one of the less confident children. Thus the child learns that his teacher and his classmates help him with his problems. His sense of his own importance and his sense of belonging to the group are increased at the same time that he is freed from fear of getting lost en route to or from school.

Finding their way around the school by themselves is also valuable experience to five-year-old children. The teacher plans a trip early in the year to help the children know what makes up a school and where each part is in relation to other parts. "Where is the office of the principal?" "How do we get there?" "Who would like to show us the way?"

Learning the Compass. As the children learn their way around the school, the teacher helps them learn the four directions. "Which is the south door?" "Shall we go out the south door or the north door to get to the auditorium?"

On science walks, too, the teacher helps the children think in terms of north, south, east, and west. She explains the directions in relation to each other, and in relation to the sun and the length and directions of shadows in the morning, at noon, and in the afternoon. In their play area outdoors and in their classroom, the children also learn which side is north, which side is south, which is east, and which is west.

If aerial photographs are available showing the school and the immediate surroundings, the teacher uses them with the children in planning walks and in locating their position on the photograph at different points during the walks. The children also like to try to identify their own houses on the aerial photograph. They discover, too, that landmarks on the photograph are the same as the landmarks they have picked out on their walks.

Interest in Water Put to Use. Five-year-old children have a great interest in water and in water play. The kindergarten teacher capitalizes on this enthusiasm and guides the children to see that a stream of water is a kind of highway. The tiny rivulet crossing the sidewalk carries leaves just the way big rivers carry boats with produce and people.

On a warm sunny day the children thoroughly enjoy making a river which runs downhill to a lake or ocean. The teacher guides them in recognizing islands and bays. Another day she may call attention to tributary streams, or to peninsulas. She helps them see one or two relationships each time they play. For instance, little boats go up and down the little river; big ocean liners and cargo ships go on the ocean carrying big loads to other countries and other big loads back again; at the mouth of the river people are needed to take the big loads from the cargo ships and put them on many little boats going up the river, and the many people working at the mouth of the river are the beginning of a city.

World Concepts

Five-year-old children quickly expand their mental horizons if new ideas are presented clearly and in relation to their current interests. Many children, for instance, easily orient themselves to world concepts. "The earth pulled that right out of my hand," a little kindergarten child said as he dropped a book he was carrying. His teacher had been using some of the excellent geography story books that are now available. She had shown the children pictures of the world ball with large figures of people at different places on the world and had explained that "down" for all of them was toward the center of the ball and "up" was away from it. The children learned that the earth was always pulling everything "down": their feet, anything top-heavy, balls and other things thrown into the air, and even the moon. The simple, accurate concept of the earth's pull helps the kindergarten child understand everyday happenings, and the concept of living on a world ball enlarges its meaning as he grows. Although the teacher may not actually use the word gravitation, she is building an experience background which will invest the word with meaning when it is encountered and explained. Certain children may have heard the word used at home in answering their questions; if so, the teacher should accept it, use it naturally in subsequent conversation, but feel under no compulsion to have all the children add the word to their vocabularies.

Changes Expected in Children

Through their experiences with space relationships the kindergarten children are different at the end of the year from what they were at the beginning. They have improved and added to their attitudes and interests, their skills, and their generalizations. They get around in their enlarged life space with greater sureness. They replace their fears about getting lost with confidence in locating and using landmarks with their new found sense of direction. And they develop new interests in maps and in exploring their neighborhood.

The kindergarten child develops new skills as well as new attitudes through his experiences with space. He makes models of the devices that move him through space, especially boats, trains, cars, airplanes, and rockets, and he plays with them imaginatively and dramatically day after day. He moves himself through the enlarging life space of his community, selecting and using landmarks to reach a destination and to return. He recognizes changes in size and in color with increasing distance. He reads aerial photographs and simple maps, and he likes to draw imagined maps. Indeed he has added materially to his practical skills in relating himself to space.

The kindergarten child continually enlarges his ability to judge distances. Jumping from a level a little higher than those he has jumped from before, he carefully estimates the distance he will go. Selecting materials with which to make a boat or a building, he makes a choice of relative sizes as well as of kinds of materials. Putting away blocks with which he has built a garage, an air control tower, or some other object, he estimates the size of the blocks and space required for each of them. In short, as a child goes into a larger life space and more complex activities, he is constantly relating space measurements to himself. His teacher helps him put into words the concepts which he is developing: "You can jump safely from heights that are less than your own height," "Two of the shorter blocks take as much room as one of the longer blocks," or "That book is too tall for that narrow shelf, isn't it? Does it fit into this shelf?"

The child has enriched his understandings about space relationships and has come to understand in part such concepts as the relative speeds of walking and going by automobile, bus or train, and of travel by train or ship compared with travel by airplane. He understands somewhat, but not as fully as he will later, the basic geographic concepts that water runs downhill bringing produce in small river boats down to the city at the mouth of the river and that the ocean-going ships take the produce to other countries and trade it for different produce which they bring back to the city at the mouth of the river. But of most importance is the child's understanding of the value of landmarks in guiding a person in a straight line or back to safety.

The following list shows outcomes that a kindergarten teacher expected of the children as a result of their experiences in space relationships:

Attitudes

Confidence in going back the way they came
Interest in maps
Interest in exploring the community

Skills

Know a building from the back as well as the front
Select landmarks and use them
Observe changes in size and color with increasing distance

Draw an imagined map
Read an item or two in an aerial photograph
Judge space needed for toys
Judge distances needed for moving oneself through space

Generalizations
Water runs downhill into other streams and into lakes and oceans
Boats carry produce and people
Walking is slower than driving or going by train
Driving is slower than going by airplane
Landmarks make it possible to walk in a straight line and to find the
way back
Our community is a part of a state in a country of the world

UNDERSTANDING QUANTITATIVE RELATIONS

By the time he is five years old the child has made considerable progress
with quantitative relations. Probably during his second year he con-
ceived the idea of himself as a separate entity, different from his mother.
This beginning idea of unity developed further as he differentiated others
in his immediate family. "One — and others" is basic to later ideas about
counting. The ability to consider each unit separately is also basic to
counting. The two-year-old child who is taught to say the counting
words, "one, two, three," may use them while pointing to a single object
or to many more than three objects. At five, some children often need
guidance in counting each item only once.

Counting

The kindergarten teacher provides only simple counting experiences,
but she provides them with endless variation so that the children realize
that counting is an integral part of many, many situations.

Birthdays are probably the most meaningful number experience for
kindergarten children. Being "five years old" has made it possible for
the child to "go to school" as do his older friends and siblings, and has
given him all the attention that his family and friends associate with
birthdays. Certainly the teacher sees that each fifth birthday is mentioned at school. In fact she probably uses the birthday number several
times during the day. She may use a simple finger play:

Is John one year old today? (*One finger up, much shaking of head*)
Is John two years old today? (*Two fingers up, much shaking of head*)
Is John three years old today? (*Three fingers up, much shaking of head*)
Is John four years old today? (*Four fingers up, much shaking of head*)
Is John five years old today? (*Five fingers up, "yes"*)

She may have a picture of a birthday cake or an actual birthday cake for the children to put candles on — five candles. She may show the children a fifth birthday card with an amusing picture as well as a "5" on it and then give the card to the child having the birthday. Or she may find other ways of emphasizing the number five.

As a child learns how people use numbers, he becomes more interested in numbers and in learning how to use them himself. Science walks offer opportunity for noticing that each house has a number on it. Later, at least some of the children will notice that all the house numbers in the block start with the same number. Soon children know the shape of certain numbers and call them by name.

On walks, children observe other uses of numbers. Sometimes signs at the corner of the block show the numbers used by houses in that block. Sometimes signs along streets use numbers (e.g. "3 blocks to Motel"). The teacher is alert to find signs with numbers and talks with the children about them.

In their classroom the children like to make use of numbers. They make signs copying the shapes of numbers or putting them down from memory. They provide their playhouse with a house number. In the sandbox they build streets and put up signs with numbers. In short, they play with using numbers in the ways they have seen the numbers used.

Time

The teacher shares her use of numbers with the group. From time to time she tells the children something about what numbers the hands of the clock point to. When she uses an old alarm clock as a timer, she explains that it will ring after a certain number of minutes (a number less than five). If she uses a thermometer or a barometer, she tells the children how she uses the numbers on the instrument. Whenever she can, the teacher points out situations in which numbers are used and helps the children see the importance of learning more about numbers.

The kindergarten has a calendar with large numbers on it hung at the eye level of the children. When one month is ending and the next month beginning, the teacher introduces an activity which will help the children observe the sequence of days throughout the month. Perhaps the children would like to watch for birds. Each day that a child reports seeing one, he puts a bird seal on the calendar in the right space. Or perhaps in March the children would like to observe the weather to see if March really is a windy month. They may choose some symbol to mark each windy day, each sunny day, and each rainy day. Through such daily use of the calendar the children see its helpfulness and observe the days of the week as well as the sequence of the numbers.

The biological laboratory shows the closeup
detail of the plant or animal.

The kindergarten child makes models of the
devices that move him through space and enlarges
his ability to judge distances.

For children to learn to count, counting must be an integral part of meaningful situations. One bright boy of kindergarten age had an individual scholastic test in which he was asked to say numbers backwards. He had never thought about saying numbers backwards and was unable to comply with the request. However, a week later after he had seen a television program showing rockets blasting off, he was launching tinker toy rockets by saying: "Five, four, three, two, one, zero, blast off!"

When children are playing with blocks, the teacher guides them in seeing that the different sizes of the blocks are related numerically. "How many small blocks does it take to cover the big block?" When children want to divide some space, the teacher helps them measure, using units clearly marked with numbers under ten, or preferably under five.

Not only must counting situations be meaningful, they should also be satisfying ones. If a group of children needs shovels to play in the sandbox, the child who goes and asks for them feels important when he comes back to count the number of children and then returns with that number of shovels. His achievement is satisfying in itself and is also satisfying because it furthers his feeling of belonging to the group.

The teacher sometimes uses numbers in breaking a large group of children into smaller groups. Each child in turn says a number until "three" is said. Then those three children are one group. Thus the children see another way in which numbers are useful.

Numbers as Words

Besides providing meaningful use of numbers, kindergarten teachers provide occasional opportunity for experience with numbers purely as words. Children like the pattern of sounds, and by repeating them become, at length, able to say numbers automatically in correct series. Teachers use a slow and rhythmical pattern in leading the group and provide a correct pattern without interruption. "Everyone misses some at first. It doesn't matter. Just keep on going. One of these times you will get each one right."

Children also enjoy the many rhymes and jingles and finger plays that use numbers. Besides such favorites as "Ten Little Indians," they like:

> One, two, put on my shoe.
> Three, four, close the door.
> Five, six, pick up sticks;
> Seven, eight, lay them straight.
> Nine, ten, do it again.

> One, two, three, four, five,
> I caught a hare alive.

Six, seven, eight, nine, ten,
I let him go again.

Here's a beehive. (*Hold up a fist*)
Where are the bees?
Hiding away where nobody sees.
Soon they'll come creeping
Out of the hive.
Watch now: (*Fingers come out one at a time*)
One, two, three, four, five! Bzzzzzz!

Five little jack-o'-lanterns sitting on a gate. (*Right hand fingers up*)
The first one said, "Ohhhh, it's getting late!"
The second one said, "There are witches in the air."
The third one said, "Pooh, I don't care."
The fourth one said, "Let's run, run, run!"
The fifth one said, "It's just hallowe'en fun!"
Oooooooo went the wind and out went the light,
And five little jack-o'-lanterns jumped out of sight. (*Right hand behind left*)

Practical Experiences in Numbers

In talking with parents, the kindergarten teacher encourages them to share number situations at home with their children. Dial telephones are of great interest to children. They like to dial grandmother's number and the time of day. When they are out for a walk with daddy, they like to call mother at home. By saying the numbers as they are dialed, the adult helps the child learn to recognize the numbers on the dial. Parents should also teach their children to remember their telephone number and to use it if they lose their way.

Any moving of furniture or estimating cost of redecorating brings out the ruler, yardstick, or measuring tape. If children have their own inexpensive dime store measuring tape, they feel they are participating realistically in this activity. They are also delighted participants in family shopping expeditions when they have their own pennies to spend for whatever is important at the moment. With their own money in their own purse or wallet, they learn to make decisions about what should be bought and what can be done without.

Changes Expected in Children

At the end of their kindergarten year, children have different attitudes toward quantitative situations, new skills with numbers, and new ideas of relationships involving numbers. Paralleling and underlying awareness of these quantitative relations is increasing awareness of qualitative relations which prepares them further for moving forward into quantitative relationships.

The five-year-old is also interested in using simple numbers in making comparisons: "I've got a shovel, and you don't." "Gimme one. I don't have any, and you have two." Such comments show readiness for working further with numbers.

Three five-year-old boys who were constructing airplanes out of tinker toys were making qualitative comparisons typical of their age range:

MIKE: See mine! It's bigger than yours.

DAVID: I don't care. Mine is neater.

PHILIP: Mine is big too.

Such comparisons sometimes lead to conflict situations until children learn to verbalize more completely. Yet they are a necessary step toward making more exact and quantitative comparisons later.

Qualitative Concepts in Quantity Relations

The teacher guides the children in making qualitative comparisons. If the school yard has a planting of three trees, she encourages the children to observe them. "Here are three tall trees. Which one of them is tallest? Are the trees taller than we are?" Through such observations the children come to know such comparisons as the following:

small	smaller	smallest	big	bigger	biggest
short	shorter	shortest	far	farther	farthest
wide	wider	widest	low	lower	lowest

The teacher also guides the children in observing contrasts. "You remember that I took a picture of our group last week. Here is the picture. It's really too small for you to see it easily, so I had an enlargement made. Here is the large picture. It's just like the small picture except that every person is larger. I'll put the large and the small pictures here on the table so you can look at them sometime during the day and see how they are alike and how they are different." Through such comparisons the children come to understand such contrasts as the following:

low — high	early — late
short — tall	more — less
small — large	near — far
thin — fat	slow — fast

One kindergarten teacher made a list of attitudes, skills, and generalizations that she thought reasonable to expect of her group of kindergarten children.

In listing these expected outcomes, the kindergarten teacher realized that mathematically minded children may far exceed what can be expected of the average child in the group. With guidance and encouragement certain children may learn many number combinations while other children may have neither skill nor interest in learning combinations. Whatever their abilities with quantitative relations, their teacher knows that each of them will develop quantitative interests and skills as he is ready.

Attitudes

Interested in making comparisons
Interested in where numbers are used
Likes to count how many
Likes to say a few numbers backwards
Likes combining numbers
Likes taking away numbers

Skills

Compares qualitatively
Counts in correct order as far as he goes
Counts each item only once
Knows one or two combinations within five
Recognizes a penny, nickel, and dime

Generalizations

Birthdays are counted
Counting is useful to people
Things of a kind can be counted
Houses and streets are numbered
Every telephone has a number
Money is counted

SITUATIONS FOR DISCUSSION

In the following situations select each course of action that seems desirable to you basing your choices and omissions on the ideas presented in this chapter. Add one or more alternate courses of action.

SITUATION I. On the first science walk of the year you plan to take the children down to the corner and back. In planning the trip with them, you should:

Talk about the corner as a landmark.
Draw a map of the walk.
Show the children the route on an aerial photograph.
Ask the children to estimate how much time is needed for the walk.
Discuss the school as a landmark for the way back.

SITUATION II. On a warm, sunny day you hear the water running and go outside to investigate. Several of the children have found a hose and are well started flooding the sandbox. As the teacher you should:

Turn the water off.

Find out who turned the water on.

Ask the children why the water came out of the hose.

With the children plan a small stream running down from hills.

Let the children enjoy the wet sand as they wish.

SITUATION III. John and Henry have been building bridges out of sticks of wood in the sandbox.

JOHN: My bridge is better than yours.

HENRY: Mine is better.

JOHN: Mine is. I'll hit you.

John hits Henry. As the teacher you should separate the boys and say:

Let's talk about this.

Both your bridges are good.

Bridges are good for something. What is yours good for, John? And yours, Henry?

Together how many bridges have you built?

Why do you think your bridge is better, John?

And Henry, why do you think your bridge is better?

SITUATION IV. A shy and sensitive little boy named Pat comes to you one morning and tells you a secret: "I can count to twenty." As his teacher, you should:

Have him do it right then.

Tell him how pleased you are.

Ask him if he would like to do it for the other children.

Have all the children who count to ten be leaders of little groups which count to ten.

Have him count out the 18 paint brushes needed for the easels.

BIBLIOGRAPHY

Professional Books and Pamphlets

Beatty, Leslie. *Guide to the Teaching of Arithmetic in Kindergarten and Grades 1 and 2.* Bulletin, California State Department of Education, Vol. XVIII, No. 8. Sacramento, California: 1949.

Discusses how to teach small children arithmetic that will function in their everyday lives and in their later lives as adults.

Deans, Edwina. *Arithmetic: Children Use It.* Bulletin #94. Washington: Association for Childhood Education International, 1954.

Describes both the incidental and planned use of number concepts with children from age four through eleven with specific suggestions for making arithmetic functional and interesting.

National Society for the Study of Education. *The Teaching of Arithmetic.* Part II, Fiftieth Yearbook. Chicago: University of Chicago Press, 1951.

Chapter IV, pages 53–75, deals with "Arithmetic for Preschool and Primary Grade Children" and emphasizes the concept of readiness.

Books for Children

QUANTITY

Counting Rhymes. Little Golden Book #12. New York: Simon and Schuster, Inc., 1942.

Included in this book of nursery rhymes are "Two Cats," "One, Two, Three," and "Seven Days of the Week."

Kuskin, Karla. *James and the Rain.* New York: Harper and Brothers, 1957.

"What do you do in the rain?" James asked a cow, two ducks, and eight cats.

Langstaff, John. *Over in the Meadow.* New York: Harcourt, Brace and Co., 1957.

Poems and pictures count to ten as they describe the families of animals.

Schlein, Miriam. *It's About Time.* New York: Young Scott Books, 1955.

This book describes in pictures and in simple words what time is. *Heavy Is a Hippopotamus*, (1954) presents relative concepts about weight as well as numerical concepts which are for more mature children.

Seignoboš¢, Françoise. *Jeanne-Marie Counts Her Sheep.* New York: Charles Scribner's Sons, 1951.

Both illustrations and text encourage children in counting along with Jeanne-Marie.

——. *Springtime for Jeanne-Marie.* New York: Charles Scribner's Sons, 1955.

Slobodkin, E., *The Wonderful Feast.* New York: Lothrop, Lee & Shepard, Co., Inc., 1955.

What is left by a bigger animal is a feast for a smaller one.

Slobodkin, Louis. *Millions, Millions, Millions.* New York: The Vanguard Press, 1955.

Millions of lakes, ducks and drakes — but only one me, and you.

Watson, Nancy D. *When Is Tomorrow?* New York: Alfred A. Knopf, Inc., 1955.

Linda and Peter plan for tomorrow during several days of boating in Maine. *What Is One?* by the same author is an introduction to number concepts.

Zolotow, Charlotte. *Over and Over.* New York: Harper and Brothers, 1957.

On her birthday the little girl wishes that Christmas and each of the other special days of the year will happen again.

SPACE

Broderick, Jessica P. *Find the Way Home.* Chicago: Rand McNally and Company, 1953.

David uses landmarks in finding his way home.

Hengesbaugh, Jane. *I Live in So Many Places.* Chicago: Childrens Press, 1956.

In a house, in a town, in a state, in a country, and in the world.

Schneider, Herman and Nina. *Follow the Sunset.* Garden City, New York: Doubleday and Company, Inc., 1952.

Family activities at sunset are described for different countries around the world.

Slobodkin, Louis. *Dinny and Danny.* New York: The Macmillan Company, 1951.
Danny and his friend the dinosaur rescue each other.

Werner, Jane. *Our World.* Golden Book. New York: Simon and Schuster, Inc., 1955.
The meaning of an island, a volcano, a glacier, and other geographic terms is presented in words and in pictures.

Weisgard, Leonard. *Pelican Here, Pelican There.* New York: Charles Scribner's Sons, 1948.
As the pelican flies here and there he finds different kinds of terrain.

Films for Children

A Day Without Numbers. Detroit, Michigan: Audio-visual Materials Consultation Bureau, Wayne University, 1953.
A disappointing day without numbers makes a boy eager for school and arithmetic. 9 minutes, black and white, or color.

Let's Count. Chicago: Coronet Instructional Films, 1948.
Cardinal numbers up to 17, and some ordinal numbers, are used in counting different kinds of objects in life situations. 10 minutes, sound, black and white, or color.

11

Developing Control of Language

At a round table several kindergarten children were happily cutting and pasting to make valentines. Gail and Martha pasted quietly, each intent on what she was doing. Across the table, Larry was talkative. He had made a remark or two that Ricky, seated next to him, had appreciated. Now he drew the girls into a delightful, humorous conversation.

LARRY: Hello, little girl.

GAIL: Hello, little boy.

LARRY: Hello, little boy.

GAIL: Hi, little girl.

LARRY: Hi, little boy.

GAIL: We aren't Mrs. Saunders.

LARRY: I know your name.

MARTHA: Your name is cuckoo clock.

GAIL: Your name is mama.

MARTHA: Your name is Ricky.

Then all the children chuckled at their jokes about whether they were boys or girls, themselves or someone else.

At her desk nearby, Mrs. Saunders seemed to be paying attention only to what she was writing. Inwardly, she too chuckled over this five-year-old humor and was pleased to be teaching such interesting little people. She felt that the group of children were alert, skillful enough to talk at the same time that they cut and pasted, and sufficiently at home with each other to talk together quietly and humorously. Here, she thought, was evidence that her attention to the social development of children also furthered their control of language. Her acceptance of children as sincere people each trying to do his best at his own level of development created an atmosphere in which children communicated with each other. They learned to express their ideas, listen to the ideas of others, and improve

204

their grammar and diction. Through their functional use of language they developed increasing control of it.

FIVE–YEAR–OLD LANGUAGE AND THOUGHT

Kindergarten children have considerable skill with language. During the three years they have concerned themselves with its use, they have learned more than two thousand words and are still delighted with their sounds. "I threw it up high, into the sky," says a five-year-old and adds, "That rhymes!"

The Growth of Language

Five-year-old children have learned to arrange words into phrases and simple sentences like those used by older people. They are able even to use compound sentences and complex ones on occasion. "I want to see what I can make out of it," Johnny said when his teacher asked about the reflector light he had found in a trash barrel.

Later the children will perfect their use of irregular verbs, unusual verb forms, and colloquial expressions. Now they are apt to make remarks like these:

If you don't have a gun, you can't be shotten.
Where's that book you had? That book you just reading?
Don't take it to parts.
Bomb away!
Can't you watch out where you're going!
I don't got no kitty.

Egocentrism in Language

Very young children are completely egocentric. As they mature, their egocentrism lessens. Piaget, the French psychologist who observed the spontaneous conversation of children, describes their egocentric speech as follows:

"The child does not bother to know to whom he is speaking nor whether he is being listened to. He talks either for himself or for the pleasure of associating anyone who happens to be there with the activity of the moment . . . He does not attempt to place himself at the point of view of his hearer." [1]

Four-year-olds playing with other children carry on egocentric monologues in which they use social expressions just as part of the talking. "You've got a sweater on, I haven't, Mummy said it wasn't cold," is the

---

[1] Jean Piaget. *The Language and Thought of the Child.* New York: H. Wolff Book Manufacturing Company (a Meridian Book), 1955, page 9.

remark of a four-year-old "talking volubly as she works." [2]   She expects no answer, and she receives none.   A five-year-old is like the four-year-old in talking almost exclusively about himself, but is different from him in that he expects others to talk, and he understands what they say.

> "Here is an example.   The children are busy with their drawings, and each one tells the story which his drawing illustrates.   Yet at the same time they are talking about the same subject and pay attention to each other:
>
> > Lev (5;11): 'It begins with Goldylocks.   I'm writing the story of the three bears.   The daddy bear is dead.   Only the daddy was too ill.'
> > Gen (5;11): 'I used to live at Saleve.   I lived in a little house and you had to take the funicular railway to go and buy things.'
> > Geo (6;0): 'I can't do the bear.'
> > Lev: 'I haven't got curls.'
>
> This example is very clear.   It is a conversation, since they are all speaking about the same thing, the class drawing, and yet each is talking for himself, without any attempt at co-operation." [3]

Beginnings of Real Communication

Understanding what other children say constitutes an important step forward in language development.   Such understanding leads on to thinking and communication about the "why and wherefore of phenomena." [4] Five-year-old "arguing consists simply in a clash of affirmations," [5] but seven- and eight-year-old arguing bears "upon logical or causal relations." [6] "Genuine argument and collaboration in abstract thought . . . only intervene after the age of 7," [7] when children "try to improve upon their methods of interchanging ideas and upon their mutual understanding of one another." [8]   Five-year-old understanding of what others say is the gateway to the land of logical thinking where egocentrism is at a minimum.

By the time children are five and a half or six, they have ability to recall common experiences, such as something seen on a study trip.   Furthermore, on occasion, they are able to use language in helping younger children.   For instance, Lev helps a little girl who wants to draw a flag.   He

---

[2] *Ibid.*, page 75.
[3] *Ibid.*, p. 77.
[4] *Ibid.*, p. 45.
[5] *Ibid.*, p. 45.
[6] *Ibid.*, p. 92.
[7] *Ibid.*, p. 90.
[8] *Ibid.*, p. 68.

advises her "first as to color, then as to shape, and finally checks the result.

'Do you know the one my daddy has? — It isn't yours, it's mine. It's red and blue. — It's red, black and white, that's it — yes, first red, white and first black — I've got the right color; I shall take a square — No, you must take two little long things — And now a square — You must let me see if it's right when you've finished' (which she did)." [9]

Role Playing

Kindergarten children enlarge their earlier interest in the roles of people in the family and usually assign roles verbally when they begin family play. "I'm my husband, and you're my wife. Okay?" asks one little girl of her girl friend as they enter the play house. Their teacher realizes that this verbal exploration of the roles they have observed in others helps them move away from egocentrism.

The children explore various channels of imagination so rapidly that they often seem to contradict themselves within a matter of minutes.

"Here, hold this," says Gail thrusting a dish into Martha's hand. But before Martha has time to set the dish down, Gail snatches the dish back saying, "Where's the salad? I need it."

Such inconsistencies are apparent only to the adult. Five-year-olds do not notice them. This behavior of the five-year-old Piaget contrasts with that of the seven-year-old by saying that five-year-old children "adopt successively opinions which, if they were compared, would contradict one another. . . . Up till the age of 7 or 8 children make no effort to stick to one opinion on any given subject." [10]

The teacher recognizes the kindergarten age as the beginning of the transition from egocentrism toward socialized conversation and logical thinking. She therefore makes every effort to encourage each child to express ideas of interest to himself and to listen to and understand what others say.

STIMULATING VERBAL EXPRESSION

During the entire school day, the teacher keeps in mind the importance of stimulating language development. She encourages talking whenever possible and helps the children talk quietly so that they do not interfere with what they are trying to accomplish. "Let's use our indoor voices," she reminds the children instead of demanding, "Let's have it quiet!" "We talk softly while we work," encourages the children to control their

[9] *Ibid.*, p. 79.
[10] *Ibid.*, p. 91,

voices. The teacher knows that children are more comfortable if they have opportunity for talking. Furthermore, when a child has the choice of talking or not, he learns when he needs his attention completely for his work and when he can divide his attention between working and talking.

Craft Activities

When she provides modeling with clay, finger painting, cutting and pasting, and other craft activities children like to do in small groups, the teacher knows that the children develop their control of language and their social skills at the same time that they develop skill in the activity.

A group of six boys were seated at a table where each was enjoying finger painting. From time to time this sensory and satisfying experience led to exchange of glances among the children and to verbal exchange as well as verbal expression.

Bert had one of his fingers glide around the sheet. "He's ice skating," he said with delight. A little later he was half chanting to himself, "Look at the finger go round and round and round," making his finger circle around in time with his speaking.

Presently Jerry stopped to admire his blue fingers. Then he carefully wiped the blue paint off his little finger, saying, "Look at my little finger." Noticing a hair stuck to it he said, "Oh, no!" and plucked it off.

Tommy attempted to elicit interest on the part of his table mates. "There's a little rabbit, folks." A few minutes later he again looked hopefully around as he said, "Hey, there's a bunny rabbit." But no one seemed especially interested in a rabbit at that time.

John was successful in initiating a verbal exchange. With one finger on the paper and the other fingers of that hand carefully extended in mid-air, he said, "I have to make a whirlybird." Erich held both his hands away from his paper for a second so that he could see what John had drawn. "That's no whirlybird," he said. He continued looking at it and then said, "Say, that is a whirlybird."

Philip, the other boy at the table, worked quickly and silently. He finished his painting by making a letter "Z" across the center of it. Then he washed his hands, selected a book, and sat down near his teacher. "Did you notice I got through first?" he asked. "Yes," said his teacher, "and I noticed that you made the sign of the 'Z.' Do you watch 'Zorro' on television?" By working rapidly and silently at the table, Philip was able to have a brief conversation with his teacher.

Sharing Time

The kindergarten teacher provides time regularly for the children to show the other children objects of importance or to tell them about an interesting happening. This sharing time is brief because the teacher knows that children find it difficult to center their attention outside of themselves. To ask them to think about what is of personal interest to other children for as much as fifteen minutes is to ask a great deal of them.

The teacher guides the group by asking stimulating questions and clarifying the discussion. She provides a comfortable and co-operative atmosphere and encourages the timid children to express themselves. The following examples illustrate teacher guidance with the children gathered together on the rug:

TEACHER: How many of us have something to share this morning? Raise your hands if you do so that I may write down your name. (*Writes names.*) Thank you.
Janet, what did you bring?
(*Janet holds up a well-worn teddy bear which now has only one eye.*)

TEACHER: Bring him over here by me where we can all see him.
(*Janet comes shyly over to the teacher.*)

TEACHER: (*Puts an arm around Janet.*) Where did you get your teddy bear?

JANET: Daddy gave it to me.

TEACHER: What happened to his eye?

JANET: It broke off.

TEACHER: (*Realizing that Janet has said a great deal, turns to group.*) How many of us like to sleep with an animal?

This question initiates a discussion in which several children participate by telling about their favorite cuddle toy. When the conversation veers to another topic, the teacher brings the group back to sharing ideas each child has planned to discuss.

TEACHER: What do you want to tell us, Kay?
(*Kay sits silent and uncomfortable. She has forgotten what she was going to say.*)

TEACHER: When you remember, you tell us about it. (*Smiles reassuringly.*)

TEACHER: What do you want to tell us, Jeanie?

JEANIE: One more week till my big papa and little mama come.

TEACHER: Are they your grandparents?
(*Jeanie nods head in agreement.*)

TEACHER: Will they take an airplane?
(*Jeanie nods again.*)
(*Teacher realizes that Jeanie is not able to say anything further.*)

MARIE: I'm going to Bishop.

TEACHER: (*Recognizes Bishop as a mountain town.*) It will be cold there. What will you wear?
(*Marie is silent. She has not thought about what she will wear.*)

TEACHER: (*To the group.*) What do we wear when we go to the snow?

TOMMY: I went to the snow. I wore a snow suit.

TEACHER: Yes, the snow is cold and wet and a snow suit keeps us warm and dry.

ALICE: I'm going to the snow.

TEACHER: When are you going?

ALICE: When my daddy gets home.

TEACHER: Can you bring us back some snow?

ALICE: No.

TEACHER: Why not?
(*Alice is silent.*)

TEACHER: Can anyone tell us why we can't bring snow back from the mountains?

LARRY: It melts.

TEACHER: Yes, it's like a popsicle. You have to eat a popsicle fast. If you don't, it melts and you don't have it.
(*Chris holds up a green tractor with a driver whose head is now missing.*)

TEACHER: What do you have, Chris?

CHRIS: A put put.

TEACHER: Is it a tractor?

CHRIS: It's a put put.

TEACHER: (*To group.*) What do farmers call this?

LARRY: A tractor.

TEACHER: Yes. The driver doesn't have his head any more.

CHRIS: He can't know where he's going.
(*With considerable poise Tony displays a model airplane. He needs a minimum of teacher support.*)

TONY: This is a B-52 jet bomber. Air pushes the jet and it goes through these things.

JOHN: Make it go.

TONY: (*Shakes his head.*) It's only a model.

TEACHER: Where did you get it?

TONY: Over at the toy store. My mother said it cost fifty cents, and she gave fifty cents to the lady. By the time we got out it was raining.

Play House Activities

The wise teacher provides either a corner indoors or a simple outdoor play house as a play center for language development as well as social development. She knows that there boys as well as girls have opportunity for playing the roles they observe in their own homes.

Five-year-old Kathy and Susan and almost-six-year-old Kimmy are using sand for preparing pretend food. Trips to the sand box and to the water faucet are interspersed through the mixing, pouring, and patting activities. From time to time the action and the social relations lead to verbal expression.

KATHY: Guess what? Guess how many pieces of pie? Ten pieces.

KIMMY: We need a piece for daddy.

KATHY: He gets this biga piece.
(*The mixing continues. Presently Susan goes to the sand box and returns with a bowl full of sand.*)

SUSAN: Here, Mom. Here's some more butter. I got some butter.
(*Kathy goes to the water faucet with a dish and returns with it full of water.*)

KATHY: Here's some more butter. I got a pan full.

SUSAN: Put in here. Wait a minute. Have to wait till full.
(*Almost-six-year-old Philip approaches the play house.*)

PHILIP: (*Announces.*) I'm going to play house. (*He looks into the play house and sees the three girls at work.*) Two girls are a half a girl. Three girls are no girl at all. (*Enters the play house and joins the mixing activities.*) May I have some butter?

SUSAN: Yeah.

KIMMY: Sure.

PHILIP: (*Takes a container and goes to the sand box.*) I'm going to make my own butter. Fresh. Homemade.

KATHY: (*Discovers the bowl in which Philip has been mixing.*) Hey, everybody. Here's a whole lot of butter.

PHILIP: (*Returns to play house.*) Hey, that's mine, and I'll show you how much I want, and how much I don't want. (*Puts some into another bowl.*) That's all I want. (*Goes back to sand box.*)

KIMMY: I'm the mother.

SUSAN: I know.

KIMMY: (*To Susan.*) Get the baby's bottle out of the stove and feed the baby.

KATHY: I will.

KIMMY: I said Susan.

SUSAN: I'll feed her. (*She gets the bottle and takes it to the crib.*)

KIMMY: Don't feed her too much.

SUSAN: I won't. (*Some time passes while she feeds the baby.*)

KIMMY: Kathy, did you feed the baby? Go feed the baby.

KATHY: Okay. (*She gets a bottle and takes it to the baby.*)

Using ten as a number for pieces of pie, calling either sand or water "butter," and feeding a baby who has just been fed are typical of the age level. Logical refinements come with an older age. Also typical was the fact that the entire dramatic play was carried on as a group activity, not as a group conversation. Five-year-old Kathy talked in monologues or responded to remarks made by six-year-old Kimmy. Five-year-old Susan showed unusual social ability by responding individually to each of the other children, an ability probably related to early years in an orphanage.

Also noticeable was the difference in social and verbal maturity between five- and six-year-old children. Kimmy as the oldest girl was the mother. Philip, also six years old, managed an entrance into an on-going group and was able to share at the same time that he looked after his own rights. The younger girls played minor roles accepting the leadership of the older children.

The teacher supervised the dramatic play of the children by listening while she carried on her own activities nearby. Having observed the characteristics of the children's play, she knew that her guidance was not apt to be needed by these children in the next few weeks. When they played in the play house, she could work with other children.

Other Dramatic Play

The teacher plans stimulating experiences outside as well as inside the classroom and then provides the materials that children need to reproduce these experiences. After taking the group to the airport, she gets out the sturdy airplanes and the blocks with which to build the hangars, control tower, and other features of the airport. She plans with the children as they begin their block construction, using vivid words and recalling scenes full of action. She encourages the children in using sound effects quietly to show the airplanes warming up, taking off, or crashing in flames. As the play progresses, she takes less part in it. Soon she is an observer who notes which children need further social development and what equipment is in need of repair or of being supplemented with other play materials. From time to time she has opportunity to help a child learn the precise term he wants to use, pronounce a word correctly, enjoy his achievement, or work out some problem in sharing play materials.

Planned Activities

When the teacher develops kindergarten activities in terms of the immediate community, she keeps in mind the need for stimulating verbal expression. One teacher worked out a series of visits to the homes of kindergarten children, including homes of families of various racial, religious, and economic backgrounds. Her description of these visits shows their value for language as well as for social development:

Our visits to the homes were very happy experiences. The mothers in these homes each sent us special invitations through their children. All welcomed us warmly.

The children had many opportunities for planning in connection with these walks. Before each visit we decided on the guests we wanted to ask to go with us, whether or not we would sing some songs on the way, what we would do when we arrived, and who should thank our hostess. Because the thirty-five children often had to crowd into small quarters, there was need to talk about behaving in such a way that everyone would have a pleasant time. Courtesies to small brothers and sisters were considered. Behavior toward pets needed careful thought.

At their homes we often sang songs, recited poems and finger plays together, or listened to a record. . . .

The trips gave the children many shared experiences to talk about. Vocabulary was increased and ideas were clarified. The children's ability to plan improved through having several opportunities to arrange similar experiences. A few of the children whose homes were visited had been shy and had not volunteered in class. In each case after a child's home was visited he seemed more at ease with the group and began to share his outside experiences in school. [11]

Actual visits to homes accomplished in this kindergarten what could not have been accomplished by merely talking about homes. In general, verbal expression is stimulated by experience in real situations. Realizing this, the kindergarten teacher provides a program of experiences, not of empty words.

Other Verbal Stimulation

In kindergartens that have a small number of children for each adult, a child has opportunity to dictate a story, letter, report, or even a song. He enjoys having the complete attention of an appreciative adult who is recording what he says. His words take on importance, and he is stimulated to gain further opportunities for dictation.

Philip, a verbal almost-six-year-old, reported at length about his hamster while a mother assistant recorded it:

Hamster is the nicest pet that I have ever had. And it does not bite very much any more. I talk with him. I pick him up. I take him places in the jeep. I take hamster everywhere. I have taken hamster to both corners and back. Hamster enjoys the scenery and I take him places. I just love to go also. Say, someday, I might take hamster and go around the block, and then he would have the best scenery he has ever had before.

[11] "Outline of Abilities to Be Developed," Volume I, Kindergarten through Grade Three. San Diego, California: Office of the Superintendent of Schools, San Diego County, 1952. Pages 18–19.

A few minutes later he enlarged his report:

> Now more about hamster. Well, I take hamster and talk with him every day. I pick him up. His fur is soft. He tickles me by his whiskers. I lay down on the floor and put hamster on my stomach. He comes up. With his whiskers he tickles me in my face.

Philip also enjoyed recording little songs. He was interested in the recording process and the fact that lines on a paper could show the sounds that both he and the piano made. Here are the words of one of the songs he had written down for him: "Run, chug. I'm a little tug."

Mother Assistants Promote Language Development

A kindergarten boy, after two weeks of school, was talking with his older brother:

> BROTHER: How do you like kindergarten, Bill?
>
> BILL: I never get a chance to talk.
>
> BROTHER: You talked the other day when you took your balloon pump to school.
>
> BILL: Yes, I know. But I never get a chance to talk with the teacher.

Bill, as one of thirty-five children, of course had had no opportunity for a real conversation with his teacher. At recess time and during certain activities, he talked briefly with other children. But, with only one adult in his room, he had no opportunity to communicate his thoughts about how to make a submarine or what the building crew were doing on the new house he saw daily on his way to school.

Bill's teacher also felt the need for conversation with him. She realized that the ideas he expressed in his drawings were beyond those he had yet expressed in words. But two and one half hours of teacher time divided among thirty-five children gave each child only a few minutes of attention. How could she have time for listening to individual children?

Recognizing the need that a child has for communicating his feelings and ideas to a sympathetic adult, many kindergartens now have qualified mother assistants. These people are especially helpful both to gifted children and to those who are timid in establishing relationships with other people. Strengthening their rapport with mothers and teacher helps them feel at home in the kindergarten. As for gifted children, if they do not have adults with whom to talk, they are continuously frustrated in their attempts to communicate their more mature thoughts and are motivated to express only immature verbalizations. As Piaget points out, "Questions of causality are confined to conversations between children and adults, or to those between younger and older children." [12] How-

---

[12] Jean Piaget. *The Language and Thought of the Child*, page 45.

ever, if adults are present in sufficient numbers, children have opportunity for logical conversations.

Some children are planting seeds in their garden. A mother assistant is at hand to help if needed.

> PHILIP: I make one hole and put in two seeds. Do you know why?
>
> MOTHER ASSISTANT: Why?
>
> PHILIP: In case it doesn't grow.
>
> MOTHER ASSISTANT: (*Nods understandingly.*) That's a very good idea.

Children need experience with more mature conversation in the same way that they need to listen to music more mature than that which they can produce. With older companions and grown-ups, children preview conversations which they will be able later to use with companions their own age.

The child who picks up a stick and finds a friendly little sow bug underneath is delighted to share his discovery with the nearest person. If that person is another child, he gets brief attention and probably the suggestion, "Step on it." But if that person is an adult, the child gets sustained attention and additional information about sow bugs. "Let's watch it," says the mother assistant. Then the child and the adult watch the sow bug and communicate their observations to each other. The adult stays as long as the child needs her and talks with her.

In the spontaneous dramatic situations of the kindergarten, mother assistants play another role that the teacher seldom has time for, the role of helping five-and-one-half-year-old children cope with their fears by playing them out in drama. One group of children, for instance, wanted to play "Haunted House" but none of them was willing to be the person coming into the scary situation. They solved their problem by having a mother assistant play the difficult role.

> SANDY: Let's play "Haunted House."
>
> JANE: I'll do the squeaks.
>
> MIKE: I'll be a ghost.
>
> SANDY: No, I'll be a ghost.
>
> JANE: I don't want to get scared. Who gets scared?
>
> SANDY: I'll get mother. She'll help. (*Runs over to mother.*) Mrs. Long! Mrs. Long! We need you.
>
> MRS. LONG: What is it, Sandy?
>
> SANDY: We want you to come to the haunted house.
>
> MRS. LONG: Oh, I'd like to! Are the ghosts all ready?
>
> SANDY: No.

MRS. LONG: You help them get ready, and then come and get me. I'll be waiting right here.
(*When the haunts are ready, Mrs. Long comes into the haunted play house.*)

MRS. LONG: Well, here I am in the haunted house. I wonder where the haunts are.
(*The children scream and make weird noises.*)

MRS. LONG: Say, there really are some good haunts here.
(*The children make more weird noises.*)

MRS. LONG: I wonder what will happen next.
(*A light flashes on.*)

MRS. LONG: Ah, an eerie light moving around. I like an eerie light. I hope it comes on again.
(*The light flashes again. More screams.*)

MRS. LONG: Good, there's that eerie light again, and some more weird noises. I think they are supposed to frighten me. I'll act scared now. Eeeeeeeek! Let me out of here! This place is full of ghosts and eerie lights. Eeeeeeeeeeeeeeeeek!
(*Runs out of the play house.*)

The children ran after Mrs. Long making their ghost noises and laughing. The mother assistant helped the children cope with their fears and at the same time helped them enlarge their vocabularies.

HELPING CHILDREN SOLVE PROBLEMS WITH WORDS

An important objective of kindergarten teachers is to help the children work out solutions to their problems with words as well as with action. The child who finds it difficult to unscrew a lid learns to ask another child to help him. The child who snatches something he wants out of the hands of another child learns to talk about what he wants. The child who runs away from the mess of a spilled paint can, learns instead to say, "I'm sorry I spilled it," and help clean it up. Whenever a child has such problems, his teacher is ready to guide him in working out a solution verbally.

The large sandbox in Miss Reynolds' kindergarten play area was alive with boys and girls all busily at work. Suddenly two of the boys were standing with one large truck between them. Each was pulling on the truck and saying over and over, "It's mine" and "I got it first!" When one fist swung out, Miss Reynolds was there to catch it. Then with an arm around each of the boys she said calmly, "Let's talk about it." First she helped them think about what each was interested in doing. Then she helped them work out a plan whereby each would do what he wanted to do and use the truck in one large co-operative enterprise. A few minutes later Miss Reynolds handled a similar conflict. "Let's talk it over," she said calmly again. But this time she helped the children by finding another truck so that each of them could continue what he was doing on his own. Another conflict situation she handled quickly by diverting one of the children, whom she knew was not sufficiently mature to discuss the problem at that time, and by saying to the other child, "Let's talk about what happened."

Miss Reynolds with her "Let's talk about it" was helping the children experience the value of language in solving their own problems. In each case she helped them work out a solution appropriate to the level of their verbal as well as social and emotional maturity. She felt that her guidance was important in helping children solve their social problems with such words as:

Let's talk about it.
Let's share.
I'll take turns with you.
When is it my turn?
I'm sorry I hurt you.

HELPING CHILDREN LISTEN TO OTHERS

The importance of learning to listen is pointed out by Piaget, who notes that children "talk only for themselves, without listening to anyone else," [13] when they are together in the school playroom. Thus the kindergarten teacher is challenged to help the children to listen to each other, as well as to her. She keeps large group activities to a minimum knowing that each child has little opportunity to talk when the number of children in the group is large. She has the children come together in a single group only to make plans for the entire group (e.g. to plan for a study trip), to show others prized possessions or tell them about experiences, to solve a problem of general interest (e.g. to work with less noise), to enjoy a story, a moving picture or other short program, and to discuss or evaluate an activity of the entire group.

Group Discussions

In these group discussions the teacher avoids relaying messages and insists that children communicate directly with each other. During planning, sharing, and evaluation periods she avoids repeating what is said, and by her attentive listening she encourages each child to listen and to speak audibly when it is his turn.

TEACHER: Who else has something to share?
   (*Becky holds up a brown paper bag bulging at various points.*)
TEACHER: Give us a hint about what it is.

[13] *Ibid.*, page 61.

BECKY: Something that's got legs.

JANE: Doll?

BOBBY: Teddy bear?
(*Becky nods.*)

TEACHER: (*Smiles knowingly.*) Maybe we should stand up for a minute and stretch.

In this conversation the teacher was one member of the group. When she spoke she recognized what others had said and carried the conversation forward to a new point. A less skillful teacher might have been tempted to announce or emphasize Bobby's discovery, but this teacher had confidence in the listening ability of the children and in Bobby's ability to communicate his ideas himself. Such teacher confidence is essential to developing optimal control of language on the part of the children.

Games

The teacher can use the telephone game to help children appreciate the importance of listening carefully and talking clearly.

The children seat themselves in a circle.

TEACHER: I'm going to say something slowly and very clearly. I'll say it to Chris. Then he will say it to the person next to him very clearly. When it is your turn, listen carefully. Then say what you hear to the person sitting next to you. Be sure to say it clearly so that the right message will get through. Now I'll think of something really good to say.
(*Whispers to Chris:* "It rained yesterday.")
(*To Chris.*) Did you hear me?
(*Chris nods.*)

TEACHER: Tell Tommy next to you what you heard. Say it clearly.

When the message has gone around the circle, the class traces the changes in the message en route. Thus the children participate in an experience demonstrating the importance of listening to receive the message correctly and of speaking clearly in order to be understood.

Mechanical Reproductions

Besides games like "Telephone" and "Echo," the teacher can use sound moving pictures and radio or television programs to help children learn to listen to what others say. In one city school system, the kindergartens have a weekly radio broadcast especially prepared for five-year-old children. "The Sounds of the City" was a program which presented a boy driving around the city in a car driven by his father. From the sounds that he heard, the boy knew, for instance, when his father started the engine, stopped before entering the highway, passed an oil well pump, pulled out of the way of a fire engine, and stopped finally at home. This program stimulated the children to listen and to interpret what they heard.

IMPROVING SPEECH

The Teacher's Example

The kindergarten teacher constantly encourages the children to express themselves, knowing that such expression gradually takes on the speech forms that the children hear daily. She is careful to have her own voice a desirable pattern and talks quietly, clearly, and correctly at all times. Especially with children who lisp, stutter, or have other difficulty in speaking she bends down to their level to listen calmly and attentively to what each has to say.

Difficult Sounds

Five-year-old children are old enough to profit from direct attention to difficult sounds, the past and perfect tenses of irregular verbs, and other difficult expressions. Practice of accepted language forms, however, should be group, not individual, and should be so brief as to be incidental to the on-going group activity. The teacher acquaints herself with exactly how to pronounce the sounds children are most apt to be slow in learning, namely *s*, *z*, *f*, *v*, *l*, *r*, and *th*. She learns brief games, finger plays, and stories to use whenever she is with a group which includes children who have not yet mastered some of these sounds. She is prepared to use these aids to good speech at any appropriate time.

Games

One teacher, newly aware of the sounds children are slow in learning, went over her repertoire of games enlarging many of them with speech practice. For instance, she improved the game in which a hidden object is to be discovered by chosen lookers each of whom must return to his place commenting on his discovery. She made a point of selecting an object which would give the children practice with a difficult sound, perhaps a thimble. Then she said, "I'm going to hide a silver thimble where you can easily see it. When you do see it, go quietly back to your place and tell us, 'I see the thimble.' Let's all practice what we are going to say. . . ."

The teacher also learned additional games for helping children develop correct language sounds. When a teacher of a higher grade told her about the guessing game in which children guess what object the person who is "It" is thinking about by asking, "Is that the thing you are thinking about?" she simplified the game. She put a few objects on a table, carefully selecting them according to their initial sounds — a box, a feather, a vase, a letter, a ribbon — and had the children name them with her as she put them there. The question to be asked of "It" she simplified to "Is —— the thing?"

The teacher collected finger plays and action rhymes which emphasized the sounds that children are slow in learning. When children were coming together into a large group, she sometimes used, for instance:

A little ball, (*Makes a ball with thumb and forefinger of one hand.*)
A bigger ball, (*Makes a ball with thumbs and forefingers of both hands.*)
A great big ball I see. (*Makes a ball with both arms.*)
Now let us count the balls we have:
One, two, three. (*Makes each of the balls again.*)

The speech-minded teacher learns how to help children make the difficult sounds. When she tells the children the story of Sunny Snake, she takes a few minutes to help them say his name correctly.

The teacher gets out her flannel board and pictures.

"We have a story about Sunny Snake today. He goes happily down the road and meets several of his friends — the rooster, the goose, the horse, and finally his best friend, Sally Snake.

Since you are going to help me with the story, you will want to say their names the way they like them to be said. 'Sunny' starts with the snake sound. 'S—unny.' When we make the 's' sound, our teeth are closed, and we can feel the air blowing out through them. . . ."

The teacher guides the children to make the "s" sound correctly and to blend it into the word "Sunny" and then "Snake." She follows this brief practice immediately by the story. Since individual children have turns in selecting the next friend to place on the flannel board and since all the children in the group together say such lines as "Sunny Snake meets the goose," the story becomes a favorite one. Each time the children ask for it, the teacher helps them with the "snake sound." They learn to hear and say it at the beginning of words (e.g. snake, Sally), later in the middle (e.g. goose, horse), and then at the end of words (e.g. meets, starts).

Whenever she is helping the children hear and say difficult sounds, the teacher is careful to pronounce the words clearly and without exaggeration. Sometimes she shows the children the difference between good and poor pronunciation. Always she makes practice in articulation a delightful, friendly game which she plays briefly with a group of children. Invariably the game ends with self-satisfaction on the part of the children in response to an appreciative smile on the part of the teacher. "That was a good try," she may comment, and each child feels that his teacher helps him say what he wants to say.

Speech Situations

Sometimes the teacher guides the children in thinking about how to talk in different situations. For instance, reading *Let's Play House* [14] leads to talk about how to order groceries or call the doctor by means of the telephone. In one kindergarten the story led to installation of a telephone in the play house and discussion about how to use the telephone.

TEACHER: Isn't it nice to have a telephone in our play house now. Has anyone used the telephone? What did you use it for, Marie?

MARIE: Daddy called.

TEACHER: What did you say when you started talking with him?

MARIE: Hello, Daddy.

TEACHER: Whenever we start talking on the telephone, we always say, "Hello." When we finish talking, what do we say?

JERRY: Goodbye.

TEACHER: Do we talk more softly or loudly than we usually do?

JANET: Softly.

TOM: Loudly.

TEACHER: Well, we really talk the way we usually do, but we have to talk clearly. Suppose we were ordering from the store and said, "Send me some spoons." If the store man did not understand, he might send some "prunes."

Working with Bilingual Children

Fortunate is the kindergarten group which has one or more children from homes that have a different culture. The teacher uses the songs and stories of their culture to enrich the experiences of the other children as well as to help the children of different background feel that they are valued. She realizes that the child with limited experience in the English language will have to go through successive stages of language development at his own rate and that he needs time for hearing the new language accurately and practicing it. She realizes, too, that the child is under great pressure to communicate with her and with the other children. She tries to lessen the pressure by making him feel that she and the children are helpful and understanding friends who enjoy him as he is and have confidence in his ability to learn their language. As she notes his progress she praises both him and the group:

TEACHER: Have you noticed that Ramon is using many new words? I've heard some of you helping him learn what we call different things in our language. You are good teachers, and Ramon is a good student.

[14] Lois Lenski. *Let's Play House.* New York: Oxford University Press, 1956.

The teacher of a bilingual child encourages the other children to learn a few of the commonly used phrases in the other language.[15] This activity helps the child of different background to appreciate his own language. It also helps the other children to develop an awareness of other languages and the desirability of learning to speak them.

DEVELOPMENTS EXPECTED IN CHILDREN'S LANGUAGE

At the first of the school year the teacher should learn quickly what language control the group of children have developed and what their needs are. She therefore observes the children both in a group and at play. Then she is ready to plan activities which will give them the opportunity they need for further language development. At the end of the kindergarten year, the teacher again observes the children as she did at the first of the year. The changes she notices show the progress they have made under her guidance. She can take satisfaction in their progress and can plan for even more effectual guidance in future teaching.

The teacher gets acquainted first by noticing which children:

    remain silent without regard for others near them
    go on talking whether someone is listening or not
    take turns in talking
    communicate with others

The children who are repeatedly silent and isolated from the group the teacher helps to feel at home in their new situation and in expressing their reactions to it. The children who talk without communicating the teacher guides into co-operative play, dramatic play, and other activities that make necessary a functional use of language. By providing a permissive atmosphere in which each child feels free to express himself verbally, the teacher encourages all the children to communicate with her and with others.

Observations When She Leads the Group

On occasions when she is the center of the group, the teacher probably finds that most of the children are able to talk effectively and courteously. She studies them further as she guides them in planning, problem-solving, and evaluation discussions. How do the children participate in the group discussion? Which children

listen and nod approval?	disagree?
repeat what is said?	suggest a new idea?
add to what is said?	

[15] I. A. Richards, M. H. Ilsey and Christine Gibson. *French Self-Taught with Pictures.* New York: Pocket Books, Inc., 1950. Similar books are available in other languages, giving the basic words of the language.

While observing how the children participate in a group discussion, the teacher uses the discussions to help the children become more effective members of the group. "Do you think we can do that?" she asks the nodding child and waits for a verbal answer. "Should we use the light color or the dark one?" she asks the repeater, encouraging him to express a point of view. "You think that will not work. What do you think will work?" she asks the disagreeing child. Always she listens carefully to what is said and is ready to point out how a suggestion helps move the group thinking forward: "That's a good idea." Her permissive attitude encourages each child to express his views, and her fairness and respect make each child feel that his ideas are understood and appreciated.

Later in the year the teacher uses the group discussion for more detailed observation of the children. Displaying an action picture she notices how the children solve the problem of interpreting it. She observes which children:

name objects in the picture
describe action portrayed
describe qualities portrayed
interpret the scene in terms of feelings
interpret the scene in terms of relationships
tell a story about what is happening
point out a moral

With other pictured and real situations, the teacher guides the children who name objects into describing action and quality, and the children who describe into interpreting the scene more fully. In short, she helps the children have a richer experience and express their reactions to it more vividly and completely.

When the teacher introduces new words to the group of children, she again has opportunity for observing them in more detail. She notices which children:

do not evidence understanding of the word
repeat the word
give the use of the object named (e.g. "Cut. Cut.")
describe the object (e.g. "The red one.")
define the word, classifying it correctly (e.g. "A B-52 is an airplane.")

By observing how the children react to her introduction of a new word, the teacher can present other new words more effectively and select stories and other materials especially appropriate for her group of children.

Observations of Children's Play

The teacher also observes the children individually as they talk and work on projects of their own selection. The free play situation, especially when mother assistants or other adults are available to help the children on request, gives the teacher opportunity to observe the language development of individual children as well as their social development as it is revealed through conversations that the child initiates. She observes the activities which the child does without talking, and with talking. The latter are activities through which he can enlarge his co-operative play. For instance, the child who hammers while he talks is the one the teacher thinks of when the play house group asks, "Please help us put up a picture." She may say, "You know, Johnny can help you with that. He is skillful in hammering nails."

The teacher observes the conversational situations in which the child talks freely with others. Does he talk with:

another child
a group of children
an adult
a group of children and adults

The teacher helps each child broaden his scope of conversation. The children who talk primarily with adults need guidance in finding children of similar or complementary interests and abilities with whom to work and talk. The children who talk more freely with children than with adults profit especially from opportunity to know a mother assistant who can give them attention over a period of time as they develop verbal ease and competence.

When a child talks with her, the teacher has opportunity to observe the extent to which he can express relationships. She observes whether as a general rule he uses:

words and phrases
simple sentences
compound subjects or predicates
conjunctions other than "and"
sentences with more than one dependent clause

She recognizes the verbally gifted child and the less verbal child by the way each relates ideas.

One other type of observation aids the teacher in understanding and helping the individual child. Listening to his conversation she observes which sounds are not yet pronounced clearly. She makes a note of these in the child's record folder, reports them to a speech therapist if one is available, and plans group activities which help the child hear and use the correct sounds. She knows that she can at least provide a clear-cut pattern in her own voice and encourage the child to talk frequently.

THE TEACHER EVALUATES HER WORK THROUGH THE PUPIL'S LANGUAGE

Teachers wonder how effective they are in their teaching. "How am I doing?" the teacher asks herself. Daily the children answer her, and the wise teacher listens to what they say.

Evidence of Co-operation

One teacher who was especially concerned that the children in her room learn to be considerate of each other and work together co-operatively listened for evidence of co-operation. When the group planned how to go from their room to the auditorium at the other end of the building, the teacher asked for helpers to open and close each of the doors as the group passed through. Every child raised his hand to volunteer for helping the group in this way. At the end of the program in the auditorium, the teacher noticed that one of the little girls stepped over to the teacher in charge to say, "Thank you." During the outdoor period, when two boys both wanted the same garden tool, she heard Philip say, "Why don't you talk things over instead of fighting them?" She heard two other gardeners work out a trade: "You can have my hoe and I'll take your rake." When the children were putting on their wraps at the end of the morning, she saw several children helping each other. "Denny's hat," said a boy picking up the hat off the floor and taking it to Denny across the room.

This teacher also heard conversations which showed that individual children were finding it difficult to be co-operative. She heard Mary, an only child, addressed by one of her companions in the play house: "Mary, you don't share. You always want to be the mother." Later the teacher planned situations in which an only child had further opportunities for taking turns and sharing. She wanted Mary to develop more mature behavior like that of Brian playing checkers:

RICKY: You always get the first shot.

BRIAN: Okay. You get the first shot.

(Ricky made the first move in the game.)

A teacher who had emphasized good work habits was pleased to overhear the conversation between two children using the colored slides and the viewer:

JERRY: Hey, aren't you going to look at these.

(Marie shakes her head.)

JERRY: Okay. You got to put them back.

(Helps Marie put them back.)

At pick-up time she heard John urge Tommy to complete the puzzle he had started before he took a book he wanted to look at:

JOHN: Put your puzzle together.
(*Tommy continues looking at the book.*)
JOHN: Go fix the puzzle.
(*Tommy closes the book and goes back to his puzzle.*)
MARY: (*To Tommy.*) Are you ready? (*Notices that the puzzle is only started.*) No, you're not. (*Starts to help Tommy complete the puzzle.*)
TOMMY: No, no. I don't need no help. (*Turns his back toward Mary and works busily at the puzzle.*)

Evidence of Reading Level

A teacher who had taught second grade before teaching kindergarten used the conversation of the children as a means for helping her find books at their level. The day she read them a second-grade favorite, *Five Chinese Brothers,* [16] she wondered whether her selection was appropriate for kindergarten children. Although the children enjoyed it along with her, she noticed that she, rather than the children, was thinking the story amusing. A few days later she heard one of the children telling a visitor the story. Pointing to the cover illustration of the five brothers, he said, "Three pigtails. Pigtail. Pigtail." Then he stopped, apparently bothered by the fact that there were other pigtails besides those to which he had pointed. As he turned the pages and commented on each of them, she realized how little the story had meant to him. She thought that the complexity of the story made it difficult for the children to follow when one of the older girls in the group also tried to explain the story to the visitor: "He swallowed the whole sea. He didn't drown 'cause at the end he was all bandaged up." Her decision to remove the book came when she observed two other children reject the book. One child glanced through a few pages and said, "Aw, this is for grown-ups." The other child looked at the book a few minutes later. He put it aside saying, "This one's no good," and then he picked up *Indian, Indian* [17] saying, "This is nice."

Identifying Gifted Children

The teacher who listens to children is able to identify not only the child who needs help with his problems but also the child who has unusual talents. She notices the child who comes to her with his evaluative remarks and evidence of reasoning in advance of his chronological years:

PHILIP: You know the valentine I made? with the hearts?
TEACHER: Yes, Philip.

[16] Claire Bishop and Kurt Wiese. *Five Chinese Brothers.* Eau Claire, Wisconsin: E. M. Hale and Co., 1938.
[17] Charlotte Zolotow. *Indian, Indian.* New York: Simon and Schuster, 1952.

PHILIP: (*Confidingly.*) No one else used a white one. They used big red ones and pink ones.

Walking up the aisle in the auditorium, Erich ran his hand over the number plates on the arm of each end seat.

ERICH: The numbers tell which row you're in.

This ability to observe and report evaluatively is characteristic of a kindergarten child with intelligence above the average in the group.

The teacher recognized Peter's unusual ability when she heard him tell his mother what he had seen that day at the airport. With gestures he reported the numerical order in which the engines of a four-motor plane were fired:

"And, Mommy, we saw an airplane land. A big one, a four-engine.

"And, Mommy, they don't do counting like we do on the engine for the airplanes. They go '3—4—' and then '2—1—'. And see, Mom, they go '3' (*Makes a circle in the air with his finger*), and when the finger goes around that means start engine number 3.

"And, Mommy, first the prop starts going slow. Then it goes fast —

"Then, Mommy, when he goes like this (*Makes a circle in the air*), engine number 4 starting. And then he goes like this, engine number 2 starting. Then when he goes like this, engine number 1 starting.

"See, Mom, they go 3, 4, 2, 1. (*Uses his fingers to show her.*) That's the way they go."

Peter's teacher thought that observing and reporting accurately an unusual use of numbers was more than a five-year-old is expected to do. She made a note of this incident in Peter's folder and reported it as evidence that Peter should have an enriched school program.

SITUATIONS FOR DISCUSSION

In the following situations select each course of action that seems desirable to you basing your choices and omissions on the ideas presented in this chapter. Add one or more alternate courses of action.

SITUATION I. Philip is fishing with a magnet for a hook and is catching paper fish that have a paper-clip mouth. "I caught a fis!" he exclaims excitedly. As the teacher, you should:

Exclaim, "A fish! Philip caught a fish!"

Tell Philip, "The word is 'fish.' Can you say 'fish'?"

Say nothing about fish.

Provide practice with "sh" words.

Show the children how to make the "sh" sound.

SITUATION II. Edgar's family has just moved to your community. Edgar speaks with a noticeable accent. As his teacher, you should:

Pay no attention to Edgar's speech.

Identify the sounds which Edgar pronounces differently.

Have Edgar participate in speech exercises.

Listen attentively to whatever he has to say.

Guide him to work with children who talk clearly and fluently.

SITUATION III. At the sink Teddy is quietly washing the clay off his hands. When Stephen finishes with his clay, he strides over to the sink saying, "I want to wash my hands." He pushes Teddy aside and starts washing his hands. Teddy stands where he was pushed for a minute. Then he puts his wet hands on Stephen's neck. Stephen whirls around with his wet fists ready for a fight. As the teacher you should:

Call across the room, "Boys!"

Let the boys solve their own problem.

Walk over to the sink and stand quietly next to the boys.

Say, "Boys, let's talk about it."

Reprimand Stephen for his aggressiveness.

SITUATION IV. In observing the language development of the children in your kindergarten, you should:

Study the group as a whole.

Observe each child individually.

Tell the children you are going to watch how they talk.

Show the children a picture that some, but not all, of the children have studied.

Observe language apart from social development.

BIBLIOGRAPHY

Professional Books and Pamphlets

Beasley, Jane. *Slow to Talk*. New York: Bureau of Publications, Teachers College, Columbia University, 1956.

The teacher aids the child in his speech problem by accepting him, giving him needed attention, and being companionable with him.

Chapin, Amy B., and Ruth Lundin. *Your Child's Speech and How to Improve It*. Cleveland, Ohio: Western Reserve University Press, 1949.

This pamphlet discusses how to detect incorrect sounds and how to teach a young child correct speech.

Dawson, Mildred A. *Language Teaching in Grades One and Two*. Yonkers-on-Hudson, New York: World Book Company, 1957.

This booklet about language teaching in grades one and two has many practical suggestions for helping children develop in oral communication, speech and choral speaking as well as in written expression and correct usage.

Durland, Francis. *Creative Dramatics for Children*. Yellow Springs, Ohio: Antioch Press, 1952.

This book describes a "working method that is clear, concise and interesting" for teachers to use in developing creative dramatics with children.

Herrick, Virgil, and Leland B. Jacobs, editors. *Children and the Language Arts*. Englewood Cliffs, New Jersey: Prentice-Hall, Inc., 1955.

Language arts are taught within a broad setting. This book has many suggestions for improved teaching.

The teacher can use telephone games to help
children appreciate the importance of listening
carefully and talking clearly.

Through the art of telling a story the teacher
guides the children into the world of written words,
into the storehouse of literature, and into the
role of a good listener in the audience.

Monroe, Marion. *Growing into Reading.* Chicago: Scott, Foresman and Company, 1951.

This book describes various levels of language abilities and their relation to how a child is able to express himself.

National Council of Teachers of English. *Factors That Influence Language Growth.* Chicago, 1953.

This pamphlet discusses and gives a bibliography of research findings regarding factors that influence language growth: personal equipment; home, school, and community influences.

Scott, Louise B., and J. J. Thompson. *Talking Time for Speech Correction and Speech Improvement.* St. Louis: Webster Publishing Company, 1951.

The group situation in the classroom can be used to help normal children with speech problems. This book gives practical teaching helps for each special sound.

Slade, Peter. *Child Drama.* New York: The Philosophical Library, Inc., 1955.

Drama aids education and can be carried out even in classrooms with limited space.

Strickland, Ruth G. *Language Arts in the Elementary School.* Boston: D. C. Heath and Company, 1957.

This book traces speaking, listening, reading, and writing through the elementary school curriculum, and points out that language is used throughout the kindergarten day.

Ward, Winifred. *Playmaking with Children.* New York: Appleton-Century-Crofts Co., Inc., 1957.

Creative dramatics enriches the program from kindergarten through junior high school.

Current Books for Children

Brown, Margaret Wise. *Where Have You Been?* New York: The Thomas Y. Crowell Company, 1952.

Children enjoy repeating the delightful short rhymes asking each animal "Where have you been?"

De Angeli, Marguerite. *Book of Nursery and Mother Goose Rhymes.* New York: Doubleday and Company, Inc., 1954.

Both at home and at school children like to say nursery rhymes.

Hamilton, Elizabeth. *P–Zoo.* New York: Coward-McCann, Inc., 1945.

An interesting "p" story which helps children distinguish "p" from "ph."

Jaszi, Jean. *Everybody Has Two Eyes.* New York: Lothrop, Lee & Shepard Co., Inc., 1956.

"A cloud only goes
When the wind blows," and other short, action poems.

Lenski, Lois. *I Like Winter.* New York: Oxford University Press, 1950.

Simple verses tell the pleasures of the winter season. *Now It's Fall* (1948), *On a Summer Day* (1953), and *Spring Is Here* (1945) also have verses that are fun for five-year-olds to say.

McGinley, Phyllis. *All Around the Town.* Philadelphia: J. B. Lippincott Company, 1948.

Children like to repeat some of these "A, B, C" rhymes about the city.

12

Introducing Children to Literature

ATTITUDES AND SKILLS TO BE DEVELOPED

In every land, children flock around the storyteller and are thrilled with his words. In the United States, this interest in hearing a story is the basis for developing other literary interests: interest in books, in pictures, in words, and in reading. Interest in stories, under the guidance of the kindergarten teacher, leads to skill in reading in the years ahead. Immediately interest in stories is expanded into certain attitudes and skills. One kindergarten teacher thought it important for the children in her group to develop the following attitudes and skills:

Attitudes

Likes to handle books
Considers books important and prized objects
Likes to look at pictures for their story
Likes to listen to simple realistic stories
Likes to listen to simple imaginative stories
Enjoys words and rhymes
Enjoys dramatic action

Skills

Listens attentively
Reacts to the story with sympathetic feeling
Asks questions about what is shown in the pictures
Makes comments relative to the story
Asks questions about what he does not understand
Distinguishes fact from fancy

To develop such attitudes and skills is a challenge to every kindergarten teacher. She learns to select stories appropriate to the children in her group. She continues to improve her ability as a storyteller and to further her skill in helping children enjoy stories. Above all she enjoys

230

children's stories herself. Her enthusiasms for them carry over into her storytelling and are reflected in the enthusiasms of the children.

The teacher discusses children's books with the librarians at school and at the public library. With the librarians she identifies the books especially appropriate for five-year-old children and for the individual children in her group. The teacher arranges for the librarian to come and tell stories to the children from time to time, and she talks with her about stories used most successfully with the children. She also encourages the librarian in having story hours for the children to enjoy at the library — a picture book hour that includes such books as *Mike's House* by Julia L. Sauer.[1]

Talking with other teachers, the kindergarten teacher extends her acquaintance with books for five-year-old children. As the teachers talk about books, they find that each of them has her own taste in children's books. A book that is a favorite of one teacher may be of interest to another — or it may not. Each teacher selects those books which she will enjoy using with her group of children. By borrowing books judiciously from other teachers, she is able to provide a wider selection of stories for her children.

BOOKS AVAILABLE

Stories Containing Factual Information

Authors of books for young children have provided many informational books which enrich the child's understanding of the social and the physical world around him. For instance, Nina Schneider has described the science aspects of the community in *While Susie Sleeps*,[2] and Charlotte S. Zolotow has written *The Storm Book*,[3] a description of how a summer storm passes over the country, city, and seashore. Books of this kind tie in with experiences that the teacher plans to help children develop basic attitudes, skills, and generalizations in social studies, science, and other phases of the curriculum. Current examples of such books are listed in the brief bibliographies at the ends of chapters VI through XV. The teacher is familiar with such books and reads them to the children whenever the stories seem appropriate.

Stories for Enjoyment

Besides the books which are primarily informational, there are many picture books of stories and poetry which take the five-year-old child into the world of literature at his level. He responds to the well-chosen words

[1] Sauer, Julia L. *Mike's House*. New York: The Viking Press, 1954.
[2] Schneider, Nina. *While Susie Sleeps*. New York: William R. Scott, Inc., 1948.
[3] Zolotow, Charlotte S. *The Storm Book*. New York: Harper and Brothers, 1952.

and repeats the recurring phrases of these books. He identifies with the heroes who move quickly through a succession of brief events to something of a climax situation. The stories describe what he would do and see if he were there, and the illustrations help him imagine the situations. Through the stories, he gains understanding about himself and his relations to other people. He develops sympathy and a sense of humor.

The kindergarten child who learns to enjoy stories and to appreciate the treasures found in books is getting ready to learn how to read and enjoy stories on his own. The teacher who has introduced her kindergarten children to the literary storehouse available to them has opened to them a new world which will enrich their lives for years to come.

The kindergarten child is ready for realistic stories and for the pretend stories related to his five-year-old experiences. These stories are so numerous that it is easy to stay within their limits and to leave to later years stories which introduce extended difficulties, stories with intense or prolonged emotion, or stories which emphasize negative aspects of living. "He'll get you if you don't watch out," has no place in the kindergarten, nor has *Hansel and Gretel*. Fairy stories and folk tales of that type are for older children.

SELECTING APPROPRIATE BOOKS

For the first of the kindergarten year the teacher selects picture-book stories that are short, happy, realistic, and familiar. *A Walk in the City* by Rosemary and Richard Dawson[4] and *Two for a Walk* by Nathan Kravetz[5] are such books for urban children. As the year progresses, the teacher introduces realistic books which show other children in both urban and rural settings, in mountains and on plains, inland and by the ocean, in the United States and in other countries, now and in earlier times. Through simple imaginative books the teacher emphasizes the difference between reality and imagination. She helps the children see the humor in books and the beauty of their wording. She introduces them to poetry and rhyme. By the end of the kindergarten year many children are enjoying longer stories, fanciful as well as realistic stories, descriptive as well as action stories, stories with more incidents, and an occasional continued story. But in the entire year, the teacher has presented only stories with a high proportion of happiness and with only a happy ending.

Of course for school use, the teacher selects only cloth-bound books which can be handled by many children. Good stories published inexpensively can be obtained in suitable bindings.

[4] Dawson, Rosemary and Richard. *A Walk in the City*. New York 17: The Viking Press, 1950.
[5] Kravetz, Nathan. *Two for a Walk*. New York: Oxford University Press, 1954.

Books Suitable to Abilities and Tastes

In selecting books to read to the children, the kindergarten teacher chooses a wide menu that will fit in with the interests of each child at one or more points. Her primary objective is to have the children enjoy books. She has books with familiar stories and poems for them. *Mother Goose* [6] in well-illustrated form helps them think of stories and books as something at school as well as at home. She has a fund of realistic books to further their understanding and appreciation of their everyday living. She also has fantasy books to stretch their imaginations and books of poetry to introduce them to rhymes and the beauty of language.

Should a teacher select large books with large illustrations or books of more usual size? Certainly the size and appropriateness of illustrations are important factors in selecting books. Publishers recognize the need for books with pictures large enough for a large group of children to see as the teacher reads to them. Many such books are now available. Mostly, of course, the teacher uses well-illustrated books of usual size to read to a small group of children. The children who have just worked hard to put out a "pretend" fire are delighted to rest while their teacher reads *Five Little Firemen* [7] to them. One or two of the children probably will want to rest further while rereading the book through its pictures.

Should a teacher select books in terms of the children's needs, or in terms of her own interests? The kindergarten year provides ample time for reading both. A wise teacher does not stop with choosing books that the children enjoy. She also selects the children's books which she enjoys most. She knows that the books she likes are the books that she reads especially well. Her pleasure in the books makes them a pleasure to the children. Fortunate are the children whose teacher shares her selection and interpretation of books with them, at the same time pointing out that these are her views and that other people have other favorites and think of books differently. The children know the personality of their teacher through her selection of books and her comments about them.

Books with Suitable Illustrations

The large picture books enjoyed in nursery school, for instance, *Baby Farm Animals* [8] and *Pussy Willow*,[9] also have their place in kindergarten. For some of the children they are familiar friends, but for many of the

---

[6] De Angeli, Marguerite. *Book of Nursery and Mother Goose Rhymes.* New York: Doubleday and Company, Inc., 1954.

[7] Brown, Margaret Wise, and Hurd, Edith Thacher. *Five Little Firemen.* Golden Book 64. New York: Simon and Schuster, Inc., 1948.

[8] *Baby Farm Animals.* Big and Giant Golden Books 481. New York: Simon and Schuster, Inc., 1953.

[9] Brown, Margaret Wise. *Pussy Willow.* Big and Giant Golden Books 564. New York: Simon and Schuster, Inc., 1952.

children they are an excellent introduction to the reading of pictures and to the use of books. Also attractive to five-year-olds is a book like *Bears*.[10] This book by Ruth Krauss is illustrated so that a child is delighted and surprised when he finds yet another bear peeking out from a familiar picture. The child who enjoys finding the bears is furthering his visual readiness for reading.

Of course, the kindergarten teacher selects books with pictures appropriate to the story. *The Village Tree* [11] by Taro Yashima for instance is a story worked out in words and in pictures to show the out-of-school fun of children in a Japanese village. Its bright colors and pictured activities appeal to children. Text, illustrations, and format are unified. Such a volume is one that a group of children can enjoy when they look at the pictures as the teacher reads it. Later, children enjoy the book individually, rereading the story as they turn the pages and look at each picture. The interesting details of the pictures add to the main idea expressed in them.

When author and artist are two different people, the pictures and the text may not be completely in accord. Erroneous details in illustrations puzzle some children. The alert teacher can often change the text to fit in with the pictures. Occasionally it is interesting to the more mature and observant child to detect an inconsistency which he can discuss with his teacher.

Over the years picture books have been constantly improved. One factor in this improvement is the annual award of the Caldecott Medal to the illustrator of the most distinguished picture book for children. Recent awards have included books appropriate for kindergarten and have been made as follows:

1948	*White Snow, Bright Snow*	Duvoisin
1949	*The Big Snow*	Hader
1950	*Song of the Swallows*	Politi
1951	*The Egg Tree*	Milhous
1952	*Finders Keepers*	Mordvinoff
1953	*The Biggest Bear*	Ward
1954	*Madeline's Rescue*	Bemelmans
1955	*Cinderella*	Brown
1956	*Frog Went A-Courtin'*	Langstaff
1957	*A Tree Is Nice*	Udry
1958	*Time of Wonder*	McCloskey
1959	*Chanticleer and the Fox*	Cooney

[10] Krauss, Ruth. *Bears*. New York: Harper and Brothers, 1948.
[11] Yashima, Taro. *The Village Tree*. The Viking Press, 1953. See also, *Crow Boy*. The Viking Press.

Suitable Kinds of Stories

Realistic Stories

Stories that recount experiences well within the living that the five-year-old children already know are the stories read at the first of the kindergarten year. The five-year-old child is still much concerned with understanding what goes on in his own living. He is also ready to explore deviations from it as they are presented in story form. But he enjoys coming back to the realistic story that gives him perspective on his own experience, the realistic story that puts into words the pleasant feelings which he has felt, the realistic story like *Two for a Walk* [12] that enlarges his experience by extending his living into new surroundings interpreted in his own terms, and the realistic story that gives him experiences he would like to have.

Through such a book as *Papa Small*,[13] the children have an opportunity to see familiar activities at home and to organize those activities from the point of view of what father does. The clear-cut and simple drawings in this book by Lois Lenski are excellent reminders of similar situations in their own homes. Reading about the Small family, the child gains perspective about his own family and its activities.

Little Red Nose [14] puts into words the feeling of spring. A child hearing the story on a spring day learns about another child who feels the way he does. Furthermore, the story sharpens his awareness of various facets and activities of spring. The positive tone of the story gives the child pleasant feelings which enrich his pleasure in the season. A story such as *Little Red Nose* enlarges and enhances the child's emotional reaction to a familiar situation.

Not every child can live in Capistrano in California nor can most children be there to see the return of the swallows in the spring. But every child can have that experience vicariously through the lovely story and illustrations that Leo Politi has put into *The Song of the Swallows*.[15] And the teacher reading the book to a group of mature kindergarten children can talk with them about the birds they see returning to their own community in the spring. How they feel about the birds as harbingers of spring is enriched by knowing how the boy in the story felt about the swallows when they returned.

---

[12] Kravetz, Nathan. *Two for a Walk, op. cit.*
[13] Lenski, Lois. *Papa Small.* New York: Oxford University Press, 1951.
[14] Schlein, Miriam. *Little Red Nose.* New York: Abelard-Schuman, 1955.
[15] Politi, Leo. *The Song of the Swallows.* New York: Charles Scribner's Sons, 1949.

The child who lives in the city can learn about rural life through books like *A Year on the Farm* [16] by Lucy Sprague Mitchell or *Wake Up, Farm!* [17] by Alvin Tresselt, and the child who lives in the country can learn about city life through books like *A Year in the City* [18] by Lucy Sprague Mitchell and *Wake Up, City!* [19] by Alvin Tresselt. Stories set in different parts of the country help the child broaden his experience when the stories are told simply and in terms of everyday living. After children are at home with their own kind of living, they need and enjoy the stimulation of stories in different settings. The teacher makes such stories available to the children and talks with them about the relation of the story activities to their own.

The realistic story can also bring children experiences which they would like to have, but are not apt to have. With the hero of Jerrold Beim's *Country Fireman,* [20] they can get the fireman to put out the fire and save the little old lady's house. Or with Seth they can help at the *Country Garage,* [21] and do their part in spite of the annoyance of another boy. As the children enjoy realistic stories with well-developed plots they broaden their experience by exploring other roles vicariously.

Realistic stories are a means for helping children assimilate their experiences and gain perspective on them. When something strange happens to a child, he often needs help in coping with it. Real help comes from hearing a story about someone else who had such an experience, who felt the way he felt, and who got command of the situation in one way or another. He identifies with the hero and solves his problem as the hero solves his.

When Philip got into the automatic elevator at the department store, the doors closed automatically before his father could get into the elevator with him. He was all by himself. Automatically the elevator carried him to the next floor; automatically the doors opened. Philip ran through the opening and found himself in a strange place. His father was not

[16] Mitchell, Lucy Sprague. *A Year on the Farm.* Golden Book 37. New York: Simon and Schuster, Inc., 1947.
[17] Tresselt, Alvin. *Wake Up, Farm!* New York: Lothrop, Lee and Shepard Co., Inc., 1955.
[18] Mitchell, Lucy Sprague. *A Year in the City.* Golden Book 48. New York: Simon and Schuster, Inc., 1948.
[19] Tresselt, Alvin. *Wake Up, City!* New York: Lothrop, Lee and Shepard Co., Inc., 1957.
[20] Beim, Jerrold. *Country Fireman.* New York: William Morrow and Company, Inc., 1948.
[21] Beim, Jerrold. *Country Garage.* New York: William Morrow and Company, Inc., 1952.

there. No one he knew was in sight. He felt very much alone, and he began to cry.

When his father found Philip a few minutes later, he comforted him and started telling him about how Philip ran the automatic elevator all by himself. Recounting the story with Philip as the hero and emphasizing its positive aspects, they re-enacted it, Daddy going with Philip in the elevator. Hearing his story helped Philip put his experience into perspective.

That night Philip told his own story, not about what had happened, but about what he was going to do when he grew up. "You know what? When I grow up, I'm going to be an elevator operator." By telling this story, Philip gained control of the elevator with the doors that closed automatically. He thus assimilated the experience and slept that night without troubled dreams. A few days later at school when *A Day Downtown with Daddy* [22] was read to him, he recalled his experience in the elevator and retold the story by which he put it into perspective. "I'm going to chop the motor out," he concluded.

Imaginative Stories

Much fiction takes adults out of their everyday lives into delightful situations where their problems of living are solved with the hero. Imaginative stories do this for children. The problem of finding playmates is understandable to any child. He therefore enjoys *Me and the Bears* [23] by Robert Bright. He also likes to think about being big, so he enjoys *The Giant Story* [24] by Beatrice S. de Regniers. With Horton, the dependable elephant created by Theodor Seuss Geisel in *Horton Hatches the Egg*,[25] he experiences the rewards of doing what he says he will do and with Maxie,[26] the Austrian dachshund, the rewards of always doing one's best. Constructive stories of this kind reinforce the five-year-old's interest in doing what is expected of him.

Kindergarten children also like to think a little about the role of being "bad." With Virginia Lee Burton's *Choo Choo*,[27] the children explore

---

[22] Horwich, Frances R., and Werrenrath, Reinald, Jr. *A Day Downtown with Daddy*. Chicago: Rand McNally and Company, 1953.

[23] Bright, Robert. *Me and the Bears*. New York: Doubleday and Company, Inc., 1951.

[24] de Regniers, Beatrice S. *The Giant Story*. New York: Harper and Brothers, 1953.

[25] Geisel, Theodor Seuss. *Horton Hatches the Egg*. Eau Claire, Wisconsin: E. M. Hale and Company, 1940.

[26] Kahl, Virginia. *Maxie*. New York: Charles Scribner's Sons, 1956.

[27] Burton, Virginia Lee. *Choo Choo*. Boston, Massachusetts: Houghton Mifflin Company, 1937.

the possibility of running away dramatically on their own and find out that it is better to help other people with the daily routine. Or they explore the idea of not co-operating. With Marie Hall Ets' *Little Old Automobile*[28] they imagine what might happen if they did not stop what they were told to. Vicarious exploration of what not to do is safer than real exploration.

The more abstract-minded and imaginative kindergarten child enjoys thinking, for instance, "What if I and my kitty went for a ride in a submarine?" Delightedly such a child goes off on a submarine trip wearing the seaweed hat devised by Slobodkin[29] or thinks with Du Bois[30] about how the lion got its characteristics. But most of the children like their imaginings tied more closely to reality. "What if I had seventeen balloons?" is an intriguing question for a five-year-old as he imagines himself in the situation that Jane Thayer describes in *Sandy and the Seventeen Balloons.*[31]

Stories and poems about animals help a child establish satisfying relationships with animals and with people. For instance, the nursery rhyme "I Love Little Kitty" makes it quite clear that "if I don't hurt her, she'll do me no harm." *Another Day*[32] by Marie Hall Ets points out the value of a child's laughter. The child in the story watches each of the forest animals show what he can do. But when the child laughs the animals all agree that that is the best trick of all. Such a story helps the child who hears it feel important. The child who hears *Little Wild Horse*[33] by Hetty Burlingame Beatty identifies with the little boy who tames the wild horse until it chooses to stay with him. He gains a feeling of achievement and is happy in reading the story. With *Timid Timothy*,[34] the cat, a child learns the desirability of appearing big and brave and not looking for trouble.

Sometimes children with problems of family relationships get help from animal stories more readily than they can from direct and realistic stories. A child who finds it difficult to think about the relationship of a

[28] Ets, Marie Hall. *Little Old Automobile.* New York: The Viking Press, 1948.
[29] Slobodkin, Louis. *The Seaweed Hat.* New York: The Macmillan Company, 1947.
[30] Du Bois, William P. *Lion.* New York: The Viking Press, 1956.
[31] Thayer, Jane. *Sandy and the Seventeen Balloons.* New York: William Morrow and Company, 1955.
[32] Ets, Marie Hall. *Another Day.* New York: The Viking Press, 1953.
[33] Beatty, Hetty Burlingame. *Little Wild Horse.* Boston: Houghton Mifflin Company, 1949.
[34] Williams, Gweneira. *Timid Timothy.* Eau Claire, Wisconsin: E. M. Hale and Co., 1954.

child to his parents can nevertheless think about animals and their relationships. Reading *Babar's Cousin: That Rascal Arthur* [35] for instance can be an intermediary step in learning that parents love their children at the same time that they scold them for wrongdoing.

Stories for Holidays and Special Occasions

Margot Austin has written and illustrated *William's Shadow*,[36] a pleasant story for ground-hog day early in February. *Over and Over* [37] the teacher uses so that the children learn the sequence of major holidays throughout the year. With the more mature children, she reads *The Columbus Story* [38] and *The Thanksgiving Story* [39] to further their interest in what happened years ago. Such books help children come to know the legends that have been handed down from generation to generation.

TELLING A STORY

Telling a story is a unique experience. The way a person tells a story depends on the teller, the listeners, and the situation. A person tells a story today; tomorrow he tells the same story but somehow it is a little different.

Preparing the Children

The kindergarten teacher prepares the children for a story by questions which stimulate them to recall their experiences: "Have any of you had a day downtown with Daddy during the vacation?" "How did you and your Daddy go downtown, Jane?" "Did you go into a tall building and ride in an elevator?" After the children have talked about their experiences, the teacher feels when they are ready to listen to the story: "Let's read about Bobby and Joan, and their day downtown with their Daddy. Are you ready to listen quietly to the story?" As she reads the story, the teacher ties it into the experiences the children have mentioned, usually with an understanding smile and, occasionally, with a comment if the child's attention is wandering, or an accepting response if the child offers an addition.

[35] de Brunhoff, Laurent. *Babar's Cousin: That Rascal Arthur.* New York: Random House, 1948.
[36] Austin, Margot. *William's Shadow.* New York: E. P. Dutton & Company, Inc., 1954.
[37] Zolotow, Charlotte. *Over and Over.* New York: Harper and Brothers, 1957.
[38] Dalgliesh, Alice. *The Columbus Story.* New York: Charles Scribner's Sons, 1955.
[39] Dalgliesh, Alice. *The Thanksgiving Story.* New York: Charles Scribner's Sons, 1954.

Children's Participation

When a story is a good story and is well told, the children live it. The story is a unique experience for them right then. Children like to help in telling the story. If the duck is talking they like to help him say "Quack." When the storyteller can handle the group of children, letting them participate in the storytelling, the story is more alive for listeners and teller.

Children also like to participate by asking questions of the storyteller; their questions help them assimilate the story. These questions enrich the story experience if they are interpreted as an addition, not an interruption to the story. For instance:

> (*The teacher is reading an action story.*)
>
> MARVIN: I did that once.
>
> TEACHER: Did you? Then you know how the boy in the story felt. Let's listen now while we read about what he does next.

Or:

> (*Teacher is reading* The Big Snow [40] *by Berta and Elmer Hader.*)
>
> JANE: Mother is going to buy me a new dress.
>
> TEACHER: We'll talk about it later. Now we're reading a story about how the animals get food in the winter. All fall they found seeds and nuts and other food on the ground and in the trees. Now the snow has come and covered up the food. What do you think the animals will do now?

Most stories have points at which questions can be asked. When the story is finished is also an appropriate time for questions. The questions show what the children got out of the story. The storyteller may alter the story a bit the next time she tells it, perhaps clarifying the plot, pointing out a bit of humor, or emphasizing something of interest to the children.

The Good Storyteller

The beginning kindergarten teacher is usually a good storyteller with her adult friends. Realizing that the children are also her friends, she soon becomes a good storyteller with them. She is interested in telling the story and feels that her audience wants to hear it. Attention to several factors helps the teacher with the story:

1. A few minutes ahead of time, she quietly goes from group to group telling the children to finish their activity and put away their things. "Then we shall have our story."

2. She arranges the setting for the story group and gets out any properties needed. For instance, she arranges pictures in the order of their showing.

[40] Hader, Berta H., and Elmer. *The Big Snow.* New York: The Macmillan Company, 1948.

3. When the children gather for the story, she helps each one make himself comfortable in a place where he will be able to see the pictures.

4. She talks quietly and directly to the children, perhaps asking questions to start them thinking about experiences of their own like those mentioned in the story. Perhaps she uses key words from the story, especially words which may be new to the children.

5. She reminds the children they are going to listen: "Are you ready now to listen to the story?"

6. She places pictures so they can be easily seen. A picture book, for instance, she holds out to the side, tipped slightly forward and at the eye level of the children. She turns the book slowly and continuously so that each child has a turn to see each picture and so that she can glance at the words. She moves the book so that the eyes of the children follow it from left to right.

7. She is so familiar with the story that she gives her attention to the children rather than to the book.

8. After the story, she lets the children comment spontaneously. She avoids asking general questions such as "How did you like the story?"

Each teacher works out her own arrangements about letting the children comment and ask questions at story time. Ideas that teachers have found useful include:

Let the children ask questions and talk in turn before the reading starts. This gives the children a chance to express themselves before listening. It also establishes rapport between the children and the teacher, a necessary prelude to enjoying the story.

At nodal points in the story, ask a question of the children or give them opportunity to participate in the sound effects of the story. After a minute of relaxation, ask the children if they are ready to listen to the rest of the story. When they are quiet, continue in a clear, distinct, but not loud voice.

Follow the story with a brief talking time and encourage the children to hold their questions and comments until the story is finished. Toward the end of the school year the children use less time during the story and more time following the story for expressing their reactions.

Storytelling is an art that the kindergarten teacher practices and studies continuously. She listens to expert storytellers and picks up ideas to try in her own storytelling. Some days she feels that the children thoroughly enjoyed the stories, and she tries to figure out factors in her success, for instance:

Knowing the needs and interests of the children and selecting books according to those needs and interests.

Observing the postures, movements, and facial expressions of children as cues to their liking that part of the story. If they like it, she spins it out a bit. If they do not like it, she moves quickly on to the next part.

Bringing out the feeling qualities of the story through the sounds of the words and through her posture, movements, and facial expressions.

Four Ways to Tell a Story

The kindergarten teacher develops competence in four types of story-telling:

Reading the story as the author wrote it, showing the pictures in the book.

Telling the story in her own words, showing the pictures in the book.

Telling the story, using the flannel board, other pictures, or puppets.

Telling the story traditionally, dramatizing the action.

The way in which the teacher chooses to tell the story depends on the story, her familiarity with it, and her liking for it. Some stories have words so well chosen that the teacher likes to use them as the author set them down. Descriptive stories are usually better read verbatim unless the storyteller is unusually expert in her choice of words. Action stories lend themselves more easily to telling and to dramatizing. As a teacher becomes practiced in telling stories, she is more free to choose sometimes one presentation and sometimes another.

Although such childhood classics as *The Three Bears*, *The Three Little Pigs*,[41] and *The Billy Goats Gruff*,[42] are available in book form, they are much better told to children just as they have always been told without the distraction of turning pages. Looking directly at the children the teacher creates for them the story. When she moves, her movement is part of the story. Both she and the children are enthralled with the telling of it.

When recounting the story, the teacher has opportunity for voice modulation, dramatic action, and pantomime. In *The Three Bears* she is Father Bear with a deep voice moving heavily and sitting heavily. Then she is Mother Bear with a middle-range voice. And she is Little Bear with a high voice moving lightly and easily. The teacher makes the characters of the three bears and of Goldilocks so interesting that the children want to do the characterizations too. She makes the dramatic action so alive that the children want to participate. Soon the children are creating their own version of *The Three Bears*. Traditional storytelling is a bridge into creative dramatics.

Experienced kindergarten teachers distinguish between reading and telling stories and pride themselves on skill in both techniques. This distinction is recognized by older children as they develop ability to read but not by kindergarten children, who are aware only of their mutual feel-

[41] *Children's Books.* 4 volumes illustrated by Leslie L. Brooke. New York: Frederick Warne and Company, Inc. Volume I has the story of *The Three Little Pigs.* Volume II has the story of *The Three Bears.*

[42] Hutchinson, Veronica S. *Chimney Corner Stories.* New York: Minton, Balch and Company, 1925.

ing with the teacher throughout the story experience. "Tell us a story," they say and are happy to have the teacher read or tell a story as she wishes so long as the book does not interfere with the rapport between them and their teacher.

Over the years the kindergarten teacher becomes increasingly skillful as a storyteller. She knows the stories and she knows how to show the pictures. She gives most of her attention to watching the children's reactions and to timing her telling or reading in accordance with their feelings. And she enjoys telling the story. She knows she is delighting the children, and she has that satisfying and exciting feeling of an actress who plays her scene well.

HELPING CHILDREN WITH STORIES

All children enjoy stories. Whether they also develop desirable skills and attitudes depends on their teacher. She asks questions which help five-year-old children relate the story to other experiences. She leads the children into appreciation of words: the sound of a word, words that rhyme, picturesque phrases, and words that convey humor. Her appreciation of these words encourages the children to imitate her expressions of appreciation as well as to express their own. She enriches the story so that it is a real experience in itself and stimulates the children to express their feelings and ideas about it, both in words and in art media.

The teacher helps the children understand stories and to reject or otherwise handle stories which are not appropriate to their age level and interests. She helps the children think of books as important treasures to be enjoyed at home, at school, and at the library. She also helps the children understand what it means to be a member of a group listening to a story. Under her guidance they develop beginning concepts of democracy. They learn to enjoy the story in such a way that those around them also enjoy it. Through the art of telling a story the teacher guides the children into the world of written words, into the storehouse of literature, and into the role of the good listener in the audience.

RELATING STORIES TO OTHER PARTS OF THE PROGRAM

Many stories are delightful in themselves, but most stories are enhanced by having the teacher relate them to other stories and to other experiences that the children have at home or in kindergarten. Children who are of high intelligence make many associations for themselves, but most children are helped by having relationships pointed out.

The Wonderful Feast [43] by Esphyr Slobodkina is a story of a feast for a

[43] Slobodkina, Esphyr. The Wonderful Feast. New York: Lothrop, Lee & Shepard Co., Inc., 1955.

horse that was shared by successively smaller animals until the ant feasted on the final grain. The story takes on increased meaning for five-year-old children whose science experiences help them understand that the size of an animal is one factor in how much an animal eats and that each child eats less than his mother or his father.

Yen Liang's stories about *Dee Dee* [44,45] point out that a boy in China and a boy in the United States are basically alike in what they do although the way they are dressed and other details of their living may differ. This theme is an important social studies concept to be developed with children as they widen their peer relationships in school. *Plenty to Watch,* [46] *The Village Tree,* [47] and *Crow Boy* [48] by Taro Yashima and *Little Leo* [49] by Leo Politi are other stories that can be used to emphasize the same theme. The wise teacher capitalizes on the interest in such stories to lead the children into activities with ships that carry goods between Dee Dee's country and Tommy's country, activities with dolls from other lands, [50] and activities with children whose parents have come from other countries.

With moving picture and filmstrip equipment easily available, the teacher can use it in varying her presentation of a story. For instance, *Golden Book Filmstrips* [51] can be used either to introduce or enrich the Golden Book stories they present. As more stories are presented in films, they will acquaint children with stories and will help them relate audio-visual materials to storybooks.

The kindergarten teacher uses records to enhance stories. Rhymes from *Mother Goose* are available in clearly sung records. [52] Certain companies also produce records in relation to favorite children's stories. For instance, *The Carrot Seed* [53] by Ruth Krauss is the basis for *The Carrot Seed* record [54] which enlarges musically on the simple story presented in book form. Using both the record and the book enables the kindergarten teacher to give the children a fuller and richer experience.

[44] Liang, Yen. *Dee Dee's Birthday.* New York: Oxford University Press, 1952.
[45] Liang, Yen. *Tommy and Dee Dee.* New York: Oxford University Press, 1953.
[46] Yashima, Mitsu and Taro. *Plenty to Watch.* New York: The Viking Press, Inc., 1954.
[47] Yashima, Taro. *The Village Tree.* New York: The Viking Press, Inc., 1953.
[48] Yashima, Taro. *Crow Boy.* New York: The Viking Press, Inc., 1955.
[49] Politi, Leo. *Little Leo.* New York: Charles Scribner's Sons, 1951.
[50] Horwich, Frances R., and Werrenrath, Reinald, Jr. *Dolls of Other Lands.* Chicago: Rand McNally and Company, 1954.
[51] *Golden Book Filmstrips.* Sets I and II. Silent, color, 8 frames each. New York: Young America Films, Inc., 1950. Teacher guides are available.
[52] *The Harrison Catalog of Children's Records.* New York: M. & N. Harrison, Inc., 274 Madison Avenue. This listing by titles, subjects and age levels is available on request. Child Craft records are not listed in it.
[53] Krauss, Ruth. *The Carrot Seed.* New York: Harper & Brothers, 1945.
[54] *The Carrot Seed.* The Children's Record Guild.

Picture storybooks further the children's appreciation of art when the pictures are well done and when the teacher comments on them: "The picture shows how surprised the boy was. See how big and round his eyes are." Meaningful and beautiful pictures enrich the story experiences and help bring children to the point where they want to express their feelings in whatever art media are at hand.

HELPING CHILDREN TO BE IN CONTROL OF STORIES

Outside of school a large number of children watch stories on television. If kindergarten children are the oldest or the only children in the family, their television diet may be limited to cartoons and other programs they can assimilate. Or their diet may include adult television programs from which they take portions which are within their experience. However, a kindergarten child with older brothers and sisters may often be exposed to cowboy and other stories that are inappropriate to his age level. If so, he needs to understand that the good people always triumph over the bad ones, and that the same heroes will reappear on the next program. If he is disturbed by ghosts he has seen on television, *Georgie to the Rescue*[55] will introduce him to a likable ghost he is better able to understand. Knowing that he can watch or not watch a television program, that he can close a book when he wants to, and that he can make his own version of a story gives a child a sense of power and of control. No story is going to frighten him; he can change it. He is in command of the stories.

Reality and Fiction. Basically, of course, children need to distinguish between reality and fiction. "Pretend that I'm your neighbor, and pretend that you come to visit me." When such conversations occur daily, it is evidence that the children speaking are aware of what is real and what is imagined. Other conversations that occur in such a kindergarten are:

JANE: We need some milk for our party.

TEACHER: Could you use water this morning and pretend it's milk? Have you something to put it in?

JANE: I'll get the pitcher.

Or:

TEACHER: I have a delightful story for you this morning. When I finish reading it, I shall ask you whether the story really happened or whether the author pretended it happened.

JOHNNY: (*Inspired by hearing* The Noon Balloon.[56]) When I was little I went up in a balloon all by myself.

[55] Bright, Robert. *Georgie to the Rescue.* Garden City, New York: Doubleday and Company, Inc., 1956.

[56] Brown, Margaret Wise. *The Noon Balloon.* New York: Harper and Brothers, 1952.

TEACHER: (*Smiling at him.*) That's what you would *like* to do, Johnny. You would like to go up in a balloon just the way the kitten did, all by itself. You have not been up in a balloon, but you can think about it. What if you went up in a balloon all by yourself, Johnny? What would you see?

JOHNNY: Trees.

TEACHER: What do you think you would see, Bob? We're all pretending we're up in a balloon the way the kitty was. We're looking down at the ground below us. What do we see?

At four years of age many children distinguish between fact and fancy. It is important for the kindergarten teacher to help each five-year-old make such distinctions. Each person must cope with the world as it is and must recognize what the limits of the world are. Flights of imagination are useful, but their limits must be clear. The kindergarten child who has not learned to distinguish reality from fantasy needs the daily guidance of his teacher in realizing the importance and the nature of the distinction.

HELPING CHILDREN TO RESPECT AND APPRECIATE BOOKS

The kindergarten teacher shares her appreciation of books with the children. Books are something to treasure, something that people are careful with. Books are for reading. They are not cushions to sit on, nor balls to toss about. The teacher helps the children learn how to hold a book and how to turn its pages. The children learn to have clean hands when they use the books. They learn to put books back where they belong, because a book can trip someone and a book can be damaged by someone stepping on it. Some incident in the course of the year usually serves to show the children that water hurts books. Books are kept indoors and away from splashes.

How to care for books is not taught all at once. It begins with teaching children to enjoy books. In first one way and then another children see that books are valuable sources of fun and information. Then as the occasion arises, they see how their pleasure in books is interfered with by carelessness in handling them. Taking care of books is part of enjoying them.

Having a comfortable place to sit and browse encourages the use of books. A low table is a good place to display a few attractive picture books. Others are easily available on nearby racks or low shelves. Exhibits enhance the books. For instance, fall fruits and leaves add to a display featuring *Johnny Mapleleaf*[57] by Alvin R. Tresselt. Large books

[57] Tresselt, Alvin R. *Johnny Mapleleaf.* New York: Lothrop, Lee and Shepard Co., Inc., 1948.

that the children have enjoyed in a large group are on the table to be enjoyed further. But there are also smaller books that are comfortable to read with the book in one's lap. Smaller books that are read to smaller groups of children are often favorites for rereading individually.

ENCOURAGING CHILDREN TO BRING BOOKS FROM HOME

As children develop an interest in books, they enjoy them both at home and at school. At home Jimmy says to his older sister, "Read me a story." The sister picks up any book within her reading ability and obliges. Jimmy is delighted with this experience and his pleasure in having his sister's attention colors his appreciation of the book. In his enthusiasm, he brings the book to school. The teacher recognizes it as a book appropriate for an older grade and inappropriate for kindergarten. What does she do? She would like to encourage Jimmy's interest in books, but she does not want to read the book to the other children.

The wise teacher expresses appreciation of the effort the child made in bringing a book to school. "How good of you to bring your book! I do appreciate your showing it to me." She may capitalize on the situation in order to encourage other children to interest themselves in books. "Jimmy brought a book to school today. He enjoyed the book and he wanted us to know about it. Maybe you will want to bring a book that you like." When a child brings a suitable book, she makes use of it with children who would enjoy hearing the story and looking at the pictures.

Whenever a child brings a book to school, the teacher is careful about having him take it home the same day. When his interest in the book is high, he is apt to get home with it safely. Unhappiness in losing a book might dampen his interest in books. When experiences are happy ones for the children, their pleasure in books continues to grow.

The teacher is pleased to talk with parents about books for kindergarten children. She shows them books that she uses and answers their questions about her selection. She emphasizes that books should be enjoyable and that children learn from pleasant experiences with books. Books appropriate for five-year-olds are simple, realistic, sometimes fanciful, but always happy. Fairy tales and folk tales, with few exceptions, are for older children. Kindergarten children enjoy picture books. Collections of stories are not useful with children directly but are useful to adults in providing stories to be told in the traditional manner. Books need not be expensive. Many of the books sold at the book stands are well worth adding to the library of a five-year-old. However, many others are not. Children can be taught to take care of books and use them properly. Then a paper-bound book lasts as long as a child's interest in it. When the teacher brings out such ideas in talking with parents, the children are apt to bring suitable books to school. More important, the teacher and the parents are working together to further the children's interest in books.

HELPING CHILDREN DEVELOP A SENSE OF HUMOR

The beginnings of humor are found in the kindergarten. They are very simple: a repeated phrase, well timed at each repetition; an alliterative phrase or some other catchy wording; or a surprise. Simple words or ideas that make the storyteller chuckle will make the children chuckle and laugh. Children are imitative, and they like to imitate humor. Of course some types of humor that adults enjoy are beyond the five-year-old. His explorations of the world of sense have not reached the point of appreciating nonsense. The subtleties of sarcasm are also beyond him.

No story is funny unless the storyteller thinks it is funny. The teacher who is amused by *Horton Hatches the Egg*[58] will find the kindergarten sharing her amusement. "Isn't that funny to have a great big elephant sitting on a little nest out on the end of a tiny branch?" the teacher points out as she shows the book and gets the children thinking about funny things. If the children are expecting to be amused by the book, they are more apt to be. Besides dramatizing her amusement with a story, the teacher sometimes interrupts to explain why she is laughing or to repeat the idea that is funny.

Kindergarten children enjoy surprises as much as four-year-olds. Knowing this the teacher selects *The Box with Red Wheels*[59] by Maud and Miska Petersham and with the children enjoys the surprise that the puzzling box contains a new playmate for the animals — a baby. The teacher who is obviously pleased and surprised each time she reads the story is the teacher who really helps children enjoy stories. Children learn how to express their reactions to a story by imitating the reactions of others.

Much humor is built on the pun. In the kindergarten, children take a first step toward appreciating that type of humor as they relate laughter to words that seem like other words. Louis Slobodkin in *Mr. Mushroom*[60] provides a delightful introduction to such humor by telling a story with key words beginning with "m." Mr. Mushroom ate "mush, of course" and married "Miss Mite, of course." The repetitive phrase is also humorous, "of course." And the surprise of Mr. and Mrs. Mushroom living happily "forever and ever" — of course, but not in keeping with the "m's."

[58] Geisel, Theodor Seuss. *Horton Hatches the Egg, op. cit.*
[59] Petersham, Maud and Miska. *The Box with Red Wheels.* New York: The Macmillan Company, 1949.
[60] Slobodkin, Louis. *Mr. Mushroom.* New York: The Macmillan Company, 1950.

The book also suggests to the teacher how to use simple questions to further the children's interest and increase their anticipation of what is coming next. This participation in the story is, of course, another reason for the five-year-olds enjoying *Mr. Mushroom* when it is read and reread to them.

HELPING CHILDREN APPRECIATE THE POETRY OF WORDS

The five-year-old child who enjoys nursery rhymes and listening to the sounds of words is beginning his acquaintance with poetry. To help him, the teacher puts aside her adult taste for new and original wordings and rediscovers the simple rhymes. "There's a dog on the log," says Philip pointing out the detail of a picture. "That rhymes!" he exclaims. The teacher echoes his pleasure, "It certainly does. Dog, log. 'There's a dog on the log.' It rhymes!"

The teacher knows the nursery rhymes and is prepared to say or sing one at any time it may be apropos. The children learn the rhymes by saying them sometimes with the teacher and sometimes by themselves. Knowing the nursery rhymes gives children a common background experience which enriches their entire lives. A reference to "Mary's lamb" or "Simple Simon" is understood by young and old.

The teacher is also familiar with such poetry as *A Child's Garden of Verses* [61] by Robert Louis Stevenson and *When We Were Very Young* [62] and *Now We Are Six* [63] by A. A. Milne. She has selected those verses which five-year-olds enjoy and has copies of them in her files. When it is a rainy day, she finds in her folder on "rain" the Stevenson poem entitled "Rain." Another folder contains his poem, "The Swing." Having poetry at hand makes it possible for the teacher to enrich a simple experience, making it stand out sharply in a child's day.

No Christmas time in kindergarten is complete without the favorite narrative poem that begins *'Twas the Night Before Christmas.* [64] An occasional five-year-old child can say the entire poem and most of the children can say at least a rhyme or two. The poem is eminently suitable for kindergarten children. It has continuous action, an easy meter, simple words, and phrases that suggest pictures. Furthermore, it is a

[61] Stevenson, Robert Louis. *A Child's Garden of Verses.* Big and Giant Golden Books 557. New York: Simon and Schuster, Inc.
[62] Milne, A. A. *When We Were Very Young.* New York: E. P. Dutton and Company, Inc., 1924.
[63] Milne, A. A. *Now We Are Six.* New York: E. P. Dutton and Company, 1927.
[64] Clement C. Moore. *The Night Before Christmas.* New York: Garden City Books, 1954.

happy poem telling a good story. What could be more appropriate for five-year-olds?

Other narrative poems which capture the interest of five-year-olds are *Madeline* [65] and *Madeline's Rescue* [66] by Ludwig Bemelmans. They, too, have continuous action, an easy meter, simple words, and phrases that suggest pictures. Besides, they have a little girl as their heroine. Her adventures are fascinating to other children.

The kindergarten teacher who especially enjoys poetry occasionally shares her enthusiasm for it by playing a record of beautiful poetry [67] or reading a short poem herself. She realizes that children are interested in any experience which gives them a new glimpse into the world of older people. But she also keeps in mind that children must have much, much experience with words before they distinguish poetry as such. Mostly she reads the children suitable stories which have rhyme and rhythm, and short descriptive poems of about two lines. [68]

HELPING CHILDREN BE GOOD LISTENERS

Children need to learn how to be part of an audience for the brief time that it takes to listen to a story. Their interest in hearing the story can be used to help them learn democratic processes and develop attitudes that underlie democracy. Early in the school term, the children and their teacher discuss how to be good listeners. Listening oneself, and letting everyone else listen too means:

Sitting relaxed and comfortable
Keeping hands and feet to oneself
Taking turns in asking questions or commenting

Listening at Home

Discussions from time to time bring out that listening to stories at home is different from listening to stories in a group situation. At home the story can be interrupted for going to the bathroom or doing something else. But at school the story goes on for the group even though one person may leave the group for a few minutes. At home a person can move around if he wants to without disturbing anyone. But in a group a per-

---

[65] Bemelmans, Ludwig. *Madeline.* A Golden Book. New York: Simon and Schuster, Inc., 1939, 1954.

[66] Bemelmans, Ludwig. *Madeline's Rescue.* New York: The Viking Press, 1953.

[67] "Poetry Time," EOCB 4562, RCA Victor Album 378, for ages 5–9.

[68] Jaszi, Jean. *Everybody Has Two Eyes.* New York: Lothrop, Lee & Shepard Co., Inc., 1956.

For other modern books containing poems suitable for kindergarten children, see the bibliography of "Current Books for Children" at the conclusion of Chapter XI.

son who wiggles makes it difficult for others to see the pictures and keep track of the story.

Individual children sometimes need individual help in learning to listen. Sooner or later some child tries to get attention from his neighbors, perhaps by poking at one of them or by whispering to one of them. Before stories are read the next time, a group discussion brings out ways of helping others be good listeners:

Being good listeners ourselves
Paying no attention to persons who do not wish to listen

When a child persists in trying to get attention, the teacher talks with him individually about it. At some transition point in his activities during a free play period, she may say, "I'm glad you are playing with other children now. This is play time. Later when we have stories is listening time. Play now and be ready to listen later." In this way the teacher guides the child in learning that playing is desirable at certain times, but not at other times.

The wise teacher takes up individual problems with the individual child concerned. As a general rule, she does not discuss individual problems with a group of children. Singling out a child is apt to disturb his feelings of belonging to the group. Furthermore, singling out a child for undesirable behavior makes that behavior attractive to attention-seekers. A child may find it easier to repeat the undesirable behavior than to learn some desirable behavior that gets little attention. On the other hand, the child who puts on a temper tantrum during a story finds it disconcerting to have the group quietly relocate itself where it can hear the story. Such a child needs help in developing desirable ways of getting attention at kindergarten and in becoming a good listener during stories. It will be easier for him to throw more tantrums for a while, but failure to gain attention from the tantrums makes such unrewarded behavior drop out of use. If other practices are gaining attention meanwhile, they will presently supplant the tantrums.

Of course, the teacher helps children be good listeners primarily by being a good storyteller. She reads or tells them stories carefully selected in terms of their interests and abilities. She makes each story a vivid and satisfying experience. She and the children enjoy the stories so much that there is room only for good listening.

SITUATIONS FOR DISCUSSION

In the following situations select each course of action that seems desirable to you basing your choices and omissions on the ideas presented in this chapter. Add one or more alternate courses of action.

SITUATION I. The children have asked for another story and you are reading a second book to them. At the back of the group, Tommy loses interest and is quietly jabbing his fists at Mary who is sitting next to him and trying to listen to the story. As the teacher you should say:

"Tommy, are you listening?"

"Let's all be good listeners now."

"Mary is trying to help you listen, Tommy."

"Tommy, do you want me to stop reading the story?"

"You may sit up here by me, Tommy."

SITUATION II. Just as you are starting to read a rather long story, one of the little girls jumps up and goes over to the bathroom. When she returns, a couple of other children want to go too. As the teacher, you should:

Say, "We'll finish the story before we use the bathroom again."

Move quickly into a more absorbing part of the story.

Stop reading the story until everyone who wishes has been to the bathroom.

Talk with the children about their experiences related to the story.

Shorten the story as you read it.

SITUATION III. When you are in the middle of reading a story to a group of more mature children, Henry's mother, Mrs. Thompson, comes to visit for the first time. She is an officer of the Parent-Teacher Association, and her husband is on the school board. As the teacher, you should:

Go over to Mrs. Thompson and tell her how happy you are to have her visit.

Continue reading the story.

Smile and nod pleasantly to Mrs. Thompson as you are showing pictures to the children.

Interrupt the story to let Henry introduce his mother.

Ask Henry to help his mother find a seat at the back of the room.

SITUATION IV. Johnny is a large and active boy who does what the other children do and then has energy for exploring his environment further. Today he finishes his painting and then goes over to browse among the books. Presently he is playing catch with one of the books. As the teacher you should:

Ask Johnny if he wants to play catch.

Say, "Books are for reading."

Explain to Johnny that books are precious.

Give Johnny bean bags and a target box for playing catch.

Tell Johnny, "We don't toss books around."

BIBLIOGRAPHY

Professional Books and Pamphlets

Adams, Beth Porter. *About Books and Children.* New York: Henry Holt and Co., Inc., 1953.

A survey of books for children.

Association for Childhood Education International. *Adventuring in Literature with Children.* Membership Service Bulletin #92. Washington, D. C., 1953.

Twelve leaflets to help parents and teachers enrich the lives of children through poetry and stories.

——. *Bibliography of Books for Children.* Bulletin #37. Washington, D. C., 1954.

This annotated bibliography is classified by subject and age level, with indexes of titles, authors, and publishers.

——. *Children's Books for $1.25 or Less.* General Service Bulletin #36. Washington, D. C., 1955.

This annotated bibliography is a classified list of "inexpensive books which meet recognized standards in form and illustration."

Children's Catalog, 9th ed. New York: The H. W. Wilson Company, 1956.

Annual supplements bring this dictionary catalog of 3400 titles up to date. The books are classified by subject and author and by the Dewey Decimal System.

Frank, Josette. *Your Child's Reading Today.* Garden City, New York: Doubleday and Company, Inc., 1954.

This book for parents is useful to kindergarten teachers because of its book lists and Chapter 7, "The Early Reading Years."

Lewis, Claudia. *Writing for Young Children.* New York: Simon and Schuster, Inc., 1954.

This book to help writers discusses such matters as "Language," "Rhythm," "What Are Children Looking For?" — factors important also in selecting and reading books.

Lewis, Howard C. *Children and Their Books.* New York: Exposition Press, 1952.

This revised edition gives lessons in how to hold books, turn leaves, take books from shelves, carry them, and get new books ready to use.

Shedlock, Marie L. *Art of the Story-Teller.* New York: Dover Publications, Inc., 1951.

This third edition has practical suggestions for the storyteller.

Smith, Lillian. *The Unreluctant Years.* Chicago: American Library Association, 1953.

Chapter eight discusses "Picture Books."

Collections for Use with Children

Arbuthnot, May Hill (Compiler). *Time for Fairy Tales, Old and New.* Chicago: Scott, Foresman and Company, 1952.

A collection of folk tales, fables, myths, epics, and modern tales of fancy for adults to use with children of all ages.

——. *Time for Poetry.* Chicago: Scott, Foresman and Company, 1951. Pp. 438.

An anthology of classical and current poetry grouped according to children's everyday experiences with a foreword helpful to the teacher.

Association for Childhood Education International, Literature Committee. *Told Under the Christmas Tree.* New York: The Macmillan Company, 1948.

A collection of holiday and Christmas stories by well-known authors.

Ward, Winifred. *Stories to Dramatize.* Anchorage, Kentucky: Children's Theatre Press, 1952.

Stories and poems for children from five to fourteen years of age are presented with suggestions for dramatization.

Witty, Paul, and Educational Research Staff of Encyclopaedia Britannica Films, Inc. *It's Fun to Find Out — Film-Story Books.* Boston: D. C. Heath and Company, 1950. "Shep, the Farm Dog," "Three Little Kittens," "The Mailman," "The Food Store," and other simple stories are illustrated from the films by the same name and have a short question and answer section.

Books for Children

REALISTIC STORIES

Beim, Jerrold. *Country Garage.* New York 16: William Morrow and Company, Inc., 1952.

> In this book, as in *Country Fireman* (1948), a boy helps with an adult activity of the village community.

Brown, Margaret Wise, and Edith Thacher Hurd. *Two Little Gardeners.* Little Golden Book #108. New York: Simon and Schuster, Inc., 1951.

> A boy and a girl prepare the soil, plant a garden, tend it, harvest its crop, and eat and can what they have grown.

Cook, Bernadine. *The Little Fish That Got Away.* New York: William R. Scott, Inc., 1956.

> The little boy caught and ate the great big fish; the little fish got away.

Kraus, Ruth. *The Birthday Party.* New York: Harper and Brothers, 1957.

> David had been everywhere except to a birthday party.

Lenski, Lois. *A Dog Came to School.* New York: Oxford University Press, 1955.

> Spot enjoys the first grade activities at school with Davy. *Big Little Davy* (1956) grows up and goes to school in another book by the same author.

Politi, Leo. *The Butterflies Come.* New York: Charles Scribner's Sons, 1957.

> Lucia and Stephen get costumes for the Monarch Butterfly Festival.

Sauer, Julia L. *Mike's House.* New York: The Viking Press, 1954.

> When Mike gets lost en route to the story hour at the library, a policeman helps him.

Schlein, Miriam. *Little Red Nose.* New York: Abelard-Schuman, 1955.

> The feel of spring as well as its activities are described.

Simon, Norma. *The Daddy Days.* New York: Abelard-Schuman, 1958.

> The week end is for doing things with daddy.

Steiner, Charlotte. *Patsy's Pet.* Garden City, New York: Doubleday & Company, Inc., 1955.

> A little girl who wanted a pet had first a mouse and then a bird.

Tresselt, Alvin R. *I Saw the Sea Come In.* New York: Lothrop, Lee & Shepard Company, Inc., 1954.

> Tresselt captures the feeling of the sea in this book, as he captured the feeling of the fall season in *Johnny Maple-Leaf* (1948) and in *Autumn Harvest* (1951), and the feeling of the warm summer morning in *Sun Up* (1949).

Yashima, Taro. *Umbrella.* New York: The Viking Press, 1958.

> Three-year-old Nomo has to wait for the rain before she can use her birthday presents of red boots and an umbrella.

FANCIFUL STORIES

Bright, Robert. *Me and the Bears.* New York: Doubleday and Company, Inc., 1951.

The four little bears come one night to play with the little girl.

Chalmers, Mary. *George Appleton.* New York: Harper and Brothers, 1957.

When Trilly, the cat, goes into the deep woods, he meets a dragon named George Appleton.

de Regniers, Beatrice S. *The Giant Story.* New York: Harper and Brothers, 1953.

One day Tommy decides to be a giant.

Fischer, Hans. *Pitschi.* New York: Harcourt, Brace and Company, Inc., 1953.

Pitschi was a kitten who always wanted to be something else.

Hurd, Edith Thacher and Clement. *The Cat from Telegraph Hill.* New York: Lothrop, Lee & Shepard Co., Inc., 1955.

One night the artist's cat explores San Francisco by himself.

Koffer, Ylla. *The Little Elephant.* New York: Harper and Brothers, 1956.

Japu's dream of being the lead elephant in the king's parade comes true.

Krasilovsky, Phyllis. *The Very Little Girl.* Garden City, New York: Doubleday and Company, Inc., 1953.

The very little girl was yet big enough to help with the baby.

Krauss, Ruth. *A Very Special House.* New York: Harper and Brothers, 1953.

A child imagines a house in which he can do and have whatever he wants.

McLeod, Emilie W. *The Seven Remarkable Polar Bears.* Boston: Houghton Mifflin Company, 1954.

A hungry polar bear increases his rations with the help of six, but only six, imaginary bears.

Minarik, Else M. *Little Bear.* New York: Harper and Brothers, 1957.

"Little Bear Goes to the Moon," one of four stories in the book, distinguishes between reality and "foolin'."

Thayer, Jane. *Sandy and the Seventeen Balloons.* New York: William Morrow and Company, 1955.

Shopping one day with his mother, Sandy gets seventeen balloons, enough to carry him up in the air above the shoppers.

STORIES FOR DRAMATIZING

Brown, Margaret Wise. *The Dead Bird.* New York: Young Scott Books, 1958.

The children find a dead bird and bury it. By the same author are *The Little Fir Tree*, Thomas Y. Crowell Co., 1954 and *Willie's Adventures*, William R. Scott, Inc., 1954.

Ilsey, Velma. *The Pink Hat.* Philadelphia: J. B. Lippincott Co., 1956.

Penelope learns to put away her things with the help of her bunnies and her pink hat.

Kay, Helen. *One-Mitten Lewis.* New York: Lothrop, Lee & Shepard Co., Inc., 1955.

Lewis had difficulty having two mittens alike until Sally came with her Lonesome Mitten Box.

Krause, Ruth. *I'll Be You and You Be Me.* New York: Harper and Brothers, 1954.

"I think I'll grow up and be a bunny" and other sketches in words and pictures suggest short dramatizations.

256 THE KINDERGARTEN TEACHER

Lenski, Lois. *On a Summer's Day.* New York: Oxford University Press, 1953.
Activities children enjoy in the summer are pictured and described in verse.

MacGregor, Ellen. *Theodore Turtle.* New York: Whittlesey House, 1954.
When the turtle gets on his back, each of his animal friends tries to help him.

Slobodkin, Louis. *Mr. Mushroom.* New York: The Macmillan Company, 1950.
The simple, alliterative wording and the humor of Mr. Mushroom soon make the story a familiar one that children like to dramatize.

Willard, Annmary. *Pillow-Time Tales.* New York: Rand, McNally & Co., 1954.
This Book-Elf Giant has 14 classical nursery stories including "The Three Bears," and "The Three Little Pigs," favorites for dramatizing.

Woodcock, Louise. *This Is the Way the Animals Walk.* New York: William R. Scott, Inc., 1946.
Imitating different animals is a simple activity for dramatizing.

Films for Children

Little Black Lamb. Wilmette, Illinois: Encyclopaedia Britannica Films, Inc., 1955.
Mary's lamb gets lost the day of the school pet show, but the postman returns it in time. 10 minutes, sound, black and white, or color.

Night Before Christmas. Wilmette, Illinois: Encyclopaedia Britannica Films, Inc., 1955.
11 minutes, black and white, or color.

13

Furthering Artistic Expression

Kindergarten children like to express their feelings and ideas through drawing and painting and through working with clay and other materials. In order to do this they must have three things: (1) they must have something to express, (2) they must have sufficient experience with art media so that handling the media helps rather than hinders their expression, and (3) they must have a favorable physical and social environment which encourages artistic expression and does not interfere with it.

Art activities are carried on individually or in small groups. The materials are easily available to the children. They are enticing. When a child wishes to use some of them, he can. Occasionally he must do something else until he may have a turn, but usually the art materials are available in sufficient quantity for everyone who wishes to have a turn at once. Of course, when new materials are introduced, many more children want to use them. Later the children distribute themselves among the various activities available, using art materials or engaging in other activities as they wish.

As the children work with different art media, they become increasingly interested in them and increasingly pleased with the creative process. They like to "read" the mood and story shown in different situations and in pictures. They like to express their feelings and their ideas with art materials. As their pleasure in doing so increases, so does their skill. By the end of the kindergarten year, children develop considerable skill in observing movement, color, texture, and shape, and in expressing their reactions to their experiences through different art media.

OUTCOMES OF THE ART PROGRAM

One kindergarten teacher listed the following attitudes and skills as desirable outcomes for the children in her group:

Attitudes

Enjoys the creative process
Likes to work with at least one art medium
Likes to notice texture, color, or shape
Likes to read the story or the mood shown in pictures

Skills

Experiments with several art and craft media
Expresses his feelings or ideas in at least one art medium
Observes movement and texture, color, or line composition
Reads the story or the mood represented in pictures
Handles art media and tools appropriately

It is to be noted that the list of objectives does not include the ability to "talk about what he has made." The teacher realized that children are not equally verbal and that many children express themselves through various art media rather than through words. Furthermore kindergarten children who are highly verbal about their activities are not at all verbal about their feelings. As John Dewey has pointed out in *Art As Experience*,[1] "Art is a more universal mode of language than is the speech that exists in a multitude of mutually unintelligible forms." Kindergarten teachers who appreciate this point of view listen with interest whenever a child volunteers comment on his art work, but avoid having group discussions about the children's paintings or other artistic expressions. Group evaluation of their compositions is appropriate for older children but not for five-year-old children. Too early emphasis on products and techniques is inhibiting during a period which aims primarily at helping children to express themselves freely and to feel a sense of satisfactory achievement without undue regard for the end product. The kindergarten teacher encourages the children in their artistic expression and carefully avoids any situation which might inhibit them or might force them to move too quickly toward representation before they have worked through earlier phases of manipulation and experimentation.

EXPERIENCES THAT STIMULATE ARTISTIC EXPRESSION

People and Objects

The rich program of the modern kindergarten includes a wealth of experiences in social studies, science, physical activities, literature, music, and rhythms and provides an excellent background for artistic expression. People and objects brought into the kindergarten and study trips from the classroom into the neighborhood stimulate children to express

---

[1] John Dewey. *Art As Experience*. New York: Minton Balch & Co., 1939, p. 335.

themselves creatively. Dramatic play both in and out of school and the relationships and activities of their homes inspire children's artistic expressions. Opportunity for manipulating and experimenting with paints and other materials of many colors or of many textures stimulates children to express their feelings and their ideas.

The Teacher

The teacher is the principal resource for stimulating creative expression. She can make even a simple learning situation alive with vivid action in a setting that is clear and understandable. Instead of talking abstractly about something like a litter of puppies, she brings the puppies into the classroom and shows them to the children or takes them out to a nearby home to see them. She knows the value of firsthand sensory experience. She plans activities so that children are stimulated through as many of their senses as possible. For instance, when she is telling a story, she has many apt and attractive illustrations for the children to look at while they hear what she is saying. Often she pantomimes the story and makes the sound patterns of her voice carry additional meaning. Whenever she can, she dramatizes what she has to say, making a vivid impression on the children. Thus, she uses visual and auditory stimuli to reinforce each other.

Learning through the Senses

The teacher encourages children to learn through as many senses as possible. The mental phases of learning are reinforced by the physical movements that the children make in converting their ideas into concrete form in the sand pile, at the workbench, or in working with art materials. Tactile and kinesthetic sensations add to visual sensations in making a fuller experience which spills over into creative expression.

As she plans and as she works with the children, the teacher constantly checks to see that she is using all sensory stimuli that relate to the activity. She tries to make use of as many of the six senses as possible: sight, hearing, taste, smell, tactile, and kinesthetic sensations. In doing this she not only provides opportunity for reinforcing sensations, she also helps the children develop awareness of their sensations. A good way of doing that arises naturally when a teacher enjoys a situation fully and shares her joyous response to it with the children by saying, "Aren't we having fun!"

There is a world of feeling difference between a guinea pig's visit to Miss Gates' kindergarten and its visit to Miss Ching's. Recalling the visit the next day, Miss Gates said to her class, "Yesterday John brought his guinea pig in its cage for us to watch. He told us that he fed it carrots and lettuce as well as a special feed." In contrast, Miss Ching talked with the children in this way: "We surely enjoyed having John's guinea pig visit us yesterday. Do you remember how we all sat close together with our knees touching so he could be out of his cage and run around in the circle we made? We thought he was a little frightened by so many of us because he watched us instead of eating. What did John have for him to eat? Do we eat what guinea pigs eat? He likes to crunch raw carrots in his teeth. What does it feel like when you crunch a carrot stick in your teeth? It feels good, doesn't it? When John took his guinea pig home in its cage, was any of the carrot or any of the lettuce left? Lettuce and carrots are good and they are good for us. They helped the guinea pig have a nice, sleek coat. Do you remember what his short fur felt like when John held him and you stroked him very gently?" When Miss Ching's group finished talking about the visit of the guinea pig, they had had a vivid experience in which they had opportunity for learning the same science facts as Miss Gates' group. But, in addition, they had feelings and remembered sensations: kinesthetic, visual, auditory, taste, and tactile. Although art materials were as equally available in Miss Gates' room as in Miss Ching's, the children in Miss Gates' room made little use of them and none of the children used the guinea pig in their drawings. In Miss Ching's room, several children took home pictures which they said were about a guinea pig. One child said her orange scribble was a carrot, and indeed the long lines of the scribble were a significant step forward for her.

Tactile Sensations. Nerve endings in the skin respond to heat, cold, and pressure. Children learn to interpret and use these sensations and to distinguish tactile experiences and label them with words like smooth, rough, furry, sharp, cold, warm, and woolly. They learn to identify different kinds of materials like plastic, wood, metal, paper, plaster, and glass on the basis of both visual and tactile sensations. Blind children depend on their tactile sensations for many of their learning experiences. Normal children should also be encouraged to use their tactile sensations and to enrich their lives by enjoying the feel of things.

A teacher can ask each child to bring an old tie which his father no longer needs. Then she can organize the ties on a rack so that the children can enjoy feeling them and distinguishing among them. From time to time children like to play tie salesman and customer. When the teacher joins this activity, she enriches it and encourages the children in using their tactile sensations:

TEACHER: Is it my turn to buy a necktie?

JOHN: Yes, which one?

TEACHER: Do you have a red one that feels nice and smooth?

JOHN: Here's a red one.

TEACHER: I like that color, but I think I like a smooth feel better. Have you any more red ones?

JOHN: Here's one.

TEACHER: Oh, I like the feel of that. Doesn't that feel smooth, though. I'll take that one. How much is it?

JOHN: Five dollars.

TEACHER: That seems a bit high. I usually pay about two dollars for a necktie. Would that be all right?

JOHN: That's O.K.

The girls also enjoy playing with samples of dress materials, and the boys with samples of shirt materials. Both boys and girls like to play with samples of papers, especially wallpapers. Sometimes they use these in dramatic play, sometimes they use them for sorting and piling, and sometimes they just play with them and then dump them back in the box. Children explore the sensory realm each in his own way.

Taste Sensations. In talking about foods, the teacher does not neglect mention of tastes. For instance, when she is showing pictures of nutritious foods on the flannel board, she makes the discussion vivid by referring to taste, smell, and touch sensations: "If you hold jello in your mouth, what does it feel like?" "Did you know that if you chew a piece of bread long enough, it tastes sweet?" "Do you like to smell bacon cooking for your breakfast? When you eat it, does it taste the way it smells?"

Olfactory Sensations. Teachers who want children to have a full sensory experience guide them in noticing and in identifying different odors. One kindergarten teacher kept her desk supplied with a single flower and encouraged the children to enjoy its smell as well as its visual beauty. The children came to know that roses, gardenias, and red carnations had odors that were easily noticed but that other flowers such as camellias did not.

On science walks the teacher sometimes has the children stop to sniff. They learn to identify the odors of their community. There are strong smells from refineries, gas fumes from passing cars, and odors of burning trash or fall leaves. Especially in the spring they can detect the sweet scents of flowers. Whatever the odors, the teacher helps the children identify what they are and avoids labeling them as good or bad. When the children notice the smell of a garbage container, their teacher guides them to think of it only as the smell of garbage. When the children notice the odors of meals cooking, the teacher talks with them about the smells and together they guess what some family is having for its meal. The day after the science walk the teacher and the children remember what they enjoyed and learned. In these discussions the teacher makes a point of including memories of olfactory sensations.

Auditory Sensations. Music enhances many experiences and brings them to the vivid level where they stimulate children to creative activities with art materials. Music can also be a sufficient stimulus by itself. When art materials are easily available, children listening to music like to express the mood created by the music. Sometimes as they listen they respond to the rhythm of the music by making rhythmic movements in their drawings. Probably their choice of colors is influenced by what they are hearing.

Children seldom express moods and feelings in words. But through art media they often show the sensitive adult how they respond to auditory stimuli. One child reacted to a rasping voice by drawing a picture of the person and then scribbling over it to get rid of the person who hurt his ears. Certainly any kindergarten teacher can widen the range of her speaking voice. If she has mostly high tones that are tiring to listen to, she can develop lower tones as well. Children are calm and happy when they hear low speaking tones, and words and phrases with spacing between. The kindergarten teacher who has trained her voice can make an ordinary story a vivid experience for the children. They are thus stimulated to express their reactions by using available art media.

Kinesthetic Sensations. When a child climbs stairs, the kinesthetic sensations in his joints give him a feeling about height. When he reaches and crawls to sail his boat around in a tub of water, he has a vivid impression which may find expression in painting or modeling. The physical movement which is an integral part of each phase of the kindergarten program enriches the child's experiences and increases the likelihood of artistic expression.

Visual Sensations. When children go for a walk, the objects that move catch their attention first. Stationary objects that have some special significance are also noticed. As children become acquainted with an object, they usually react to it as a whole at first. Later they may become acquainted with distinguishing details. However, children sometimes react first to a part of an object and then become acquainted with the entire object in relation to that part. The teacher can notice where a child focuses his gaze and infer what catches his attention. The teacher never takes it for granted that a child has observed what she wants him to. She calls his attention to one point or one relationship at a time and asks questions to help his observation.

A walk through a residential area provides opportunity for observing a great variety of colors and textures. A single house may be made with one or more colors and with several different materials each having its particular texture. Landscaping plans make use of color contrasts and similarities which the children observe. They can notice texture differences, too — for instance, smooth and shiny leaves contrasting with more bushy foliage. Every day the sensitive teacher helps the children widen their range of observation.

Emotional Experiences Leading to Artistic Expression

The visual world provides stimulation for every kind of artistic expression. Many visual experiences lead to verbal expression, but those with a high emotional quality frequently stimulate children to artistic expression. If a child sees a gray kitten crossing the street, he may say, "There's a gray kitten." But if the kitten is his and a car comes down the street so fast that the child is afraid it may squash the kitten, he will probably show how he felt about the gray kitten when he draws a picture. When children respond emotionally to what they see, they often use art media to express their reactions.

Integrating and Interpreting Sensory Experiences

What each child sees is a unique experience for him, and his artistic expression of his reaction to his experience is also unique. When the kindergarten group goes for a walk in the fall, the teacher helps them enjoy the full experience: shuffling through the crinkly leaves on the ground, feeling the brisk air, listening to the crisp sounds, smelling bonfire smoke, seeing the many colored leaves still clinging to the branches of some trees, and noticing the bare twigs on other trees. To some of the children this experience may be sufficiently emotional for them to react to it with their art materials. One child selects an autumn color paint and covers his paper with it. Another child uses crayons to draw a tree with a bit of orange on the tree and below the tree. Another child scribbles at length with red crayon. One child uses clay and rolls out a thick piece for a tree trunk and some smaller rolls for branches. In short, children who were sufficiently stimulated by the autumn walk expressed their observations about it and their reactions to it, each in his own way.

Reinforcing Sensory Experiences

In every part of the kindergarten program the teacher reinforces learning situations with visual stimulation. She makes extensive use of pictures and other visual materials: blackboard drawings, magazine pictures on the flannel board, large illustrations mounted on sturdy cardboard, and displays of objects brought in by the children. To help children "read" pictures, she has apt illustrations for them to look at while she reads a story. She has a collection of reproductions of paintings about children which she uses when the children tell the story they see in the picture. She also has a collection of reproductions of paintings which show mood and feeling. "When do you feel like this?" she asks as she shows one of them to the discussion group.

The kindergarten teacher also helps the children relate what they see in a picture to what they know from experience. For instance, if the children have their picture taken at kindergarten, they will notice when they look at it that not all parts of them show in the picture. This does not mean that they do not have those parts. It simply means that a photograph can include only the parts that the camera "sees." The teacher encourages the children to bring pictures of themselves or their homes and then helps the group interpret what they see in the picture as it relates to what they know from experience. In doing this the teacher uses real photographs about the children's world rather than any representative drawings they make of it.

EXPLORING THE WORLD OF COLOR

An important world for children to explore visually is the world of color. Their teacher helps them do this through powder paints. She makes up three solutions for each of the primary colors on the color chart: red, yellow, and blue. For each of the colors she has three clear glass quart containers: (1) a solution of the color at full intensity, (2) a solution of the tint obtained by adding white, and (3) a solution of the shade obtained by adding black to the full intensity color. So that these solutions will keep indefinitely without spoiling, she adds some oil of cloves or oil of wintergreen to each. Often she shares the fun of mixing colors with one or two of the older brothers or sisters of kindergarten children who come in to help. Only the teacher will handle the large glass jars after the paint is mixed and the jars are stored on a high shelf equipped with a guard.

When a child wishes to paint, he selects whatever colors he desires, and the teacher pours out a small quantity of those colors into containers for use at an easel. Thus the child can select one, two, three, or more colors — whatever he chooses to use that day. He can select colors of full intensity, or tints, or shades, or any combination of them that he wishes. He can explore the intensity of a single color. He can explore tints of several colors or shades of those colors. He can explore color hues within tints or within shades or within full intensities. Or he can mix colors and learn that with the primary colors he can mix all other colors.

Each day that he paints, the child has this opportunity for exploring color. He commands the world of color because each day it is he who makes the selection. He is not limited to only one color or to three colors put out for him. Instead he has the satisfaction of being responsible for his own selection of color as well as for his own use of the color in his painting. Thus his artistic expression builds his self-confidence, and his satisfaction makes for increased artistic expression.

Sometimes teachers seek to prevent inharmonious use of color by making available for the child's use only those colors which she believes "go well" together. Such a procedure stultifies creativity and perpetuates stereotype color combinations. A free selection permits the child to discover through experimentation what colors are pleasing to him.

As the children go about their activities in the kindergarten, their teacher helps them develop awareness of both color and texture. When she greets them as they come in, she may comment on what they are wearing: "What a pretty, shiny dress! It's as blue as your eyes and it looks so smooth." "Your shirt is a color that sailors wear. That is why we call it navy blue." The teacher's interest in color and texture stimulates the children's interest in them.

The teacher encourages children to notice actual colorings, and she avoids teaching them color stereotypes such as: tree trunks are brown, the sky is blue, and new leaves are green. If she has a picture of a fawn Guernsey cow to illustrate a story, she makes a point of getting a picture of a black and white Holstein cow to illustrate another story. Seeing many illustrations of the same animal helps children develop a fuller understanding of the animal and the variations found in its appearance. Children enjoy the range of color, texture, and line in the dresses that their teacher wears. The little girl whose kindergarten teacher wore a pretty red dress each day said to her mother, "You can't wear a red dress. You aren't a teacher." Children need to explore a great variety of colors and textures if they are to develop sensitivity to color and texture in nature and in their own art expression.

EXPLORING ART MEDIA

Anything the child has in his environment is potentially an art medium: flowers and vases for the playhouse, dishes and place mats for setting the table, and small pieces of wood for constructing boats and other things. Wherever the child turns his attention he finds objects with which to express himself creatively, arranging and rearranging them as he wishes. The teacher encourages the children in their sensitivity to art in everyday activities. When a child enthusiastically asks her, "What do you think of my service station? Isn't it neat-o?" she appreciates not only his accomplishment in block building but guides him to realize more fully the artistry of his construction. "It certainly is," she replies, "and I like its sloped roof. Isn't that a new design?" Thus the teacher concerns herself with the children's artistic use of everyday materials. At the same time, however, she is also concerned with their use of the art supplies for the kindergarten.

Five-year-old children enjoy trying out various art media. They like to explore the use of chalk, crayons, pencils, charcoal, finger paints, and clay, manipulating them directly with their fingers. They also like to try using brushes and scissors and other tools. They like to make designs in smooth wet sand, and they like to mold it into different shapes and structures. They like to draw in fine dust, sometimes with a finger and sometimes with a stick. The children are intrigued both by the simple materials from early times and the modern materials, especially those available in a wide range of color.

The Teacher Allows for Individual Differences

Whatever media the children are using, their teacher is interested and respectful concerning their use of the materials. She sees that each composition has the artist's name on it and that each child has the opportunity to use the medium as he wishes. Of course, if a child starts to use his paints to make one of the girls look like an Indian when she does not wish to, the teacher helps him find more suitable ways to explore the use of paint. He may like to paint a headdress of different colored feathers and give that to the girl to wear.

Letting the child work in his own way includes letting him work until he is finished. Most children carry out the suggestion about finishing what they are doing and getting ready for the next activity. However, occasionally a child is emotionally unwilling to relinquish a satisfying art activity. Recognizing this occurrence as an exceptional one, the teacher says, "You may work quietly here until you finish if you wish. The group is now going to outdoor activities. When you finish you may join us. You are sure you would rather paint this morning than play outside?" In this way she lets the child decide when he is finished and whether he prefers painting to playing outside. Of course if a child repeatedly chooses to linger, the teacher finds out if the child wants to miss the next activity, if he needs more opportunity for art work at home, or if he needs help in learning to move with the group.

The teacher does not insist that a child use every medium. Some children like to explore one medium at length before going on to another. Each child should determine when he is ready for a medium new to him. Children find security in using a familiar material. But when they have assimilated one kind of experience, they go on to another. The wise teacher talks with a child about a medium he has yet to use, but lets him decide when he is ready to start working with it. If a child has been using crayons but has not worked with paints at the easel, she may say to him, "You like working with crayons, don't you? One of these days you will find out what fun it is to work with the paints too. When you are ready to paint, you tell me, and I'll help you get started." The next week if Tim is still using only crayons, the teacher may set up an easel for use with crayons. When Tim has worked at the easel with crayons, he may be ready in a few days to work in the same situation with the paint medium that is new to him.

While Tim is getting used to the easel situation, the teacher also helps him get used to the paint medium. When she is mixing paints or cleaning up the paints and brushes, she has Tim help and talks with him, not about his painting, but about the materials — the pretty colors of the paints, their feel, the paper used, the feel of the brushes. She encourages him in handling the brushes and perhaps in trying an exploratory stroke. Always she has the very real expectation that when he is ready to paint, he will do so. The teacher's confidence makes Tim confident, too, that he will paint when he is ready. Soon he does go to the easel and paints.

Various Media

Charcoal. Children like to work with charcoal on large sheets of newsprint or butcher paper, especially when they are prepared for it by thinking about early man. When the cave men sat around their camp fires, they sometimes pulled out a burned stick and used the blackened end to help them show their friends pictures of the animals they had hunted or the sights they had seen. The children like to use charcoal and draw with it the way early man did.

The teacher provides not the thin and expensive charcoal sticks of the artist but the thick chunks sold for braziers. The children enjoy the charcoal medium occasionally, but crayons, powder paints, and water colors are more enticing because of their range of colors.

Crayons. Fortunately today children need not limit their drawings to black and white. They can use fat wax crayons suited to the size of their hands. With a box of many-colored crayons, they select first one and then another color as they explore this medium of artistic expression. Sometimes a child uses broken crayons on their sides to make wide colored places. Mostly the children use the crayons like a pencil. A soft pad of newspaper on which the children can crayon produces an interesting effect. A suggestion to one child will set a whole group experimenting with different surfaces.

The teacher is careful not to overemphasize crayons to the exclusion of other media. Crayons are so easily handled and lend themselves so easily to drawing at an easel, at a table, or on the floor that it is a temptation to overuse them. The wise teacher arranges for crayons to be available as one of several art media. Then children choose whichever medium they wish to use that day.

Pencils. Another medium that five-year-old children enjoy is the pencil. It must be a fat pencil that is easily handled, and it must have a very soft lead that marks easily. Children like red pencils and pencils with other color leads. These, too, must be very soft so that they mark easily. Pencils are a favorite medium when children explore various forms of scribbling and drawing.

Chalk. Since five-year-old children are more interested in the process than in the product, they enjoy using colored chalks sometimes on the chalkboard and sometimes on wet or dry paper. The teacher makes sure the children understand that they make a picture on the chalkboard, erase it, and then make another picture.

The Plastic Sheet. Another medium that emphasizes the fun of drawing is the transparent plastic sheet over a lightweight paper which adheres easily to the wax pad underneath. When a pencil or fingernail marks on the plastic, the design is seen until the paper is lifted up. Five-year-old children today enjoy this device as much as children used to enjoy the slate.

Finger Paints. Kindergarten children put on their paint smocks or cover-all aprons and have fun with the process of finger painting on a nonabsorbent surface, sometimes on oilcloth and sometimes on smooth paper. First they spread a spoonful of thick elastic starch around. Then they use the shakers of tempera paint to sprinkle whatever colors they want wherever they want them. When they are done, they wash off their hands in the bathroom or in a bucket of water.

The teacher encourages the children to enjoy a turn with the finger paints, but she does not insist that they explore this or any other art medium. She knows that the finger paint medium offers an emotional release for many children but can be a threatening situation to children who are constantly held back by parental admonition from being messy or getting dirty.

Powder Paints. With tints, shades, and colors of full intensity to choose from, the kindergarten child likes to explore painting at an easel. He selects a brush to fit his hand and puts one of that size in each of the juice cans, small milk cartons, or other containers that fit the holders at the bottom of the easel. With a big piece of newsprint or butcher paper tacked on the easel or attached by clothespins to the top of the easel, he is ready for big sweeping strokes as he explores this fascinating medium. His teacher has carefully written his name on the back of the paper so that he can take his composition home at the end of the kindergarten day when the paint is dry.

The teacher gives the child very little guidance after she has helped him select the materials he needs. If it is his first experience at the easel, she may emphasize that he has a brush for each color and that he uses it just for that color. Another day she may help him realize that if he wants drips, he leaves a lot of paint on his brush and if he does not want them, he wipes the brush on the edge many, many times as he takes it out of the can. If a child is covering his paper rather thickly, the teacher assures him that there is more paper if he wants to paint another picture. He decides when he has finished his painting. He may want to do a series of paintings that morning, or he may be finished after only a few strokes on a single sheet of paper.

If the child is making big round strokes, the teacher may say, "Big round strokes," encouraging him in making them. If the child wants to talk about the idea he is expressing, the teacher bends down to listen. Her only comment, however, is, "Yes, indeed." At another time, but not then, she may talk with the child again, helping him expand his awareness of the experience he expressed verbally and in his painting. While the child is painting or while he is helping hang his drawing up on the line to dry, the teacher reinforces his pleasure in his experience and in his achievement: "Isn't painting fun? Those surely are pretty colors." In general, the teacher makes the painting situation a pleasant time in which the children are free to express themselves as they wish. She uses another time for helping them expand their concepts.

Part of cleaning up after easel painting is cleaning paint brushes with water. A good grade of brush does not shed its bristles. The containers the children use are rinsed out easily with water too. The big jars of tints, shades, and colors of full intensity keep indefinitely with the oil of wintergreen or cloves as a preservative.

Powder paints are also available in earth pigments. These provide additional variety in color since they include warm browns, rich purples, and soft greens. They too are made up with water. Tints are made by adding white to the original solution, and shades are made by adding black. A child thoroughly enjoys selecting the tints, shades, and colors of full intensity that he wishes to work with that day. Then he paints in his own way, exploring the medium or using it to express some feeling or concept.

Water Colors. Kindergarten children find water colors a satisfying medium. The semi-moist colors now available are easy to use, and the medium gives children the opportunity for mixing colors and exploring the realm of color in yet another way.

The teacher encourages the children to mix their colors either on their papers or in the space provided in the lid of the water color box. However, she does not insist on their doing so because she knows that the five-year-old child's pleasure in painting is more important than his technique. If he learns to enjoy painting with water colors, later he can acquire the techniques for using his colors most efficiently and most economically. Knowing this, the kindergarten teacher does not burden the children with keeping their color tins free from other colors. If they mix colors on top of their color tins she simply reminds them that, "You can mix colors right on your paper if you like." For five-year-old children it is important to enjoy the water color medium in whatever way they wish.

Modeling Clay. A favorite medium for kindergarten children is soft modeling clay. It works easily and is less resistant to the touch than plasticene. Dough is a good substitute material, especially when it is colored with food dye. Most children enjoy squeezing their hands through it. When they are first getting acquainted with the medium, they pick off bits and pat and pound and poke. Later they learn that rolling it between their hands results in snakes or balls. Still later they move into representative sculpture and use the snake-like roll to make a handle for a basket. The teacher encourages the children to enjoy working with the medium as they wish, no matter what the stage of their development. She says, "Isn't this fun?" "My, it feels good." "Mary likes to go roll, roll, roll with her hand" (describing the way Mary is making a snake).

The teacher understands the inhibited children who are unable at first to find emotional release in the clay medium. She simply says, "When you are ready to use the clay, you will enjoy it." To the children who ask Mary why she doesn't play too, the teacher says reassuringly, "Mary will when she is ready."

The teacher creates a permissive atmosphere in which the children are free to enjoy working the clay in any way they wish. She knows that working with clay builds co-ordination and satisfies the need for manipulation as well as self-expression. Modeling is an activity which should always be available in the kindergarten as an outlet for energy. She lets each of them decide when he is finished with what he is doing and ready to go on to another activity.

The children learn to clean up their clayboard, linoleum, or oilcloth work surface by rolling a piece of clay over it to pick up small pieces of clay. They clean themselves up too. If bathrooms are not conveniently located, they use a wet sponge to clean their hands and a paper towel to dry them.

To keep the clay available for use, the teacher has the children roll all their clay into a big ball when they are finished. Flattening this and making a large thumb hole in the middle provides a place for water that will keep the clay moist and ready for working. These water-filled chunks of clay are stored in an earthen crock with a lid or in a covered galvanized pail.

In the latter part of the school year it may be desirable for the children to make some clay object to take home. Something that the child has modeled will dry out to a solid chunk which can be painted with poster paints. Although such objects are fragile, they make acceptable gifts for parents. Occasionally, some pieces may be fired so children may experience the transformation. Five-year-old children are pleased with making and presenting the gift and are usually not concerned about having it on display for any length of time at home.

Other Media. Kindergarten children like to use scissors that cut well. Sometimes they use them for only a minute or two. But they like to have scissors and paper available for cutting when they are interested in exploring the use of scissors. They like to cut newspaper into strips. They like to cut folded paper and open it into surprising designs. They enjoy free cutting of colored construction paper. Sometimes they like to paste bits of colored paper or different textures of paper on a sheet of plain paper to make a design or a collage. Sometimes they like to cut out catalogue or magazine pictures or Christmas card pictures about trains or children or animals or airplanes, and sometimes they like to paste such pictures on plain paper.

STAGES IN ARTISTIC EXPRESSION

In our culture so much emphasis is put on representative pictures that children's drawings move toward that type. Teachers and enlightened parents say, "Oh, did you draw a picture? Tell me about it." But most adults and older children say, "What is it?" They may add, "Doesn't look like it to me," or else they may attempt to be helpful by some suggestion, "If it's a house, why don't you put a chimney on it?" Such remarks may help the ego of the person who makes them, but they tend to inhibit free artistic expression on the part of the children.

Manipulation and Experimentation

Drawings of kindergarten children can be classified according to the stage of development displayed. When children first start working with an art medium, they manipulate it and get the feel of it. As they work with it, they begin to try out ideas with regard to it. This experimentation may continue for some time before it moves to the next stage of symbolism.

Symbolism and Representation

Sooner or later, however, the child labels his creative expression and it is evident that he attaches some significance to what he creates. He proudly displays a rounded ball of clay and says, "It's an egg. I made an egg." He may be discovering that what he modeled resembled an egg, or he may have expressed his idea of an egg in the medium of the clay. Whatever his thought processes, this stage of labeling art creations is called symbolism. From the symbolic stage the child moves on to representative composition.

Their first compositions are scribblings as the children acquaint themselves with the materials. Then the scribblings suggest that the children are experimenting with mass and color. After some time the scribbling suggests that they are experimenting with line and form. When they begin experimenting with the expression of ideas, they like to tell their teacher or another child about their art creation. This symbolic stage moves toward more realistic drawing. Representative drawings, as well as drawings classifiable according to each of the other stages, are made daily in the kindergarten. The kindergarten teacher is careful to appreciate each drawing, whether it be a scribble, a symbolic drawing, or a representative drawing.

Each of the four stages — *manipulation, experimentation, symbolism,* and *representation* — has its values for the child. He should be encouraged to explore each of them fully and should not be rushed into representation. He may be in the manipulative stage with an art medium that is new to him and may be in another stage with a more familiar medium. Nor should he be expected to work always at the same stage with the same medium. One day he may wish to experiment with crayons, the next day he may wish to use them in expressing an idea, and the next day he may just enjoy scribbling with them. No matter what stage describes what the child has done, the teacher helps him enjoy what he has done. Permissively she accepts the child, his art creation, and any comments he cares to make about it.

The art creations of children in kindergarten are usually experimental or symbolic. Much of the art work reveals to the understanding teacher facets of a child's observation and thinking which might otherwise go unnoticed. A child, for instance, creates parts which he puts next to each other to show relation. This haptic, or non-visual, approach shows that the child expresses what he feels rather than what he sees. When a child makes one thing very large and another relatively small, he probably shows his feeling about their importance. The teacher encourages children in non-visual composition just as she encourages children in visual representation.

Comparatively few kindergarten children are realistically visual. At an early age the optic, or visual-minded, child is not able to show the realistic view of the world which his verbal descriptions indicate. He finds it difficult to portray a three-dimensional experience using a two-dimensional piece of paper. Yet sometimes such children work out ingenious representations of their ideas. A vertical view of a fence may be drawn on each of four sides to show that the fence went all the way around. The back door of a house may appear next to a front door because the child knows that his home has a back and a front door and he wants to get them both into his drawing. The wise teacher concerns herself less with what a drawing shows and more with what the child says about it. What he says is her cue for planning experiences which will expand his observations.

PICTURES FOR PARENTS

At five, children are primarily interested in the expressive process and comparatively disinterested in the product created. They thoroughly enjoy modeling clay and then squishing it down into a ball for use at another time. Finger painting on oilcloth is as much fun to them as fingerpainting on paper because both are an artistic expression. The five-year-old child has outgrown the possessiveness which makes it important for nursery school children to take home their art creations. Yet he is willing, nevertheless, to take home whatever his teacher or his parents wish him to take. In order to further home-school relations, he takes home his drawings, his paintings, and his craft work. These art expressions become a link between the school and the home.

Parents Foster Art at Home

The teacher is concerned that the parents understand the development of their children as it is reflected in their artistic expressions, and she is concerned that the parents further and not interfere with the creative development of their children. One teacher had the following note mimeographed. She attached a copy of it to the first drawing that each child took home.

> This is the first drawing your child has made at kindergarten. He will be bringing other art work home from time to time. You encourage your child to express himself in art forms when you:

Accept his drawing as it is and say, "Thank you for bringing it home."

Listen to any explanation he wishes to make about it.

Or ask him only, "Would you like to tell me about it?" and then accept "No" or whatever answer he gives without question.

Put each art work on display and then in a folder to be cleaned out sometime when your child is at school.

Provide your child with art materials at home.

We shall talk about children's drawing and the art materials they like to use at our next meeting for parents, October 10th at 3:30 in the kindergarten room.

Discussions at P.T.A. Meetings

At the meeting this teacher had several illustrative folders of work done by children in preceding years. One folder showed drawings made at the first of the year. Another folder showed how one child's work developed from formless scribbling, through symbolic scribbling, and into the beginnings of representation. The teacher discussed these drawings as an aid to understanding the children who drew them. She emphasized that each was a unique expression — something the child wanted to express that day. She also emphasized that each child will develop his artistic expression if the adults who are important to him are interested in what he has to tell them verbally and through his drawings and paintings, but are not directive or critical about what he has done.

At parent meetings the teacher guides parents in discussing art materials for use at home. She shows them how she helps a child put on his paint smock at school and start painting. Then she asks how mothers help their children do this at home. When the discussion has brought out a vivid and practical picture of how parents help a child paint, clean up after his painting, and display his painting, the teacher leads a similar discussion on the use of clay at home and the use of crayons and other art media that the parents mention. When parents ask about coloring books, she emphasizes the importance of free expression when children are beginning to express themselves artistically. If parents persist in advocating the use of coloring books, she suggests that they also provide their children with materials for free expression and observe whether the children use the coloring books or the other materials more often.

The teacher is prepared to answer questions of individual parents. For instance, a parent may ask what to do when a child says, "You make it." The teacher helps the parent understand how to build the child's confidence in what he does himself and how to withdraw from "helping" him. When a parent asks how to get a child interested in drawing, the teacher mentions ways of making experiences vivid for the child. She also emphasizes the importance of letting a child use his art materials in whatever way he wishes, whether he appears to the adult to waste materials or not. "Are we more interested in keeping the art materials in good condition or in encouraging the children to use them?"

Inspecting Child's Work in the Classroom

When parents visit school they like to see the artistic compositions of their children. Anticipating this the teacher has a place for each child to display one of his compositions. She may enhance the paintings by putting them onto a mat, using pins to mount them on the display space. Whatever she provides for one drawing, however, she provides for each of them. The teacher realizes that each drawing is an important creative expression for the child who made it, and she respects both the child and his drawing. She helps the parents develop this point of view. If the parents admire drawings which represent what a child has seen, the teacher points out that sometimes the children paint what they see but very often they paint what they feel. The important thing, she emphasizes, is that they find some art media through which to express themselves. The display of their art shows that each kindergarten child has at least one medium for artistic expression.

SITUATIONS FOR DISCUSSION

In the following situations select each course of action that seems desirable to you, basing your choices and omissions on the ideas presented in this chapter. Add one or more alternate courses of action.

SITUATION I. The children are to take home paintings at Easter time. To motivate such expression, as the teacher you should:

> Make a drawing of an Easter bunny while the children watch.
> Tell the children Easter-time stories.
> At each easel put four or five spring colors: lavender, light green, pink, yellow, and white.
> Have a pet bunny in a cage visit the kindergarten for a week or two.
> Show the best children's drawings made for Easter a year ago.

SITUATION II. Parents are invited to open house at the school. Your kindergarten room is one of those on display. You plan to show children's drawings. You should:

> Display a drawing by each child in your room.
> Display realistic drawings made by children in previous years.

Display different kinds of drawings and label them: haptic, optic.

Frame some of the pictures.

Have the children's names on the back, not on the front of the picture.

SITUATION III. At the open house, one of the kindergarten mothers says, "I'm glad Susan has a chance to paint here at school. I don't let her have paints at home. It's so messy." As the teacher, you should say:

"You might give her a plastic apron and let her paint outside on a big piece of paper on warm days."

"Susan enjoys painting and does very well with it."

"We are going to talk about painting at the next parents' meeting."

"Painting is messy, isn't it?"

"Children need a chance to be messy sometimes."

SITUATION IV. At an institute for teachers you hear the new theory about letting children choose colors for their easel painting instead of having four or five colors set out for them to use. The next week you should:

Put in a requisition to your principal for a dozen quart jars and some oil of wintergreen.

At the next parents' meeting, ask whether you should use the new theory with the children.

Discuss the new theory with your principal.

Talk over the new theory with other kindergarten teachers.

Use the new theory only if other teachers try it too.

BIBLIOGRAPHY

Professional Books and Pamphlets

Alschuler, Rose H., and L. W. Hattwick. *Painting and Personality*. Chicago: University of Chicago Press, 1947.

A two-volume work that describes how children's personalities are reflected in their painting.

Art for Children's Growing. General Service Bulletin No. 64. Association for Childhood Education International. Washington, D. C., 1955.

Specialists in art education tell how art aids development of children and suggests ways of having a climate favorable to creativity.

Association for Childhood Education International. *Art for Children's Growing*. General Service Bulletin No. 64. Washington, D. C., 1955.

Specialists in art education tell how art aids development of children and suggest ways of having a climate favorable to creativity.

D'Amico, Victor E. *Art for the Family*. New York: Museum of Modern Arts, 1954. This book for parents is also useful to teachers.

De Francesco, Italo L. *Art Education*. New York: Harper and Brothers, 1958.

A comprehensive book on art education in the elementary and secondary school.

Ellsworth, Maud, and Michael F. Andrews. *Growing with Art.* Book I: "Fun to Begin." Chicago: B. H. Sanborn & Co., 1950.
The first book of the series contains many practical suggestions about teaching art to young children.

Eng, Helga. *The Psychology of Children's Drawings.* London, E. C.: Routledge and Kegan Paul Ltd., (Imported by Robert Brunner, 1212 Avenue of the Americas, New York 36), 1954.
Dr. Eng describes and reproduces illustrative drawings by her niece from the time she was one until she was eight years old and discusses the drawings in relation to psychological theories.

Erdt, Margaret Hamilton. *Teaching Art in the Elementary School.* New York: Rinehart & Co., 1954.
"Motivation, release, accomplishment, satisfaction — these constitute the cycle of an art experience" says Miss Erdt who brings in this book a rich professional experience to share with teachers of young children.

Gaitskell, Charles D. *Children and Their Art.* New York: Harcourt, Brace & Co., 1958.
An inclusive book on art education.

Gaitskell, Charles D., and Margaret R. Gaitskell. *Art Education in the Kindergarten.* Peoria, Illinois: Charles A. Bennett Company, 1952.
This helpful booklet is an outgrowth of the authors' experience with children.

Gans, Roma; Celia B. Stendler; and Millie Almy. *Teaching Young Children in Nursery School, Kindergarten and the Primary Grades.* Yonkers-on-Hudson, New York: World Book Co., 1952.
Chapter XII, pages 285–313, emphasizes the child's need to express himself freely through different media of art and music.

Lee, Carvel. *Kindergarten-Primary Art Activities.* Dansville, New York: F. A. Owen Publishing Company, 1956.
The author illustrates her suggestions for art activities.

Lowenfeld, Viktor. *Creative and Mental Growth.* New York: The Macmillan Company, 1957.
Chapter IV, "First Representational Attempts," discusses scribbling; representation, intended and actual; and relationship to the child himself.

——. *Your Child and His Art.* New York: The Macmillan Co., 1954.
Dr. Lowenfeld based this book on questions asked by parents attending his lectures on art. Chapters deal with the creative expression of children at different ages (*e.g.* "The Four- to Seven-Year-Old"), as well as such questions as, "How Can I Foster My Child's Art?"

Books for Children

Baer, Howard. *Now This, Now That.* New York: Holiday House, 1957.
When I'm on the climber, Daddy says "I'm upside down, but I say daddy's upside down."

Brown, Margaret Wise. *The Color Kittens.* Little Golden Book #86. New York: Simon and Schuster, Inc., 1950.
The two kittens mix and match colors.

Johnson, Crockett. *Harold and the Purple Crayon.* New York: Harper and Brothers, 1955.

With his purple crayon, Harold is able to solve every problem of his evening. By the same author, *Harold's Trip to the Sky*, 1957, and *Harold's Fairy Tale*, 1956.

Kessler, Leonard P. *What's in a Line?* New York: William R. Scott, Inc., 1951.

A line can go any place and be anything.

Krauss, Ruth, and Crockett, Johnson. *Is This You?* New York: William R. Scott, Inc., 1955.

Amusing questions and drawings stimulate expression of ideas and feelings in drawings.

Lambert, Emily W. *The Man Who Drew Cats.* New York: Harper and Brothers, 1957.

By drawing cats, Mr. Phip helped a clown regain his laughter, a shy woman be friendly, and a little girl frighten the mice away from her dolls.

Rey, Margaret E. and H. A. *Billy's Picture.* New York: Harper and Brothers, 1948.

When Billy the rabbit tries to draw a picture of himself, his animal friends add what is important to each of them.

Schlein, Miriam. *A Bunny, A Bird, A Funny Cat.* New York: Abelard-Schuman Limited, 1957.

"Something alive must grow from its own kind of seed," but "in art you can make something that no one has ever seen before."

Webber, Irma E. *It Looks Like This.* New York: William R. Scott, Inc., 1954.

The mice draw pictures of what the barn animals look like from where each of them lives, and come to appreciate each other's point of view.

Films for Teachers

A Day in the Life of a Five-Year-Old. Bureau of Publications, Teachers College, Columbia University. 2 reels, 20 minutes, sound, black and white.

Art and the Growing Child. New Haven, Connecticut: Films for Education, 1956.

Paintings of children from nursery school through high school show their emotional and intellectual development. 60 frames, 33$\frac{1}{3}$ r.p.m. disc recording, color.

Finger Painting Methods. Chicago: Coronet Instructional Films, 1954.

Techniques for children's finger painting are demonstrated. 11 minutes, sound, color.

Understanding Children's Drawings. New York 19: A. F. Films, Inc., 1949.

In art classes of the Manhattan Jewish Center in New York, children from three through seven years of age scribble, draw with form and design, and compose story-telling pictures. 10 minutes, sound, black and white.

14

Self-Expression Through Music

Music as a means of expression is an innate need and desire. Love of music is natural in children and the role of the kindergarten teacher is to foster music as part of their very nature. Before children come to school they sing as they play — sometimes a little wordless improvisation, sometimes the ubiquitous television "commercial," sometimes a phrase or sentence sung over and over accompanied by rhythmical movements, sometimes a comforting humming to accompany a task on which they are concentrating.

Kindergarten should provide many opportunities to sing in small groups or alone if a child wishes, to listen to the teacher sing a song, to learn songs, to listen to recordings, to listen to choral or instrumental music, to experiment with rhythm instruments, to try out the piano, to respond rhythmically to music, and to learn the names of a few instruments of the band or orchestra. In a world where children are surrounded with music, many opportunities for learning music and finding out how music is made occur out of school.

Children differ in the degree to which they respond to music, however, so the teacher must always be careful not to demand too much from the child of modest musical gifts nor too little from the child of exceptional ability. Children differ also in the kinds of musical activity that appeal to them. For many children, melody is the most appealing part of music and they find their greatest enjoyment in singing, in listening, or in playing tonal instruments. Other children find their great joy in rhythm and their greatest pleasure in responding to music through bodily movements or through playing rhythm instruments.

Response to music is spontaneous when children feel free, secure, and comfortable. Music provides release from tension, keen aesthetic enjoyment, and moments of explosive fun. The major purposes of all music activities in the kindergarten are to help children broaden their contact with music, increase the number of ways they can express themselves musically, and build a deep and abiding love of music as an indispensable experience in their lives.

THE WELL-BALANCED MUSIC PROGRAM

The kindergarten teacher is concerned with the five facets of a well-balanced music program: singing, listening, rhythmical response to music, playing simple instruments, and creating original music.

Singing

If a child comes from a home in which he has been encouraged to sing, has listened to the singing of others, and has realized that the adults in the family find music a pleasurable experience, he usually feels free to sing and may sing exceedingly well. But even when a child has not had so fortunate a background, a rich musical environment and friendly encouragement usually result in the child's joining in simple songs with a small group and before the end of the year may lead him to want to sing individually.

The young child expresses himself happily and naturally through singing. His spontaneous songs appear in his play as he creates little tunes about his environment. "Oh, kitty, kitty," is just as likely to be sung as spoken by the young child, and such phrases as, "Johnny has a baseball," are often chanted rhythmically. As the child matures and enjoys play with his friends at school, he participates in singing games, and he learns songs about things and people he knows, songs of counting and of things to do, and easy repetitive folk songs.

Songs should be sung within a vocal range that is easy and natural for the child so that he has a feeling of satisfaction, pleasure, and success. Failure to take account of voice range may lead to a mistaken impression of his ability to sing.[1] Many kindergarten songs are written too high for the majority of children. The young child's voice range centers nearer G above C than the C above as was previously believed.

The singing of any group of young children brought together for the first time will reveal a wide range of differences. A musically unawakened child should be neither pushed nor discouraged. Children of limited musical background should be given plenty of time to grow. Many opportunities should be provided for children to find expression in free spontaneous song. Singing should be an important part of their daily living. Lilla Belle Pitts says:

[1] Arthur T. Jersild and Sylvia F. Beinstock. "A Study of the Development of Children's Ability to Sing," *Journal of Educational Psychology*, XXV (October 1939), p. 491.

An adequate music program has to make special provision for meeting all kinds of individual differences. Short and simple songs that can be grasped with ease and many well-known singing games should be included. These little folk need a chance to join in, on their level with what the others can do. Independence is built up step by step through active, happy and successful participation.

A thoughtless or joking remark made to or in the presence of a child about his or her singing may make a deep and lasting impression on a sensitive boy or girl. It is a mistake to assume that children always know how to interpret casual statements, such as: "Tom can't carry a tune, he takes after his father's family." "You should hear Peggy sing, her voice is too funny for words." But overpraise of the more gifted child in a family and finding fault with the one who does not do so well can have even worse effect. Jealousy and resentment follow many a child to school, causing either a stubbornly negative or an openly hostile attitude toward all singing.[2]

Release from tension may be accomplished readily through singing as well as through rhythmic movement. The pleasure which singing gives the individual and his subsequent desire to sing as a member of the group are more important than vocal perfection. The child's greatest pleasure, however, will come through a feeling of success in giving his best effort to the group. The child's personal integrity and sensitivity must be respected at all times. Singing is necessary to the full expression of the child's spirit and to the growth of his personality. Every child has his important place in singing experiences and is a valuable member of the group.

Singing Experiences

Singing Throughout the Day

In the sharing period
"In School," Spear — *American Singer*, Book I, p. 13
"In School Together," Dykema — *Our First Music*, p. 5

In the work period
"Tap-a-Tap Tap," Bohemian — *Our Songs*, p. 48
"The Grocer Man," Rossman — *Our Songs*, p. 52

In the play period
"Skip-a to My Lou," Tennessee — *American Folk Songs for Children*, p. 166
"What Shall We Do When We All Go Out?" North Carolina — *American Folk Songs for Children*, p. 59
"The Mulberry Bush," Old Singing Game — *Experiences in Music for First Grade Children*, p. 102

On a study trip
"The Bus" — *Singing on Our Way*, p. 153
"Merrily We Roll Along," American — *Our First Music*, p. 337

[2] Lilla Belle Pitts, *The Kindergarten Book*. Boston: Ginn and Company, 1949, pp. viii and ix.

Singing informally with the teacher

FAVORITE SONGS FOR ENJOYMENT

"Silent Night," Gruber — *Our Songs*, p. 25

"Jimmy Crack Corn," American Singing Games — *The First Grade Book*, p. 46

"Go Tell Aunt Rhody," American — *Timothy's Tunes*, p. 41

ART AND FOLK SONGS

"Chick-A-Biddy," Brahms — *New Music Horizons*, Book II, p. 99

"How Lovely Are the Messengers," Mendelssohn — *Our First Music*, p. 62

"The Little Dustman," Brahms — *Experiences in Music for First Grade Children*, p. 116

SONGS SUGGESTING RHYTHMIC BODILY EXPRESSION

"Circus Parade" — *Our Songs*, p. 54

"Autumn Leaves" — *Rhythm Fun*, p. 10

"A Little Bridge" — *First Grade Book*, p. 47

"We'll Dance" — *Our First Music*, p. 75

SONGS SUGGESTING IMPROVISATION

"Oh, Oh, the Sunshine," Texas — *American Folk Songs for Children*, p. 64

"Toodala," Texas — *American Folk Songs for Children*, p. 54

"Roll that Brown Jug," Illinois — *American Folk Songs for Children*, p. 88

"The Grocer Man," Rossman — *Our Songs*, p. 52

SONGS SUGGESTING DRAMATIZATION

"I Had a Little Nut Tree," Traditional — *Experiences in Music for First Grade Children, New Music Horizons*, p. 41

"Ra-Ta-Ta-Ta-Boom," French — *Experiences in Music for First Grade Children, New Music Horizons*, p. 111

Songs appropriate for the use of instruments; songs about instruments

"Making Music," Italian — *Our First Music*, p. 115

"Our Band," French — *Our First Music*, p. 121

"My Tambourine," Coleman — *Singing Time*, p. 23

"Patapan," French — *Our First Music*, p. 228

SONGS SUGGESTING RHYTHM INSTRUMENT ADDITIONS

"The Daily Express," Harvey — *Our Songs* (rhythm sticks), p. 68

"The Clock," Bently — *The Kindergarten Book* (rhythm sticks), p. 125

"Spring Bells," Rossman — *Our First Music* (bells), p. 294

"Hickory, Dickory, Dock," — *Our First Songs to Sing with Descants* (sticks, xylophone, gong, woodblock), p. 8

Their own songs

Simple phrases and motifs from songs that will provide help for pitch difficulties

"Who's That Tapping at the Window," Virginia — *American Folk Songs for Children*, p. 52

Toneplay — "Mammy," "Pappy," or name of any child

"Did You Go to the Barney," Arkansas — *American Folk Songs for Children*, p. 112

Toneplay — "Yes, Ma'am"

"Hush, Little Baby," Alabama — *American Folk Songs for Children*, p. 147
Toneplay — "Mocking Birds"
"Spring Bells," Rossman — *Our First Music*, p. 294
Toneplay — "Ding, Dong, Bells"

Songs learned from recordings
"Little Red Hen," Decca Record CVS II
"When the Sun Shines," Young People's Record 617
Songs of Many Lands, Decca Album 605
"Sheep Are Coming Down the Road," African
"Go Tell Aunt Rhody," American

To keep up with new musical publications, the teacher may ask a music store to put her name on its mailing list.

Teaching a Song

The first step with children is to get the singing going. The children should sing because it is fun. The teacher pitches songs in a range where the greatest number of children will participate voluntarily. Teachers find that as children develop vocally, their tone quality and intonation will improve when songs are pitched higher. Every teacher should work for the lovely, clear tone that children alone can produce. The play spirit should be kept uppermost, especially in individual work when children are helped to find their singing voices. The informality of the seating arrangement is important in working with young children.

When the teacher introduces a new song, she makes it childlike and as beautiful as possible. She may introduce it as a song and then tell the children its story, or she may introduce it by using the story first. Its meaning should be clear to the children and they should feel that it is a song they would like to sing. Various methods of presenting a song are listed in order of preference, but these methods may be combined: voice, recording, piano, tonebell, or other melody instrument.

When the teacher sings for the children she pitches the songs to fit her voice. The pitch should be changed later if necessary for the best performance of the children.

The teacher teaches the song as a whole. Repeated hearing of the song is necessary as the children are learning it. As time goes on, special attention is given to more difficult phrases and the meaning and pronunciation of new words. The successful teacher is resourceful in promoting activities which help to focus the attention of the children on the song and aid them in learning it. The children are encouraged to join in singing the song at the earliest possible moment, and the teacher must be sensitive to their readiness to sing. For illustration, some desirable activities in relation to particular songs are listed.

Suggestions to stimulate listening while the song is being learned:

"Riding in a Wagon," MacCarteney, *Songs for the Nursery School*, p. 2
Drive a horse (first 4 measures) and rotate one arm around the other to make the motion of wheels going around. (2 measures)

"Warm Kitty," English Folk Tune, *Songs for the Nursery School*, p. 27
Pet a kitty

"So-Sow-Sowing," Old Tune — *Our Songs*, p. 109
Actions as suggested in text of song

"Mary's Lullaby," Traditional Carol — *Rime, Rhythm and Song*, p. 39
Rock a baby

"The Saucy Sue," Stevens — *Merry Music*, p. 76
Hoist the sails

IMPROVISATION OF SONG TEXTS:
"Oh, Oh, the Sunshine," *American Folk Songs for Children*, p. 64
"Mary Wore Her Red Dress," *American Folk Songs for Children*, p. 130
"Walk Along John," *American Folk Songs for Children*, p. 134

STANZAS TO SUIT THE WEATHER OR OCCASION TO:
"Toodala," *American Folk Songs for Children*, p. 54

Dramatization

"Tin Soldiers and Pussy," Hartford — *Kindergarten and First Grade Book*, Music Hour Series, p. 30
Fingers may march and creep, and then pussy cat and the soldiers may play the story while the teacher sings.

Use of rhythm instruments

"Rain Song," *Our First Music*, p. 130
Drums and rattles
"Spring Bells," *Our First Music*, p. 294
Bells on appropriate parts
"The Sledge," *Merry Music*, p. 104
Coconut shells and sleigh bells

Motif or part of song

"Three Little Kittens," Traditional — *New Music Horizons*, Book I, p. 6: "Miew's" last eight measures
"Hallowe'en Is Coming," Children's Songs — *Kindergarten Book*, p. 73: "Oh, What Fun"
"The Cat Is in the Snow," *Singing On Our Way*, p. 114

It is desirable to vary the presentation each day. The preceding suggestions for stimulating attention may be used for this purpose, or the teacher may play or hum partially learned songs and encourage the children to recognize and identify them.

Helping Children Listen

Listening is an integral part of life for a young child. He is fascinated by the world of sound around him. On his way to school he hears a great many interesting sounds — a bird call, a rubbing sound, the rumble of a big truck. When he comes into kindergarten he should not close the door on that world of sound, but should bring it in with him. When a child says, "I heard a fire siren," his teacher encourages him to make the sound he heard and then to share his experience with the other children near him.

JOHNNY: I heard a fire siren.

TEACHER: Did you? What did it sound like?

JOHNNY: WHEEEeeeeeee.

TEACHER: (*to children nearby*) Johnny heard a fire siren. What did it sound like, Johnny?

JOHNNY: WHEEEeeeeeee.

SAM: I heard it too.

TEACHER: How did it sound to you?

SAM: WHEEEEEEEEEEEeeeeeeeeeee.
(*The teacher asks different children to show what it sounded like to them.*)

TEACHER: It's fun to listen to sounds and to make them. We make fire sirens outdoors because they are so loud. Later today when we are outdoors we can pretend we are sirens.
(*The teacher guides the children into other interests.*)

The sensitive teacher is alert for opportunities to focus attention on sounds. An airplane flying over the school is not an interference but an occasion to decide whether the noise was made by a jet airplane or by a propeller-driven airplane. The kindergarten children develop an interest in distinguishing sounds. Is it a child or an adult coming down the hall? From what direction is the sound of the plane coming? Did the teacher say "today" or "tomorrow"? Is the word "sad" or "said"? Discrimination in listening to sounds helps children get ready for reading and for identifying the voice they hear over the telephone, the approaching footstep, or each friendly sound of the night.

In all other aspects of his music experiences except listening the child is active. He sings songs, he moves rhythmically to music, and he plays instruments. All of these are producer's enterprises. But now and throughout his life he will be a consumer of music and hence this part of his musical experience needs stimulation and guidance. As a matter of fact, effective singing, dancing, and playing of instruments depends upon discriminating listening. The child must be able to listen to his own singing, listen to the accompaniment for his rhythmic movements, and listen to his instrument and the other instruments being played with his, in order to correct and improve the quality of his performance.

Facilities for Listening

The modern kindergarten has excellent facilities for training children in quiet listening. It is not necessary for all the children to listen to recorded music at the same time. With the Listening Post, a small companionable group may enjoy music together. The Listening Post is a control box, with headsets, which may be attached to any type of phonograph. When it is attached, the regular speaker is silenced. Matched earphones of good quality bring high fidelity reproduction to the children. The vibrations of music permeate ears, sinuses, and bony structure of the head so the music really becomes a part of the listener. A control for each headset permits the child to adjust the volume to his desire. The headset shuts off the ambient noises of the room and the child is off in a world of music. As he listens he relaxes, and as he relaxes he hears more music and the music takes on more meaning. Thus do children discover the joy of quiet listening. They grow in ability to discriminate. They become acquainted with their cultural heritage and are on their way to becoming appreciative consumers of the musical riches of their world.

Some listening in the kindergarten may involve all or nearly all of the children. Through the use of recordings, children can respond with understanding to music far beyond their ability in musical performance. Since tone color plays a major part in the appeal of music, it is important that both the records and the machines that play them be of good tone quality. The teacher recognizes that the attention span of children differs and avoids musical compositions that are too long. Descriptive music or music that tells a story usually holds attention. Dramatization of the music by playing instruments to accompany it or free interpretation in movement are enjoyed for a long time.

Many children find their richest response to music through listening to it without attempting to perform it. Music education has a place for experiences that are impressive as well as expressive. Mursell says:

> Often music can be brought to children for no other reason than that it is beautiful and appealing and likely to be enjoyed — and a very good reason too. Listening, in fact, is a prime and many-sided musical influence. It reveals standards rather than imposes them, suggests all kinds of enterprises including creation, and incites to achievement. A program of music for children should be saturated with listening.[3]

[3] James L. Mursell. "Music for Children," *Children and Music.* Bulletin of the Association for Childhood Education. Washington: Association for Childhood Education, 1948, p. 5.

Listening may be incidental to other activity, but it may also be the focus of the child's attention and involve reaction on the part of the child. This reaction can be creative and it can be one of the most rewarding of all the child's musical experiences. Children listen attentively when they know what to listen for and know also that they will have an opportunity to respond in their own way to what they have heard. On days when children feel tension either in or out of school, quiet listening can be a source of relaxation and serenity.

In relation to musical growth, however, incidental listening is incomplete; the response of children should involve the head as well as the heart. Very young children can recognize differences between loud and soft, high and low, heavy and light, and can relate them appropriately to situations they have experienced. Although music, strictly speaking, conveys only musical meaning, the recognition of certain instruments as appropriate to certain characterizations, animals, or objects can provide a foundation for future musical discrimination at a much higher level. Little children, for example, can enjoy laughing at the humor of the elephant trying to do a toe dance in "The Carnival of Animals" by Saint-Saëns even though strictly speaking the humor really consists of the bass viols playing a melody originally written for the delicately muted tones of the violins.

It is important to recognize that feeling about music and the development of a warm-hearted response to it are of first consideration in listening. Teachers need not hesitate to play the same recording many times. Children, like adults, enjoy what they know. They develop favorites among musical compositions as they do among their friends, and they crave the continuing company of each.

Choosing Music for Listening

In choosing music for children's listening, teachers should include only the best and strive for variety. The fundamental criterion in selecting music is its aesthetic appeal to the children and their potential response to it. Certain compositions may be too long to be practical for the listening of young children, but *no* music is too good for them. No intrinsic value in the whole world of music is too good to be introduced to children. Children can respond to the expressive message and appeal of the greatest music in their own way, which need not be the way of adults. If children are given the opportunity to hear fine music it will serve as a rich foundation for future musical growth. A lasting appreciation of the world's great music is built only on a basis of many pleasurable experiences with it.

Listening Experiences
Listening to Sounds in the Environment
Pitch, such as bells, clocks, whistles, sirens
Rhythm, such as trains, hoofbeats, patter of rain
Voices of teacher and classmates speaking and singing
Tones of piano, and other musical instruments and recordings

Listening for Relaxation
"Air on the G String" — Suite in D Major — Bach — Victor Record 7103
"Lullaby" — Brahms — RCA Victor Album, Listening, Vol. I, 45-5024
"Nocturne" from *Midsummer Night's Dream* — Mendelssohn — Victor, DM 1280
"Night Soliloquy" — Kennan — Victor Record 15659

Listening to Create Congenial Atmosphere
"Moment Musicale" — Schubert — Victor Record 11-9174
"On Wings of Song" — Mendelssohn — Victor Record 6848
"Schwanda" — Polka and Fugue — Weinberger — Victor Record 7958

Listening Associated with Childhood Interests
RECORDINGS BROUGHT TO SCHOOL BY THE CHILDREN
With music — especially recorded music — receiving so much attention at
home these days, possibilities for musical development in early childhood are
ever increasing. Through the careful selection and use of worthy music in school,
the opportunity arises to continue the rich musical environment provided in
many homes. In addition, the teacher may be helpful to parents in advising them
concerning recordings desirable for children.

GOOD EXAMPLES OF CHILDREN'S RECORDINGS
"Mother Goose Land" — Read, Look and Listen Series, Victor Y-34
"Tubby, the Tuba"[4] — Victor Jory — Decca CU 106
"The Lost Sheep" — Young People's Records
"The Mulberry Bush" — Allegro Junior

EXAMPLES OF RECORDINGS OF STANDARD COMPOSITIONS WHICH CHILDREN ENJOY
"March of Toys" — Herbert — Victor 12592
"Hungarian Dances 5 and 6" — Brahms — Fiedler, Boston Pops, Victor
Record 4321
"Hansel and Gretel" — Humperdinck — Victor P-38
"American Folk Songs" — Siegmeister — Victor P-41

Rhythmic Activities
Rhythm is basic to every aspect of human life. During infancy and
continuing through childhood, rhythmic experiences help fulfill the need
for release from emotional tension, help provide satisfaction and pleasure,
and bring a sense of relief and security. Ribble says:

[4] Paul Tripp. *Tubby, the Tuba.* New York: Treasure Books, 1954. This book is
one of several which tell a story also told by a record.

Along with its rhythmic swing, the lullaby holds a time-honored place as a means of helping the infant to establish his sleeping function. So through the years, lullabies help bring a feeling of relaxation.[5]

Since motor activity is so important, bodily movement is essential to physical, emotional, and social development. Many of the activities of the kindergarten give children opportunity to express ideas through rhythmic movement. Swinging on the swing, rocking the doll, skipping, running, hopping, being a rabbit, being a galloping cowboy, and dancing in a circle are some of the rhythmic activities which contribute to the child's motor development at the same time that he is identifying himself with his world.

According to Helen Christianson, the child's "whole body becomes an instrument vibrating in response to gay, rhythmic music."[6] As a child satisfies his individual need for rhythm he tends to share his rhythmic experiences with his classmates and to join in group activities. Jersild says, "The use of markedly rhythmic music was found to help some shy children to become more expressive and to participate more freely in group activities."[7]

Creative bodily rhythms may develop as an outgrowth of any experience. They may come from a study trip, from play, hearing a story, looking at a picture book, seeing a film, hearing music, or from the innate love of movement for its own sake. A child's first response through rhythmic bodily movement may seem limited and incomplete. But when these tentative beginnings are recognized, valued, and nurtured by the teacher, the child becomes more confident in his rhythmic efforts.[8]

Teachers should not expect children to be socially comfortable doing rhythms in large groups of twenty-five or thirty. In the kindergarten, children respond best either alone or in small groups of three or four. With this in mind, the teacher offers opportunity for rhythmic experience in accordance with each child's development.

Recognizing that the desire for rhythmic expression is inborn in children, teachers may direct and aid its development by first providing opportuni-

[5] Margaret A. Ribble, M.D. *The Rights of Infants.* New York: Columbia University Press, 1943, p. 45.

[6] Helen Christianson. *Bodily Rhythmic Movements.* New York: Bureau of Publications, Teachers College, Columbia University, 1938, p. 16.

[7] Arthur T. Jersild. "Music" in the 38th Yearbook of the *National Society for the Study of Education.* Bloomington: Public School Publishing Company, 1939, p. 140.

[8] Natalie Cole. *Arts in the Classroom.* New York: John Day Company, 1940. Rhythmic activities are suitable for kindergarten children.

ties for simple, natural, free expressions and then proceeding gradually
to more complex patterns and understandings. Basic rhythms are the
starting point. Rhythm must be "felt in the bones."

Opportunities for rhythmic expression and growth may be offered in a
variety of ways. The teacher may improvise simple accompaniments for
rhythms created by the children. She may provide songs or chants, piano
selections, and recorded music, or she may use percussion instruments
such as drums, tone blocks, or coconut shells. A rich program includes
them all. Such variety makes it possible for any teacher to provide
rhythms for children.

Since the first approach should be a recognition and encouragement of
each child's bodily movement, desirable procedure calls for adjusting
accompaniments to the rhythm of the child rather than asking him to
adjust to a set piece of music. Teachers need not be hesitant in attempting
to provide such accompaniments. A few chords on the piano or the auto-
harp or rhythms produced on percussion instruments which capture the
child's movement will enrich and encourage his early rhythmic expressions.
The alert teacher will also adjust the tempo of songs and piano selections
to the rhythm of the children.

Children extend and refine their rhythmic activities progressing from
broad, bodily movement to the playing of percussion instruments. For
example, first the child gallops and later he plays a galloping rhythm on
coconut shells.

The following are a few examples of materials that have proved unusually successful in stimulating rhythmic activities. The musical notation
suggests patterns for the percussion instruments when the teacher cares to
use them.

Rhythmic Experiences

Natural Rhythms

Patty-cake to clapping
  "Pat-a-Cake" — Traditional — *The Kindergarten Book*, p. 49
  "Pat-a-Cake" — Jewish — *The First Grade Book*, p. 60
  "Clap Your Hands" — Folk Tune — *The First Grade Book*, p. 20

Rocking and swaying
  "Rocking" — Folk Tune — *Timothy's Tunes*, p. 23
  "Rock-a-bye-Baby" — Traditional — *New Music Horizons*, Book I, p. 40

Swinging
  "Swing Song" — Coleman — *Singing Time*, p. 37
  "Swing Song" — Hartford — *Experiences in Music for First Grade Children*,
    p. 66

Dancing
"Come Dance" — Swedish — *Our First Songs*, p. 104
"I'm Learning to Dance" — Alsatian — *Our Songs*, p. 107
"Mignon" — Gavotte — Thomas — RCA Victor Record 7456

Walking
"Let's Go Walking" — Coleman — *Another Singing Time*, p. 13
"Will You Come?" — Porter — *The Kindergarten Book*, p. 23
"Walk Along, John" — Oklahoma — *American Folk Songs for Children*, p. 134
"March" — Gurlitt — RCA Victor Album E-72, Rhythms, Vol. II, 45-5005

Walking on Tip Toe
"Tip Toe March" — Italian — *The Kindergarten Book*, p. 20
"Tip Toe March" — Italian — RCA Victor Album E-71, Rhythms, Vol. I, 45-5002

Sliding
"I'll Skate on My Roller Skates" — Castle — *The Kindergarten Book*, p. 32
"Song of the Roller Skates" — Allen — *Our First Music*, p. 338
"Skating" — Kullak — RCA Victor Album E-72, Rhythms, Vol. II, 45-5005

Running and Trotting
"Run a Little" — Coleman — *Another Singing Time*, p. 19
"Running" — Children's Song — *The Kindergarten Book*, p. 10
"Trot, Trot, Trot" — Rossman — *Our Songs*, p. 20
"The Race Track" — Strauss — Columbia Record 12543-D
"Running" — Anderson — RCA Victor Album E-71, Rhythms, Vol. I, 45-5002
"Running Game" — Gurlitt — RCA Victor Album E-72, Rhythms, Vol. II, 45-5006

Jumping
"See Me Jump" — Children's Song — *The Kindergarten Book*, p. 19
"Jumping" — Gurlitt — RCA Victor Album E-72, Rhythms, Vol. II, 45-5005
"See, How I'm Jumping" — Finnish — *Songs for the Nursery School*, p. 95

Bouncing
"Bounce Ball" — Children's Song — *The First Grade Book*, p. 26

Galloping
"We're Galloping" — Children's Song — *The Kindergarten Book*, p. 18
"Galloping" — Engels — *Our First Music*, p. 114
"The Wild Horseman" — Schumann — RCA Victor Album E-78, Listening, Vol. II, 45-5028

Hopping
"Hop Up, Hop Down" — Motion Song — *The Kindergarten Book*, p. 21

Marching
"Marching Song" — Coleman — *Singing Time*, p. 7
"Marching" — English — *Our First Music*, p. 103
"Yankee Doodle" — *Our Songs*, p. 94
"Soldiers' March" — Schumann — *Our First Music*, p. 97
"Stars and Stripes" — Sousa — Victor Record 18-0053

Skipping
"Rigga Jig Jig" — Folk Song — *Twice 55 Games with Music*, No. 24
"Happy and Light of Heart" — Balfe — RCA Victor Album E-72, Rhythms, Vol. II, 45-5007
"Skipping Theme" — Anderson — RCA Victor Album E-71, Rhythms, Vol. I, 45-5002

Imitative Rhythms

Rhythms in imitation of nature, animals, and means of transportation are a rich source for growth in freedom of expression. The following suggestions can be worked out through two approaches. Sometimes bodily rhythmic movements are a means of expression of an idea to which music is added later as an accompaniment. In most instances, however, music is played for the children and they interpret what they hear and feel by means of bodily movement.

Nature
Wind
"Berceuse" — Ilyinsky — RCA Victor Album E-73, Rhythms, Vol. III, 45-5010. Glissando accompaniment may be played on melody bells by running mallet up and down the bars.

Waves
"Waves" — Wentworth — *Our Songs*, p. 138
"Barcarolle" — Offenbach — Victor Record 11-9174
Sand block accompaniment is effective.

Trees
"Waltz No. 9" — Brahms — RCA Victor Album E-72, Rhythms, Vol. II, 45-5006

Animals
FOUR-LEGGED
"Hop Old Squirrel" — Virginia — *American Folk Songs for Children*, p. 109
"Running Horses" — Mendelssohn — *Our First Music*, p. 329
"See That Elephant" — Loomis — *Our Songs*, p. 58
"March of the Lions" — Carnival of Animals — Saint-Saëns, Victor Album MO 785
"The Little White Donkey" — Ibert — Animal Pictures in Music, Decca Record Album 55

CRAWLING
"Tortoises" — *Carnival of Animals* — Saint-Saëns — Victor Album MO 785

FLYING
"Garden Varieties" (bees, butterflies) — Phoebe James Record AED 4-A
"Papillons No. 8" — Schumann — RCA Victor Album E-73, Rhythms, Vol. III, 45-5008

Means of Transportation
Boats
"Allegretto" from *Faust* ballet — Gounod — RCA Victor Album E-79, Listening, Vol. III, 45-5033

With tints, shades, and colors of full
intensity to choose from, the kindergarten child likes
to explore painting at an easel.

Children learn the difference in sound when a
bell is hit hard and when it is struck gently to
produce a singing tone.

Trains
"Clickity-Clack" — *Our First Music*, p. 336
"Planes and Trains" — Mendelssohn — *First Grade Book*, p. 181
"Here We Go A-Riding on a Train" — *First Grade Book*, p. 178
Airplanes
"Airplane" — Phoebe James Record AED 3
Buses
"The Bus" — *Singing on Our Way*, p. 153
Action Songs
"Open, Shut Them" — MacCarteney — *Songs for the Nursery School*, p. 8
"The Do-It Song" — French — *Rime, Rhythm and Song*, p. 36
"Did You Go to the Barney?" — Arkansas — *American Folk Songs for Children*, p. 112
"This Old Man" — English — New Music Horizons, Book II, p. 120

Playing Instruments

If innate and lasting interests are guides in planning a program of music education, provision for the use of musical instruments will be included throughout the child's school life. No child should be called unmusical because either through choice or limited ability he does not achieve success in the singing program. For many children a musical instrument serves their needs and desires more effectively than singing. Likewise, musical instruments provide an added challenge to the child who is particularly musical. The resourceful teacher develops a close relationship between instrumental and singing activities so that each enriches the other.

Musical instruments should be regarded *not* as external gadgets that a child may learn to manipulate but as an extension of the child's being through which he sings in an expressive way. Musical instruments provide children with an added avenue of musical growth and the contribution the children may make to their group through the use of instruments makes them feel more secure socially. Musical instruments are not solely for a gifted few. All children in the kindergarten should have the opportunity to grow musically through exploratory experiences with appropriate instruments.

When the playing of instruments is approached with an exploratory and experimental attitude, children have opened to them a new array of sounds with the possibilities of developing discrimination in their use. As the child uses instruments, he becomes aware of the appropriate instrument for the effect he desires. Many children find the rhythmic rattle of a gourd satisfying as an accompaniment to an Indian tune. Sensitivity to the tone quality of an instrument and awareness of mood in music will develop artistry in playing the simplest of instruments.

As he matures, the child enjoys choosing his instrument and playing it in the rhythm and tempo in which he feels most comfortable. Muscular co-ordination is an important factor in this choice. Later, as he becomes more adjusted socially, he plays his instrument to accompany the group. He may be one of the tom-tom players accompanying his friends as they dance.

More acceptable procedures in the childlike, experimental use of rhythm instruments are replacing the formal rhythm band. Helen Christianson tells us:

> When numbers of five-year-olds are assembled in a rhythm band, insistence on set timing dulls creative sensitivity, fatigue results from too long periods of conformity, and overstimulation is induced by the volume of discordant sounds. Far too frequently the rhythm band situation eliminates the possibility of rhythmic expression growing out of or being a part of play activities and checks a child's ability to advance at his own rate.[9]

In order that experiences with percussion instruments become a part of kindergarten activity, a child must have opportunity to experiment, to discuss, to listen, and to evaluate. Before a satisfying choice of an instrument can be made, he must manipulate it. For example, he finds the triangle does not suit his slow-moving freight train nearly so well as a pair of sand blocks.

The placing of instruments in a convenient corner indoors or outdoors encourages experimentation and stimulates independent activity. It also promotes the playing of instruments by individuals and small groups. The music corner should be out of the general path of activity. In this way the sounds of other activities do not interfere with tonal thinking on the part of the child and the instruments likewise do not disturb other activities. The instruments should be varied from time to time. Two or three sizes of drums differing in tone quality are desirable. Tone bells with *Timothy Tunes* or a similar book open to an interesting song, a variety of shaker instruments, bells of different sizes, and tambourines for dancing are useful. An illustrated songbook placed upon the piano interests children in using it. This may be either a published book or a collection of the original songs of children.

Playing Experiences

Opportunities for playing a variety of percussion instruments
  Rhythm tone block or coconut shells for galloping pony
  "My Pony," *Rime, Rhythm and Song*, p. 61

---

[9] Helen Christianson. "Producers or Consumers: Which Shall We Foster?" *Children and Music.* Bulletin of the Association for Childhood Education. Washington: Association for Childhood Education, 1948, p. 10.

"Trot, Trot, Trot," *Our Songs*, p. 20

"Wild Horseman," RCA Victor Album E-78, Listening, Vol. II, 45-5028

Deep-toned drum, preferably homemade
"Big Tall Indian," *Singing Time*, p. 26

"Follow My Leader," *Our Songs*, p. 79

"Grinding Corn," *American Singer*, Book II, p. 37

"Rain Song," *Our First Music*, p. 130

"Down Came a Lady," *American Folk Songs for Children*, p. 51

Bells worn as a necklace or at wrist or ankle for fun in skipping
"A Skipping Song," *Our First Music*, p. 75

"Skip-a to My Lou," *American Folk Songs for Children*, p. 166

"Jingle at the Windows," *American Folk Songs for Children*, p. 173

"Happy and Light of Heart," RCA Victor Album E-72, Rhythms, Vol. II, 45-5007

Sand blocks for waves and trains
"Here We Go A-Riding on a Train," *The First Grade Book*, p. 178

"Train That's Going West," *Merry Music*, p. 77

"The Train Is A-Coming," *American Folk Songs for Children*, p. 150

"Sailing in the Boat," *American Folk Songs for Children*, p. 16

"Boat Song," *Merry Music*, p. 79

"Run, Run, Run," RCA Victor Album E-72, Rhythmic Activities, Vol. II, 45-5006

Given an opportunity children experiment freely with instruments. In order that the tonal quality of instruments may be easily distinguished it is wise to play them singly and in small combinations in the early stages of experimentation. The children learn the difference in sound when a bell is hit hard and when it is struck gently to produce a singing tone. Likewise, they become sensitive to the variety of sounds produced by a variety of drums and recognize the ringing tone of a triangle as distinguished from the sound of the song bells. In this way children come to identify the sounds of instruments as being appropriate to situations.

A well-equipped kindergarten is provided with a piano and a three-speed phonograph. In addition, an autoharp, a collection of drums, song bells, cymbals, jingle bells, rhythm sticks, sand blocks, tambourines, and triangles should be available. An ingenious teacher finds many ways to construct additional rhythm instruments such as beans in cans, beans in cardboard containers, small pieces of metal, and drums made from kegs. By manipulation and experimentation the children discover pitch, tension, vibration, and tone quality.

Creating Music

In the music-minded kindergarten, a child feels free to come to the teacher with the little song he has created, for instance. The teacher shares his delight with his composition and listens attentively while he sings it. Frequently she sings it back to him so he hears it too. Sometimes she has him share it with other children nearby. Such appreciation encourages children in listening as well as in creating music.

Although creativity is frequently interpreted to mean the production of something new and original, there are elements of creation in every satisfying musical experience the child has. Interpretation enters into his singing of a song, his developing of a rhythm, his playing of an instrument, or his listening to a musical composition. Creativity is a deeply personal experience; all such creative experiences may become the reservoir from which eventually will flow a unique expression.

It is the natural urge of all children to explore the world in which they live. In expressing their enthusiasm for this world young children are continually creating little songs, chants, rhythms, or games. They are endlessly exploring the sounds in their environment and experimenting with tones of simple musical instruments, many times for the love of the sound itself. Young children "act out" or dramatize familiar songs and rhymes as readily as they sing or speak them; they enjoy responding rhythmically to music to which they listen. Children's experiences in music are direct, simple, and increasingly creative.

Faith in the creative, exploring nature of children eliminates any hesitancy or fear on the part of the teacher to encourage creative expression. The teacher should be constantly alert to the child's expression of his ideas and encourage his eager enthusiasm. Creativity in children is often stimulated by simply having an appreciative audience listening to and supporting the ideas which they express.

Many opportunities should be provided for children to experiment with music. The fun of exploring and the satisfying enjoyment which results are important to children. The teacher's role is to allow children to find out for themselves rather than to expect them to "do this the way I do it." Children should feel free to express their feelings and ideas in their own way and in their own time, with little direction from the teacher.

PARENTAL ATTITUDES TOWARD MUSIC

In meetings with parents and in conferences with them, the kindergarten teacher encourages interest in music for children. Parents sometimes say, "I never liked music, and my George is just like me." The teacher can reassure such parents by telling them that almost all children like music and like to express themselves in music. Some children show their interest earlier than others. But each child will express his musical interests when he is ready and will choose his own means of expression. Some children want to move to music, some like to repeat the words or the ideas of songs, some like to be part of a singing group, and others just enjoy listening. Each child, if he is encouraged at home and at school, enjoys music and finds some means of reacting to it.

Teachers can help parents understand what kind of comments encourage children. If parents think a child will learn when he is ready, the child thinks so, too. But if parents think, "He's just like his grandfather, tone-deaf," they discourage the child. "She'll never learn. It's not in her," is a parental attitude that can make the difference between a child's enjoying music or avoiding it.

Teachers can help parents to understand the importance of musical experiences at home, the effect on children of the musical interests of other members of the family, the ways in which children may respond to various informal musical experiences at home and to records, and the simple instruments of particular value in encouraging children's interest in musical expression.

MUSIC IN A TYPICAL DAY

"Tell me the part music plays in your kindergarten day," was the request addressed to a kindergarten teacher in a city school.[10] Here is her reply:

"Because the kindergarten is such a perfect example of music in general education, I will give you a brief picture of the many-faceted program in which many of our children have their first musical experience. In kindergarten music is not a short period for songs, recordings, and rhythmic response, but it is a part of the entire day. Sometimes a beautiful recording is being played as the children come in, and sometimes the teacher improvises words to an American folk tune, thus personalizing a greeting for each child. Soon we honor our country and sing a song to show our love for our flag. On special patriotic days, we may have a rhythmic response such as waving little flags or marching to the drum. A day in kindergarten never begins "without a song."

When work time is under way, a group of block builders may make a boat or a train. Someone may begin a chant expressing the sound or movement of the thing that they have built. Another child may remember that the group knows a song about a train, or perhaps the teacher has a new song or a record that is just perfect for the group to hear right then.

Always at work time a few children are at the instrument table finding out how the triangle sounds or how many different things you can do with a tambourine. One may be improvising a tune on the tone bells or experimenting with the coconut shells while a playmate may trot or gallop or stamp or prance, pretending that he is a pony. The teacher may pick up the child's rhythm at the piano or with tone blocks.

[10] Statement of Anna Grace Poindexter, Kindergarten Teacher, San Diego City Schools.

A musical instrument often is used to give signals for change of activity or to facilitate quiet and unexcited movement from one period of the day to the next. Instruments are also a part of outdoor equipment. A big drum may be freely used and the fine large rhythmic movement is discovered. Individual use of instruments gradually becomes co-operative and sometimes a leader will take over and direct a group — singing as he does — while others dance or skip. Thus, there develops a great deal of discrimination in the choice of suitable instruments to use with songs or free rhythmic action.

At rest time, the teacher may play the piano, sing, or strum the auto-harp. There are songs of home, of patriotism, or perhaps the Brahms' "Lullaby" or the song that a Mexican or a Filipino mother would sing to her baby. One day a child might gently play the piano or tone bells or another day a beautiful record might be played softly.

At midmorning snack time grace is often sung, and what a wonderful thrill to sing along with the recorded "Grace for a Child," from *New Music Horizons*. If grace is said, it may be prefaced with the ringing of a chime as a church bell.

Then comes Music Time. We take off our shoes and have rhythms, some very free and some that fall in a pattern, such as skipping, running, and galloping. Sometimes the teacher will improvise at the piano to match the movement of a child who may be joined by a few friends. Perhaps movement is accompanied by a chant or the rhythmic pattern is picked up with a percussion instrument. It is a delight to see little feet scampering around the kindergarten and little hands pretending to make or do helpful things as we pretend to be brownies when the lovely scherzo from *Midsummer Night's Dream* is the record. Some times there is a slower, more graceful arm movement, as of the wings of a butterfly, with little faces seeking the nectar in the flowers around the room.

Even at story or science time, there may be a song. In kindergarten, music is a part of our lives; it makes us feel good and it helps us to be happy. Should Bobbie fall and skin his knee, there is a song to praise his bravery; if Susie has not yet learned to share, we sing "Your turn, My turn, That's Our Way," if there is restlessness on the rug — perhaps legs have become tired of being doubled up — there is the American folk tune "Come on Boys and Stop Your Talking" and everyone takes a brief walk around the room.

In all, the teacher uses music that is *good* and tries to avoid materials that are trite, poorly harmonized, or lacking in good rhythm. Many excerpts from the finest recordings may be used by the teacher of the very young and still be suitable for use by the teacher of sixth grade music. The supervisor is always happy to help with resource materials or to work with the teacher in conference or with the class. She is also happy to arrange "in service" workshops for groups of teachers so that we may continue to grow with the children.

So you can see in the kindergarten the beginnings of the music program in all its aspects: singing, listening, playing instruments, and responding both rhythmically and creatively. This is truly music's part in understanding our American heritage.

SITUATIONS FOR DISCUSSION

In the following situations select each course of action that seems desirable to you basing your choices and omissions on the ideas presented in this chapter. Add one or more alternate courses of action.

SITUATION I. Jane's mother stops for a few minutes to talk with you before taking Jane home from kindergarten. She says: "Don't feel you have to include Jane in the group that sings for PTA next time. She's just like her Aunt Jane. There isn't a note of music in her." As the teacher, you should say:

"Thank you for telling me how you feel about Jane's singing."

"Many five-year-olds are not ready to sing yet."

"Every child learns to enjoy music in his own way."

"When the class sings for PTA, all the children are in the group, but we ask some of them to use their lips quietly."

"The next parents' meeting will be about helping children with music."

SITUATION II. One morning when you are teaching the children a song, Tommy says, "John did it wrong." As the teacher, you should say:

"Let's each listen just to himself."

"Let's try it again."

"Let me draw a picture of how it goes."

"Tommy, will you sing it for us?"

"Listen, now, while I sing it for you."

SITUATION III. One day during singing, Marie asks, "Why doesn't Rose sing?" As the teacher, you should say:

"Why don't you sing, Rose?"

"Maybe Rose will help sing the next song."

"Marie, what song would you like to sing today?"

"Rose will sing with us when she is ready."

"Sometimes we like to listen, and sometimes we like to sing."

SITUATION IV. Recently you have been having rhythmic activities the latter part of the morning. Early this morning while the children are busy in the playhouse, at the painting easels, and in a variety of other activities, Emily comes skipping up to you saying, "I want to dance." As the teacher, you reply:

"Good. We are going to dance after juice time, the way we did the other day."

"You came skipping up to me. Let's find a record for skipping."

"Does anyone else want to dance now?"

"How would you like to use the Listening Post now?"

"Let's go outdoors where the big drum is."

BIBLIOGRAPHY

Current Professional Books and Pamphlets

Association for Childhood Education International. *Music for Children's Living.* Bulletin No. 96. Washington, D. C., 1955.

If music is to give meaning to life, children must learn its value through rich experiences at home and in school.

Children's Reading Service. Annotated List of Phonograph Records (Kindergarten–Grade 9). New York, 1950.

Five-hundred selected recordings to enrich language arts, science, and social studies as well as music are classified according to subject and grade level.

Landeck, Beatrice. *Children and Music.* New York: William Sloan Associates, Inc., 1952.

A teacher writes for parents emphasizing fun and creativity in various music media. "Good Song Material," "Records and Keeping the Child Interested," and "What to Expect of the School," are helpful chapters.

Mathews, Paul R. *You Can Teach Music.* New York: E. P. Dutton and Co., Inc., 1953.

A lively reassuring book for the classroom teacher who thinks music is the realm of the specialist.

Mursell, James L. *Music Education Principles and Programs.* New York: Silver Burdett Company, 1956.

This latest contribution of one of the nation's outstanding music educators and educational philosophers describes music as a program of learning experiences including singing, playing instruments, rhythm, and listening; and as a means for developing creative capacity. Other books by the same author include *Education for Musical Growth* (1948) and *Music for the Classroom Teacher* (1951).

Music Educators National Conference. "Selected Bibliography of Music Education Materials." Chicago, 1951.

This useful bibliography was published in a limited edition.

Nye, R. E. and V. T. *Music in the Elementary School.* Englewood Cliffs, New Jersey: Prentice-Hall, Inc., 1957.

A modern creative approach applied to the teaching of music.

Sheey, Emma Dickson. *There's Music in Children.* New York: Henry Holt and Co., 1952.

A brisk style distinguishes this book designed to help parents and teachers with small children.

Suggested Music Materials for Use with Children

Andrews, Gladys. *Creative Rhythmic Movement for Children.* New York: Prentice-Hall, Inc., 1954.

Armitage, Theresa. *Singing School Series.* Chicago: C. C. Birchard and Company, 1940–1944.

Baldwin, Lillian. *Music for Young Listeners.* New York: Silver Burdett Company, 1951. Recordings available.

Beattie, John. *American Singer.* Book I. New York: American Book Company, 1944.

Clarke, Irma. *Rhythm Ensemble.* Boston: Boston Music Company, 1950.

Coleman, Satis N. *Singing Time.* New York: John Day Publishing Company, 1929.

——. *Another Singing Time.* New York: John Day Publishing Company, 1937.

Crowninshield, Ethel. *New Songs and Games.* Boston: Boston Music Company, 1941.

——. *Songs and Stories about Animals.* Boston: Boston Music Company, 1947.

——. *Stories That Sing.* Boston: Boston Music Company, 1946.

Dykema, Peter. *Twice 55 Games for Children.* (Piano Accompaniment). Chicago: C. C. Birchard and Company, 1924.

Hood, Marguerite. *On Wings of Song.* New York: Ginn and Company, 1945.

Horwich, Frances R. *Here Comes the Band.* Chicago: Rand McNally & Company, 1956.

Hunt, Evelyn H. *Music Time.* New York: Viking Press, 1947.

Kent, A. T. *Tiptoe Tunes for Tiny Tots.* Waterloo, Ontario: Waterloo Music Company, Ltd., 1952.

Krone, Beatrice. *Our First Songs to Sing with Descants.* Chicago: Neil A. Kjos Co., 1949 (revised edition).

Landeck, Beatrice. *Songs to Grow On.* New York: Marks and Sloan, 1950.

——. *More Songs to Grow On.* New York: Marks and Sloan, 1954.

Langstaff, John. *Frog Went A Courtin'.* New York: Harcourt Brace and Co., Inc., 1955.

Martin, Burnett. *Rime, Rhythm and Song, for the Child of Today.* Chicago: Hall McCreary Publishing Company, 1942.

McCall, Adeline D. *Timothy's Tunes.* Boston: Boston Music Company, 1943.

McCarteney, L. P. *Songs for the Nursery School and Kindergarten.* Cincinnati: Willis Music Company, 1937.

McConathy, Osbourne. *Experiences in Music for First Grade Children.* New Music Horizons Series. New York: Silver Burdett Company, 1949.

——. *Music for Early Childhood.* New Music Horizons Series. New York: Silver Burdett Company, 1952. Recordings available.

Mursell, James, and Others. *Music for Living Series.* New York: Silver Burdett Co., 1956.

Pitts, Lila Belle, and Others. *The Kindergarten Book.* Our Singing World. New York: Ginn and Company, 1949.

Pitts, Lila Belle. *The First Grade Book.* Our Singing World. New York: Ginn and Company, 1949.

Renstrom, Moiselle. *Rhythm Fun.* Salt Lake City: Pioneer Press, 1944.

Seeger, Ruth Porter. *American Folk Songs for Children.* New York: Doubleday and Company, Inc., 1948.

——. *Animal Folk Songs for Children.* New York: Doubleday and Company, Inc., 1950.

Steiner, Charlotte. *Kiki Loves Music.* New York: Doubleday and Company, Inc., 1954.

Wessels, Katherine Tyler. *Golden Song Book.* New York: Simon and Schuster, 1945.

——. *Singing Games.* New York: Simon and Schuster, 1947.

Wheeler, Opal. *Sing for Christmas.* New York: E. P. Dutton Company, 1943.

Wolfe, Irving. *Together We Sing.* Chicago: Follett Publishing Company, 1950.

Suggested Record Bibliography

I. Standard Recordings
   A. *Single Recordings*
      Victor 7103
      "Ave Maria"   Schubert   Wilhelm ⎫
      "Air on G String"   Suite in D Major   Bach ⎬ Elman

      Victor 11–9174
      "Barcarolle"   Offenbach ⎫   Stokowski
      "Moment Musicale"   Schubert ⎬ Hollywood Symphony

      Victor 15425
      "Blue Danube Waltz"   Strauss ⎫   Stokowski
      "Tales of the Vienna Woods"   Strauss ⎬ Philadelphia Orchestra

      Capitol 89–80151
      "Little Train of the Caipira"   Villa-Lobos Janssen Symphony

      Victor 7256
      "Minuet"   Boccherini ⎫   Stokowski
      "Eighteenth Century Dance" ⎬ Philadelphia Orchestra

      Victor 15659
      "Night Soliloquy"   Kennan ⎫   Hanson
      "White Peacock"   Griffes ⎬ Eastman Symphony

      Columbia 12543–D
      "Race Track" Thunder and Lightning Polka   Strauss ⎫   Leinsdorf
      "Perpetuum Mobile"   Radetzky March   ⎬ Cleveland Orchestra

      Victor 7958
      "Schwanda"   Polka and Fugue   Weinberger ⎫
      "Arkansas Traveler"   Arranged by Guion ⎬ Brockman
      "Semper Fidelis"   Sousa   ⎭ Carnegie Pops Orchestra

      Victor 11932
      "Sleeping Beauty"   Tschaikowsky ⎫   Fiedler
      "Dagger Dance"   Herbert   ⎬ Boston Pops Orchestra

      Victor 18–0053 (vinylite)
      "Stars and Stripes"   Sousa ⎫   Koussevitsky
      "Semper Fidelis"   Sousa ⎬ Boston Symphony

      Columbia 7119
      "Symphony No. 39 in E Flat Major"   (Minuet) ⎫   Beecham
      Mozart   ⎬ London Philharmonic

      Victor 4390
      "Turkey in the Straw"   Arranged by Guion ⎫   Fiedler
      "Music Box"   Liadow   ⎬ Boston Pops Orchestra

   B. *Albums*
      Victor MO 785
      "Carnival of the Animals"   Saint-Saëns ⎫   Stokowski
                                             ⎬ Philadelphia Orchestra

Victor MO 1077
"Christmas Hymns and Carols" Shaw and Victor Chorale

Victor DM 1280
"Incidental Music to a Midsummer Night's Dream" } Toscanini
(Mendelssohn) } N.B.C. Orchestra

Victor Record Library for Elementary Schools
Indian Album

Columbia MX 151
"Mother Goose Suite" Ravel } Barlow
} Columbia Broadcasting Company Orchestra

Columbia MM 627
"Nutcracker Suite" Tschaikowsky } Rodzinski
} Philadelphia Orchestra

Columbia MX 180
"Peer Gynt Suite, No. 1" Grieg } Beecham
} London Philharmonic

Columbia MM 447
"Peter and the Wolf" Prokofieff } Rathbone
} Boston Symphony

Columbia 631
"Symphony No. 6 in F Major" (Pastoral) Beethoven } Ormandy
} Philadelphia Orchestra

Victor MO 1186
"Sea Chanties" Traditional Warren

Decca 605
"Songs of Many Lands" Marais and Miranda

RCA Victor Albums for Elementary Schools
Vol. E71, E72, E73, E77, E78, E79

II. Recordings Which Lead to More Discriminating Music Experiences
 A. *Rhythms*
   Ruth Evans Childhood Rhythms (Albums)
     Series I R.E. 101, 102, 103, 104, 105, 106
     Series II Record 201, 202, 203, 204, 205, 206
   AED 1-2-3
     Elementary Rhythms Phoebe James, U.C.L.A., Box 134, Pacific Palisades
   Allegro
     Junior 303 "Ring-a-Round the Rosy" and Other Singing Games
 B. *Musical Stories*
   Decca CV110
     "Chicken Licken" Luther
     "Gingerbread Boy"
   Decca CVS-9
     "Goldilocks and the Three Bears" Luther
   Decca CVS-11
     "Little Red Hen" Luther
   Young People's Record
     #619 "Little Indian Drum"

Young People's Record
#724 "Out-of-Doors"

Young People's Record
#702 "What the Lighthouse Sees"

Young People's Record
#617 "When the Sun Shines"

15

Helping Children Relate to Others

Five-year-old children vary greatly in their ability to relate themselves to adults and to other children. A child who is one of several children in a family may have learned to give and take, to share and take turns, and to play co-operatively with others. Or he may have been a family pet who has learned to expect special privileges and continuing attention. An only child may have had playmates and a wise mother who have helped him learn to go readily to other people's homes and to work independently. Or he may have remained emotionally dependent on his mother, unwilling to leave her for new surroundings. Whatever the stage of maturity of the five-year-old, his kindergarten teacher must help him improve his ability to cope with new situations and to work with other children individually, in small groups, and eventually in larger groups.

When the five-year-old comes to kindergarten, he has two spheres in which to grow: his home and his school. Ideally, in each sphere he should be self-confident, accepted by the adults and children as a desirable member of the group, and successful in doing what he wants to do. Realistically, however, the kindergarten can help the child directly in only the school situation. No matter what his home situation may be, the kindergarten teacher is challenged to make his in-school experience a happy and satisfying one. If the kindergarten can provide each child with what he needs for a few hours each day, he is better able to cope with his out-of-school situations.

THE TEACHER – CHILD RELATIONSHIP

In many ways, the most important relationship that a child establishes during his kindergarten year is his relationship to his teacher. For many children the teacher may be the first woman, other than his mother, whom he has known in a day-to-day situation. For all of the children, it is important that the teacher appreciate each of them as an individual. This

305

first relationship with a teacher must be a happy and successful one on which other teachers may build in the years to come.

Through what she does and says, a teacher helps the kindergarten children build a concept of "teacher." A teacher is different from a mother; she must be shared with many other children. A teacher is like a mother in that she loves children, understands what they are trying to do, and helps them do it. She lets a child do what he wants, but keeps him from hurting others or getting in their way. She shows children many interesting things and talks with them about new ideas. Through knowing her, the five-year-old should develop a concept of "teacher" which will make him ready to enjoy and learn from succeeding teachers as he goes through school.

The Teacher's Responses

Especially important is the kind of response that a teacher makes to a child. A child runs to the teacher for approval and admiration of his creation. Does the teacher respond directly and appreciatively? Or does she respond indirectly, tangentially, or negatively?

> PHILIP: Listen to my song! I just made it up!
>
> TEACHER: (*Stooping down to be on his eye level*) A new song! Will you sing it for me?
> (*Philip sings the song while the teacher gives him her complete attention.*)

If another child clamors for attention at the same time, the teacher has a chance to help the children learn to take turns in getting attention. "Just a minute, Mary. Philip is singing a song." When she gives Mary her attention after the song, she says, "Thank you for waiting until I could help you. We take turns in getting help just the way we take turns on the slide."

The teacher who is intent on moving the children from one activity into the next or in meeting a time schedule is apt to respond tangentially when Philip has a song he wishes her to hear. If the teacher says, "Let's put our things away now," she gives Philip the idea that his song is not very important. "I'll listen to it later, Philip," overlooks the fact that a five-year-old has a song only for a moment. Only an immediate, direct, and appreciative response to a child encourages him in feeling a real importance in himself and in his activity and helps him relate directly, affectionately, and satisfyingly to his teacher.

When a teacher is intent on having children learn "the right way" she is apt to respond negatively: "No, not that way. Do it this way." Actually it is much better if she lets the child have a first experience and then plans subsequent activities so that clear and simple directions as he works give him the guidance needed for carrying out the activity more easily and satisfactorily. Negative responses and emphasis on technique before the activity is well begun tend to frustrate the child and discourage him from further attempts.

TEDDY: I finished my boat, and here's the captain on the flagpole!

TEACHER: Isn't that a nice boat! And the captain certainly can see where the boat is going.

TEDDY: Toot! Toot! Here goes the boat!

TEACHER: Does the captain have a steering wheel to guide the boat?

TEDDY: Toot! Toot! Here goes the boat!

The teacher encouraged Ted at his level. He thought the captain should be up high, but he was not interested in how the captain would steer the boat. Later when he is ready for another idea, the teacher will help him understand why the captain should be on the bridge rather than on the flagpole. Meanwhile, she does not frustrate him with undue expectations of performance.

The Teacher Makes the Kindergarten Pleasant

The skillful teacher provides pleasant experiences for the children, and avoids unpleasant situations. She helps each child channel his energy into desirable patterns. Rather than stop him or put frustrations in his way, she encourages him and guides his activities. She is careful to plan with the children before they begin an activity, and she does not hurry them through it. She knows that small children move slowly and require considerable time in beginning or finishing a project. When the activity is nearing completion she reminds them of the next activity. At five, children learn the sequence of activities, but completing an activity within a given time limit is far beyond them.

One reason kindergarten is pleasant is that the teacher allows time for the children to plan, to do, and to clean up. If an activity requires more time than she had anticipated, she does not hurry the children. Instead she replans the day as it goes along, leaving activities for another day rather than trying to crowd them in. Thus children are not forced to cut off an activity before they feel finished with it. This avoidance of time pressures makes for self-confidence and is especially helpful to the timid children and the attention-seekers.

The skillful teacher probably gives as many commands as does the teacher lacking skill, but her commands are explained in terms of the good of the group rather than in terms of what she wants as an individual. By using such explanations the teacher is setting an example which potential leaders in the kindergarten soon follow. She says, "As soon as we are finished, it will be time to pick up our things," rather than, "I want you to pick up your things now." She says, "Sit where you can see comfortably," rather than "Sit down and be still."

Helps the Child to Carry Out His Plans

The teacher who is permissive and understanding makes kindergarten a pleasure for the children. She helps each child do what he wants to do, provided it does no harm to himself, to others, or to the school property. The teacher knows that what the child asks for is important to him or he would not ask. Therefore, she complies with his request or tries out his suggestions. If the request is impractical or unrealistic, she works on it with the child until he understands its impracticality. In this way, the child feels that the teacher respects his ideas, helps him carry them out, but at the same time helps him keep safe.

JOHN: I want my shoes off.

TEACHER: It's a warm spring day, and the sand would feel good between your toes. I'd like to take my shoes off too. But I'm not going to. Do you know why?

JOHN: Why?

TEACHER: Because if you take off your shoes, or if I take off my shoes, other people will want to take off their shoes. Tom will want his shoes off. Then maybe tomorrow Tom will sneeze and have a runny nose and have to stay home from school. I guess we had better leave our shoes on at school.

JOHN: I guess so.

TEACHER: But when you get home from school, if it's still warm, you ask your mother if you may go barefooted then. How's that?

JOHN: Fine.

John went off feeling understood. His teacher knew that it is often more important to be understood than agreed with.

The permissive kindergarten teacher gives the unusual request the same consideration that she gives an expected one. One morning when the swings were "pretend" rocket ships, the teacher helped each of the children take off for the destination of his choice: the moon, Mars, Fantasyland. Sandy, the sensitive daughter of a leader in one of the local churches, said, "I want to go to the Devil." The teacher helped her start as casually as she had helped each of the others: "Loading for the Devil. Gate 3. All aboard. Blast off!" A few minutes later, Sandy announced to the teacher triumphantly, "He wasn't there!" The teacher's confident acceptance of what the child wanted to do had helped Sandy cope with a somewhat obscure problem.

Helps Him to Realize the Limits of a Situation

At the same time that she is permissive, the kindergarten teacher helps the children learn the limits in a given situation. She helps them set up and follow rules which make their activities go more smoothly and happily. She knows that five-year-olds are interested in rules and that they feel insecure in a situation until they know definitely what its limits are. They like to be reminded of the rules. Pleasant reminders help them learn the rules, but unpleasant ones may interfere with their learning.

When a child is late for school, he is delighted that he receives the same warm welcome that he gets other mornings. As he leaves for home at the end of the session, his teacher may remind him, "See if you can get an earlier start from home tomorrow morning, Ken. We want to start building our warehouse first thing, and we need your help."

When George ran down the hall and landed in a heap, his teacher sympathized with him about his bruised knee.

GEORGE: Oh, my poor knee!

TEACHER: (*Looking at the knee*) No blood. But I know how it hurts! Now you know why we have the rule about no running in the halls.

GEORGE: I won't do it again.

TEACHER: I'm sure you'll remember to walk after this.

The sympathetic and understanding teacher makes the kindergarten a pleasant situation. If she appreciates the children and enjoys working with them, the whole emotional climate of the kindergarten is happy and co-operative.

HELPING CHILDREN RELATE TO OTHER ADULTS

In kindergarten, children develop satisfying relationships with their teacher and with other children. They also develop friendly relationships with other adults at the school: the principal, school secretary, doctor, dentist, nurse, and other school personnel. When mothers of other children come to the kindergarten as mother assistants to the teacher, the children find that other parents are understanding and helpful in the same way that their own parents are. They realize that mothers and fathers help all children, not just their own. When a workman comes to the kindergarten either on business or on invitation, the teacher and the children talk with him and find out not only how he helps them but also that he likes children and probably has children or grandchildren of his own. When the kindergarten goes into the community on study trips, the teacher points out that other fathers and mothers are the workers in the post office, the house under construction, the fire station, the market, and the other places he visits. Through these repeated introductions to friendly adults and through his teacher's explanations, the child comes to realize that the people whom he meets at school and in working situations, as well as in his own home, are friendly people who will help him as long as he helps them do their jobs.

The teacher also talks with parents about how to protect their children from kidnapping and other crimes by teaching the children two simple rules:

> Get into a car, bus, or streetcar only when your parents or friends of long standing invite you to go with them. Do not go with anyone else.
>
> Eat what your family or friends of long standing offer you. Do not eat what anyone else offers you.

The teacher and parents work together to have the children learn that people are helpful and friendly, as long as they or their property are not hurt. A stranger is friendly and helpful, too, except in the rare case when he tries to make a child eat something or go with him without asking his parents.

HELPING CHILDREN TO BE PART OF A GROUP

For most five-year-olds, kindergarten is a first experience as a member of a large group. In the course of the year each child develops skills, attitudes, and understandings which will help him relate himself to the large group throughout succeeding years of school. He also develops skills, attitudes, and understandings which make him an effective member of a small group. Getting along with another child while working with him on some project is followed by brief participation in projects carried on by two or three children. More lengthy participation ensues. Gradually each child gains confidence in himself in small and large group situations.

Some kindergarten activities lend themselves to large group situations: rhythmic activities, listening to a story, having fruit juice, resting, and study trips. Other activities lend themselves especially well to small group situations: block building, housekeeping in the playhouse, and dressing up. Certain activities are best carried on individually: reading the pictures of a book, modeling with clay, painting a picture, and construction work. Yet even individual activities take on a social aspect within the group situation of the kindergarten. Looking at a book alone at home is different from looking at a book in kindergarten where another child may share a picture or listen to a comment.

Often children coming into the kindergarten group are overawed by its size and inhibited in their activities. This is evident in what they are able to do in the group as compared with what they are able to do at home. "At home Janet makes much better pictures than this" is probably an accurate observation for a parent to make on a first visit to school. Yet the child who has had nursery school experience may enter the kindergarten group and go on almost immediately to improved performance. Having already learned how to adjust to the group situation, the child from nursery school can give his attention to other learnings.

During the kindergarten year the skillful teacher helps each child develop the social techniques which make the large and small group situations of school enjoyable. These techniques include taking turns, planning, and developing sympathy and co-operation.

Learning to Take Turns

A kindergarten child learns that the rules of possession for a group are different from the rules for a single child. At home a child can leave his tricycle at the back door and expect it to be there when he comes out again fifteen minutes later. But at school, if he leaves a tricycle to go into the playhouse, he may not find it waiting for him when he comes out. On the other hand, if he sees a tricycle not in use, he is free to have a turn with it. Early in the year the teacher talks with the children about how equipment is used. She may use the flannel board in explaining and discussing the rules with a large group of children. Certainly she will also explain the rule each time that a conflict situation arises between children as they learn how to use equipment.

The teacher went over to where George and Sandy were each tugging at the red wagon, trying to pull it in opposite directions and shouting at each other, "It's mine!" Calmly she sat down in the wagon to talk with the children.

TEACHER: What's the problem?
GEORGE: It's mine! I got it first!
SANDY: It's mine! I was using it!
TEACHER: (*Noticing Sandy's dress-up hat*) Did you take the wagon over to get your pretty hat?
SANDY: Yes.
TEACHER: Then you left the wagon while you tried on the hats. George came along, saw no one using the wagon, and started using it. You see, Sandy, when you leave the wagon someone else may have a turn. The wagon is yours only while you use it. You can get it again when George has had his turn with it. Ask George to let you have it next.

SANDY: I want it next.

GEORGE: O.K., as soon as I deliver my packages.

Learning to Plan

Children need to know what will happen and what to do. Planning their activities gives them confidence. If plans are made realistically to cover the major aspects of the situation, and they are carried out as planned, the children feel secure as they take responsibility for their part. But if plans are haphazard or incomplete, children do not know what to anticipate. Their insecurity is evident in undesirable byplay, inattention, withdrawing, or aggressive behavior.

Planning an activity before doing it is especially helpful to timid children and makes them more ready to participate. However, such planning must be in line with what is done. Planning to go out the south door of the building and then actually going out the east door is disconcerting to timid children and confusing to others. Any deviations from the accustomed routine should be talked over with the children. "Today we are going for a walk. When we come back we shall have juice and rest the way we usually do." In this way children are prepared for the change and also have the security of knowing that they can depend on following the routine or on being informed about changes in it.

Especially at the first of the year, the skillful teacher does much of the planning with the children, individually, in small groups, and in the large group. With the individual child, she helps him identify his problem and then plan how to solve it.

TED: (*Crying*) Sam hit me!

TEACHER: I'm sorry about that. How did it happen?

TED: I wanted the big bike. He held it.

TEACHER: (*Smiling and understanding*) So you grabbed and he hit. Let's talk it over with Sam and figure out turns.
(*While the teacher sat on her heels talking it over with Sam and Ted, Janet joined the group.*)

JANET: I want the big bike.

TEACHER: (*Calmly*) So do Ted and Sam. We're going to take turns with it. Sam just had a ride on it. How far did you go, Sam?

SAM: To the hydrant.

TEACHER: Fine. Out to the hydrant and back is a turn. O.K.?

CHILDREN: (*Nodding*) O.K.

TEACHER: Sam just had a turn. Ted, your turn is next because you asked first. Then Janet. And then Sam gets another turn. Then Ted and Janet again. Is that all right?

CHILDREN: O.K.

TEACHER: Work out your turns so everyone is happy.

At the first of the year the teacher plans with the children how to carry out their large group activities. For instance, about fifteen minutes before the close of school on the first day, she probably gathers the children in front of her on the rug for a final planning session. When they are seated comfortably, they plan what to do in leaving school.

TEACHER: We are going to plan now what we want to do before we go home. We have plenty of time for planning because school is not over until both hands of the clock are pointing straight up. Is our room the way we want to leave it?
(*The children talked about what needs to be put away. Individual children volunteered to put away each item.*)

TEACHER: Some of us wore jackets and sweaters when we came this morning. What did we do with them?

CHILDREN: Hung them up.

TEACHER: Yes, we hung them up. How can we get them without getting in each other's way? Robin has an idea to suggest.

ROBIN: Take turns.

TEACHER: That's a good idea. We'll take turns. First, . . .
(*The teacher suggested in detail just how taking turns could result in each child getting his jacket or sweater.*)

As the year progresses the children participate more and more in the planning. At the first of the year, the teacher asks key questions and makes many suggestions. Later the children make more and more of the suggestions. Accepting or rejecting an idea is followed later by choosing between two good ideas. By the end of the year some of the more mature children will ask a key question as well as suggest a practical solution. This growth in ability to plan is an important outcome of the kindergarten experience. Each child progresses as he is able and lays a foundation for further participation in democratic group experience.

Developing Sympathy

As they relate themselves to other people, children not only develop standards of what is good co-operative behavior, but as individuals they also learn more and more to see the other person's point of view. The child who could build only by himself at the first of the year learns to have someone else work with him. He learns to tell his helper what he needs: "Bring big blocks" and later "I want two small blocks." As he works with other children, he may go on to see how to help another child work out his plan. "May I help saw?" and "Let me have a turn now" are succeeded by "What do you need?" and "How do you want me to hold it? This way?" This growth in seeing another person's point of view is one of the satisfactions for the kindergarten teacher who has watched and guided this social development. It is also a fundamental requisite for democratic group participation.

Many kindergarten children have not learned to feel and express sympathy for other children. Yet four-year-old children easily learn to express such feelings. The skillful kindergarten teacher looks for opportunities to help individual children develop sympathy.

Billy was an only child with large, tall parents. He knew what he wanted to do, and he went quickly and directly about his work. As he darted toward the painting easel, he did not see Tim carefully taking his wet painting over to the drying line. When they collided, Tim and his painting landed on the floor. Tim burst into tears, and Billy stopped for a minute and then went on over to the easel.

The teacher picked up two sponges as she walked toward Billy on her way to help and comfort Tim. "Billy," she said, "Tim needs our help." Billy helped sponge paint off Tim and off the floor. When Billy had had time to sense how Tim felt, the teacher said, "I think Tim would feel better if you told him you were sorry you bumped into him." When Billy went back to the easel, the teacher thanked him for helping Tim. Her sympathy and understanding helped the boys feel sympathy for each other.

Building Co-operation

The child who relates himself easily to others in small and large groups is the child with co-operative attitudes and skills. Realizing this, the wise teacher furthers co-operation and avoids competitive situations. Competition has no place in the kindergarten. Co-operation does.

Often children bring with them competitive behavior which the teacher skillfully channels into co-operative behavior. "Me first!" clamors Jeff. The teacher smiles at him and reassures him that each child will have a turn.

The wise teacher emphasizes what is to be done rather than who is going to do it. For instance, when the children have rhythm instruments she casually selects a leader for marching around in a line, "Let's see. How about a drum in front today?" The teacher makes a point of seeing that each child has leadership experience, but she does not overly emphasize the selection of a leader.

"I want to be leader!" "May I be leader?" If being leader is highly prized, then children compete for the place. "We take turns trying out different places in the line," says the teacher calmly. "Let's start at the back. Who wants to be last today?" Another day she may respond to a child's request to be first by saying, "Jane says she wants to be first today. Who wants to be second?" In this way, the teacher helps the children learn ordinal numbers at the same time that they are learning that each place is important.

The wise teacher realizes the subtle but important difference between praise through realistic description and praise which calls attention to a child. Praise by description helps children in having realistic standards for their behavior. Praise for the child rather than for what he does makes for competition, frustration, and resentment.

Jimmy rushed over to show his first construction project to his teacher. He had hammered nails to fasten a small board across a somewhat larger board. "See my plane! I made it!" Jimmy's teacher shared his satisfaction in what he had done, "You made a plane! And these are the wings. Say, that's a nice plane."

A less desirable situation occurred when Tim made a plane and showed it to his teacher. She hugged him and said, "You darling child! I think you're just wonderful!" Jimmy, who was standing nearby asked, "Why don't you hug me like that?" The teacher's reaction, resented by an observant child, showed a favoritism which excluded other children in the group at the same time that it singled out Tim.

The kindergarten teacher is careful to avoid belittling and competitive remarks as well as personalized praise. She knows that parents encourage sibling rivalry by such remarks as, "Why can't you be neat the way your sister is?" "Jane is the student of the family," or "Marie is so careful of her clothes, but getting Tom to school with his shirt still clean is certainly a problem." In the kindergarten, personal comparisons have no place. The only comparisons made are comparisons of what the child has done with what he was able to do yesterday and what he wants to do today. Children need to know that they are growing and achieving as persons rather than that they are growing and achieving more or less than some other person.

When Evelyn reported to the teacher, "I can't close the gate," the teacher said, "The fastener may be sticking again. Let's see what is the matter with it." After Evelyn oiled it with the teacher's guidance, she was able to open and close it smoothly. "There!" the teacher pointed out, "You oiled it, and now you can close it easily."

A few weeks later Tony had trouble in closing the gate. Again the teacher furthered co-operative attitudes in the way that she handled the situation.

TONY: The gate won't close.

TEACHER: Yes, it sticks sometimes. A little oil fixes it.

EVELYN: I can fix it! Let me do it!

TEACHER: Evelyn fixed it the other day. Could you show Tony the little place that needs oil?

EVELYN: Yes! (*To Tony*) I'll get the oil can for you.

TEACHER: (*To Evelyn*) That's good of you. (*To Tony.*) Evelyn will help you fix it.

The teacher made the situation a co-operative one. If she had acceded to Evelyn's request, she would have encouraged Evelyn in competitive behavior and would have left Tony with a sense of failure.

The wise teacher does not settle the children's arguments for them when they are able to settle the arguments themselves. As rapidly as possible she lets them take responsibility for working out turns and playing together happily and co-operatively.

On several days the big bike had been a source of contention between Sam and Ted. Each time the teacher had given them help in working out turns. Today she tried a different tactic: "If the big bike is making you boys unhappy, we shall just have to put it away until you can work out turns with it." Confronted with the possible loss of the big bike, the boys worked out turns. Usually, their teacher found, the threat of removal was sufficient motivation for working co-operatively. Only once did she actually remove the desired article and then only for a few moments. However, the children knew that she would remove it if necessary in order to help them.

Kindergarten children make great progress in getting along with other children. By the end of the year their free play situations reveal the skills, attitudes, and understandings they have acquired.

Judy and David were working on puzzles when Jenny knocked on the playhouse door. Judy quickly turned over each of the puzzles and thinking it a great trick giggled behind David as he went to the door.

DAVID: Hello, Jenny. Judy turned over all the puzzles and dumped them out.

JENNY: Did she?

DAVID: I think she should put them back. What do you think, Jenny?

JENNY: I think she should too.

DAVID: You put them back, Judy. I'll help you with one of them.

JENNY: I'll do one.

The children returned to the puzzles and soon had them all back in place. Such spontaneous planning and co-operation would not have been possible at the beginning of the kindergarten year.

HELPING THE CHILD AS AN INDIVIDUAL

The kindergarten teacher works with children individually as well as in groups and helps each solve his long-range developmental problems as well as his immediate problems. The teacher is especially aware of the children who lack self-confidence. Their feeling of inadequacy may express itself in different ways. A child may react to only part of his environment, avoiding potential pressures or demands he feels unable to meet. Such a child is often described as a timid child. Another child may rush into a situation in which he lacks confidence. He hits, teases, or otherwise attacks children, teacher, or objects that are part of the overwhelming situation. His strength and lack of control may result in his being termed a destructive child. Usually he is described as overly aggressive.

The Use of Labels

Labeling a child as timid or as overly aggressive shows that the teacher working with such a child is aware of his problems and is working with him in overcoming them. But using such a label with a child is apt to destroy his self-confidence further. "Well, you certainly are destructive!" is no help to a child who has just broken a toy airplane. Standing there with the pieces in his hand he is wishing that the airplane were back in one piece, and he is feeling insecure about the breaking. He is relieved to hear his teacher say, "Well, that airplane is not as strong as I thought it was. Let's see where it broke." Such an objective remark shifts attention away from the self-conscious child to the kinds of material things are made of.

Inspiring Confidence

It is often suggested that children who lack confidence should be praised. Such praise should be realistic and genuine. The teacher looks for real accomplishments and then praises them both with an appreciative tone of voice and with accurate description.

When a group of children were working at the clay table, the teacher knelt beside each one in turn and admired each child's handiwork.

> MARIE: I made a snowman.
>
> TEACHER: You certainly did. He has arms and a head with eyes and nose and mouth. What a fine snowman!

When a child did not volunteer a realistic explanation of what he was doing, the teacher continued using a commendatory tone of voice. "What fun you are having!" or "So many bits and pieces!" To each child in turn the teacher communicated appreciation of his activities. Even the child who was using his heel to flatten out lumps of clay on the floor felt that the teacher appreciated his work. "My, you certainly make those lumps of clay flatten out. Can you do it on the table, too, with the heel of your hand? The custodian has a hard time getting clay off the floor, so we try to keep it on the table."

It is often said that there is no such thing as "a problem child" but that every child is a child with problems. The wise teacher studies how to help each child solve his problems and becomes increasingly skillful in helping the child who is withdrawing from a situation or the child who is rushing into it impetuously because of his lack of confidence in himself.

Readiness and Confidence

The kindergarten teacher keeps in mind the concept of readiness and is continuously confident about a child's eventual success. She knows that when a child is at home in a situation, is sufficiently mature, and has the information he needs about getting started, he will approach an activity and will learn. Her confidence is shown in what she says: "Jane is just getting acquainted with the blocks today. When she is ready, she will build with them." Her confidence gives the child increasing self-confidence and assures the other children that no one is going to force a person into an activity. Furthermore, her genuine belief in readiness prevents the teacher from having expectations of performance that are unrealistic for a particular child. Each day the teacher's confidence is reflected in the way she works with individual children who are timid about a new situation.

When Johnny's mother brought him to kindergarten she helped him find a place in the library corner. After his mother left, Johnny clung to this place. That first day he did not venture away from the corner at all, and in the next few days he made only short sallies away from it. His teacher accepted his emotional dependence on the library corner and realized that he needed to become familiar with the new setting as well as with the activities of kindergarten. Developing relations with the other children would come later. The teacher therefore arranged with Johnny's mother for him to come to school before the other children. Each morning while she was getting ready for the children, Johnny had free rein to explore the physical setting of the kindergarten. Soon he used this simplified situation for trying out activities he had observed. This period enabled him to enter gradually into the activities with the other children. Furthermore, he knew he could always retreat to the library corner whenever he needed to regain his confidence. Successful participation in the kindergarten activities gave him readiness to explore farther and farther away from the library corner.

The teacher knows that the child who spends time watching what other children are doing is getting ready to participate in their activity. Her encouragement furthers his readiness.

Arthur was playing by himself in the sandbox, but he really wanted to be at the workbench nearby. Often he stopped his play with a dump truck to watch the sawing and hammering. The teacher noticed his interest and came over to sit on the edge of the sandbox. When she was sure that she was seeing what Arthur was seeing, she established rapport with him by describing the sawing: "Tom pulls the saw back and forth, back and forth, back and forth."

When Tom put down the saw, the teacher said, "Tom has finished his turn. Do you want to saw next? I'll help you to get started." The first time she encouraged him, Arthur withdrew and went back to play with the dump truck. The understanding teacher accepted his withdrawal and said, "When you are ready, you can make the saw go back and forth." Another time she said, "Maybe tomorrow you will want to try sawing."

One day when the other children went away from the workbench, Arthur stepped out of the sandbox and picked up the saw. He used it until another child came over to the bench. The teacher ignored his retreat to the sandbox but shared his victory, "You were sawing! Isn't it fun!" A week or so later Arthur was able to continue sawing while another child hammered. Gradually he mastered the group relationship as he gained skill in sawing. The understanding comments of his teacher helped him acquire confidence.   ·

Success and Confidence

The teacher can also help the timid child develop confidence through success. If an activity is complex, she helps the timid child set up the first step as his goal and then successive steps one at a time. Completion of each step is a success and the teacher shares the child's pleasure in achieving it. When Marie joined the children in the playhouse for the first time, her teacher smiled at her and remarked, "You had a good time in the playhouse this morning making pies with Margie and Flora."

The teacher realizes that a child who is timid in a group of more mature children can be successful and admired in a group of less mature children. Skillfully she guides such a child toward more congenial playmates: "Kathy is going to cut out the handles for our baskets. Who would like to help her?" When several children volunteered, the teacher spoke to Janie, a shy girl and the youngest of several children in a family: "Would you like to help with the handles, Janie? Good. Kathy and Janie will take care of that for us."

Although the teacher is aware of the needs of the timid child and makes every effort to have him gain confidence through simplified activities and through working with less aggressive children, she avoids favoring him unduly. A child whose timidity keeps him from opportunities for developing skills and social relationships needs more interaction with other children. If he is thought of as a "teacher's pet," he may have less opportunity.

Information and Confidence

The wise teacher realizes that children are timid about situations they do not understand. Arthur who stands each day watching children slide down the fireman's pole in the jungle gym is not only developing an emotional readiness for that experience, he is also getting information he needs to try the experience himself. How does Billy start his slide? How can I start my slide? When Arthur is ready emotionally and intellectually, he slides down the pole, provided, of course, that sliding down the pole has not become involved with some unsatisfactory interpersonal relationship. The teacher does not push Arthur into trying the pole before he is ready to try it. She encourages him only as he needs encouragement.

BILLY: 'Fraidy cat! 'Fraidy cat! Arthur's a 'fraidy cat!

ARTHUR: I am not! I don't want to slide down your old pole.

TEACHER: (*To Billy*) You slid down the pole when you got ready to. When Arthur gets ready, he will too. Now he's watching and learning how it's done. Show us how you get onto the pole, Billy.

Billy demonstrates, and then the teacher helps Arthur try it, first from part way up the pole, then from the next higher level, and finally from the top.

The teacher notices when a child needs information he does not have, and gives it to him right then.

SUSIE: Janet won't let me have the big trike.

TEACHER: Did you say, "*When* may I have the big trike?"

SUSIE: No, she won't let me have it.

TEACHER: I think she will. You ask her *when* you may have it.

In this way the teacher gives the child the information he needs to solve his problem. She may go with Susie while she arranges for her turn. And she may, if Susie needs further help, talk with Janet about when Susie will have her turn. But as rapidly as Susie is able to make her arrangements, the teacher encourages her to do so. As much as possible, the teacher avoids having the children use her as a crutch. Her objective is to help each child depend upon himself.

Understanding the Child

The Attention-Seeker

The skillful kindergarten teacher is constantly helping each child feel understood, appreciated, and at home in the group situation. At the same time she is prepared to cope with the child who tries to get more than his share of attention. She knows that the usual kindergarten experiences will soon channel his aggressive behavior into helpful activities. She realizes that as he gains satisfaction from desirable activities, his undesirable actions will occur less and less frequently. Meanwhile she is prepared to show him how to substitute more socially desirable for less desirable behavior.

Dale was a sociable five-year-old, an only child in a family with many adult relatives in the community. She was delighted to know the kindergarten teacher and each morning engaged her in conversation. Each morning the teacher enjoyed talking with Dale as she walked with her to a play situation with other children. Especially in the playhouse, Dale immediately transferred her attention to her playmates, secure in knowing that she had a firm place in the thought and affection of her teacher. If her teacher had not been responsive or had tried to shut off Dale's conversation prematurely, Dale would have felt insecure and kept on talking, trying to get the teacher's attention by this, her best developed skill.

The Destructive Child

Sometimes the kindergarten teacher finds it difficult to be understanding and sympathetic with the child who is destructive. In our culture so much emphasis is put on being neat, clean, and tidy that a child who brings with him "messes," disarrangement, and breakage is often unconsciously resented. Yet the destructiveness is only a symptom of a child who needs help in developing self-confidence.

Jimmy was the third child in a large family. His older siblings built up their own egos by berating what Jimmy did. His accomplishments and helpfulness were taken for granted but his shortcomings brought him attention. Jimmy also got attention by "accidentally" breaking the toys of his younger siblings. At kindergarten he found the sturdy toys difficult to break, but he sometimes succeeded in removing a part. His teacher understood his need for feeling competent and gave him sincere praise and affection as an individual. In group situations, she helped him realize that he was treated on a par with the other children. Whenever opportunity arose, she helped Jimmy understand how others felt and helped him build desirable ways of getting along with other children.

Jimmy was walking along behind Mary when her drawing slipped out of her hand onto the floor. Jimmy stepped deliberately and squarely in the middle of the paper. Mary looked hurt and unhappy. The teacher came over to reassure her and brush off the paper. Then she talked with Jimmy.

TEACHER: Would you like someone to step on your drawing?

JIMMY: No.

TEACHER: How would you feel if someone did? That's the way Mary feels now.

JIMMY: I'm sorry.

TEACHER: How would you feel if someone picked up your paper and handed it to you?

JIMMY: I'd like it.

TEACHER: I would too. Next time let's be a picker-upper. O.K., Jimmy?

JIMMY: O.K.

The Pugnacious Child

Some children come to kindergarten prepared to make their way against a competitive world by hitting and pushing. Even well-meaning parents tell their children, "Stick up for yourself and fight." Their teacher is prepared to help them learn that the kindergarten is a co-operative and friendly world where competition has no place. She also is prepared to deal with any hitting, pushing, or grabbing which may occur while they learn. She knows that they will learn more rapidly if the other children know how to defend themselves against hitting.

TEACHER: (*Talking to the large group of children*) Here in kindergarten we talk about our problems, and we don't hit. But outside of school you may have playmates who have not learned to talk over problems. What do you do if a boy hits or pushes you?

CHILDREN: Hit him back.

DAVID: Tell him, "Don't hit me!"

TEACHER: But if you hit him back, then he hits you, and all you've gotten is a lot of hitting. David, what do you think you should do if a boy hits you?

DAVID: Tell him, "Don't hit me!"

TEACHER: Good. When a boy hits you, then you start talking to him. You say, "Don't hit me!" How do you say it?
(*The children and the teacher try out different tones of voice for discouraging the hitter.*)

TEACHER: What do you do if he still tries to hit you again?

CHILDREN: Hit him back.

TEACHER: But that just gets more hitting. Here's a better idea: Keep him from hitting you.

The discussion that followed brought out how to grab a hitter's hands and hold them until he is willing to stop hitting and talk about the problem. Various ways of blocking a hit were also demonstrated. The teacher summarized the discussion by saying, "We can help a hitter by keeping him from hitting us. We don't hit back. Instead we say, 'Don't hit me!' We hold his wrists, or we block his blow until we can get him to talk it over."

Occasionally the skillful teacher finds it necessary to help a child remove himself from the group. She does this in such a way as to reassure the child and build his confidence in her as someone who helps him do what he really wants to do.

Reggie's arrival at kindergarten showed his reaction to his home environment. His mother thought of her children as an aid to her social status. Her high standards of performance for them were accompanied by rejection of them whenever they interfered with her activities. For several mornings Reggie, under pressure at home, exploded into the kindergarten, pushing and hitting as he entered. One morning he went to the record player and played one record after another. Anyone who came over to him was at once rebuffed. However, after about an hour of record playing, Reggie was able to participate in activities with the other children.

Later in the day the teacher talked with Reggie about his problem.

TEACHER: You certainly felt like hitting and pushing when you came to school this morning.

REGGIE: I sure did.

TEACHER: Then you played records for a while and pretty soon you felt like playing with the other children. I think you have a good idea. Whenever you feel like hitting when you come to school, you just go over and play records.

REGGIE: (*Nodding*) O.K.

Reggie had found an outlet for his emotions. His teacher, observing him, helped him to realize that this was a way to handle his emotions acceptably. This help recognized Reggie's responsibility for his own behavior and was much better than selecting an emotional outlet for him. A child must learn to handle his feelings of aggression himself. One aggressive child may find pounding and hammering an effective emotional outlet; another, tricycle riding; or another, painting. The teacher of the emotionally upset child helps him find for himself at least one socially acceptable emotional outlet.

Ordinarily the teacher uses understanding, co-operation, and appreciation as her techniques for helping each child gain the self-confidence he needs for becoming a desirable member of the group. Occasionally she uses the techniques of ignoring undesirable behavior. This she can do when the undesirable behavior is not dangerous either to the disturbing child or to any other child. Sometimes she ignores undesirable behavior when she thinks the child is emotionally involved to the point where he cannot profit from talking over the problem at that time.

Chris had been feeling that the world was mostly against him. At home the new baby was getting all the favorable attention. Daddy was out of a job again and mother was all tired out when she came home from the office. Grandmother was always wanting him to be quiet while she rested. This morning at school everyone else seemed to be getting attention except him.

TEACHER: (*Planning with the children in a large group*) Today let's let Tim have the big bike first. He hasn't had a turn with it. . . .

CHRIS: I want the big bike! Nobody let's me have anything!

Chris burst into tears and threw himself into a tantrum, the kind that always got him what he wanted at home.

TEACHER: We'll go outside now. Tim has the first turn with the big bike. Chris will probably want a turn later when he's himself again.

The teacher went out on the playground with the group of children. When she returned to the room a few minutes later, she busied herself putting away and getting out materials and paid no attention to Chris. After a time he quieted down. When he went outside with the other children, the teacher stood by to help him have a turn with the big bike, but he got it successfully by himself.

Later in the day when he was no longer emotionally upset, the teacher talked sympathetically with Chris about his tantrum: "That was quite a tantrum you put on this morning. Is that what you do at home to get what you want?" With genuine interest and understanding, she pointed out that tantrums at kindergarten do not get you what you want: "All your tantrum did this morning was to take up time you could have used playing with the other children and riding the big bike." Individually, in the next few weeks, the teacher made it a point to see that Chris had much evidence of her understanding and appreciation. In group situations she helped Chris to see that everyone else took turns on the same basis that he did.

The Teacher Interprets for the Child

Five-year-old children are only beginning to develop the ability to interpret themselves to other children. The teacher therefore frequently steps into situations in the role of interpreter. By doing so she helps children understand such concepts as: a child learns when he is ready to learn; a person does not expect someone else to do what he does; telling someone what to do may or may not result in getting it done; a person does what he wants to do so long as he does not hurt himself or others.

John and Teddy were building a ship together when Teddy got the doll figure for the captain and placed it on the flagpole for the teacher to admire.

Some children come to kindergarten prepared to
make their way against a competitive world
by hitting and pushing.   The teacher helps them
learn that kindergarten is a co-operative
and friendly place.

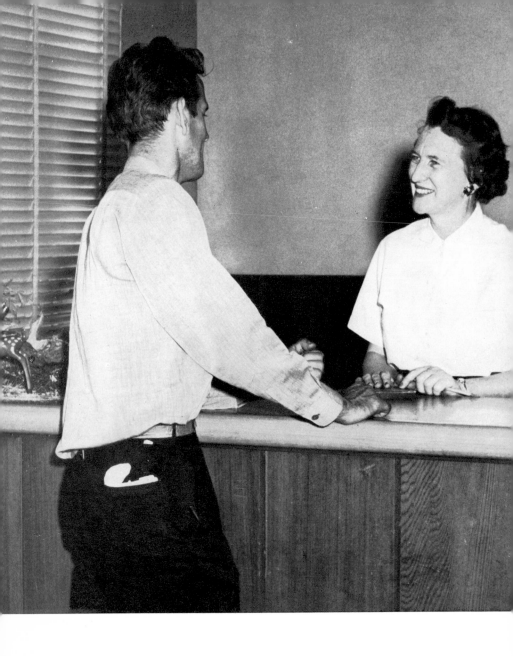

By putting together what they know, parents
and teachers each achieve a more complete
understanding of the child.

TEDDY: Here's the engineer on the flagpole!

JOHN: That's wrong. The captain is on the bridge.

TEACHER: (*To John*) You think the engineer runs the ship from the bridge.

JOHN: (*To Teddy*) Put the engineer here in the engine room, or I'll hit you.

TEACHER: (*To John*) Let Teddy put the engineer where he wants to. When it's your turn with the engineer, you put him where you want to. We each do what we want to, if it doesn't hurt someone else.

On the playground Miriam often tried to reassert her command over Tommy, a younger boy, who lived next door to her.

MIRIAM: You be my horsey, Tommy! I need a horsey!
(*Tommy obediently got down on all fours to be the horse.*)

TEACHER: Tommy, do you want to play horsey? You know you don't have to unless you want to. Miriam can get a hobby horse to ride if she wants.
(*Tommy started playing horsey for Miriam. But a few minutes later he ran away from her to where others were playing in the sandbox.*)

In the kindergarten situation most five-year-olds make the most of the opportunity to be with other children. However, occasionally a child is intent in working out some individual idea by himself. He needs freedom from interruption to enable him to do this, and he may need help in keeping other children from interfering. His teacher provides these conditions and interprets his behavior to the other children.

David volunteered to build a barber shop, usually a two-person project.

TEACHER: Whom do you want to help you?

DAVID: Nobody.

TEACHER: You want to build it yourself without any helper?

DAVID: (*With determination*) Yes.
(*David worked intently, breathing hard. He was obviously working out something that he had thought through.*)
(*Mike, an especially good friend of David's, came over to help him.*)

MIKE: May I help?

DAVID: Go 'way.

MIKE: (*Picking up a block*) Does this go here?

DAVID: (*Angrily*) Leave it alone.

TEACHER: (*To Mike*) I think David wants to do it by himself this morning. Sometimes we like to work with others, and sometimes we like to work alone. Tommy over there is looking around as if he needs help. See if you can help him, Mike.

The teacher protected David's right to solitude and interpreted his behavior to his friend. Her wisdom in handling the situation as she did may contribute to the future careers of the boys, perhaps a research career for David and a salesman's career for Mike.

When five-year-old children come to kindergarten, they must work out relationships with their teacher and with other children as individuals and as members of large and small groups. Their teacher helps them develop self-confidence and a feeling of belonging to the kindergarten group. She does this by being genuinely interested in each child, listening to what he has to say, helping him do what he wants to do without hurting others, and trying to understand his point of view. She helps the children plan their activities and work together co-operatively, taking turns and learning to see how the other person feels. Her belief that each child learns when he is ready, emotionally and intellectually, gives the timid child confidence. Her understanding of the attention-getter helps him develop socially acceptable channels for his energy. By planning in terms of the needs of the children, the teacher makes the kindergarten a co-operative and happy situation in which children develop satisfying relationships with others.

SITUATIONS FOR DISCUSSION

In the following situations select each course of action that seems desirable to you basing your choices and omissions on the ideas presented in this chapter. Add one or more alternate courses of action.

SITUATION I. Stanley goes to great lengths to get attention from other children. Today he has come in late and is entertaining several children by the way he is taking off his jacket and hanging it in the cupboard.

As the teacher you should say:

"Stanley, you're disturbing us."

"Boys and girls, do we think acting silly is funny?"

"While some of us finish hanging up our jackets, the rest of us can start planning our work."

"Stanley wants us to laugh at the way he is hanging up his jacket."

"Show Miss Teacher you know how to hang up your jacket, Stanley."

SITUATIONS II AND III. David is building "an underground tunnel," as he calls it, out of blocks. Just as he is putting on the finishing touches of ladders, Billy walks by on his way to the clay table. Billy's toe takes off a corner of David's structure. Crying and with clenched fists David starts after Billy.

As the teacher you should help David by:

Paying attention to him first.

Letting him get one good hit before you start talking with him.

Telling him that Billy did not mean to break off the blocks.

Encouraging him in rebuilding his tunnel.

Listening while he talks out his anger.

As the teacher you should help Billy by:

Bringing him back to where David is working.

Telling him to say, "I'm sorry."

Helping him feel ashamed of himself for knocking over David's building.

Asking him, "How can we make David feel happy again?"

Asking him, "When are you going to learn to watch where you're going?"

SITUATION IV. Charles, Mary, and Kathy live on the same street and walk to school each day. At the first of the year the three children walked together. Lately Mary and Kathy have gone by themselves, leaving Charles to walk alone. Today Charles arrives at school looking very unhappy. "Mary and Kathy won't walk with me," he says. "They don't like me."

As the teacher you should say:

"Well, I like you," and give him a big hug.

"Mary and Kathy enjoy playing and talking about what girls do."

"The girls like you. They think you are a good friend."

"I'll talk with your mother. Maybe we can figure out a plan."

(To Mary and Kathy) "Charles feels left out when you girls walk by yourselves."

BIBLIOGRAPHY

Professional Books and Pamphlets

Baruch, Dorothy Walter. *New Ways in Discipline.* New York: McGraw-Hill Book Company, Inc., 1949.

Advice on how to handle crucial situations, how to forestall crises, and how to make discipline easier is included.

Bettelheim, Bruno. *Love Is Not Enough.* Glencoe, Illinois: Free Press, 1950.

This interesting report of daily life at the Orthogenic School of the University of Chicago describes behavior of children with severe emotional disturbances and emphasizes the similar needs of all children.

D'Evelyn, Katherine. *Meeting Children's Emotional Needs.* Englewood Cliffs, New Jersey: Prentice-Hall, Inc., 1957.

Chapters two through six suggest how teachers can meet emotional needs of school children.

Hemming, James, and Josephine Bells. *The Child Is Right: A Challenge to Parents and Other Adults.* New York: Longmans, Green and Company, 1948.

A series of case studies regarding the conflict between the drive for security and that for achievement and new experience, and the effect of this conflict on child development.

Montagu, Ashley. *Helping Children Develop Moral Values.* Better Living Booklet. Chicago: Science Research Associates, Inc., 1953.

This pamphlet emphasizes the role of the adult in helping a child develop a sense of right and wrong.

Moustakas, Clark E. *Children in Play Therapy.* New York: McGraw-Hill Book Company, Inc., 1955.

Acceptance of and respect for the child's values and ideals help both normal and abnormal children with their problems.

Moustakas, Clark E. *The Teacher and the Child.* New York: McGraw-Hill Book Company, Inc., 1956.

Interpersonal relationships between teacher and child are discussed.

Neisser, Edith G. *Children in the Family: Rivals and Friends.* Parent-Teacher Series. New York: Bureau of Publications, Teachers College, Columbia University, 1951.

Teasing and quarreling are basic to learning how to get along with others co-operatively. This booklet suggests how teachers may control competitive behavior.

Redl, Fritz, and David Wineman. *Children Who Hate.* Glencoe, Illinois: Free Press, 1951.

Analysis of case studies of highly aggressive eight- and nine-year-old children at Pioneer House in Detroit brings out factors helpful in preventing hate and aggression and in aiding children in making a good adjustment.

Taylor, Katharine Whiteside. *Parent Cooperative Nursery Schools.* New York: Bureau of Publications, Teachers College, Columbia University, 1954.

Chapters VII, VIII, and X deal with "The Three R's of Discipline:" relationship, readiness, and responsibility; "Helping Children Channel Emotions;" and "Helping Children Develop Sympathy."

Books for Children

Beim, Jerrold, and Lorraine. *Two Is a Team.* New York: Harcourt, Brace and Company, Inc., 1945.

Working together, Ted and Paul are able to pay for the damage they brought about when they were competing against each other.

de Regniers, Beatrice S. *A Little House of Your Own.* New York: Harcourt, Brace and Company, Inc., 1954.

A child conjures up many secret houses for being alone or with friends, and learns the rules for secret houses.

Ets, Marie Hall. *Another Day.* New York: The Viking Press, 1953.

A child's laughter is more valuable than any stunt the animals think of, and is admired by his father as well.

Johnson, Crockett. *Terrible Terrifying Toby.* New York: Harper and Brothers, 1957.

Looking in the mirror, Toby scares even a terrible terrifying dog like himself.

Langstaff, Nancy. *A Tiny Baby for You.* New York: Harcourt, Brace and Company, Inc., 1955.

Johnny helps his mother with their new baby.

Lenski, Lois. *Papa Small.* New York: Oxford University Press, 1951.

A clear account of Papa Small's activities at home with his family.

Liang, Yen. *Tommy and Dee Dee.* New York: Oxford University Press, 1953.

A boy in the United States and a boy in China are very much alike in this story.

Lipkind, Will, and Nicolas. *Finders Keepers.* New York: Harcourt, Brace and Company, Inc., 1951.

Two shaggy dogs with one bone try to decide what to do with it.

Rowand, Phyllis. *George.* Boston: Little, Brown and Company, 1956.

When George disappeared, the busy family discovered that the difficulties the big dog got them into were part of loving him.

Steiner, Charlotte. *Lulu's Play School.* Garden City, New York: Doubleday and Company, Inc., 1948.

Lulu, by making a play school for others to enjoy, has fun herself.

Thayer, Jane. *Where's Andy?* New York: William Morrow and Company, 1954.

A delightful game of hide-and-seek is played by Andy and his mother.

Zion, Gene. *Jeffie's Party.* New York: Harper and Brothers, 1957.

Jeffie's costume birthday party was an experience in being different.

Films for Teachers

Fears of Children. Chicago: International Film Bureau, 1951.

A mother who tends to coddle her five-year-old son and a father who is friendly but stern magnify the boy's rudimentary fears. 30 minutes, sound, black and white.

Helping the Child to Accept the Do's. Wilmette, Illinois: Encyclopaedia Britannica Films, Inc., 1948.

A child learns to accept the "do's" for personal living, for his role as boy or girl, and for human relations. The companion film, *Helping the Child to Accept the Don'ts*, deals with the "don'ts" that protect him from change and from taking what is not his, and teach him to have respect for others. 11 minutes, sound, black and white.

A Long Time to Grow, Part II. New York: New York University Press, 1954.

Four- and five-year-old children play at nursery school. 35 minutes, sound, black and white.

Preface to a Life. New York: United World Films, Inc., 1950.

Parental attitudes and expectations influence the development of a child. 29 minutes, sound, black and white.

Shyness. New York: McGraw-Hill Book Company, 1953.

This study of three shy children shows how the methods of handling them affected their shyness. 23 minutes, sound, black and white.

Films for Children

Animal Friends. Chicago, Illinois: Coronet Films, 1956.

A kitten is friendly with a watch dog, and, on a walk in the country, meets such friends as a gopher, a toad, and an owl. 11 minutes, sound, color.

Developing Responsibility. Chicago: Coronet Instructional Films, 1949.

A small boy learns to make sacrifices and plan carefully to get the little dog he wants. 10 minutes, sound, black and white, or color.

Fox and the Rooster. Wilmette, Illinois: Encyclopaedia Britannica Films, Inc., 1951.

The adaptation of an Aesop fable shows a clever schemer being outwitted by good friends helping each other. 10 minutes, sound, black and white.

Let's Play Fair. Chicago: Coronet Instructional Films, 1949.

Sharing, taking turns, respecting property and making up for mistakes are shown, 10 minutes, sound, black and white, or color.

16

Planning the Kindergarten Day

To make each day profitable in promoting the growth and development of children, the teacher thinks first about the long-range goals of the experiences provided in the kindergarten program. She knows that every activity planned should help the children:

To learn to work and play with others

To learn desirable ways of behaving which will serve them well throughout life

To develop present interests and stimulate new interests

To expand their store of useful information

To acquire increasing skill in observing, manipulating, experimenting, talking, dramatizing, building, playing, and creating

To grow in power to initiate, think, judge, and evaluate

To finish what they start and so develop a feeling of power and attainment

To increase interest in and appreciation of stories, poems, pictures

To participate joyously in dramatic play, in singing together, in playing games together, and in listening to each other's stories

To express themselves freely through a wide variety of art media

SUGGESTED SCHEDULE

To meet all of these needs, the teacher evolves a flexible plan which provides indoor and outdoor activities, a rhythm of activity and rest, and a wide choice for children's selection of materials, equipment, and experiences. A typical schedule for a kindergarten day follows, but the specific activities will not be the same for any two children, nor will the major centers of interest to which the children are attracted be identical on any two consecutive days.

330

SCHEDULE FOR KINDERGARTEN DAY

8:30–8:45
Arrival and Nurse Inspection
Teacher greets children, helps adjust wraps for indoor or outdoor activities, helps make disposition of properties and possessions which have been brought from home.

8:45–9:40
Work and Play Activities — Indoors
These may be alternated with outdoor activities in warm weather.

Choice of work and play period activities including:

Playhouse and doll play — house cleaning, "cooking," dish washing, care of babies, calling on friends, enacting the roles of workers who come to the house, telephoning, taking trips on airplanes and trains, washing doll clothes, performing simple cooking experiments.

Building with small floor blocks. In connection with these, children use accessory toys such as trucks, trains, boats, planes, and stand-pat dolls. Using large hollow blocks to build houses, trains, airplanes, boats, accompanied by play with structures created. More and more interchange between these building centers and the "house play" will occur as the year progresses.

Painting at easels or using finger paint.

Using crayons or chalk.

Modeling with clay.

Constructing with wood.

Looking at books.

Working with puzzles.

Culmination of the hour's experience may take the form of:
Short evaluation involving small groups, song concerning a selected interest, playing of records related to the activity.

Clean up period.

9:40–10:15
Midmorning Toilet and Juice and Rest
Following toileting and washing, each child goes immediately to the juice table and then to his cot for rest.

10:15–11:30
Outdoor Activities in Play Yard
These activities include the use of the following:

Large physical apparatus, such as swings, bouncing boards, the jungle gym, rocking boat, climbing bars, climbing ladders.

Tricycles, wagons for hauling and pulling.

Large platforms and large packing boxes adapted for use and combined with ladders, hollow-yard blocks, small boxes, planks, boards, reels, and hose. These are used for a variety of purposes according to whatever ideas are in the ascendancy for the day. These ideas may stem from child suggestion, arranged environment, teacher suggestion, or a group study trip.

Outdoor playhouse or tree house.

Digging and gardening tools.

Sandbox, with a hose and running water in warm weather, sand toys, and models such as road scrapers, concrete mixers, steam shovels, steam rollers, boats, and trains.

Pets, which are cared for as well as played with by the children.

Experimentation with science aspects of the environment.

Free and guided activities with musical instruments.

11:30–12:00
Games, Rhythmic Activities, Singing, Stories, Listening to Records

12:00
Dismissal
The teacher talks briefly at dismissal with parents who call for children about the events of the session.

The teacher modifies the schedule as she observes the children because she recognizes their growth needs:

Are they having adequate opportunity to develop large and small muscles?

Is there a sufficient variety in the activities provided?

Does the schedule provide for a proper rhythm of activity and relaxation?

Are the children communicating freely with each other?

Are they planning, working, and evaluating at a level appropriate to their maturity?

Are they using books, pictures, and observation to find answers to their questions?

Are all children having opportunity for the leadership role?

Are the children growing in recognition of the worth and rights of others?

Would some modification in the schedule for a day or two help a child solve his problems of development?

VARIATIONS IN THE SCHEDULE

Although an orderly plan is indispensable to the effective guidance of children, occasional changes add adventure and develop ability to make adaptations to new circumstances.

As children mature, more time will be spent in planning and evaluating activities although even at the end of the year, these periods will seldom involve more than a part of the total group, nor will the period exceed five to ten minutes. These brief periods may be devoted to setting up standards for block-building, construction, cleanup, and rest periods. Seasonal events like Halloween, Thanksgiving, Christmas, Valentine's Day, Easter, Mother's Day, or the birthdays of the children all call for special planning, special stories and poems, special activities in painting, modeling, construction, and special opportunities for children to enter into the cultural heritage.

The danger to children of overstimulation in relation to special events is always in the mind of the wise kindergarten teacher. A few days of preparation ending in a simple culminating observance in which the major purpose is sharing a happy experience with others is probably the safest way to manage these occasional departures from the well-considered schedule of a typical kindergarten day. Children build a feeling of security when an interesting schedule is followed regularly with a change now and then for some definite reason.

A TYPICAL DAY

The children began to arrive at the door of the spacious double room of the Whittier School Kindergarten at a quarter after eight; Mrs. Smiley, the school nurse, was sitting on a low chair near the door. According to his temperament, every child greeted her either with a "Hi, Mrs. Smiley!", a grave nod, a smile, a timidly offered hand, or an exuberant hug. To the casual observer, this ritual might have seemed little more than a friendly greeting, but to this public health nurse trained to observe the early symptoms of communicable disease it was enough to insure the safety of a group of children who had not yet developed much immunity.

The children devoted little time to farewells for the occasional parents who accompanied them. They were eager to get into the intriguing activities arranged to stimulate their interest. By coming early a child may have a treasured bit of private conversation with his teacher or an opportunity to use unhindered some piece of favorite equipment greatly in demand by more aggressive classmates. Sometimes schools lose precious opportunities by keeping children outside until an appointed hour. But Whittier School had no such regulations and from a quarter after eight children began to come — to greet Mrs. Smiley, to rush to their adored Miss Carpenter for a special word, and then to begin the real business of their day.

Two little girls went to the table labeled "Our Look and Listen Corner." Here were musical instruments, colorful music books, and a Listening Post — a phonograph equipped with three sets of headphones so children could enjoy the carefully selected phonograph records. These children knew exactly what they wanted, adjusted the earphones, selected a record, and sat down companionably to absorbed listening which continued for more than forty minutes.

Shortly after, a child who gave evidence of little physical vigor joined them, adjusted the earphones, listened until the record was finished, took off the earphones, played briefly with a tambourine, went to the library table and looked at the books for a minute or two, strummed briefly on the piano, and then went to the clay table and began to manipulate the clay with little evidence of any purpose.

A blue-sweatered boy clutching a woolly brown dog under his arm came over to the playhouse, picked up the baby doll from its crib, and dropped it on the floor. He looked at it there for a moment or two and then gave it an impatient push with his foot and turned away, clutching the brown woolly dog more closely. Only for a brief moment when he played the piano with thundering crashes was the brown woolly dog out of his hands.

Three little girls arrived together in high spirits and headed straight for the playhouse. Maternal cluckings accompanied the immediate restoration of the baby to its crib and then the ladies made an attack on the clothes rack of dress-up clothing and the chest of feminine accessories —

veils, purses, hats, and shoes. After they were dressed up, they did a few dance steps accompanied by a chorus of their own giggles. One lady immediately got to work scrubbing the woodwork, another initiated a tea party, and the third launched into cooking with a great opening and shutting of cupboard and oven doors. These children had been in kindergarten for weeks but there was little actual playing together — most of the play was solitary or parallel play.

Miss Carpenter was observing all these ways children were responding to the environment. A little girl picked up a "freighter" from the harbor, looked at it appreciatively for a moment, and then stood looking around the room. Miss Carpenter took her hand and together they walked around the room looking at the play centers until finally she handed the freighter to Miss Carpenter and with the assurance Miss Carpenter's presence afforded joined the group of girls in the housekeeping center.

Here a boy experimented with a pair of scissors with indifferent success.

Two boys were at the clay table. Tommy was pounding the clay vigorously; Lionel was modeling a large circular object. A brief conversation ensued:

TOMMY: Do you like red?

LIONEL: Yes, sir! I like red. I like blue too. What do you think this is? What do you think this is? It's a pie — pie — pie!

TOMMY: Is it a pie?

LIONEL: Yes, yes!
Because I *said* it is a pie.
(*Lionel finished his pie, took a container of red paint from an easel and painted the "pie" vigorously.*)
How does my pie look?

TOMMY: It looks very red.

The train center attracted five vigorous little boys who were soon engaged in propelling trains at break-neck speed around tracks painted on the floor. Trouble developed fast, and the inevitable collision brought Miss Carpenter with a calm "Just a minute, engineers." All talked at once but soon the need for signals at crossings, for a train dispatcher, and for engineers who realized how responsible they are for the welfare of their passengers emerged out of the evaluation of this exciting play. The talk was vigorous and purposeful, information was shared, plans were made, and agreements were reached. For a while at least there would be a "clear track ahead" in the Whittier kindergarten.

Although many of the activities reported might be called "free play," they were really guided activities. The teacher provided guidance in her arrangement of the work and play centers to attract the children. As children live and work and play together, it is desirable and necessary occasionally for the adult guide and counselor to step in to help children secure new knowledge, evaluate the success of their present activities, and build standards of behavior which will create better values. As Miss Carpenter talked with the "engineers," she gave them the values of the culture which they could learn in no other way than by the understanding guidance of a sympathetic adult at hand while they played.

In this situation, the teacher stood by observing and making a few notes for her later guidance; she entered into the situation as an active participant only as need arose, as illustrated by the collision of the trains.

This kindergarten had a "Look and Listen Corner," a piano and musical instruments available for use by the children, a clay table with clay ready to use, easels and cold water paints, housekeeping corner, small building blocks, engines and all types of freight cars and passenger cars, a library table with a selection of attractive books, a table with crayons and paper, and a harbor setup with blue oilcloth on the floor and with tugs, freighters, and steamships.

The Teacher's Role

With such a rich environment in two spacious rooms to challenge the interest of the children, the teacher had opportunity to jot down some notes about the things she observed. Her notes follow:

> No children painted at the easels. Change their location tomorrow so children won't feel out of the group when painting.
>
> Is this environment better suited to the boys than the girls?
>
> No girl engaged in train or harbor activities this morning.
>
> Johnny had a terrible time with the scissors. They *are* dull. Is it safe to supply some sharp ones?
>
> The boys got overstimulated with the train play. Should I have stopped them before the collision?
>
> Gail repulsed Sandra two or three times this morning and made it even more pointed by her eager acceptance of Anne. What to do?
>
> Did Lionel work at the clay such a long time because of his interest in the clay or his inability to hold his own in the more vigorous train and harbor activities?
>
> Robby really knows a lot of things. He said, "Mine was a streamliner. They go fast. Everyone clears the track for the streamliners." What use of language — Robby won't be five for two months!
>
> Teddy still has his woolly dog. Why is that child so insecure and unhappy?

Evaluating the Events of the Day

And so Miss Carpenter's plans gave her the opportunity to watch these fives in action in a situation which met their needs. Their interest and curiosity were challenged; space and freedom made it possible for them to be active; they were free to share and communicate with her and with one another; materials were available so they could manipulate, construct, and build with blocks; many centers encouraged creative play; and others encouraged aesthetic expression. Only in such a situation could an observant teacher discover the actual points at which her guidance was needed to help children meet their developmental tasks.

Adjusting to New Circumstances

Knowing that an unforeseen happening may offer opportunity for much learning, the teacher is always sensitive to community events in which the children may participate actively or at least in the role of observer. She capitalizes on landscaping of the school ground, a kitten mewing in a schoolyard tree, or the fire truck parked in front of the school while firemen distribute leaflets to householders. She notices the fresh red, white, and blue paint on the postbox at the corner and uses it as a springboard into a brief study of postmen and post offices. When a new stop sign is placed at a neighborhood crossing, she makes the most of the event as a means for teaching safety. Incidentally, of course, her awareness of happenings in the neighborhood helps the children to become good observers themselves.

On her way to school Mrs. Mitchell had the serene and relaxing feeling that she was well prepared to meet the needs of the children in her group. After school the day before she had mixed paints and cut large sheets of paper for use at the easels. She had selected story and flannel board material leading up to the study of house construction, for in a week or two a contractor would start to build a group of new houses a few blocks from school.

Mrs. Mitchell thought comfortably about the finger play "All for Baby" [1] which she would use when Tommy told about the family birthday party for his baby brother. *Timothy Turtle*,[2] the book she was fortunate to find in the boys and girls department of the public library, should help Mary and the other children who had been turning their pet turtle over on his back. Jerry's mother was coming the latter part of the morn-

---

[1] June Pierce (compiler). *The Wonder Book of Finger Plays and Action Rhymes.* New York: Wonder Books, Inc., 1955.

[2] Alice Vaught Davis. *Timothy Turtle.* Eau Claire, Wisconsin: E. M. Hale and Company (Cadmus Books), 1940.

ing with some dress-up clothes including a few carpenter's aprons that should capture the imagination of the boys and prepare the children for studying about house construction.

Now Mrs. Mitchell was passing the houses in the same block as the school. A concrete mixer rumbled down the street and came to a stop at the curb in front of her. She watched as the driver went up to one of the houses and rang the bell. A few minutes later she went up to the same house and introduced herself to the owner's wife, Mrs. Cox. She found that the Coxes were having a patio poured in their garden. Three concrete mixer trucks were scheduled to come at intervals of half an hour. Mrs. Cox would be pleased to have Mrs. Mitchell bring the kindergarten children in time to see the last truck pour its load at 9:30. They could watch from the living room, looking out the sliding glass doors. "I'll come after school and clean the children's finger prints off the windows," offered Mrs. Mitchell. "That's good of you," smiled Mrs. Cox, "but my cleaning woman comes tomorrow and would be disappointed not to do them." "We shall be here about 9:20," said Mrs. Mitchell as she left.

At the school Mrs. Mitchell quickly rearranged the kindergarten as she revised her plans for the day. She added *The Big Book of Real Trucks*[3] and the *Wonder Book of Trucks*[4] to the library corner, as well as *Timothy Turtle*.[5] From her file she took pictures of a concrete mixer, of children riding their tricycles on a sidewalk, and of a car standing in the driveway next to a house. These she put with the flannel board ready for talking with the children about uses of concrete. Looking at her file notes on "Concrete Mixer," she hummed the suggested songs. As she closed the file drawer she glanced at the fat folder labeled "House Construction." She was glad that the concrete mixer would help lead the group to use of that folder.

The children were arriving now. Jane had her turn arranging the bouquet of fall leaves the way she wanted them for the day. Teddy had a turn feeding the guppies while his good friend Sammy trotted along beside him. Then Sammy fed the turtle while Teddy watched. The doll house and the library corner were put to use by other children. Just as the bell was ringing Peter and Jerry burst breathlessly into the room. "We saw a cement mixer!" "It's right near here!" Mrs. Mitchell listened

[3] George J. Zaffo. *The Big Book of Real Trucks*. New York: Grosset and Dunlap, Inc., 1950.

[4] Lisa Peters. *The Wonder Book of Trucks* (#616). New York 10: Wonder Books, Inc., 1954.

[5] *Op. cit.*

with interest but calmness while the boys told their story and quieted down. Then she said, "Maybe this is something we should all talk about." She signaled for the whole group to gather on the rug.

When Peter and Jerry told what they had seen, the whole group wanted to go to see the mixer too. Carefully they planned how they might do this. They would have to stand where they could see but not get in the way of the workers. Maybe they could watch from a window at the Cox's house. They would be careful not to touch the Cox's things, and would say "Thank you" afterwards. They would all stay together as a group. They would walk with a friend because the sidewalk is just wide enough for two people.

At 9:20 the kindergarten children rang the bell at the Cox home. Mrs. Cox helped the children find places at the window. Mrs. Mitchell asked questions to help them observe the making of the patio: What keeps the concrete in place? What are Mr. Cox and his helpers doing to get the rocks to sink down to the bottom? What color is the concrete? What color does it change to as it dries?

Rumble, rumble, rumble. The yellow concrete mixer turned the corner of the house and backed around into position for pouring. The children watched in fascination as the driver swung the trough into place, gave the mixture a final mix, and then let it come tumbling down the trough to spread out over the patio. Mr. Cox and his helpers started working it, puddling the rocks down and smoothing the concrete on top.

When the mixer was empty, the driver got back into the cab and drove the mixer out to the curb. Quickly the children thanked Mrs. Cox and went out to see what happened next. They watched the driver uncoil a small hose and carefully wash the residue of concrete off the blades, off the trough, and off the truck. When he finally rolled up the little hose, laid the troughs along the side of the truck, and climbed back into the cab, they waved "Goodbye" and called, "Thank you for letting us watch."

Back at the kindergarten, the children found places on the rug. Again Mrs. Mitchell guided their comments with questions about relationships: What is concrete made of? What shapes it into the form of a patio or a sidewalk? What will the patio be like tomorrow? Why did the driver wash off his truck so carefully?

The excellent science discussion shifted briefly to a planning session as the children asked to see the patio the next day. Mrs. Mitchell helped them think about how well they had managed the study trip today. Together they planned how to arrange for the trip the next day. After school Mary and Tom and Mrs. Mitchell would go to thank Mrs. Cox for letting them come and would ask her if they might come again the next morning.

Then Mrs. Mitchell remembered the song "Cement Mixer, Put-ty, Put-ty" and sang it with an autoharp accompaniment. This led to other songs and presently to an action play about "Pouring Concrete."

By midmorning lunch the children were ready to talk about many things other than concrete mixers. Then as the children rested Mrs. Mitchell sang one last song about the mixer to the tune of "I Dreamt I Dwelt in Marble Halls." She adapted her memory of a song about the old mill to make this rhyme:

> The cement mixer goes 'round and 'round;
> 'Round and 'round; 'round and 'round;
> With such a pleasant whirring sound
> Until the mix is on the ground.

But many of the children were still thinking about the concrete mixer during the remainder of the morning. As they enjoyed painting at the easels, yellow seemed to be a favorite color. "Here's the mixer," said Jane pointing to a yellow mass in her painting. The mixer appeared that morning and other mornings in various settings.

The children in the library corner found the pictures of concrete mixers and the children with blocks were busy laying forms for patios. How glad Mrs. Mitchell was that the supply of cars and trucks included two concrete mixers.

The children who were not especially interested in their first experience with a concrete mixer also found things to do. Homemakers were at work in the playhouse. Jerry's mother was supervising the carpenter's bench where Jerry and other children dressed in carpenter's aprons were busy with hammer and saw. Girls as well as boys were enjoying the new dress-up clothes as they made polite calls on the playhouse ladies. So much constructive activity was under way that Mrs. Mitchell decided to use the flannel board and pictures the next day, rather than introduce a new activity at that time.

Soon it was time to put things away and clean the kindergarten to get it ready for the next day. After the other children left, Mary and Tom and Mrs. Mitchell made arrangements with Mrs. Cox for the study trip the next morning. Then Mrs. Mitchell went back to her desk to make brief records about the individual children who had been outstanding that day. For the first time Peter and Jerry had initiated an activity. Are they especially interested in mechanical things? Maybe the unit on house construction will give each of them further opportunity for leadership. Mary had been suddenly shy in talking with Mrs. Cox. Perhaps she should have more opportunity for meeting adults. Mrs. Mitchell made a mental note to have mother assistants talk with her. Jenny showed no interest in the mixer. Each day she just goes along with the other children. What does interest her?

On her way home Mrs. Mitchell suddenly remembered that she was to say a few words at the parents' meeting scheduled for that evening. "I'll just tell them about today," she thought. "It certainly illustrates the flexibility that the kindergarten and the home must have in meeting the needs of five-year-olds. Today we took part in a neighborhood activity, and we experienced how to get along with neighbors at the same time that we learned much about the scientific process of making concrete. We had opportunity for planning a study trip, evaluating the success of the plans, and planning a follow-up study trip. The whole activity was so interesting that for many of the children it was the springboard for art, music, construction, and language projects for the rest of the day and probably for many tomorrows as well."

SITUATIONS FOR DISCUSSION

In the following situations select each course of action that seems desirable to you basing your choices and omissions on the ideas presented in this chapter. Add one or more alternate courses of action.

SITUATION I. All term Jimmy has often played just outside the playhouse. During the last week, for minutes at a time, he has looked at what the girls were doing inside the playhouse. This morning while you are taking off your hat twenty minutes before opening time, Jimmy knocks at the door: "May I play in the playhouse?" As the teacher you should tell Jimmy:

"Of course you may play in the playhouse. It's for everyone to play in."

"You must wait until opening time. Then you may have the first turn in the playhouse."

"Wait until others come to help you play."

"We play outside until opening time. Would you like to use the boxes to build a playhouse outside now?"

"I have a great many things to do to get ready for school today."

SITUATION II. You are one of several teachers talking informally about making notes while the kindergarten children have "free play."

TEACHER A: You don't catch me taking notes. I finished that when I finished college.

TEACHER B: I couldn't get along without my notebook. I keep it open on top of a cupboard just the right height for writing.

TEACHER C: I like to give my attention completely to the children while they are playing, but I spend a few minutes making notes after each session.

As a beginning teacher you should:

Postpone note taking until you gain more experience in teaching.

Try making notes at the end of the session.

Try making notes during the free play period.

Observe Teachers A, B and C to determine whether note taking is associated with better teaching.

Talk with Teacher C about what kind of notes she takes and how she uses them.

SITUATION III. Several of the boys have been using large wooden boxes to make a playhouse. They made a roof by putting long, lightweight boards across the top. These are not fastened and probably will fall when anyone brushes against them. As the teacher you should:

Have the boys take down the roof because it is unsafe.

Have the whole class discuss safety.

Join the boys in their play and have the roof come down on you.

Watch, but do nothing until part of the roof tumbles down.

Get the builders together for an evaluative session about the roof.

SITUATION IV. Every Wednesday the children bring money for the thrift project sponsored by the parents. This Wednesday, the last day before Thanksgiving vacation, you have planned the kindergarten activities around the holiday theme. But shy and sweet Susan who has not participated in leadership activities comes in with her eyes shining to tell you, "I have a new baby sister!" As the teacher you should:

Have Susan share her news with the group.

Begin the week of activities you have planned around the new baby theme.

Carry out your plans for using the Thanksgiving theme.

Cut out the thrift project in order to have time for other activities.

Instead of having the usual rest period, use that time for quiet talk about babies.

BIBLIOGRAPHY

Professional Books and Pamphlets

Foster, Josephine C., and Neith E. Headley. *Education in the Kindergarten.* New York: American Book Company, 1948.

Chapter VIII, pages 108–125, discusses "Starting the Kindergarten Year," and contains practical suggestions regarding the kindergarten day.

Heffernan, Helen, ed. *Guiding the Young Child, Kindergarten to Grade Three, Second Edition.* Boston: D. C. Heath and Company, 1959.

Chapter III, pages 21–35, describes "A Teacher's Day with the Five-Year-Olds."

New York State Education Department. *Child Development Guides.* Albany, New York: 1955.

Part IV, "The Program," pages 74–81 emphasizes program planning in terms of the needs of the children in the group.

Wills, C. D., and William H. Stegeman. *Living in the Kindergarten.* Chicago: Follett Publishing Company, 1951.

Chapter 7, pages 84–109, discusses "The Program: What to Include and When."

Films for Teachers

A Day in the Life of a Five-Year-Old. New York: Bureau of Publications, Teachers College, Columbia University, 1949.

The National Association of Nursery Education shows the role of a teacher in guiding children through a happy day in a well-planned kindergarten setting. 20 minutes, sound, black and white.

Filmstrip

A Good Day in the Kindergarten. Produced by Helen Heffernan in 1956 at the University Elementary School, University of California, Los Angeles. Long Film-Slide Service, 750 S. Farrmount Ave., El Cerrito, California. A filmstrip of sixty pictures with accompanying phonograph recording.

17

Exceptional Children in Kindergarten

The kindergarten teacher realizes the importance of identifying and helping exceptional children. She knows that the public school must not deny the benefit of education to any child who can profit from the school program. She understands what constitutes an exceptional child and how to help him develop to the point of profiting from the school activities that lie ahead. By identifying an exceptional child early she helps to prevent the development of unfortunate social and emotional problems. Her help sometimes makes it possible to salvage a child who might otherwise become lost to the school and to society.

The teacher also realizes that the kindergarten is unique in being a social experience free from pressures for performance. In the later years of the school, attention is focused to an extent on the development of skills in reading, writing, and arithmetic. But in kindergarten the focus is almost wholly on the child and his development as he relates to other personalities. Adult guidance and a variety of materials are provided to help him in achieving his purposes. Through his successes, he gains confidence in himself and a feeling of belonging to the group. All children, exceptional and normal, thrive in the permissive atmosphere of the kindergarten.

The teacher needs to know what kinds of children are exceptional so that she can make the school aware of them and their need for special services and teaching skills. She learns to identify children with vision and hearing defects, with conditions that interfere with their locomotion, with speech difficulties, with disturbed personalities, with retarded intellectual development, and with exceptional abilities. She also works with their parents in getting the children and themselves ready to co-operate in the special activities that schools and communities provide in later

343

years. She is always willing to work with the parents and with the local guidance and health service personnel as a member of a team working to develop a program for the exceptional child.

The teacher also works with specialists in helping decide more precisely the extent of a handicap and the kind of remediation needed or the nature and extent of unusual abilities. These specialists include the physician; the people making audiometric, visual, and speech tests; the psychologist who administers the Wechsler Intelligence Scale for Children, the Stanford-Binet, and other tests of mental abilities or who makes studies of emotional disturbances.

Of course what the teacher does primarily is to help the exceptional child feel that he is an important individual and a worthwhile member of the group. He is a unique person among other unique people, all of whom are helpful and co-operative the way he is.

PROVIDING A NORMAL ENVIRONMENT FOR THE EXCEPTIONAL CHILD

When a teacher has an exceptional child in the kindergarten group, she keeps in mind that such a child is more like, than unlike, other children. He will grow and develop best only in the kind of environment he will live in, the kind of environment with which any child must learn to cope. The sooner he starts living realistically, the better for his emotional, social, and educational development. The teacher provides a simplified but realistic environment in which the exceptional as well as the so-called normal five-year-old thrives and develops.

ASSISTING THE GROUP IN AIDING THE EXCEPTIONAL CHILD

The teacher who has one or more children with obvious handicaps in the group takes advantage of the situation to help all the children, including the handicapped, to learn that each child is unique in one or more ways and like other children in most ways. Enrolled in Miss McDonald's group was a boy whose hand had not fully developed before he was born. She said nothing about Lester's hand until one of the more observant boys asked her about it. She answered his questions quietly:

PETER: Lester's hand is funny.

MISS MCDONALD: Oh? What's funny about it?

PETER: It has only two thick fingers.

MISS MCDONALD: And yours has five fingers, doesn't it? Now you know that a person can be born with five fingers like yours, or with two fingers like Lester's.

PETER: Was he born that way?

MISS MCDONALD: Yes, each of us is born different from everyone else in some way or other. That's the way Lester is different. Do you know how you are different?

PETER: How?

MISS MCDONALD: I don't think I have ever seen eyes that were quite as blue as yours.
Have you been playing with Lester? He's lots of fun to play with. Let's see what he's doing now.

A few days later Miss McDonald talked with the large group of children briefly about how each person is unique but yet like everyone else. She had thought about each child and was prepared to point out some desirable characteristic of each one: the smallest girl and the smallest boy whom the French would describe by the lovely word *petite*, the girl with eyes like a brown-eyed Susan, the boy whose two-fingered hand does everything a hand needs to do, the boy with cheeks of tan, the girl who likes very small toys as well as large ones, and the girl whose favorite color is green.

A kindergarten teacher like Miss McDonald is careful to have the children see the handicapped child as someone like themselves. When the children hold hands, the teacher unobtrusively clasps the withered hand of a handicapped child. She encourages the handicapped child to have his first turn on a piece of apparatus when other children are busy elsewhere on the playground. At the same time she helps him feel at home in a group of children whose interests are similar or complementary to his. In short, she helps him learn how to participate in group activities and when to try an activity by himself. Thus he develops a realistic understanding of what he can do with others.

The teacher of exceptional and normal children also emphasizes co-operation and helpfulness among all the children. The handicapped child is given only enough help to participate in the group activity. "Hand Jim a rag so he can help polish the boat." Sometimes the handicap of the child can be capitalized on for the benefit of the group. "Maybe Jim can poke it with his crutch." Such matter of fact co-operation gives Jim a feeling of successful achievement, as well as a feeling of belonging to the group. Withdrawal and egocentricity are easy to avoid in a kindergarten where teacher and children are working together on projects of their own choosing.

ADJUSTING TO THE SPECIFIC PROBLEMS OF THE EXCEPTIONAL CHILD

Although the greatest need of the exceptional child is to be treated like any other child, he also needs consideration in terms of his particular handicap or unusual talent. The kindergarten teacher thinks of the child with an aural handicap differently from the way in which she thinks about the mentally retarded child. She develops skills in terms of the special problems of the exceptional children in her group. Furthermore she needs to know what helps are available for exceptional children through the local school system, community agencies, and educational and welfare services of both county and state. When a specific case comes to her attention, she knows that she can write to the Bureau of Special Education in the State Department of Education for current information.

Visually Handicapped Children [1]

The kindergarten teacher knows the importance of identifying early any child with visual handicaps. Each child should have good eyesight if he is to cope with the school program, which puts great emphasis on visual skills. The teacher is alert to notice any signs of an actual or potential visual handicap, including:

> holding a book very close
> squinting
> rubbing eyes or saying that they hurt

When she notices such symptoms of visual difficulty over a period of time, the teacher records typical anecdotes which verify her opinion. Then she takes her observation records to the school nurse. The school nurse finds such written observations especially useful in talking with the child's parents. Often their observations are in line with those of the teacher, and they realize that they should have the child's eyes examined. Thus the teacher is able to help a child be ready for the reading and other visual activities of the elementary school.

Blind children and children with a visual handicap that will necessitate special education provisions later can participate in kindergarten if they have been taught how to help themselves with such things as doors and toilets. Both the blind and the sighted children can enjoy and profit from the socializing experience of the kindergarten. They learn to accept and get along with each other. Both become increasingly independent.

Of course the key to a wholesome kindergarten for both blind and sighted children is the teacher. She must accept the blind and partially sighted children as individuals in the same way that she accepts other children. She knows what five-year-old children can and cannot do. She knows, for instance, that any five-year-old can participate in simple games and do stunts on the bars. She praises their accomplishments realistically,

---

[1] The National Society for Prevention of Blindness, 1790 Broadway, New York 19, supplies a catalog of free literature regarding eyes and visual difficulties.

and she avoids expecting more of them than they are yet able to do. She does not let a handicapped child use his visual difficulty as a crutch for getting overprotection. In short, she is interested in helping each child no matter what the extent of his visual acuity to develop his abilities, widen his interests, and enjoy the social experiences of the kindergarten.

At the same time the teacher is considerate of children's eyes. She avoids glares; she uses soft-colored rather than bright and shiny papers. She gives the blind child something to do with his hands so that he will not rub his eyes. She takes advantage of his disability to help him develop his auditory and other abilities and to help other children develop their verbal ability by relating what they have seen. But mostly she accepts each child and is confident of his ability to be one of the kindergarten group.

Aurally Handicapped Children

As the teacher becomes acquainted with the children in her group, she has opportunity to observe symptoms of hearing impairment. By reporting children with symptoms of hearing loss to the school nurse she may make it possible to get medical attention that will enable them to profit more fully from their educational opportunities. The symptoms that she looks for include:

inattention to what is said
failure to follow directions
request for a repetition of what was said
difficulty in speaking clearly
restlessness
turning head to hear better
earaches and frequent colds
marked aggression or timidity
reluctance in entering group activities
excessive fatigue
persistent attempts to watch the face of a person speaking

The importance of identifying children with hearing loss as early as possible has led to audiometer testing programs for many kindergartens. School administrators realize that hearing loss can be cured or alleviated in about sixty percent of the cases.

Not only does the teacher identify children with hearing loss, she also thoughtfully helps to meet their needs by the way she works with both handicapped and normal children. Each day she is careful to:

get the attention of each child when giving directions
give simple and brief instructions

use complete sentences, and round out each thought

stand where light, but not shadow, falls on her face

keep hands away from her face

speak naturally and without exaggerated movement

Early attention of parents to hearing difficulties has resulted in an occasional child's coming to kindergarten with a small portable amplifying unit or personal hearing aid. The casual acceptance of the hearing aid on the part of the teacher has much to do with the aurally handicapped child's feeling at home in the kindergarten. Suggestions for helping the child with an amplifier include accepting the hearing aid, and helping the child in using it.

If a child finds a hearing aid uncomfortable, his teacher reassures him by telling him it will be comfortable when he gets used to wearing it. If he thinks it too loud or if he turns it to the "off" position frequently, his instrument may need adjustment. His teacher feels free to get assistance from a specialist and to find out about the construction and operation of hearing aids. As she does so, she feels increasingly at home with the hearing aid and with the child who uses one. Her increased ease is reflected in calm acceptance of the handicapped child by the other children.

Speech-Handicapped Children

In the kindergarten many children are still perfecting their speech patterns. The teacher works with all of them in ways that help them to improve their speech. She speaks slowly, using correct pronunciation and clear enunciation. In this way she provides a clear pattern for children to imitate. She also provides a good pattern for listening by the way in which she pays complete attention to what a child is telling her. At no time does she make a child aware of his or anyone else's speech imperfections.

In a teacher-centered kindergarten, the great demands upon children tend to increase speech difficulties that have an emotional basis. But the kindergarten in which children and teacher co-operate in worthwhile activities without expectations of prescribed performance is helpful to anxious or fearful children who stutter or have voice problems. The teacher is calm, unhurried, interested in *what* a child says, not *how* he says it, and is highly permissive. She helps children be successful in what they want to do. She accepts the speech of the children as it is. She knows that most apparent speech difficulties will disappear in the situation she provides. Any that do not, she will refer to the speech therapist if one is available or to the school nurse in case there may be malformation of the speech mechanism or need for surgical care.

Meanwhile the teacher provides many activities which build good listening and speaking habits. She makes up simple games in which children listen to sounds and identify them. She encourages the children to imitate sounds that they hear. With the teacher, the children chant jingles, rhymes, and little poems and sing songs. Probably the principal way in which the kindergarten provides for speech development of both handicapped and normal children is by much opportunity for talking together, with mother assistants as well as with the teacher. Children improve their speech by communicating their ideas to other people and by having them appreciated, understood, and responded to.

Mentally Retarded Children

As the kindergarten teacher works with and observes the group of children she soon identifies those who are alert, interested, and able. Identifying the children at the other end of the distribution is not so easy because they include the child who placidly and unobtrusively goes along with the activities. However, the teacher soon notices and records instances of behavior which are her bases for referring a child to the school authority who arranges for further examination and observation of the child. Such behavior includes:

not wanting to learn
being unable to cope with new or unusual situations
having little or no ability to associate ideas
having a very short memory
paying attention for only brief intervals
finding abstract concepts difficult
being unable to take care of himself the way other five-year-olds do

When a teacher has children enrolled who are known to have low mentality, she does not bother them with abstractions and she minimizes their need to cope with new and unusual experiences. Instead, she emphasizes routine personal habits: toileting, washing hands before eating, and other health habits; safety habits such as crossing the street only with the help of a crossing guard; and looking after personal and school property. She encourages them in play about home experiences and in their relationships to other members of the family. She provides concrete experiences in the school and the community. Depending upon the child, the teacher encourages him in experiences which train his senses: recognizing his name when it is said, enjoying the physical world around him; and recognizing things by sound, smell, touch, and color. She provides training in manual skills: hammering nails, carrying household articles, stringing beads or buttons, doing coarse needle work, cutting paper and cloth, carrying blocks, and moving sand or dirt. She encourages activities conducive to the development of muscular co-ordination: marching, creative dancing, climbing a ladder, and walking up and down stairs and on walking boards. She uses clear speech and simple words. She encourages any special interest such as taking care of a pet or gardening. In working with mentally retarded as well as other children, the teacher furthers the total development of the child in terms of his abilities.

The teacher keeps in mind the general principles of working with mentally retarded children:

Use the child's immediate goals as the basis for teaching. Distant or abstract goals may be beyond his comprehension.

In each new situation, patiently interpret the facts to the child.

Supplement the usual classroom supplies with concrete materials.

Recognize that the child must adjust to the school and the community as well as his home.

Emphasize that the home and the school must work together for the good of the child.

Crippled Children

The kindergarten teacher should detect and report any symptoms which point toward an orthopedic condition. By doing so she may make it possible to prevent serious injury to bones, muscles, and joints. She watches for any evidence that a child is overly protecting or supporting any part of his body and for any dysfunction, misuse, or imperfect muscle co-ordination he may show in his play. She listens permissively whenever a child complains of a hurt and observes quietly whether the problem persists or is forgotten. She observes drowsiness, excessive thirst, frequent trips to the toilet, a tendency to cry, frequent tiredness, persistent irritability and negativism, as well as glassy and dull eyes, lusterless hair, unusual facial coloring, and scaly or dry skin. Her alertness in observing such symptoms and in reporting them immediately to the school medical personnel may make it possible for a child to benefit from the offering of the school as he might not otherwise be able to.

Children with Special Health Problems

When the kindergarten teacher has a child with a special health problem in the group, she co-operates with the school physician in carrying out suggested modifications in the program of activities. For children restricted in activity she provides picture books, art materials within easy reach, and invitations to join groups listening to stories or to music. For a child recovering from some debilitating illness she may arrange rest periods or additional food. The teacher also helps the child accept a program that is unique for him. If the other children become aware of any differences, she helps them understand that each child is unique and that she helps each child to have what is best for him.

Epilepsy

Miss Watson's introduction to the *petit mal*, a mild type of epileptic seizure, occurred during the first weeks of school. She had noticed first that Marie was unusually restless. Now she noticed how pale Marie was and how large the pupils of her eyes seemed. She went over to her quickly and quietly lowered her to the floor. One of the children looked up from his block building to ask, "What's the matter?" Miss Watson managed to yawn before she answered calmly, "I think Marie is not feeling well. I may have to take her to the nurse's office to rest." Reassured, the children continued their activities.

The next day the school nurse told Miss Watson that Marie's parents knew the child had epilepsy, but they had not mentioned it because they thought she might have outgrown it. When the parents, the nurse, and Miss Watson talked over Marie's problem, they agreed that Marie should have additional medical care and should remain in the kindergarten. After talking further with the school nurse, Miss Watson realized that she had handled the *petit mal* situation most satisfactorily and felt that she could cope equally well with any recurrence of the seizure.

Emotionally Disturbed Children

The kindergarten teacher can also identify the child with marked emotional problems, the child who finds it difficult to relate himself to other children or to the teacher, and the child who exhibits abnormal behavior. She records observations of the behavior of such children and then discusses what she has observed with the school counselor. Further observations and testing by a psychologist follow in order to determine more precisely the nature and extent of the child's disturbance. Then the teacher, school counselor, and the parents of the child discuss the problem and work out mutually some plan for helping him. Unusual behavior which the teacher observes includes:

submission
withdrawal
nervous habits
sex problems
temper tantrums
cruelty and destruction
fighting

Her observations and the early recognition of the problem make it more likely that therapy will be successful in lessening or even eliminating the child's difficulty.

The Gifted Child

Since the kindergarten emphasizes social development of children, the gifted child has much to gain from this experience. Later his exceptional abilities and interests may tend to take him away from others. It is therefore highly important that he learn successful ways of getting along with children during his kindergarten year.

The teacher who identifies the gifted child easily is the teacher who observes children primarily in terms of their own purposes rather than in terms of the purposes of others. The gifted child in a teacher-centered kindergarten may appear to be a discipline problem. But in a kindergarten where children and teacher work together, his questions and his comments help the group activities, and the permissive atmosphere gives him scope for developing his unusual abilities. In such a situation, he is easily identified. His teacher observes and records instances of:

a persistent interest in musical, mechanical, or artistic matters

high verbal facility

an unusual number of questions about the world around him

ability to carry out suggestions with a minimum of guidance

interests and vocabulary typical of older children

disinterest in what he already understands

When her observations suggest that a child is gifted, the teacher discusses her recorded observations with the school counselor or principal, who arranges for testing by the school psychologist. Later the psychologist, counselor, and teacher discuss the findings of the test and consider how best the school may help the child develop his abilities. This early identification of the child who is gifted, combined with discussions with his parents, may make it possible for the child to contribute to society as he might not otherwise be able to.

Many of the suggestions made throughout *The Kindergarten Teacher* are especially pertinent to the gifted child. They include provisions for:

A variety of experiences so that the child may develop physically, socially, and emotionally as well as intellectually

Planning and evaluating discussions to which he can make an able contribution

A wide selection of picture books, phonograph records, visual aids, and construction materials which he is prepared to use

Study trips to widen his interests in the community and to give him a basis for discussion

Practice only to the extent of his interest

Clear explanations in answer to his questions

Encouragement of independent thinking and action

Probably the important suggestion for helping the gifted child is really the suggestion which helps any exceptional child: Encourage him in feeling like the other children in the kindergarten group.

SITUATIONS FOR DISCUSSION

In the following situations select each course of action that seems desirable to you basing your choices and omissions on the ideas presented in this chapter. Add one or more alternate courses of action.

SITUATION I. With her hip in a cast, Marie lies on a board with wheels to roll her around the kindergarten. She enjoys stories and likes to look at the pictures after the story is read. She lays the book on the floor in front of her where she can see the pictures and turn the pages easily.

Today when you finish reading *The Little Fir Tree*,[2] you start to hand the book to Marie when Tommy says, "I want to look at it!" As the teacher, you should:

Tell Tommy that Marie needs the book.

Interest Tommy in painting a picture of a Christmas tree.

Later talk with Tommy about helping crippled people.

Help Marie and Tommy plan how to take turns with the book.

Avoid the argument by putting the book away.

SITUATION II. Marilyn, a blind girl, who has had special teaching for over a year, is coming into your kindergarten class. As the teacher, you should:

Tell the other children what it means to be blind.

Check your supplies to be sure that they include aluminum foil and off-white paper.

Talk with the children about how to help Marilyn.

Emphasize that Marilyn is different from other children.

Plan how to interest Marilyn in art materials like clay, paints, and crayons.

SITUATION III. In taking the children on a nature walk around a nearby block, you keep in mind the needs of each individual child. For instance, as the teacher, you should think of the walk as an opportunity for teaching:

The mentally retarded children to cross the street safely.

Each child to stay with the group.

The gifted children to notice street signs.

The children with verbal fluency to tell the blind children what they see.

Each child to observe the signs of the season.

SITUATION IV. Jerry is a healthy, normal child who has unclear speech. He enjoys kindergarten and is well liked by the other children. When his mother talks with you one day, she asks about his "speech problem." As the teacher, you should:

[2] Brown, Margaret Wise. *The Little Fir Tree.* New York: Thomas Y. Crowell Company, 1954.

Refer her to the school nurse.

Tell her that many children even in the first grade are continuing to improve their speech.

Suggest that she talk slowly and clearly with Jerry.

Ask what she thinks his "speech problem" is.

Tell her a word game she may play with Jerry if she wants to help him.

BIBLIOGRAPHY

Professional Books and Pamphlets

Buck, Pearl S. *The Child Who Never Grew.* New York: The John Day Company, 1950.

Both parents and teachers will be interested in this sympathetically presented account of a sub-normal child by a well-known author.

De Haan, Robert F., and R. J. Havighurst. *Educating Gifted Children.* Chicago: University of Chicago Press, 1957.

Goodenough, Florence L. *Exceptional Children.* New York: Appleton-Century-Crofts, Inc., 1956.

"Those who are defective in mind or body may be handicapped as much by their attitude toward their defect as by the defect itself."

Hathaway, Winifred. *Education and Health of the Partially-Seeing Child.* New York: Columbia University Press, 1954.

This third edition is for people concerned with the health and education of partially-seeing children.

Johnson, Wendell, and Others. *Speech Handicapped School Children.* New York: Harper and Brothers, 1956.

The teacher, the speech correctionist, or both help with speech disorders and speech education in the classroom.

Joseph, Henry, and Gordon Zern. *Emotional Problems of Children.* New York: Crown Publishers, 1954.

This book guides parents and teachers in working effectively in the difficult situations of home, school, and community.

Martens, Elise H. "Curriculum Adjustments for the Mentally Retarded." Bulletin No. 2. Washington, D. C.: U. S. Office of Education, Federal Security Agency, Printing Office, 1950.

This helpful pamphlet contains suggestions for teaching the mentally retarded child.

The National Society for the Study of Education. *Education of Exceptional Children.* Part II, 49th Yearbook. Chicago: The University of Chicago Press, 1950.

Anyone concerned with the education of exceptional children will find this book most useful.

Witty, Paul A., ed. *The Gifted Child.* Boston: D. C. Heath and Company, 1951.

The American Association for Gifted Children reports progress made and problems to be solved in educating brilliant and talented children.

Films for Parents and Teachers

Broken Dream. East Lansing, Michigan: Capital Film Service, 1956.

A couple, who are happy in a pregnancy, experience the discovery that their child is retarded and eventually understand the problem. 22 minutes, sound, black and white.

For Those Who Are Exceptional. Chicago 3: National Society for Crippled Children and Adults, 1956.

Describes special educational facilities for handicapped children in many Illinois school districts. 45 minutes, sound, color.

Filmstrips for Parents and Teachers

A Child's Road to Independence. Chicago: National Society for Crippled Children and Adults, 1957.

"Fingers, Families and Fun," 75 frames; "Upon His Feet," 56 frames; "What Parents Should Know about Cerebral Palsy," 39 frames show the progress of handicapped children. Silent, color.

Living Is Learning. Chicago: National Society for Crippled Children and Adults, 1957.

Social and play activities, together with family life, bring happiness to cerebral palsied children. 37 frames, silent, color.

18

Parents and Teachers Work
Together for Kindergarten Children

Parents and teachers are both vitally interested in kindergarten children, but they need to work together to obtain the optimum development of each child. Parents know aspects of their child's life which teachers do not know, and teachers know other aspects of the child's life which parents do not know. By putting together what they know, parents and teachers each achieve a more complete understanding of the child.

THE PARENTS' KNOWLEDGE

Parents have known their kindergarten child as he has developed up to the age of five and as he has tackled and mastered the developmental problems of successive age levels. Parents know how their child gets along in his own back yard with his siblings and his friends. They know the interests, activities, and emotional reactions of their child in his out-of-school hours. And they know how he reacts to the people close to him: his mother, his father, and other members of his household. What the parents know is highly important to understanding their child and should be communicated to the teacher or anyone else who works with the child.

THE TEACHER'S KNOWLEDGE

What the kindergarten teacher knows about each child is also highly important to understanding the child and should be communicated to the parents. The teacher knows the child in terms of what a five-year-old is like in a kindergarten. The teacher has worked each year with groups of such children until she is an expert on what a five-year-old does in a kindergarten group. She knows the skills, the attitudes, and the kinds of ideas he develops through the kindergarten activities. She knows how he moves

356

from activity to activity and the work habits he develops. She knows each child in relation to other five-year-olds and in relation to his teacher. What the kindergarten teacher knows about a child added to what the parents know about the child gives an excellent basis for furthering his optimum development. The following list emphasizes the need for teachers and parents to work together:

The Kindergarten Teacher:	*The Mother of the Kindergarten Child:*
Knows the five-year-old through working with groups of them	Knows the longitudinal development of the child up to age five
Knows how each child approaches and participates in each of the kindergarten activities	Knows the out-of-school activities and interests of the child
Knows how each child gets along with his classmates at school	Knows how the child gets along in his own back yard with his siblings and his friends
Knows how each child gets along with his teacher	Knows how the child gets along with his daddy and his mother

School personnel realize the importance of the kindergarten in introducing parents and children to the school. The kindergarten is the institutional starting point for an educational process that the community will continue for many years to come. How important it is then for parents to appreciate the school, to understand its purposes and its methods, and to begin working constructively with its personnel. When parents think well of the school, their children go willingly to school and are more likely to profit from its educational offering.

PLANNING A PARENT-SCHOOL PROGRAM

In one school system the kindergarten teachers got together as a group to consider what parents need to know about the kindergarten and what methods of communication would reach the greatest number of parents in the most effective way. They realized that their plans should take into account the attitudes, interests, and habits of the people in that community. Although the teachers were interested in similar plans for other communities, they considered each part of those plans in terms of adaptability to their own community. Mostly the teachers used their records and recollections of the questions asked by parents of kindergarten children as a basis for planning a parent information program.

Communicating with the Parents

The schedule that this group of kindergarten teachers developed for communicating with parents was as follows:

May 27 — Article in the *Town Herald* regarding legal requirements for entering a child in kindergarten.

May 28 — Letter to parents of prospective kindergarten children inviting them to register their child on June 3 and to bring him to a party the afternoon of June 10.

June 3 — Registration of prospective kindergarten children, with a page of suggestions distributed to parents, titled: "Helping Your Child Get Ready for Kindergarten."

June 10 — Kindergarten party for prospective kindergarten children.

September 14 — First day of school. Opportunity for getting acquainted with each child and his mother personally and through the use of the "Get Acquainted Sheet."

September 15 — "A Day of High Adventure for Your Child," a booklet developed by the kindergarten teachers for the parents of each child.

September 30 — A note about how to help children enjoy their art experience, attached to the first drawing that each child takes home.

October or November — A meeting for the parents. Show the filmstrip *A Good Day in the Kindergarten* [1] or the film *Your Child in Kindergarten.*

Throughout the year drawings and other art work of the children are to be used as a continuing means of communication with parents.

Registration Invitation

The letter which was worked out by the kindergarten teachers to be sent home on May 28 is on the opposite page.

Registration Day

In preparing for parents to register their five-year-old children for kindergarten, the teachers asked kindergarten mothers to volunteer as hostesses for the pre-school children and their mothers. The volunteers included several mothers who had been members of a co-operative nursery and were accustomed to assisting the nursery school teacher in supervising activities of three- and four-year-old children. Two of the kindergarten mothers who had taught in kindergarten and primary grades before they were married also volunteered to help with the children. So did one or two of the mothers who had arrived at effective ways of working with small children through their own family experience.

Each of the mothers helping with the children brought discarded paper cartons for free play and smooth-edged juice cans for use in the sandbox. The kindergarten teachers provided sand toys, large rubber balls, wagons and tricycles, and other attractions for pre-school children. A box of crackers and a box of tissues were available in case of need.

---

[1] *A Good Day in the Kindergarten.* Filmstrip produced by Helen Heffernan with accompanying phonograph record (20 minutes), California Association for Childhood Education, Long Film Service, 750 S. Fairmount El Cerrito, California.

Dear Parent:

    If your child will be four years and nine months old by next September 2, our State law will permit him to enter kindergarten on that date.

    The school will be ready to receive him, and we invite you to come to Washington School on Wednesday, June 3, to register him. Will you please bring his birth certificate with you? The school is required to make a record of the legal evidence of his correct birth date.

    We would also like you and your child to visit the kindergarten on June 10. A visit now will help your child to feel more secure as he thinks about coming to kindergarten. Leaving home for school is a big step for a five-year-old child. On Wednesday afternoon, June 10, from 2 to 3 p.m., the kindergarten group will entertain all of the children who will be entering next year. You and your child will receive an invitation to be present.

    If you have neighbors or friends who have children of kindergarten age, will you please tell them about registration day and the get-acquainted party?

    We hope that you will come to the school on many occasions so that we can work together to make school a happy, successful experience for your child.

Most sincerely,

_____

Teacher

_____

Principal

    Other mothers volunteered to act as hostesses to help the prospective kindergarten mothers register their children. Depending upon their skills, these hostesses served as friendly welcomers, dispensers of school forms to be filled out, guides to vacant seats, or card checkers. One kindergarten mother received the completed registration cards and gave the visiting mother a mimeographed sheet with suggestions for getting her child ready for school in the fall. These suggestions included teaching him the route to school, toileting habits in keeping with the kindergarten schedule, how to tie his shoe laces, and how to recognize his name in his jacket. With many volunteer helpers, the kindergarten teacher was free to meet each prospective kindergarten mother and establish a friendly relationship with her.

The First Day of School

The teachers also asked kindergarten mothers from the preceding year to help with the first day of school. Again those mothers who enjoyed being with pre-school children served as hostesses for them, and those mothers who enjoyed being with adults served as hostesses for the incoming group of kindergarten mothers. These arrangements made it possible for the teacher to welcome each child and his mother, fixing their names in her mind and furthering friendly relationships with them individually and then in a group.

Talking with the group of mothers, the kindergarten teacher asked their help in getting acquainted quickly with each five-year-old child. Then, while the teacher worked with the group of children, a hostess passed out the questionnaire on the next page to be completed for each child.

During the first few weeks of school, the kindergarten teachers found the information sheets as useful as they had anticipated when they devised them.

Information Booklets for Parents

The booklet "A Day of High Adventure for Your Child" was taken home by each child the second day of school. The kindergarten teachers had put into it suggestions about ways in which parents may help their child maintain good health, develop habits of responsibility, increase his knowledge and powers of observation, further his language development, get along well with others, and develop desirable means of emotional expression.

In another school system, the kindergarten teachers working with administrative personnel developed an informational booklet which was given to each mother when she registered her child. This booklet discussed briefly the purpose of kindergarten; some of the changes expected in children through different phases of the kindergarten program; habits that contribute to health, effective work, and getting along with others; information about entrance requirements, schedule, traffic guards, accidents or emergencies, excuses for absence; an invitation to visit the kindergarten; symptoms of common contagious diseases; and a bibliography of books about children and about family life.

The kindergarten teachers were concerned that the booklet be easily read. They drew simple child-like drawings to decorate the cover and several of the pages. They used different colored paper for different pages of the booklet, and they arranged the pages so that the bottom edges made

GETTING ACQUAINTED

PLEASE help us get acquainted with your child by completing the following items and writing in additional information:

Name of parent describing the child_____

Name of child_____Age on September 1st_____ _____
                                                    Years   Months

Name of sister(s)_____Age_____ _____Grade in school_____

_____Age_____ _____Grade in school_____

_____Age_____ _____Grade in school_____

Name of brother(s)_____Age_____ _____Grade in school_____

_____Age_____ _____Grade in school_____

_____Age_____ _____Grade in school_____

Usually my child plays with: _____his brother(s)

                               _____his sister(s)

                               _____a friend

                               _____the neighborhood children

                               _____by himself

                               _____ _____

My child likes to play with: ____dolls   ____guns   ____crayons

                             ____farm figures ____tricycle ____paints

                             ____toy cars   ____books   _____

                             _____   _____ _____

My child likes to pretend:_____

_____

_____

When I am with my child, we usually:_____

_____

_____

My child needs especially to learn:_____

_____

To go to the bathroom, my child says:_____

I would like my child's teacher to know also that_____

_____

_____

an index. Each page was one line longer that the preceding page and its title was printed at the bottom edge. This indexing scheme made it easy for parents to find whatever information they wanted in the booklet.

Almost every good school develops a handbook for parents of kindergarten children. It is an excellent means of providing parents with the information they need for doing their part in facilitating the work of the school. But even though the school has made the information available to parents, it cannot be sure that parents have absorbed the information unless it has some means of "feedback." The parents must have a channel for communicating with the school and must have some means of showing what they have learned. Handing a parent a booklet is no assurance that the parent will read the booklet and will know what it says. An invitation to a parents' meeting pinned on a child's jacket is a way of sending a message home, but only the parent's attendance at the meeting or his reply to the invitation are evidence that the message was communicated. When kindergarten teachers and administrators develop plans for communicating information to parents, they need to include plans for feedback.

The Parents Visit the School

The teacher invites parents to visit and shows them what the kindergarten is doing. The parents observe the activities, feel the emotional climate of the group, and better understand how their child benefits from going to school. When the value of good parent relationships is appreciated, schools are cordial in inviting parents to visit. On the opposite page is the letter that one principal wrote to encourage parents to visit the kindergarten and to suggest procedures for doing so. The kindergarten teachers worked with the principal in composing the letter.

Effect of the Classroom Situation on the Visit. Whether parents find it easy to visit the kindergarten depends in large measure on whether the classroom is teacher centered or is a co-operative situation with children and teacher working together on interesting activities. When a mother comes to Miss Inkopf's room to visit, she is quickly guided to a seat at the rear of the room where she can watch what Miss Inkopf is doing with the children. If the mother can stay until the end of the session, she will find Miss Inkopf a delightful and friendly person interested in talking with the mother about how the child is fitting into the kindergarten activities. But if the mother can stay for only a few minutes, she may feel that she has turned her child over to Miss Inkopf for the kindergarten period and that she should leave Miss Inkopf alone with the children. Since she does not want to disturb the activities, she probably will find that she does not have time to visit kindergarten except on special request by the teacher.

Dear Parents:

You are invited to visit kindergarten and to
confer with the teacher concerning your child's
progress. In this way, he will sense your interest
and your co-operation with the school. It will give
him an added sense of security to know that you, the
teacher, and the principal are working together for
his good.

It is usually better to wait about a month before
your first visit to allow the child to adjust to the
new life at school. While kindergarten is in session,
the teacher is occupied with the children, but she
will welcome your visit. She is glad to talk with
you for a few minutes at the close of the session, or
by appointment.

It is suggested that frequent short visits of
about 30 minutes to an hour be made, rather than
longer and fewer visits. This gives you a better
opportunity to see the growth which has been made
since your previous visit. As a safety measure, all
visitors are requested to secure permits from the
principal's office.

In visiting, you will have an opportunity to see
your child in comparison with others of his age and
to learn how he is adjusting to the kindergarten situation. You may want to observe your child from the
following points of view:

Does he approach a new project with enthusiasm?
with disinterest?

Does he usually share and take turns? sometimes?

Does he respond to signals and directions willingly? unwillingly?

Is his attitude toward the class friendly? shy?
antagonistic?

Please visit the kindergarten soon. Together we
can build the best possible program for your child.

Sincerely yours,

_____

Teacher

_____

Principal

When a mother comes to visit in Miss Shimizu's room, she finds a different emotional climate. She is immediately welcomed as Tommy's mother in much the way she would be welcomed in the home of a busy family. A child or a group of children working near the door may be the first to greet the visitor. Tommy may come over to her, or he may smile at her and go on with his work. Miss Shimizu comes over to greet Tommy's mother and to help her feel at home with the group. As she explains briefly what is going on, she suggests how to observe the activities without interfering with what the children are doing:

TEACHER: Good morning, I'm Miss Shimizu.

MOTHER: I'm Mrs. Holtz, Tommy's mother.

TEACHER: We're glad you came. Can you stay and visit us?

MOTHER: I'm on my way to a dental appointment. I can stay a few minutes if it won't be disturbing.

TEACHER: Not at all. When Tommy finishes what he is doing, he will want to show you around our room. Perhaps you would like to sit here at the back of the room for a while where you can see what the children are doing. You will be near enough to Tommy's group so that you can hear what the children say without attracting their attention.

When Mrs. Holtz leaves for her appointment, she will have a friendly feeling toward Miss Shimizu. Probably she will tell her friends about visiting school and encourage them to go too. She will come back again.

Establishing Rapport with the Mothers. Mothers need reassurance when they come to the kindergarten. When a mother brings her oldest child, she has all the diffidence that goes with approaching an unfamiliar situation. "Will the teacher like me?" she wonders. "What will the children think of me?" "Will the teacher admire my child?" When the teacher is friendly and casual, the mother is reassured about herself, and when the teacher points out some praiseworthy characteristic of the child, she is reassured about her child.

A kindergarten teacher needs to recognize that differences in age and in social status between a mother and herself may contribute to feelings of inferiority on the part of the mother or on her own part. Sometimes an older person tries to build his ego by saying, "When I was your age . . ." and succeeds in making the other person feel uncomfortable. A patronizing manner makes the other person feel belligerent. Recognizing such feelings for what they are enables the teacher to shunt them aside as unrelated to the common ground of working together for the good of the children.

A kindergarten teacher also needs to understand the daily life of a mother as it contrasts with her own daily living. A teacher has her own income and can spend what she needs for her wardrobe. She has time to herself for rest and for reading. On the other hand, the mother of a kindergarten child shares a family income and probably has a limited wardrobe. If she has other pre-school children besides her five-year-old, her sleep is often interrupted at night; she probably has difficulty in finding time for housekeeping as well as meeting the needs of her children and her husband; and she probably has little or no time to herself for rest and reading. If the kindergarten teacher has a sympathetic understanding of the daily problems of mothers, she has an asset in winning their confidence.

Parents Communicate with the School

Communication is more than a monologue; it is a two-way process. School principals and kindergarten teachers are interested in informing parents about the kindergarten program. If they want the parents to listen and help with the program, they must also be willing to listen to the parents. Furthermore, principals and teachers have no way of knowing the effectiveness of their informational program unless they have some feedback arrangement by which the parents can ask questions about and comment on the material presented. It is of the utmost importance to have occasions for parents to come to the school for group discussions. Such parent meetings are not to be confused with lectures or even panel discussions, which are primarily to dispense information.

People notice and remember what they already know and what helps them meet their needs. Parents hear or read what fits in with their memories of schooling twenty or more years ago and whatever helps them solve their problems now. Lectures on topics of general interest may or may not deal with material related to the unmet needs of parents. But when parents discuss problems of their own choosing and the teacher contributes pertinent comments, what she says is likely to be noticed and remembered. In such meetings the teacher is a source of information about the characteristics of the five-year-old child and about the kindergarten program.

The School Sponsors Parents' Discussions

The desirability of discussion meetings for kindergarten parents is clear. If parents of five-year-old children can learn through these meetings what the school is doing for children, their confidence in the school and their understanding and loyal support of its program will be an asset for years to come. But the means of arranging parent meetings has not been so clear. With a heavy pupil load, the teacher is doing well to arrange two or three opportunities for parents to observe the kindergarten group of children and to discuss briefly what they have observed. It is not practical to expect the kindergarten teacher to be responsible for a series of parents' discussion meetings. Who, then, can take such responsibility?

One school system answered this question by obtaining the services of adult education workers. The adult education worker talked with the kindergarten teacher about the questions parents ask. Together they made a list of possible topics for discussions of mutual interest to parents and the teacher. The teacher felt capable of serving as a resource person in four or five meetings provided they dealt with topics selected from the following list:

> What does a five-year-old child do and what are his needs?
>
> What kind of environment does the school provide for five-year-old children?
>
> What school people does the kindergarten child meet?
>
> How does the teacher plan a kindergarten day?
>
> How can adults help a child maintain good health?
>
> How do adults further the physical development of the five-year-old?
>
> How can adults help a child understand the people around him?
>
> How can adults help a child understand the world of science?
>
> How can adults help a child count and measure?
>
> How can adults help a child with the beginnings of geography?
>
> How do adults help a child improve his language?
>
> What stories do kindergarten children enjoy?
>
> How can adults help children enjoy music?
>
> How can adults help a child express himself through art media?
>
> How can adults help children get along well with each other?
>
> How is a five-year-old child different as a result of his kindergarten year?
>
> How does kindergarten contribute to reading readiness?
>
> How does kindergarten get children ready for first grade?
>
> How can parents and teachers work together to further the development of children?

The adult education worker invited the parents to come together for an initial meeting in which the group organized itself and selected the topics for discussions spaced throughout the year. With the help of the adult education worker it was possible for the parents to have a personally satisfying group experience as well as a chance to exchange information and opinions regarding their children. The parents asked a question and found out what other parents thought and what the teacher could tell them about it. Thus they had information which met their needs and which gave them an understanding of the school and its problems.

The teacher realized that each member of the discussion group, not just herself, was a resource person. The parents were resource persons who could tell about problems of children as they were handled at home and in other out-of-school situations. The teacher was the one resource person who could tell about helping children solve their problems in the kindergarten situation. She kept the group informed about the philosophy and practices of the kindergarten. At the same time she was careful not to rob the parents of opportunities for leadership. As a general rule she contributed to the discussion only after the parents had made their points and were about to move on to another topic.

As a contributing member of the parents' discussion group, the teacher found that she often reassured parents by reminding them in different ways of one of the following points:

This type of behavior is frequently found in children of this age range, or this body build, or this sex, or some other grouping.

Within each grouping, children show marked individual differences. Each child is unique. No two children are alike.

This phase of the child's development will pass as he continues to grow and develop. Growth and development can be guided but cannot be interfered with.

Desirable behavior can be encouraged further when it reappears. The undesirable behavior drops out if it is not overly emphasized and if the desirable behavior is satisfying.

Other adults feel this way about the children they work with too.

The teacher emphasized whatever made the parents feel more comfortable in their role as parents and whatever relieved them of embarrassment and of overexpectation of both themselves and their children. Often the teacher felt she made an important contribution by being an especially attentive listener.

Providing Informative Books for Parents

Parents of kindergarten children are often interested in reading some of the excellent books, pamphlets, and magazine articles now available to help them with their problems. The teacher encourages a lending library but avoids getting into a position of responsibility for checking books in and out. She knows that embarrassment about lost books might interfere with her rapport with parents.

After parents' discussions is an excellent time for the parents to look over books and pamphlets.[2] With their problems fresh in their minds, they are likely to be sufficiently interested to take material home to read. Materials are displayed on a table with a comfortable chair or two for parents to sit on while they browse. The teacher works with the

[2] *Better Living Series.* Chicago: Science Research Associates.

librarian in helping parents find what they want: "Mrs. Jonathan and I have been talking about children who are destructive. Do you still have those pamphlets you were showing me the other day? Mrs. Jonathan may want to check one of them out."

The Parents Observe in the Kindergarten

A month or two after school begins, perhaps during American Education Week, the teacher issues a special invitation to parents to visit the kindergarten and to talk over what they observe. At one school this visit was worked out by the kindergarten teacher with the help of parents whom she had already come to know. On Thursday she sent home a note to each parent, pinning it on each child at the close of school. The note read:

```
        Some parents are interested in discussing how to
help their children develop good work habits. Espe-
cially if you have not yet visited kindergarten,
please come sometime next week, American Education
Week, and observe how the children get started and
work on their projects. Then Thursday afternoon from
3:00 until 4:00 we shall discuss how to help five-
year-old children develop good work habits. Please
come. We need you.


        _____

        Teacher


        _____

        Principal
```

On each day of the following week, one of the mothers served as a smiling and friendly hostess. She greeted the visiting mothers and helped them find separate chairs where they could observe easily without carrying on conversation among themselves. She reminded each parent, "We are observing quietly how the children get to work and how they carry on their work. We shall talk about what we observe Thursday afternoon at three o'clock, but today we are watching and not talking."

Thursday at three o'clock the mothers first listed on the chalkboard what they had observed about how kindergarten children get to work and carry through a project. Then they discussed their observations. The teacher commented and explained as needed but left the discussion mostly to the mothers. From listening to the discussion she gained insight into the problems, attitudes, and interests of the parents. At the conclusion of the meeting the chairman again emphasized that children take time to get clearly in mind what is to be done. When they know what to do they proceed to do it, but they move very slowly compared with an adult and they follow several interesting bypaths on their way to their goal. The chairman also reviewed the suggestions made for helping the children develop good work habits. These included: plan each step of the project with the child just before doing that step; let the child carry out the project himself; if he has tried unsuccessfully and asks for help, give him the assistance he needs; when the step is finished, comment favorably on some aspect of either the process or the product; and in a group activity, let those who are finished first help others carry out their part in the project.

Several points are notable in this planned observation for parents:

It was worked out co-operatively with parents

The observations were purposeful

The observations were centered on only one kind of behavior

Time for discussion was planned in connection with the observations

These are essential characteristics of observations that are of maximum benefit to parents.

The Teacher Invites the Parents for a Conference

It is common practice for kindergarten teachers to talk with parents instead of writing them a report about their child. Teachers feel that such individual conferences require about as much time as the preparation of written reports and that they are more rewarding in understanding each child in relation to his parents. Written reports usually elicit little or no response from parents, but a conference with parents reveals parental expectations and opinions about their child. In one school system, the note on the next page was sent home with each child.

Miss Flynn was well prepared for her conferences with parents. At the first of the term she had set up for each child a cumulative folder into which she dropped notes from parents, typical drawings, or any other record regarding the child. It was her practice each day to spend five or ten minutes at her desk after the children left. Thinking over the happenings of the morning, she wrote anecdotal records about different children and put the records in the children's folders. Ten days before the conferences with parents, she checked each folder to see if it had one or more anecdotal records and if its records gave a realistic and favorable picture of the child. She listed the nine or ten children whose folders needed anecdotal records and made a point of observing and recording their

Dear Parents:

During the next two weeks each afternoon from 3:00 until 5:00 o'clock and Monday and Thursday evenings from 7:00 until 9:00 o'clock, the kindergarten teachers will be in their rooms to talk with parents individually about how their child is getting along in kindergarten. The teacher will be interested also in knowing what you want your child to get out of his kindergarten experience this year.

Please check the following times to show when you can come for your half-hour conference with Miss Flynn, and pin this note on your child's jacket when he goes to school tomorrow. Miss Flynn is looking forward to talking with you and will telephone you about the time that best fits into her schedule of half-hour conferences.

Sincerely yours,

_____

Principal

- -

I can come at any of the following times:

On ____day afternoon at ____ o'clock, November ____,

or on ____day afternoon at ____ o'clock, November

____, or on ____day evening at ____ o'clock,

November ____.

_____

Parent's name

_____

Telephone number

behavior during the next few days. In this way, she was ready to show each parent objective records about his child and to interpret the records with the parent.

When Teddy Thompson's mother came for her conference, Miss Flynn welcomed her warmly and made her feel at home: "Let's sit down here at my desk where I keep my notes about the children and some of their drawings." Sitting side by side, the teacher and the mother opened the cumulative folder for Teddy. It contained a few drawings and two anecdotal records. One drawing showed a round orange ball on a green branch of a green stem: "Teddy sees the world quite realistically. Here he has drawn an orange pumpkin on a green vine. Such representative drawings are unusual at his age."

Next Miss Flynn and Mrs. Thompson considered the anecdotal records. The first one was as follows:

Name: TEDDY THOMPSON		Date: SEPTEMBER 26
What Child Did	What Teacher Did	Interpretation and Remarks
Teddy was squatting next to the sink in the bathroom	"What is it, Teddy?"	Is curious about how things work
"Did you know you can turn the water off in case of a flood?"	"Oh, is that so?"	Realistic imagination
"Yes, you just turn this valve right here. Want me to show you?"	"Yes, if you like. It may be too hard to turn, though."	Is Teddy's daddy a plumber? Does he spend quite a bit of time with Teddy helping?
Tries to turn it and is unable to do so	"It is too hard."	
"Can't do it without a wrench."	"Yes, with a wrench you could turn the valve and shut off the water. Thank you for showing me."	
Teddy goes outside	"It's time to go out doors now and play."	Follows suggestions well

Mrs. Thompson laughed about the anecdotal record and said that Teddy's father was an engineer who took care of plumbing problems at home with Teddy's help. She also said that Teddy's daddy took over the responsibilities of the children each evening while she looked after the kitchen work and that he often took the children on week-end trips.

Miss Flynn and Mrs. Thompson then read the second anecdotal record which follows on page 372.

Mrs. Thompson was most interested in the anecdote and said that she and her husband were concerned about Teddy's co-ordination. They encourage him in any physical activities and take him weekly to a class in creative dancing. They hope to build up Teddy's muscular control so

Name: TEDDY THOMPSON		Date: NOVEMBER 4
What Child Did	What Teacher Did	Interpretations and Remarks
Teddy was one of the first children to put away his mat after rest time. As he carried his mat to the closet he stumbled and fell on top of Jimmy who yelled.	I quieted Jimmy and told him he could put his mat away.	Moves slowly and awkwardly and makes me feel as if I ought to reach out to help him. Yet he usually gets where he wants to go without mishap.
Teddy picked himself up and then picked up his mat and took it to the closet.		
When Jimmy brought his mat to the closet, Teddy said, "I didn't mean to fall on you."		Is considerate of others.

that he will no longer withdraw from physical competition.   They appreciate the physical education that is part of the school program and would welcome a discussion of physical development at a parents' meeting.

Miss Flynn noticed that another parent had arrived and that it was almost time for her next appointment. She stood up, and Mrs. Thompson did too. Miss Flynn thanked her for coming and said, "I'll look forward to seeing you at the next parents' meeting."

Several aspects of this conference merit attention, namely:

> The teacher made a definite appointment with each parent at his convenience.
>
> The purpose of the conference was described as a two-way exchange of information.
>
> The conference started with favorable comments.
>
> The conference was based on objective written observations of the child.
>
> The parent helped the teacher interpret the records.
>
> The conference pointed forward to the next opportunity for discussing children's problems.

A Parent Asks the Teacher for Help with a Home Problem

Parents ask for a conference when their children's behavior at home presents them with problems. Such conferences are less numerous when parents get together regularly as a group to discuss their problems. However, they do occur and the teacher needs to know how to help the parent who asks for an appointment.

In helping the parent help himself the teacher keeps in mind the limits inherent in her training and experience and in the counseling situation itself. A teacher is trained and experienced in handling groups of five-year-olds in the kindergarten situation. In this she is expert, but she is not a psychiatrist; she is not a marriage relations counselor; and she is not a psychoanalyst for either children or their parents. If she oversteps and tries to function in any of these capacities, she may interfere with the parents' obtaining expert help when they need it.

The Teacher's Role in the Conference. But the teacher can become expert in the role of a friend who helps parents and their children by being a good listener. With real interest and sympathy, she mentally puts herself into the situation that the parent describes. She says, "Yes, I understand," but she does not say, "Yes, I approve," or "No, I do not approve," because she is in no position either to approve or disapprove. She knows only what the parent is saying, and this may be at variance with the real happening. Parents are usually not trained observers. They probably are emotionally involved in the happenings they describe, and they may be quite prejudiced both in their reporting and in their interpreting of situations. The wise teacher listens sympathetically as the parent tells his story. She says encouragingly, "Tell me more about it." Essentially, she helps the parent solve his problem by mirroring for him what he says, "You feel that. . .," or "Your problem is that. . .?" or "You want to. . ."

Throughout the entire conference with a parent, the teacher acts only as a sounding board. When the parent's problem is clear to both the parent and the teacher, then the teacher encourages the parent in thinking about possible courses of action. "You're wondering what to do about it," the teacher says, but she does not ask any suggestive questions unless she is sure that the parent has made all the suggestions he can. Then she may say, "Let's see now. You have suggested . . . And you thought about doing . . . Have you considered trying . . .?" The teacher is reluctant even to ask suggestive questions because she knows that the parent who has responsibility for the child through the greater part of each day is the person who must carry out any improved procedures. By letting the parent take the initiative in planning how to work more effectively with the child, the teacher helps the parent solve his problem himself and at the same time helps him develop a method for solving other problems.

When the parent conference is finished, the teacher thanks the parent for sharing his problem with her. She points out that the first step in solving a problem is to understand it. Certainly the conference has clarified the problem. The teacher assures the parent of her genuine in terest in the problem and urges him to discuss it with her further. "In the meantime," says the teacher, "I shall think about your problem, too, and see if there is anything we can do in school to help with it." Thus encouraged the parent is better able to cope with his problem. In fact, the opportunity to talk out his problem with the friendly sympathy of the teacher may be all that the parent needs in order to do what his better judgment has been suggesting.

Follow-up on the Conference. As a result of the parent conference, the teacher thinks of pertinent information about children and the ways in which they learn. At the next parents' discussion meeting, she finds opportunity to discuss some similar problem and to show how the pertinent information helped with its solution. After the meeting she greets the parent with whom she had the conference and says, "Weren't you interested in that problem about . . .?" The wise teacher, however, leaves the parent free either to relate the described problem to himself, or to avoid relating it.

When a parent asks for a second or third conference, the teacher finds either that the parent is still going over his problem emotionally or that he is objective about it and is genuinely interested in further information. If the parent is still emotionally involved and confused about his problem, he is in need of expert guidance. The teacher, as a sympathetic friend, is in a good position to help him in getting to the local family service association, the school psychologist, or some other appropriate counseling service. On the other hand, if the parent is really interested in learning more about children and their growth and development, the teacher is in a good position to encourage him to read some of the excellent books available for parents and to discuss with him the theory most closely related to the problem.

Two Recommendations for Parents. Whenever the kindergarten teacher is with individual parents or with a group of parents, she may feel free to recommend two simple procedures which help to alleviate most problems of children. The teacher can encourage parents to spend an hour each day, or at least once or twice a week, following the leads of their five-year-old children. And the teacher can encourage parents to have other kindergarten children play with their children.

If each parent spends an hour or a half hour alone with his child regularly, letting the child make all the decisions about what to do, the parent better understands the child and the child feels and responds to the interest and affection of the parent. What can be accomplished in an hour a week is demonstrated by the children's analyst who is able to help the child work through many difficult problems in that length of time. Of course, the parent, like the analyst, must make it clear to the child that he is really king for the hour. A mother may say, "John, we spend so much time doing what mother wants to do. How would you like to have an hour each day when we do what you want to do and talk about what you want to talk about. Mother will forget about what needs to be done around the house or in the garden and will just help you do what you want to do." Then she has to be really willing to do what John suggests, whether it results in a mess or not and whether John gets dirty or not. If the mother goes along with John's projects, she will find out what an interesting person her son is. Of course, fathers profit as much as mothers from spending an hour with their five-year-olds regularly. They come to enjoy being with them and will think of trips and activities which they can share with their newly found friends.

Besides advocating a regular time for following the leads of the child, a teacher can encourage parents to arrange playtime for their children with another five-year-old. Children enjoy other children. Playing with one child at a time gives them opportunity for knowing the other child and for developing good ways of getting along with him. With improved social techniques, the child is better able to cope with kindergarten situations as well as with out-of-school situations with several children. Success in playing with one child leads to success in more complex play situations and to a much needed sense of belonging in the play group.

Sometimes the kindergarten teacher can say to a mother of a girl who needs to improve her social skills, "In kindergarten Jean has been playing with Mary Smith a great deal lately. They both enjoy the playhouse. I wonder if Jean would like to have Mary play with her at home too. Maybe the girls could go home together some day after kindergarten." The teacher also encourages the parents of boys to invite friends home. "Tom likes to play wrestling with Conrad. It is important for boys to explore these friendly games, but they need opportunity for such play outside of school. We do not permit even friendly hitting in kindergarten. Would it be possible for Tom to have Conrad spend an afternoon with him soon? Maybe you could call Conrad's mother and work out some visits back and forth." When the teacher encourages such visiting, she is doing a service to the child and his parents as well as to herself, because the child will be a happier person both at home and at school.

The Teacher Visits Parents at Home

Whether a kindergarten teacher visits parents in their homes depends primarily on her teaching load. If she has a large group of children in the morning and another large group of children in the afternoon, she finds that preparation of materials for the children to use, reading and other professional activities, conferences with parents who come to the school, and parent and community meetings take up her out-of-school hours quite completely. But if her pupil load is small, she considers carefully the values of home visits and whether these values are better realized through visits or through some other channel of communication. She may think it better to devote her time and energy to parent meetings for instance, feeling that she can communicate with a group of parents in the time required for her to call on the parents of one child. Or, after talking with her principal, she may decide that the best use of her time is to visit parents in their homes.

The desirability of home visits depends not only on the teaching load but also upon the community and its relation to the school. In a community of average or less than average incomes, mothers who care for several children, do all the housework, and take care of the yard have more than they can accomplish easily. To entertain a guest for even half an hour is a considerable strain and not a situation which furthers desirable relations with the school. In a community of high incomes the teacher may feel ill at ease in calling at impressive homes. However, in many middle class communities, home visits are entirely feasible.

In one community where the economic level was above average and where the typical family had only two children, the school administrators thought a key factor in the public relations program was the kindergarten teacher's visit to the home of each prospective kindergarten child. The teacher was employed for two weeks prior to the opening of school so that she could make these initial visits. Each mother knew when to expect the teacher and welcomed her as a guest. The teacher brought pictures of the kindergarten activities and talked about them with the mother and the five-year-old child. For the most part the visits were polite get-acquainted occasions. Sometimes a mother took advantage of the opportunity to discuss her problems. The teacher, not wishing to discuss a child in his presence, pointed out that all parents have problems in bringing up their children. "The problems are what make it so interesting to be a parent." Then she told the mother about the parents' group discussions and suggested that her problems were the kind to bring up there. As she left, the teacher found occasion for favorable comments: "Tom is certainly an active boy, and you dress him so sensibly."

PARENTS PARTICIPATE IN KINDERGARTEN ACTIVITIES

Among the parents especially interested in children are those who by temperament and training feel at home in the classroom and welcome opportunities to assist the teacher. In most communities only one or two such parents offer their services. But in other communities, groups of parents are active in co-operative kindergartens. The parents study how to work more effectively with children, and the mothers take turns in helping the teacher with the children at school. The experience of one such group of mothers led to compiling the following list of activities for the child, the equipment he uses in the activity, the value of the activity for him, and the part that the assisting parent plays in the activity.

Parents who participate in the kindergarten feel that they handle their own children more successfully at home because of their experience in working with them and other children at school. A teacher who has such parent-assistants feels that she is able to provide a richer program for all the children. In the foreseeable future an increasing number of kindergartens will have parents participating in such ways as those shown in "Parent-Kindergarten Activities and Their Values."

PARENTS AND TEACHERS WORK TOGETHER FOR THE CHILDREN

Parents and teachers of five-year-old children must work together for the maximum benefit of the children. The teacher knows the child in the kindergarten situation as he compares with other five-year-olds. The parents know the child's interests and activities in his out-of-school life and how he gets along with his family and with the neighborhood children. As the teacher and the parents exchange information, they come to understand the child more completely and each is better able to work effectively with him.

Channels of communication between kindergarten and home begin with a good school publicity program, including a booklet for kindergarten parents. But a publicity program is only part of a two-way communication system. Parents must have channels of communicating their reactions to the school, for instance through parents' observation and discussion meetings. When parents come to the kindergarten to observe some particular aspect of child behavior and have an opportunity to discuss their observations afterwards, the teacher learns what parents are really thinking about. When an adult education leader is available to help parents organize and carry on discussions of their problems, the teacher can be a member of the group contributing the school point of view to the discussion and learning from it what parents think.

Parents benefit from group meetings, and they benefit also from individual conferences with the teacher. In such conferences they discuss the teacher's observations of their child in kindergarten, or they work out their personal problems about their five-year-old child in the presence of their sympathetic friend, the child's teacher. In such ways as these the parents and the teacher communicate with each other and work together for the benefit of kindergarten children.

PARENT-KINDERGARTEN ACTIVITIES AND THEIR VALUES [1]

Kind of Activity	Equipment Required	Value for the Child	Parent Participation
Climbing / Supporting one's weight	Climbing apparatus: large packing boxes, barrel, rope, stairs, ladders, horizontal and parallel bars	Encourages co-ordination of large muscles and releases physical energy and feelings of aggression	Arranges equipment to allow adequate space for free and creative activity
Running, chasing, throwing, kicking, punching	Space free of equipment / Ramps, runways, mounds, balls, beanbags, punching bag		Mentions limits which insure safety and group participation / Offers physical support when encouragement is needed
Walking, sliding, crawling	Posture boards, boxes, steps, hollow blocks, slide, tunnel / Any safe surfaces		Watches for fatigue and restlessness and redirects energy of children when desirable
Swaying and swinging rhythmically	Rhythm boards, swings, bars		Rearranges equipment to offer new interests and challenge
Gaining strength and skill	Tricycles, wagons, wheelbarrows		Encourages children to put away equipment
Digging and gardening	Sturdy junior garden tools, sand shovels, cans, spoons / Designated areas, sandbox		

[1] The starting point for this table was a table in "Parent Nursery Schools," a mimeographed report-manual prepared by a committee for the Berkeley Public Schools, July, 1931.

Activity	Materials	Values	Teacher's role
Using small toys	Form boards, puzzles, peg boards	Imaginative exploration of adult activities	Arranges materials on low tables and open shelves easily accessible to children
Sandbox construction	Shovels, containers, trucks, cars, trains, planes, boats	Development of small muscles, finger manipulation, and eye-hand co-ordination. Supply quiet activity for child needing individual play, experience in spatial relationship	Supplies minimum amount of direction as children make selection
Building with blocks	Solid blocks, hollow blocks, building boards, trains, airplanes, farm animals, cars, trucks, cash register		Provides tables and chairs as needed
			Offers simpler but similar materials when maturity level prevents child from being successful
Working with wood	Work bench, variety of wood pieces, hammers, large-headed nails, saws, vises, cloth pieces		Redirects energy to more active play when child indicates need
			Mentions limits which insure safety
Water play	Boats, short hose, funnels, troughs, containers, wash board, clothes line		
Planning, evaluating		Participation in democratic group processes	Encourages putting away
			Sits near restless child
			Listens attentively as teacher works with children
Pounding, patting, kneading, modeling	Clay, wet and dry sand, mud, finger paint, various textures	Opportunity for self-expression	Offers a minimum amount of direction as children use materials

Kind of Activity	Equipment Required	Value for the Child	Parent Participation
Painting, crayoning, pasting	Easel paints, water, paste, and colored paper	Hand and finger manipulation	Sets simple standards such as suggesting the wiping of a brush on side of container after dipping in paint
	Crayons	Use of a medium with a tool	
	Chalk		Emphasizes the experience rather than the product
			Shares child's satisfaction
			Labels paintings, writes child's comment upon them
			Stores products for safekeeping
			Encourages children to put away equipment
Singing, dancing, listening to music	Simple songs, drums, shakers, rattles, bells, tone sticks, records, piano, or other instruments	Experience in rhythm	Uses special talents to encourage children in musical experience
		Experience in listening	
	Music of various sorts	Experience in singing	Encourages spontaneous and informal responses
	Dress-up hats	Awareness of melody and rhythm	Encourages children to experiment with instruments and equipment which bring forth rhythmic responses
		Spontaneous musical expression	
		Dramatic expression	

Looking at books or pictures Listening to stories Selecting pictures and stories Telling and dramatizing stories Enjoying art prints	Mounted pictures A variety of books suitable for five-year-olds	Enjoyment of story experience Experience in speech Utilization of child's increasing attention span Enjoyment through stories of familiar experiences and of simple unfamiliar experiences	Arranges book corner for individual child's use Checks lighting, size of table and chairs Allows children to browse and to choose stories Demonstrates proper use of books Keeps story group small Encourages attention and children's participation Chooses books suitable to group's maturity and interest Encourages spontaneous and original storytelling and dramatization
Housekeeping play, playing with dolls, dressing up, expressing dramatically in other kinds of play	Stove, table, chairs, bed, sink, scaled to child's size Dolls, stuffed animals, doll clothes, telephone, doll dishes, dress-up clothes, purses, iron, squares of cloth, broom	Provision of natural outlets in play and emotions Easier social contacts for small children Spontaneous group play which fosters group feeling	Sits near, but does not initiate activity Provides materials as they are requested or needed Occasionally participates but withdraws as children enter into play

Kind of Activity	Equipment Required	Value for the Child	Parent Participation
Housekeeping play, playing with dolls, dressing up, expressing dramatically in other kinds of play	Tool kit, oil cans, nuts, bolts, paper punch, mesh bags, old letters, old clock, stapler	Opportunity to test roles and ideas by doing	Is ready to accept rejection if material offered is not interesting to child at the time Encourages constructive use of equipment
Watching natural phenomena, digging for worms, planting seeds, feeling the wind, going on excursions occasionally, watching mechanical equipment at work	Wooden spoons, blunt trowels, cans, watering cans, seeds, flats, soil, streamers, bird nests, leaves, rocks, pets and pet cages, aquarium	Development of natural curiosity in living things, the earth around them Development and appreciation of the mechanical aspects of community life	Observes and records children's participation and comments on the world about them Provides materials to foster interest Takes children on short excursions Answers questions simply Explains simply what she observes
Going through a health inspection	Tray, paper cups, pitchers, wastebasket, disposable tissues	Experience in taking turns, removing wraps, pouring from a pitcher to a cup Co-operation in the observation of good health habits	Sits with child in designated area Encourages child as needed Says goodbye and leaves promptly

Toileting and handwashing	Steps which enable child to reach fixtures, soap, toilet tissue, paper towels, clean cloth, wastebasket	Recognition of own physical needs Experience in good health habits Experience in unfastening and fastening clothing	Encourages self-reliance Gives child time to help himself Recognizes child's need for privacy Answers questions simply Redirects to next activity Leaves bathroom clean and ready for use
Enjoying nutrition	Table, chairs, pitcher, paper cups, napkin, juice, crackers, wastebasket, damp cloth	Opportunity for eating and talking in small groups Practice in simple table manners, pouring and helping each other to napkins, spoons, and the like	Helps child wipe off table Helps child pour juice Gives opportunities for children to help each other Sets example of courtesy and friendliness Encourages sampling of juice and crackers Helps children clean up
Resting	Labeled rugs and blankets	Prevention of fatigue and over-stimulation	Helps child get own rug from locker

Kind of Activity	Equipment Required	Value for the Child	Parent Participation
Resting	Labeled rugs and blankets	Practice in relaxation in the presence of others	Establishes a quiet atmosphere by arranging furnishings and shades in advance
			Soothes restless child
			Yawns and relaxes
			Separates children who stimulate one another
			Helps child roll rug after rest
			Checks order of restroom before leaving
Picking up the equipment	Wagons, boxes, brooms, utensils, cloths	Encouragement in sharing in a job, completing a job, in tidiness and co-operation	Gives warning for pick-up time
	Storage space		Indicates what needs to be put away and where, gives encouragement and praise
			Accepts child's help at his level of achievement
			Sends child on to rest or next activity when he has done his share

SITUATIONS FOR DISCUSSION

In the following situations select each course of action that seems desirable to you basing your choices and omissions on the ideas presented in this chapter. Add one or more alternate courses of action.

SITUATION I. At the beginning of kindergarten, Jimmy Fantail had blinked almost continuously. Now that he feels more at home, he seldom blinks. But one day just before the close of the session, Mrs. Fantail comes to visit and Jimmy starts blinking. When he is absorbed in what he is doing, he does not blink. But whenever he glances toward his mother, he blinks repeatedly for a minute or two.

Mrs. Fantail and Jimmy stop to talk with you after the close of school. Mrs. Fantail says, "I suppose you've noticed Jimmy's blinking." As the teacher you should say:

"Many five-year-olds blink."

"Blinking fits in with our discussion for the next parents' meeting."

"Yes, I have."

"He started blinking today when you came in."

"I am due at a meeting now. Can you come next Tuesday afternoon to talk with me?"

SITUATION II. In thinking about the meeting for parents to discuss their observations of children's work habits, you should:

Plan a brief talk about children's work habits.

Describe how desirable work habits are developed in kindergarten.

Ask the parents what work habits they observed in kindergarten.

Plan to list "Desirable Work Habits for a Five-Year-Old."

Let the parents ask questions about the observation.

SITUATION III. Mrs. Randall, an older woman, comes to discuss her problem about five-year-old Susan. Each school morning Susan says, "I don't want to go to school." The conversation continues:

MRS. R.: When Susan was three, she got up each morning asking, "Do I go to nursery school today?" She loved to go to her school.

YOU: She seems to enjoy kindergarten. She enters into all the activities.

MRS. R.: Well, it seems to me that something is wrong with the kindergarten when a girl does not want to go each morning.

At this point, as the teacher, you should say:

"Well, that is one possibility."

"I keep anecdotal records about what the children do. Let's see what the records show us about Susan."

"If she is like my nephew, she adds, 'And you can't make me!' "

"Children usually explore the question of going or not going to school at some time or other."

"You have a very interesting problem. How about bringing it up at the parents' discussion meeting? Probably other parents have this problem too."

SITUATION IV. As a new teacher in a suburban community built after the last war, you have a morning group of 36 children and an afternoon group of 34. You feel you need to know the kinds of homes the children live in. You should:

Make friends with the mothers who come regularly for their children.

Ask the experienced kindergarten teachers what they do about home visits.

Discuss your problem with your principal.

Dismiss the question in view of your heavy pupil load.

Call on the parents of two or three kindergarten children who seem to have many problems.

BIBLIOGRAPHY

Professional Books and Pamphlets

Association of Childhood Educational International. *Reporting on the Growth of Children.* General Service Bulletin No. 62. Washington, D. C., 1953.

The purpose of reporting, what children need and wish reported, and desirable practices in reporting are discussed briefly.

Babitz, Milton, "Handbook on Parent Education," Bulletin XXVII. Sacramento, California: State Department of Education, 1958.

The organization of a parent education program and group processes that help parents learn are discussed briefly.

Eckert, Ralph G., and Faith W. Smitter. *Home and School Work Together for Young Children.* Sacramento: California State Department of Education, Bulletin, Volume XVIII, No. 1, March, 1949.

Parents and teachers need to work together for the benefit of kindergarten children. The characteristics, needs and problems of children, and methods of controlling them are discussed in this helpful pamphlet.

Frank, Mary, and Lawrence K. *How to Help Your Child in School.* New York: The Viking Press, 1950.

The Franks have many practical suggestions for parents of children from nursery school age to age twelve.

Heffernan, Helen, ed. *Guiding the Young Child.* Second Ed. Boston: D. C. Heath and Company, 1959.

Chapter XIV, pages 221–239, discusses the effective use of nondirective techniques in parent conferences and meetings.

Hymes, James L. *Three to Six: Your Child Starts to School.* Public Affairs Pamphlet No. 163. New York: Public Affairs Committee, Inc., 1950.

Gives suggestions to parents about meeting their new responsibilities.

Ilg, F. L., and L. B. Ames. *Child Behavior.* New York: Harper and Brothers, 1955.

These authors write what parents want to know about how their children behave.

Johnson, June. *Home Play for the Preschool Child.* New York: Harper and Brothers, 1957.

Lists of activities for preschool children at home will be helpful to mothers.

Leonard, Edith M.; Dorothy D. Van Deman; and Lillian E. Miles. *Counseling with Parents.* New York: The Macmillan Company, 1954.

Teachers and others who work with parents find useful suggestions in this book.

National Education Association, and the National Congress of Parents and Teachers. *Happy Journey: Preparing Your Child for School.* Washington: Department of Elementary School Principals and the National School Public Relations Association, 1953.

Gives practical suggestions for getting a child ready physically and emotionally for school experiences, and to prepare parents for their activities in relation to the school.

Books for Children

Abel, Ruth and Ray. *The New Sitter.* New York: Oxford University Press, 1950.
A baby sitter is presented sympathetically and realistically.

Shane, Ruth and Harold. *The New Baby.* Little Golden Book #41. New York: Simon and Schuster, Inc., 1948.
Mike and his parents get ready for the new baby.

Films for Parents

A Child Went Forth. San Francisco: Grandon-Western Cinema Guild, 1942.
Children from two to seven years old explore their environment at a summer camp, make their own social adjustments, and attack new problems. 20 minutes, sound, black and white.

Children's Play. New York: McGraw-Hill Book Company, 1956.
Children play differently at different ages. Parents can help them have healthy play. 27 minutes, sound, black and white.

Helping Your Child Feel Emotionally Secure. New York: Seminar Films, 1953.
Fifteen short incidents are handled by parents in wrong and in right ways. Incidents include "Playing with Water Is Fun," and "Self-Reliance Begins Early." 30 minutes, sound, color.

Let Your Child Help You. New York: New York University Film Library, 1947.
By helping at home children gain a feeling of accomplishment and learn to take responsibility. 11 minutes, sound, black and white.

Preface to a Life. New York: United World Films, Inc., 1950.
How a child grows up depends in part on whether his parents are overly solicitous, expect too much of him, or treat him as a person. 27 minutes, sound, black and white.

Your Children's Play. New York: McGraw-Hill Book Company, 1952.
Children learn through play. Shows how adults can either help or hinder them. 21 minutes, sound, black and white.

19

The Teacher Develops in Service

DESIRABLE ATTITUDES PROMOTE TEACHER GROWTH

The student who completes her course work at a college, university, or other teacher education institution is not a finished product as a kindergarten teacher. She has merely completed the studies which should make it possible for her to continue to develop during her years of working with kindergarten children. She should grow in service, enjoying her activities in guiding children, improving the timing of her suggestions to them, and increasing her fund of ideas and materials to expand their interests. She should grow in her understanding of five-year-old children by observing and recording what they do in the kindergarten situation and by talking with and visiting parents to find out their attitudes and practices in handling their children during out-of-school hours.

Children enjoy the teacher who enjoys life and shares her enthusiasms with them. Hobbies which take her outdoors enable her to collect rocks, plants, and small animals to enrich the kindergarten. Hobbies which she carries on with other people give her stories and other ideas to share with the children. As she travels or as she goes about her usual activities she has an eye for seeing what catches the attention of a child. Thus what enriches her life enriches the lives of the children.

The teacher makes a point of keeping in good health so that she has a zest for living. She practices the desirable health habits that she teaches, and she gets professional assistance when she has a health problem. She is realistic about the negative but cultivates the happy aspects of life.

The teacher plans her activities so that her in-service development is an integral part of her work. When she is collecting anecdotal and other records for a case study of a child in her group, she does this within the framework of her regular activities, not as an additional and unrelated activity. The teacher who is developing in service is distinguished not by a great number of additional activities but rather by the ways in which she carries on the usual activities of a kindergarten teacher.

388

As the teacher develops her understanding of how to work effectively with children individually and in groups, she also develops the skills she needs to work effectively with parents, teachers, and community people. She learns more about participating in democratic group discussions and about individual interviews. With the co-operation of her principal she furthers her own development by observing other kindergarten situations and by talking with other teachers, keeping abreast of current professional books and periodicals, sharing with mother assistants her responsibility for the children, attending professional conferences, participating in curriculum development, and working with student teachers as opportunities present themselves.

The way a teacher thinks about herself and her work may determine over the years whether she finds teaching strenuous and nerve-wracking or a genuine pleasure. Does she think of herself as a performer, of her teaching as her performance, and of the children as the means for either enhancing or interfering with her work? Or does she think of herself as a person who enjoys helping and guiding children in their activities? The way in which a teacher takes responsibility for her group of kindergarten children affects the limits of their learning and also her happiness in her work.

Miss Inkopf, for instance, thinks that it is her responsibility to be in command of her group at all times, moving them as a group from one educative activity to another and seeing to it that each child takes part in the activity without interfering with any other child. She often says, "I'm waiting for Harold," or "If you can't stand quietly, I shall have to ask you to come back to your places," or "Miss Inkopf will read a story as soon as you show her you are ready." If she must be out of the room for a few minutes or if she must give her attention to a visitor, she appoints some active child to take over the leadership of the group.

Miss Inkopf is very fond of children. She worked her way through college by baby sitting and by helping in a nursery school. Yet she does find teaching strenuous and is glad when the school day is over and she is no longer responsible for the children. When the children are more noisy than usual, she is embarrassed and thinks about what she can do next time to prevent their getting noisy. She is pleased with herself when the school day seems to go well. She feels when things go wrong she is to blame. She is not a very happy person.

In contrast to the teacher-centered classroom is the kindergarten group in which the teacher and the children share the responsibility for their activities. Miss Shimizu, for instance, thinks it highly important for the children to develop skill in group planning as well as skill in planning their individual activities. She feels that they learn more fully through experience than through her telling them how to plan. When a group of children becomes noisy, she lets the noise continue until the children are aware of it and aware that it interferes with hearing each other. When the children recognize such a problem, she sits down with them to talk over how they really want to work. She may ask, "What was good about the way we were working?" and "Did our talking help our work?" When the children understand their problem and realize that its solution is their responsibility, they develop rules to help them work more effectively, and incidentally more quietly.

Miss Shimizu enjoys her work with the children. She is interested in the growth and development of each of them. Understanding them as five-year-olds with a great deal to learn about getting along with each other individually and in a group, she likes to note what they learn and what they need to learn. When the school day is over, she has already planned how to work with the children in helping them meet the individual and group problems growing out of the day's activities. When the first-grade teacher tells Miss Shimizu how pleased she is with the responsibility that the children take when they come into her room, Miss Shimizu replies, "Yes, I think the children learn to plan their activities very well by the end of the school year." Miss Shimizu feels that she is successful not in terms of how hard she has worked but in terms of what the children have done. She is developing as a person and as a teacher because her attention is focused on the children, not self-consciously on her achievement.

GAINING CONFIDENCE

Confidence Through Skill in Timing

The wise teacher knows that only practice makes for perfection. She therefore plans her work and teaches each day as well as she can knowing that constant improvement will result. When she tells a story she tries to make it the best story she has told. She watches the children and gets clues about when to elaborate and when to move on. When she helps the children with rhythmic activities, she times her suggestions according to the reactions of the children. As she helps them move from one activity to another, she watches for the moment that a child loses interest and looks around for some new activity. When the children are playing, she develops awareness of when a child has gone as far as he can by himself and needs some suggestion or other help to continue. In short, each day the teacher endeavors to time her group and individual guidance so that it furthers the optimum development of the children. Such timing is an art that comes with intelligent experience and gives the teacher confidence in her work with children.

Confidence Through Files of Materials

The kindergarten teacher who can put aside her plans for the day and capitalize on the children's interests is the teacher who has well-organized collections of useful materials. In the cupboard next to the big flannel board is a box of frequently used figures, each with a piece of sandpaper glued on the back ready to help tell a story. In the file are pictures large enough to be easily visible to a group of children. The pictures have been assembled from magazines, catalogs, and calendars. Each has been mounted on cardboard, and the best ones have been covered smoothly with cellophane to protect them as the children use them. With the pictures in the file are related materials for the teacher: music for a song; suggestions and patterns for simple craft activities; descriptions of games, finger plays, and action songs; synopses of stories; and a list of library books. The file folders for each of the special holidays during the school year are most nearly replete. The compiled materials represent many hours of teacher time, but they make it possible to use the time with the children to great advantage.

Mrs. Morgan, a kindergarten teacher with years of experience, was talking with other kindergarten teachers about the usefulness of files. "You know," she said, "when John brought a little garter snake to school the other day, I thought to myself, 'Now there's a topic I don't have anything on.' But I checked my file anyway and was amazed at what I had filed several years before: word lists for teaching the snake sound, how to do a serpentine, and suggestions for keeping a snake as a pet." The other teachers continued their interesting conversation, and in the next few days each of them found time to add to her files in the light of what she had learned from the other teachers. Such teachers are confident about their teaching because they know they can depend on their files to help them provide for the needs and interests of children.

THE TEACHER DEVELOPS THROUGH UNDERSTANDING CHILDREN

The teacher develops through understanding children individually and in groups. The more kinds of children she knows as individuals and the more she knows about effective methods of working with groups of children, the more competent she is in guiding their development.

Observing Activities of the Children

The kindergarten teacher increases her understanding of five-year-old children not only by reading about them but by observing objectively what each of them does and by writing her observations as anecdotal records or as time recordings. The brief but significant anecdote is especially useful in noting some aspect of social, emotional, or intellectual development. It can be written down either at the time or later in the same day. In doing so, the teacher should:

write descriptively and vividly what actually happens

note social contacts

record conversations

record emotional reactions both negative and positive (aggression, resentment, anger, guilt; and joy, pleasure, sympathy, and affection)

give the setting for what happens

be specific and use words that are expressive ("Jean pounded the clay" rather than "Jean played with the clay.")

report what the child does and how he does it ("Hand on hip, David looked at each child and finally pointed to the last one saying, 'I choose Clyde.' ")

keep descriptions of what was said and done separate from interpretations

The following anecdotal record illustrates many of these suggestions:

ANECDOTAL RECORD

Name: RODNEY SMITH   Date: NOVEMBER 4

Situation: BLOCK BUILDING. Tom chose Rodney and Teddy to help build a farm.

What Child Says and Does	What Teacher Says and Does	Interpretation
Rodney is busily helping build the farm	"What a nice farm you've built. You're ready to get the farmer dolls and have them work on the farm."	
Rodney walks to the shelf and returns with a doll. "Hop, hop, hop," he says as he jumps the farmer around the farm and then puts him astride the barn roof.	"Is that what a farmer does — sit on the roof?"	
Rodney says, "Mine does."		Is not ready for realistic dramatic play; still interested in manipulating materials.

Like anecdotal records, time recordings are useful in getting better acquainted with a child. The kindergarten teacher makes a running account of what the child does during a given time interval, usually twenty or thirty minutes. Every few minutes she observes and records what he is doing or saying, trying to obtain an accurate picture of the pattern of his behavior. She records vividly and specifically what the child does and says. In a separate column she records any interpretations she makes at the time. Later she often amplifies her interpretations, writing with a different colored pencil or ink.

On the following page is an illustration of a time recording.

The teacher who collects anecdotal records and time recordings for Stephen for several weeks finds that her record folder for him is a good start on a case study. The materials show Stephen's behavior in kindergarten. The teacher checks to see whether they show both classroom and playground situations; physical, social, emotional, and intellectual aspects of development; and a good sampling of curriculum areas. Any gaps are filled in with subsequent observations and recordings.

To understand Stephen more completely, the teacher extends her observations into out-of-school situations. By recording what Stephen's parents say about their child during parents' discussion meetings, individual conferences, and home visits, the teacher gains insight into his family relationships. Talking with his siblings at school also helps the teacher understand Stephen.

It is not possible for a teacher to make case studies of many children at a time. The press of daily responsibilities precludes that. But it is within the limits of the time and energy of any teacher to make one case study each term. Over the years such studies give a teacher a considerable and increasing insight into child behavior. Sometimes the teacher selects a boy for study, sometimes a girl. When she is irritated by a child or otherwise feels the need for understanding him, she makes observational records into a case study of the child. Usually long before she rounds out the study, she comes to understand and enjoy him.

Observing the Child in Relation to His Family

The teacher has two avenues for getting acquainted with children in the setting of their family. She can talk with parents and listen to what they say about their children, or she can observe the relation of parents and children in their own homes. The wise teacher uses both methods for getting acquainted with at least a sampling of children and their families.

The teacher listens attentively to what parents say, for instance, "I

TIME RECORDING

NAME: <u>Stephen Dale</u>, large for his age   DATE: <u>December 7</u>
and vigorously active.   DAY OF WEEK: <u>Wednesday</u>

SITUATION: The afternoon group came in at 12:40. A story about a Xmas tree was
a stimulus for art work around the Xmas theme. Stephen chose to work
with clay.

Time	What Child Does and Says	Interpretation and Remarks
1:00	Stephen sits down at the clay table taking the nearest chair. Pounds vigorously, and then works clay with both hands. Sings quietly as he rolls clay.	Stephen has much energy. Sings constantly when working.
1:03	Has 2 round balls, one on top of other. Rolls balls together. Turns around toward table in back of his where the children are making trees. "I wish I'd made a Xmas tree instead."	Interested in what others do.
1:06	Singing along to himself as he works the clay some more. "I'm going to make a Xmas snake. A Xmas snake. Instead of a jack-in-the-box, a snake-in-the-box. Instead of a snake-in-the-box, a Santa-in-the-box."	Imaginative. Likes to sing and talk and play with words and phrases.
1:09	Sings loudly: "Easter eggs in the Xmas basket." Then quiets down when asked to.	Disturbingly loud. Co-operates when asked directly.
1:12	Smiles at the three-ball snow man he has made complete with eyes, nose and mouth. Jane brushes past with her Xmas tree. "Oh, look at the Xmas tree," he says but gets no response. Turns and finishes snow man. "Teacher, look at my snow man, a great big snow man."	His achievement is good for his age. Likes to get the attention of others, but is not disappointed when he doesn't. Pleased with his second attempt. Has his own standards of what to do.
1:15	Takes book from rack and goes toward freshly painted window seat. When reminded of paint, goes to rug. Sits on top of a girl's work. When she ignores him, he goes and sits down on Dan's work.	Finally has to be helped to find a place on rug without disturbing others.
1:18	"Where's my snow man?" he asks and goes to shelf where it was put. Does not see it. "Did you throw it away?" Sees it, and then stops by tree-making table, getting paste on his hands from touching a tree.	
1:21	Sitting on rug, he turns pages of book. "Hi, Dan, look at this." Dan comes over and two girls nearby show interest.	Stephen is often able to get attention of those around him. The other children like him.

certainly don't let my children run out of the house with a sandwich the way my neighbor does. I have my children sit down at the table and eat the way they should." As the teacher smiles understandingly, she makes a mental note to look for other evidences of excessive parental demands and for any feelings of pressure and tension on the part of the child. As the teacher becomes increasingly familiar with the attitudes and expectations of typical parents in the community, she is better able to work effectively with the children.

No matter what the social or economic level of the community, it is important for the teacher to have firsthand knowledge of the kinds of homes the kindergarten children come from. If she makes a formal, scheduled visit to a home, she knows how such a home treats a guest but she still has little real information about the family relationships and their influence on the child. She can observe the kinds of play equipment the five-year-old has but she still needs to know whether the child is free to use the equipment as he wishes or is expected to keep it unmarred. If she is entertained in the living room, she has no way of knowing what arrangement the child has for sleeping and for keeping his own personal belongings. In short, the formalities of being a guest may prevent the teacher from gaining insight into the influence of the home on its five-year-old child.

How, then, can a teacher within the limits of her time become acquainted with at least a sampling of homes? One teacher who had come from a lower income community and a family of five children taught in a community like the one in which she grew up. When she was out for a walk and saw a five-year-old from her class, she greeted him as a friend and soon found herself right at home with his family. Drying the dishes in the kitchen she chatted with the mother and noticed how the mother responded to first one child and then another as each found some reason for coming to his mother. The teacher who feels at home in the living situation of her children soon understands the thinking of families in the community and is able to predict parent reactions to problems of children.

A kindergarten teacher in another community had an announced policy of visiting homes when a new baby was born. "There aren't enough hours in the week for me to visit the homes of all my children the way I would like to, so I just visit the homes of children with new brothers or sisters. Then my visit makes the five-year-old feel important at a time when he is finding it hard to compete with the new baby." The community understood the teacher's point of view and admired her for it. Through a comparatively small number of home visits, the teacher gained considerable insight into the family attitudes in that community and the usual parental responses to their children.

In a wealthy suburban community, the teacher wrote a letter to a kindergarten mother who was a social leader and offered to assist her in planning and having a birthday party for her five-year-old child. The mother welcomed the teacher's assistance and said, "Why, I wouldn't have thought about having a party for Janet if you hadn't written me." The teacher gained insight into a home situation she otherwise might not have known. When a teacher needs to understand a child in his home environment, she can find some way to make a home visit.

THE TEACHER DEVELOPS SKILL IN GROUP DISCUSSIONS

The teaching profession is aware of the development of its members through participation in group discussions. More and more frequently teachers' meetings are planned as round table discussions. Panels, films, or other presentations are followed by small group discussions. Or workshops are held. In each of these situations, it is important for the teacher to use and develop skill in democratic group discussion. Furthermore, with such skill, she is a more effective member of a parent discussion group and an addition to any community group. The wise teacher finds it desirable to study and practice democratic group participation.

Conducting a Discussion

Through such study she learns that each member of a group feels free to ask questions and make comments at any time. Each group member, not just the chairman, takes responsibility for keeping the discussion focused on the problems: "Is what we're talking about related to our problem?" "Maybe what we're discussing is a good problem for our next meeting, but let's get back to our problem for this meeting." Whenever any member has something to say, each member of the group listens courteously, knowing that he will have the same respect when he voices his opinions. If someone talks on, elaborating without adding any new idea, the chairman, or some other member of the group, reassures him by putting his comments into one or two concise sentences: "Your point is . . ." Then the chairman gets another member of the group into discussion by saying, "Are there other views?" or "Does someone else have another comment before we go on to our next question?" Of course the use of *Roberts' Rules of Order* also furthers democratic operation of the group. Any member of the group can move to limit discussion to a certain number of minutes. Furthermore, the chairman always recognizes a new speaker in preference to someone who has already spoken on a topic. In these ways, the teacher learns, each member of the group feels that he has as much opportunity to express his views as does any other member of the group and no more opportunity than anyone else.

Topics for Discussion

The teacher also learns that democratic meetings deal primarily with problems related to the purposes of the group. But from time to time meetings may take up problems arising from group processes, and occasionally a meeting may consider a problem arising from an unmet personal need of a member. Of course, if a group establishes its purposes and is kept constantly aware of them, it will be so constructively occupied that problems of process and personal problems probably will not appear. In meetings of teachers or parents, "How best may we further the optimum development of our children?" is a topic for endless discussion.

Occasionally it is necessary for a group of teachers or parents to consider how it wishes to function. For instance, if certain members tend to sit with friends and carry on side conversations during a meeting, the group has the problem of how to provide for meeting their social needs without interfering with the discussion. This problem must be taken up by the group in order to make the meetings of maximum benefit to everyone. The group may decide to have a social hour at the beginning of the meeting. A coffee hour on arrival gives parents or teachers a chance for the small talk they enjoy. They feel at home with each other and get their personal questions and neighborly planning taken care of before the discussion starts. Then the discussion can be carried on with everyone listening courteously as each member contributes.

Usually the personal needs of individuals can be met within the democratic operation of the group. If not, the chairman can find some opportunity outside for talking with the disturbing person. By discovering his talents, the chairman can help him find legitimate opportunities for leading the group in the direction it wants to go. When the person gets sufficient attention for helping the group, he no longer needs to try undesirable ways of being noticed.

THE TEACHER DEVELOPS THROUGH PROFESSIONAL ACTIVITIES

The teacher of small children spends much of her time guiding the development of young minds. She needs also to have interesting activities with adults at her level of maturity. With her colleagues at school she has opportunity for constructive conversation as a by-product of her teaching. But with the help of her principal she can go beyond the school into larger areas of professional activities. There she finds stimulating situations that enable her to enrich her teaching and her own living.

Working with Other Staff Members

For a beginning or an inexperienced teacher, what others can tell about their experiences in the teaching profession is an excellent source of new ideas. Realizing this the wise teacher practices interview skills which help in getting such information in usable form. If another teacher says casually, "I hope the mimeograph office has run off my anecdotal record forms," the first teacher immediately follows up the remark with, "Is it a form you worked out for your own use?" With such a lead, she soon finds out what the form is, how and when the teacher uses it, what effect the teacher thinks it has on her teaching, and anything else the teacher can tell her about it. By asking a fellow kindergarten teacher about her methods, the teacher understands more about effective ways of working with children and makes the other teacher feel pleased about being helpful and about being understood.

The skillful interviewer is essentially an interested listener and a sounding board which reflects the other person's ideas for verification. She uses the feedback principle and asks, "The point you are making is . . .?" or "Do you mean . . . or . . .?" She reassures the other person by saying, "Yes, I understand," but she does not say, "Yes, I approve what you are saying." She does not say whether her own views are similar or entirely different, but she convinces the other person that she understands the point of view presented. Any discussion of differences of opinion can come much later when many conversations have built up a feeling of mutual confidence.

The teachers in a school system differ in their training and in their expectations of children. If teachers are to work together smoothly they need to understand and respect each other's point of view. Where two kindergarten teachers must share facilities and equipment, it is necessary for their expectations of children to be similar or harmonious. For instance, one kindergarten teacher thinks it highly important for five-year-old children to have continuity in their activities from day to day as a means of developing skill in carrying on a project over several days or weeks. Another kindergarten teacher may feel that a variety of new experiences should be explored briefly by five-year-olds, but that extended projects are more appropriate for older children. These two teachers find it difficult to share the same kindergarten room unless they can discuss their views, identify this difference in their objectives, and then arrange for the first teacher to have some means of rolling the children's construction area into a large, low cupboard when the room is used by the second teacher.

With the kindergarten children, the teacher emphasizes the distinction between reality and what is pretended. With adults she makes these distinctions only mentally, but she must make them. When another teacher, Miss Dale, says, "There's that Miss Parker letting her children run all over the playground. I wish she'd learn to keep them under control,"

Miss Dale's remark shows that she is irritated by the way children in Miss Parker's group play on the playground. The remark should be interpreted only as an opinion, and not as a statement of fact. To find out more about Miss Dale's opinion, the teacher can ask, "You think the children should use less of the playground?" The wise teacher keeps the discussion objective and steers away from personal comments about other teachers. She refrains from asking, "Doesn't Miss Parker have good control of her group?" because she knows that such personal remarks interfere with good mental hygiene in a school faculty. Nor does she tell Miss Parker, "You should hear what Miss Dale said about you." By confining her remarks to constructive and objective matters, the wise teacher furthers the happiness of the staff and her own happiness as an ethical member of the teaching profession.

Stimulation from Mother Assistants and Student Teachers

Fortunate is the teacher who has mother assistants or student teachers to share her responsibilities with the children, for their co-operation is stimulating. In explaining to them why she did what she did with the children, the teacher points out relationships that might not otherwise come to her conscious attention. In talking with them about plans for the next day, the teacher thinks through the needs of the children and the ways in which those needs will be met through kindergarten activities. Thus the teacher, as well as the children and the other adults, have an enriched experience.

For adults to work effectively with the teacher in the kindergarten, it is necessary for them to learn as rapidly as possible:

the name of each child. The name is a mental peg on which to hang further information about the child — his interests and attitudes, his skills, his needs, his social sensitivities

the location of each item of equipment, and how it is used by the children

the characteristics of five-year-old children

the procedures and policies of the school as they relate to kindergarten activities

Realizing how much is to be learned, the teacher is pleased with what each adult does learn. She expects each to learn in her own way, at her own rate and in her own order. Therefore, she is not disappointed nor frustrated by what is not yet learned, but is pleased with the daily accomplishment. Her praise is an incentive for further learning.

The teacher is generous in showing other adults how she works with the children and in explaining her reasons for her methods. At the same time she does not expect any other adult to work with the children in the same way she does. Recognizing individual differences in adults as well as in children, the teacher leaves the adults free to develop their own methods and helps them see the cause of their successes. Her explanations and expressions of confidence contribute to her own competence as a teacher at the same time that they contribute to the effectiveness of the adults working with her.

Professional Opportunities on the Job

School principals and other administrative personnel are interested in furthering the professional development of their staff through observing other teachers, attending professional conferences, participating in curriculum development, acting as a master teacher for student teachers, and working with parent groups. When a teacher feels that she carries out her responsibilities with her group of children effectively and feels that she is ready to consider new ideas, she talks with her principal and her supervisors about stimulating professional experiences she would enjoy. In most school situations, it is possible to arrange for such experiences within a short time. Sometimes a substitute teacher is employed to replace teachers carrying on professional activities away from their group of children. Sometimes an assistant principal takes the children's groups and in this way gets better acquainted with the children in the school. A good administrator provides in some way for the in-service development of his faculty.

In one school system, Miss Thorsen talked with her principal about observing Mrs. Griffith, an outstanding kindergarten teacher in a nearby school. Miss Thorsen's principal called Mrs. Griffith's principal and found out that Mrs. Griffith was the kind of person who enjoyed having visitors and would welcome a visit from another kindergarten teacher. A tentative date was arranged for an afternoon two weeks later. Then Miss Thorsen's principal secured a substitute teacher for Miss Thorsen for that afternoon. Miss Thorsen described plans for the children for the afternoon and discussed them with the substitute teacher a few days in advance.

Miss Thorsen enjoyed visiting Mrs. Griffith. She talked with her over the telephone and arranged to meet her after school the day before her visit. In this way the teachers were soon at ease with each other, and Miss Thorsen was familiar with Mrs. Griffith's facilities and equipment and with her plans and the problems which she expected to help the children with the next afternoon. Mrs. Griffith also appreciated the opportunity to preview the observation. She felt that Miss Thorsen would appreciate and understand what the children did while she was visiting. Mrs. Griffith thought about how to modify her work with the children in small ways that would emphasize the points of special interest to Miss Thorsen.

After the observation, Miss Thorsen talked with Mrs. Griffith further, clarifying the cause and effect relations she had observed. Both at that time and later in other conversations, Mrs. Griffith talked freely about what she planned to do and what she actually did in meeting the needs and interests of the children. She felt that Miss Thorsen had observed her class intelligently, was interested in it, and understood sympathetically what happened in it. In short, one well-planned observation was really an introduction to a stimulating professional friendship.

Other Professional Opportunities

After some years of teaching Miss Thorsen talked with her principal about further opportunities for professional development:

MISS THORSEN: Each year when you have rated me as a teacher, you have marked me as average in professional relations.

PRINCIPAL: (*Smiling at her*) And as above average in your work with the children.

MISS THORSEN: Yes, but what concerns me is that low rating professionally. I thought I had good relations with the other teachers. I certainly try to further the ethics of our profession.

PRINCIPAL: Indeed you do have good relationships with the other teachers, and you certainly have done a great deal in planning excellent parties for our faculty. Those are reasons for rating you as average in professional relations. You have taken the responsibility that any good teacher takes in her own faculty. But outside our school is a whole professional world that you have scarcely entered.

MISS THORSEN: Oh? What is it and how do I get into it?

PRINCIPAL: Well, you are on the fringe of it when you attend institutes, and you enter it when you start taking responsibility for sharing your ideas with other teachers. And you do have some excellent ideas about working effectively with children, Miss Thorsen. When I talk with you here in the office and when I stop by your kindergarten with some message, I find you thinking creatively about children and how to guide them.

MISS THORSEN: How do I get started sharing my ideas with others?

PRINCIPAL: Well, I have a letter on my desk asking me to recommend a kindergarten teacher to work with other kindergarten teachers in preparing a booklet to send home to parents at the beginning of school next fall. How would you like to work on that committee? I should be very happy to recommend you for it.

MISS THORSEN: That sounds most interesting. Please suggest my name.

As the conversation continued, Miss Thorsen glimpsed a world of professional stimulation that she had never really thought much about. Her principal pointed out that her success in professional group activities would depend primarily on the excellence of her ideas about working with children but that whatever skill she developed in group techniques would contribute to her success. He said that the chairman of a group shares the leadership function with members of the group and that she should try assuming different phases of leadership in the group. "For instance," he said, "you might begin with suggesting some idea that has not been presented. Don't expect all your ideas to be accepted by the group. But as you become more skillful in presenting them you will find your ideas used more often. When you contribute good ideas the group soon starts looking to you for leadership through such ideas."

Toward the end of the school year, Miss Thorsen talked with her principal again. She thanked him for recommending her for membership on the committee and told him how she had used his suggestions about how to participate in the group work. Picking up a folder from his desk, her principal said, "I have heard such good reports about your committee work that I wonder if you would be interested in attending a workshop that the university is offering this summer for kindergarten and elementary school teachers. It is entitled 'Practice in Professional Leadership.' "

In the next few years, with the help of her principal and the professional leaders whom she met at the university, Miss Thorsen went on exploring new horizons she had not known existed in the teaching profession. Through her new activities, her teaching and her life were enriched. She enjoyed contributing to the leadership of her profession.

Colleges Help the Teacher Grow in Service

The teacher education institution is prepared to further the development of the teacher in service. In addition to the regular course offerings of summer sessions, it offers seminars, institutes, and workshops especially geared to the mature student. Workshops differ from courses in that they center on the problems of the members rather than on content chosen by the professor. The workshop members have professors, library materials, and each other as resources to aid them in solving their problems. Resource people are available for individual conferences or for group meetings. An experienced group leader helps the members of the workshop make effective use of their time in working with each other. Such workshops are of great value to the teacher who has identified what she wants to study as a means of improving her work with children.

Often teacher education institutions provide a summer school for children which can be used as a demonstration center for newer methods of teaching or as a laboratory situation for students wishing to try out under guidance newer methods of working with individual children or groups of children. Some institutions also offer opportunities for developing skills to use with groups of adults — teachers, parents, and community people.

Many states encourage teachers to take advantage of the offerings of teacher education institutions by requiring a certain amount of course credit to keep a teaching certificate in good standing. In many school systems, increased competence as a result of college or university study is recognized by increments on the salary scale. The greatest incentive for collegiate study, however, is the personal satisfaction that a teacher finds in being able to work more effectively with children.

SITUATIONS FOR DISCUSSION

In the following situations select each course of action that seems desirable to you basing your choices and omissions on the ideas presented in this chapter. Add one or more alternate courses of action.

SITUATION I. You think it desirable to keep anecdotal records about the children in your kindergarten group. As the teacher, you should:

> Set aside a ten-minute period each day for recording.
> Obtain record forms and a student file for putting them in.
> If an anecdote is not well written, don't waste time redoing it.
> Try to make each anecdote as vivid as possible.
> Interpret the anecdote after you have written the description.

SITUATION II. Several kindergarten teachers are discussing their problems. An experienced teacher who has a teacher-centered group says, "It's the children from the same block that make trouble. They play together outside school, and they want to play together in school." A teacher who has a co-operative situation in her kindergarten says, "Some of my children who work especially well together are friends outside school." As a new teacher in the school, you should:

> Observe children in your group who play together outside school.
> Discuss with your group of children how working together in kindergarten compares with playing together outside school.
> Ask your principal which teacher has the right idea.
> Tell the teacher with whom you agree that you think her views are right.
> Discourage parents from having their children play outside school with other children in the room.

SITUATION III. At a teachers' meeting, three of the younger teachers are sitting at the back. They take advantage of any slight lull in the discussion by talking and laughing among themselves. Several of the older teachers turn around and stare rather pointedly at the young members who soon are talking again. As a member of the group, you should:

Concentrate on the discussion and ignore the young teachers.

Speak to them after the meeting about letting other people listen.

Raise the question of having a social hour before the discussion hour.

Talk with the chairman after the meeting about how to handle the disturbance.

Rise to a point of order: "Mr. Chairman, we can't hear what is being said."

SITUATION IV. As a teacher, when you feel the need for further professional interests, you should:

Attend professional meetings.

Discuss your interest with your principal.

Help with faculty money-raising events.

Take part in a workshop on professional leadership.

When your point of view is not brought out in the discussion at a teachers' meeting, obtain the floor and present your view.

BIBLIOGRAPHY

Professional Books and Pamphlets

Kawin, Ethel. *A Guide for Child Study Groups.* Better Living Booklet for Parents and Teachers. Chicago: Science Research Associates, Inc., 1952.

This pamphlet gives specific ways for parents, teachers, and youth leaders to organize and maintain study groups in which the understanding and helping of children may be analyzed.

Miel, Alice, and Others. *Co-operative Procedures in Learning.* New York: Bureau of Publications, Teachers College, Columbia University, 1952.

Classroom teachers "tried to develop more skill in working co-operatively with their pupils" and identified opportunities for co-operative procedures as well as difficulties in the use of such procedures.

Mitchell, Lucy Sprague. *Know Your Children in School.* New York: The Macmillan Company, 1954.

"Kindergarten Scenes," pages 21–32, describe Allen, the Disturber; Freddie Who Cannot Concentrate; and Christina, Who Never Causes Any Trouble.

——. *Our Children and Our Schools.* New York: Simon and Schuster, Inc., 1950.

This book grew out of the Bank Street Workshops for Teachers. Chapter 8, "Learning Through Play and Experience in the Here-and-Now World," pages 129–141; Chapter 11, "Building a Social Studies Curriculum for Kindergarten, First and Second Grades," pages 198–215, are of special interest to kindergarten teachers.

Prescott, Daniel A. *The Child in the Educative Process.* New York: McGraw-Hill Book Company, 1957.

Part I discusses the educative process and the teacher's part in it.

Stewart, Robert A., and Arthur D. Workman. *Children and Other People Achieving Maturity through Learning.* New York: Dryden Press, 1956.

The adult helps the child with the adjustments he makes as he grows and develops from infancy through adolescence.

Films for Teachers

Helping Teachers to Understand Children. New York: United World Films, Inc., 1953.

Part I, 21 minutes: A school faculty sets up a local child study program with help and guidance from the Institute for Child Study at the University of Maryland. Sound, black and white.

Part II, 25 minutes: A summer workshop at the Institute for Child Study helps teachers develop awareness of forces affecting a child's personality, as well as his approach to others and to his studies. Sound, black and white.

Our Teacher. Chicago: Coronet Instructional Films, 1951.

Teachers are friends and helpmates as they explain and demonstrate; pupils are co-operative and self-reliant. 10 minutes, sound, black and white, or color.

Planning for Personal and Professional Growth. New York: McGraw-Hill Book Company, Inc., 1956.

Case studies of four typical teachers show how a teacher avoids failure and frustration by planning for personal and professional growth. 18 minutes, sound, black and white.

Filmstrips for Teachers

How to Make and Use the Felt Board. Columbus, Ohio: Ohio State University Teaching Aids Laboratory, 1955.

Explains the felt board as a teaching aid. 53 frames, silent, black and white.

Introducing Filmstrips. New York 20: National Film Board of Canada, 1947.

Cartoons explain what a filmstrip is and does, and how to use it. 29 frames, silent, black and white.

Current Publication Agencies

Association for Childhood Education International, 1200 15th Street, N.W., Washington 5, D. C.

A current list of many useful publications by the Association is available on request. *Childhood Education* is published monthly from September through May. It presents readable feature articles, useful news, reviews of books for children and adults, and reviews of magazine articles.

Child Study Association of America, 132 East 74th Street, New York 21, New York.

Child Study is a "quarterly journal of parent education." It includes book reviews.

Elementary School Journal. University of Chicago Press, 5750 Ellis Avenue, Chicago 37, Illinois.

This monthly magazine has one issue a year (the March issue) giving "Selected References on Kindergarten-Primary Education." These references include films as well as books and magazine articles.

Morton Edwards, editor and publisher, 1225 Broadway, New York 1, New York.

Your Today's Child, formerly "2-to-5 World News", each month presents current "news and views of the specialists in the child care field."

National Association for Nursery Education, State University of Iowa, Iowa City, Iowa.

Occasional publications by the Association deal with the development and education of kindergarten children.

National Education Association, Department of Kindergarten-Primary Education, 1201 16th Street, N.W., Washington 6, D. C.

This recently formed department of the National Education Association focuses attention on the need for preparing how to educate the four million children born last year. A newsletter and such publications as "An Annotated and Indexed Bibliography" are sent to members.

National Education Association, Department of Supervision and Curriculum Development, 1201 16th Street, N.W., Washington 6, D. C.

Publishes *Educational Leadership* monthly from September through May. Publishes an annual Yearbook and many occasional bulletins of interest to professional workers.

Parent Cooperative PreSchools of America, 2418 St. Paul St., Baltimore 18, Maryland.

Parent Cooperative PreSchools of America is the title of a quarterly newsletter of interest to parents and teachers in parent co-operative kindergartens and nursery schools.

Society for Research in Child Development, Inc., 1341 Euclid Avenue, University of Illinois, Champaign, Illinois.

Child Development is published quarterly and reports studies regarding various phases of child development.

Child Development Abstracts and Bibliography is published six times a year.

Monographs of the Society for Research in Child Development, Inc., are published with no fixed schedule.

United States Department of Health, Education and Welfare, Children's Bureau, Washington, D. C.

Children is published six times a year and is obtainable from the Superintendent of Documents, Government Printing Office, Washington 25, D. C.

United States Department of Health, Education and Welfare, Office of Education, Washington, D. C.

Publishes bulletins on many subjects of interest to teachers. List of publications available on request.

Professional Tools for the Teacher

Educational Film Guide. New York: The H. W. Wilson Company, 1953.

11,000 16 mm. motion pictures are classified by subject and listed with source, date of release, and price. A title and subject index and annual supplements add to the usefulness of the guide.

Filmstrip Guide. Third Edition. New York: The H. W. Wilson Company, 1954.

This guide contains a classified subject list of filmstrips, and an index of titles and subjects. It has an annual supplement.

Free and Inexpensive Learning Materials. Division of Surveys and Field Services. Nashville, Tennessee: George Peabody College for Teachers, 1952.

2521 entries in this booklet were selected according to accuracy of content, timeliness, presentation, and lack of bias.

Horkheimer, Patricia A. *Elementary Teachers' Guide to Free Curriculum Materials.* Randolph, Wisconsin: Educators Progress Service, 1955.

Annual revisions keep this guide of selected materials indexed by title, subject, and source up to date.

Kindergarten-Primary Education — An Annotated and Indexed Bibliography. Department of Kindergarten-Primary Education, National Education Association. Washington: National Education Association, 1955.

This bibliography is probably as complete a listing as is available.

Miller, Bruce. "So You Want to Start a Picture File?" Riverside, California: Superintendent of Schools Bruce Miller, Box 369, 1954.

This pamphlet discusses the value of a picture file, sources of materials, processing of pictures and their display. Another fifty-cent pamphlet, "Free Pictures" lists such pictures according to their subject and tells where and how to write for them.

Salisbury, Gordon, and Robert Sheridan. *Catalog of Free Teaching Aids.* Riverside, California, 1956.

Sources of Free and Inexpensive Educational Material. Chicago: Educational Division of Field Enterprises, Inc., 1955.

INDEX